TRIBES OF MIZORAM
Description, Ethnology and Bibliography (1840–1990)

TRIBES OF MIZORAM

Description, Ethnology and Bibliography (1840–1990)

By

Sipra Sen

GYAN

Tribes of Mizoram
Description, Ethnology and Bibliography (1840–1990)

Sipra Sen

ISBN : 978-81-212-0412-5

First Published 1992, reprint 2013 in India by
Gyan Publishing House
23, Main Ansari Road, Daryaganj,
New Delhi - 110002
Phones : 23282060, 23261060

Fax : (011) 23285914
E-mail: books@gyanbooks.com
website: gyanbooks.com

Printed at : Sagar Color Scan, New Delhi.

Preface

The literature on Mizoram and its tribes are scattered in several monographs, journals, edited books, reports, proceedings etc. There is an urgent need to bring together a list of main publications of this area to provide a base for future research work. This book will facilitate macro and micro level researches on the tribes of Mizoram.

From this informative document, one can get the idea about the region regarding Geography, Flora, Fauna, Climate, Religion, History, Districts, Socio-Political, Socio-Economical, Socio-Cultural and Ethnology of the tribes as well as all the references of published and unpublished research materials which has already been done so far on Mizoram and its people. This bibliographical book will indicate the gaps of work in the field of research on the people of Mizoram. It is hoped that, this will assist to fill up the gaps and to select further research-projects on Mizoram and its tribes on various disciplines. This book has covered all aspects of Social/Cultural/Biological, Anthropology, Human Population Genetics, Human Ecology, Forestry, Geography, Sociology, Ethnology, Custom, Folklore, Archaeology, Social Psychology, History, Education, Political Science, Economics, Linguistics, Botany, Zoology, Geology, Soil Conservation, Tourism, Administration etc. Thus, it presents a multi-dimensional picture of the land, its people and their aspirations.

Until some years ago, the whole of North East India was referred to as *Assam*. It is now divided into seven States and is popularly known as seven sisters of North--East India. Till 1962, Meghalaya, Nagaland and Mizoram were the districts of one State i.e. Assam. The State of *Nagaland* was born in 1963, *Meghalaya* in 1972 and *Mizoram* was separated from Assam and became an Union Territory on 21st January, 1972 and on 20th February, 1987 it became a State. *Arunachal Pradesh*, which was known as *North East Frontier Agency* (*NEFA*) was made an Union Territory and named *Arunachal Pradesh* on 21st January, 1972 and got its Statehood on 20th February, 1987. *Manipur* and *Tripura*, formerly Princely-States, were Union Territories until when they got full--flaged status of States on 21st January, 1972.

The Mizos live in Mizoram, Tripura, Manipur and some parts of Assam and Meghalaya. Some kith and kins of them are inhabited in *Burma* (*Chin Hills* and *Bangladesh* (*Chittagong Hill Tracts*). Some main tribes of Burma are :- The *Karen, Palaung, Yang, Taungthu, Kachin, Lushai Chin, Lisu* etc. In Bangladesh :—*The Chakma, Garo, Kuki, Riang, Mag, Halam, Lushai, Noatia* etc. The separation of Burma from India in 1935 and the partition of India in 1947 had badly effected a significant change in Geographical boundary which caused an economical, political and social changes among the life and culture of the *Mizos*. Since 1954, the term *Lushai* has been superseded by the generic term *MIZO* to identify all the tribes, sub-tribes of the *Lushais* those who are of the same origin and having same social and cultural affinities.

At the initial stage the studies on Mizoram and its people was undertaken in English mainly by the British Administrators, Surveyors, Defence personnels, Christian Missionaries and Travellers. Britishers like Capt. Fisher (1840), E.T. Dalton (1872), R. G. Woodthorpe (1873), W. F. Badgley (1873), W.W. Hunter (1876), George Campbell (1874), Alexander Mackenzie (1884), T.H.Lewin (1885), C.A.Soppitt (1889), O.A.Chambers (1889), EA.Gait (1892), A.R.eid (1893), E.R.Elles 1893), J.Shakespear (1895), B.S.Carey and H.N. Tuck (1896) and many others published their reports, tour diaries, ethnographic notes, articles etc. on Mizoram and its people in the shape of Hand-Book, Census Reports, District Gazetteers, Proceedings, Monographs, Journals etc. Actually, from the Britishers we heve got some earlier recorded documents on Mizoram from the year 1840.

Before that, there was no suitable recorded English documents on Mizoram and its people. In 19th century, no Indian scholar published any book on the *Mizos* except Brojo Nath Shaha (1884) whose work is an excellent one on *A grammar of the Lushai language, to which are appended a few illustrations of the Zou or Lushai popular songs and translations from Aesop's fables.* Before Independence, several excellent ethnographic monographs had been attempted in the 20th century by a good number of British scholars, specially L.A. Waddell (1901), B. C. Allen (1902, 1905, 1908), E. A. Gait (1906), J. Shakespear (1912), W. Shaw (1928), N. E. Parry (1928, 1932), L.W. Shakespear (1914, 1929) and Robert Reid (1942). After Independence, several works were written on Mizoram and its people by A.G. McCall (1949), F.K.Lehman (1963), E.R. Leach (1954, 1961), R.Pudaite (1963), Saradindu Bose (1967), B.K.Roy Burman (1970), J.D. Baveja (1970). Mrs. N. Chatterji (1975), Lal Biak Thanga (1978), B.B. Goswami (1979), Animesh Roy (1982), J.V. Hluna (1983, 1985), Suhas Chatterjee (1985), P.K. Bandyopadhyay (1985), K.K. Upadhyaya (1986), R.N. Prasad (1987), N. Nibedon (1983) and many others. Except Pudaite, Thanga and Hluna, none of these works wre carried out by any insider Mizo people. The insiders are now gradually publishing their works on Mizoram and the tribes. There are several other Indian scholars who have published their written materials on Mizoram and its people but, the major basic works came out from the pen of the Britishers. There is, however some basic authentic and dependable books such as *Descriptive Ethnology of Bengal* by E.T.Dalton (1872), *The North East Frontier of India* by Alexander Mackenzie (1979 *Reprint* Edition), *Provincial Gazetteer: Eastern Bengal and Assam* by B.C.Allen *et al* (c. 1908). *History of Assam* by E.A.Gait (1926), *The Tribes of Brahmaputra Valley* by L.A.Wadell (1901), (*History of the Frontier Areas Bordering on Assam from 1883-1941*) by

Robert Reid (1942) etc. has thrown sufficient light on many important aspects on Mizoram and its people. The basic monographs are-: *The Lusl ei Kuki Clans* by J. Shakespear (1912), *The Lakhers* by N.E.Parry (1932), *Notes on the Thadou Kukis* by W.Shaw (1928), *A Monograph on Lushai Customs and Ceremonies* by N.E. Parry, (1928) *Lushai Chrysalis* by A.G.Mc Call (1949), *Education of the Hmar people* by R.Pudaite (1963), *Land Where the Bamboo flowers* by J.D.Baveja (1970), *Carrying Capacity of Land Under Shifting Cultivation* by Saradindu Bose (1967), *The Mizos : A study in Racial Personality* by L.B.Thanga (1978), *Mizo Unrest : A Study of Politicisation of culture* by B.B.Goswami (1979), *Church and Political Upheaval in Mizoram* by J.V.Hluna (1985) etc. are obviously dependable books about the people of Mizoram. There is a most essential edited book entitled, *Demographic and Socio-Economic Profiles of the Hill Areas of North East India : Census of India 1961* by B.K.Roy Burman (1970) where from we may know about the people of Mizoram and other States.

This is a multi-disciplinary bibliography which covers the important writings on the tribes of Mizoram in the pre and post-Independence period. A detailed study of this bibliography will reveal the important gaps in our knowledge about them. A large number of publications listed here are papers published in journals and presented to various Seminars and Conferences. It is observed that, Ethnographic Monographs are now gradually published after Independence by the new scholars. Some other types of monographic books hre also published on Mizoram about its Religion, Politics etc. It is also observed that, there is a vast number of articles on ethnographical, political, historical and religious aspects by several new scholars who had published in journals and also in edited books. A large number of insiders of Mizoram had published their articles etc. since last two decades. Further this bibliographical work indicates that a large number of studies have been done on the *Lushai Mizo, Lakher, Kuki, Hmar, Pawi (Poi), Paite, Thado* etc. But not much work have been done on the *Vaiphei, Ralte, Gangte, Simte, Zou, Mag, Chakma, Riang* and many other tribes, sub-tribes, of this State.

The main purpose of compiling this bibliography is however, to assist the scholars and researchers so that, the anthropologists, sociologists, ethnologists, archaeologists, historians, geographers, psychologists, linguists, politicians, economists, botanists, zoologists, geologists as well as librarians may get quick and ready references about the reference queries without wastage of their precious time. Moreover, an individual researcher may select his own research theme from this.

In this bibliography all the maps and sketches have been drawn by myself and several old and new records, periodicals, books, newspapers, proceedings, dissertations etc. were consulted from the year 1840 onwards. I have not found it necessary to annotate the references Because, a serious scholar must read all the relevent materials by himself and cryptic annotations are rarely of much use for them. I also access here have to the unpublished research reports, papers of Proceedings, Seminars, symposia and even dissertations along with the published materials.

The preparation of bibliography is an ongoing process. I have to decide compulsorily at some point of time to stop adding entries. As a result of this, there may be some omission of publications which have been brought out after November, 1990. In spite of my best effort few references are not complete as these have bere collected from secondary sources and could not be procured for verification. The choice before me was either to reject or to include them in this Bibliographical book. I chose the latter because, some informations are better than none. Now, if this book can be of some help to make the people of Mizoram better known and understood and assist the scholars, that will be the real satisfaction for my hard and painstaking work. I shall welcome any suggestions, additional informations and comments from the users to improve this book in near future.

I must acknowledge my best thanks which are due to Mr. R.V. Leishisan, Asstt. Publicity Officer, Manipur and to Sr. Information Officer, Information and Public Relations, Mizoram. I am very much grateful to them for their kind and esteemed help which they had extended to me and the photographs which I have used here are received by their courtesy. I wish to express my sincerest gratitude to them for getting encouragement and co-operation from them. I am also grateful and indebted to Mr.F. Thanghulha, Jt.Director, E. & S., Mizoram ; Mr. Johnny Zoram Thanga, D.SO., Lunglei ; Mr. K. Thankhuma, D.S.O., Saiha ; Mr. Vabeiha Hlychho, T.I.O., Mizoram and Prof. B. B. Kumar, Secretary, N.B.P., Kohima for their kind co-operation and help rendered to me.

In the end, I must express my sense of gratefulness to the National Library, Calcutta ; Gauhati University Library, Guwahati and Anthropological Survey of India Library, Shillong. I like to record my debt to my brother Dr.Salil Ranjan Sen who helped me to get the entire manuscript typed. Finally, I must express my highest respectful regards to my mother Mrs.Malati Sen for her kind help and constant encouragement at every step to complete this work. Her immense inspiration have been of untold value. Had it not been for the active inspiration, sympathetic interest and help of my mother, the work would not have accelarated as at its present tempo.

Rehabari,
Guwahati,

SIPRA SEN

Key to Bibliography

All the references have been alphabetically arranged in a chronological order with reference to each author.

For books the author's name is followed by year, title of reference, place of publication and publisher's name with total number poges.

For journals the author's name is followed by year, title of the article, name of the journal in which it was published, volume, number, month and page numbers.

In the case of newspaper etc. the author's name or publisher's name which is followed by year, title of the article, name of the newspaper and date of publication, page number and column number.

Mast of the reference are in English but French, German, Hindi, Lushai (*Dulian*) Paite, Manipuri, Naga, Assamese and Bengali publications have also been included in this Bibliography.

For books, journals, newspapers etc. I have marked against few serial numbers as "*n·p.*". This means "not published". Similarly "*n.p.*" indicates that "no date" (i.e. date of publication is not available in the book, journal, newspaper etc.). About question mark "?" it means regarding "doubtness" about author, date of publication etc. of the reference. "*Sr*". means Senior and "*Jr.*" means Junior. *Ed.* means "Editor", *Jt.* means "joint" and Jr. means "journal".

Contents

PART—II

PART—III

PART I

ONE

INTRODUCTION

Land and People of Mizoram

Mizoram is a paradise State for social studies as it is the most fertile field to study Anthropology and Sociology, for its 93.54 per cent of tribal population with different cultural traditions, folklore, myths and legends as well as customs of the Lushai-Kuki-Chin tribes which they carry the trace of their ancient chronicles.

Previously most of them were nomads due to their agricultural practice of *Jhum* cultivation to search out better and fertile cultivable land from one place to another. Since 1950 the term *Lushai* has been superseded by the term *Mizo*. It is a matter of their pride when people recognise the tribes of Mizoram as a single tribe the *Mizo* instead of the *Lushai* etc.

Prior to 1937, the Kuki-Chin tribes were living together in Indian sub-continent. In 1937, Burma was separated from India taking with it *Chin Hills* and *Upper Chindwin*. Again when India was divided in 1947 *Chittagong Hill Tracts* have gone to East Pakistan and later on in 1971 to Bangladesh. As a result, some of the tribes of Mizoram lost geopolitically their identity and identify themselves with the neighbouring groups whoever had influenced them.

Geography

Mizoram is situated approximately between 22''02' and 24''24' North latitude and between 92''16'' and 93''29' East longitudes. It is a small State but bigger than *Nagaland* and *Tripura* with an area of 21,081 sq. km. This State runs 276,82 km. lengthwise from north to south and 120.75 km width from east to west which forme almost a trapezoid shape. This State is situated in an isolated pocket of southern most part of North East India (*Map-1*). The geographical continuity with the Indian mainland is maintained only in the north, north east and north west. The *Tropic of Cancer* passes through Aizawl district.

Mizoram is bounded 117.53km by *Cachar* district of Assam, 86.94 km by *Churachandpur* district of Manipur and 61.18km by *North Tripura* district of Tripura in its north, north east and north west borders respectively. Its 273.52 km south-eastern and 214.13 km south-western borders are sharing with the international border of the nation like Burma and Bangladesh (*Map-2*). Geopolitically it is very much sensitive State as nations such as Burma and Bangladesh has *sandwiched* it by surrounding the maximum part in its eastern, southern and western border.

Name of the State

Formerly Mizoram was an Autonomous Hill District of Assam and known as *Lushai Hills District*. It was sub-divided into *North Lushai Hills* and *South Lushai Hills*. The term *Lushai* was derived from the word *Lushei* or *Lusei* the classified name of one major tribe of the *Mizo* people. Lushai the Hills District has changed its name to *Mizo Hills District* since 29th April, 1954 by an *Act No. XVIII of 1954* of Parliament. The word *Mizo* is a generic term which means in Lushai language *a hill man* (*Mi*=man, *zo*=hill or high altitude).

Mizo Hills District became an Union Territory on 21st January, 1972, when the State of Assam was reorganised under the *North Eastern Area Reorganisation Act of 1971* and it was named *Mizoram* which means the *land of the Mizos*, those who are akin to the Lushai people in custom, language and way of living. This Mizoram became the 23rd State of India. It got the status of *State* on 20th February, 1987.

Mountain

Mizoram is fully covered with ranges of hills which runs from north to south in a parallel way separated from one another by narrow valleys. The height of the hills tends to be higher in the middle of the State (from west to east) and are tapering in the north and south. The hills are generally small and steep. The height of the hills increases from west and gradually decreases and are gentle towards east. The average height of the hills varies from 300 ft to 5000 ft above the sea level. The hills consist of sandstones and shales of tertiary age. Mizo Hills (*nee* Lushai Hills) are intermediate in height towards the west (*Chittagong Hills* of Bangladesh) the average height is 1500 ft but in the central portion of Mizo Hills is about 3500 ft and towards the east (*Chin Hills* of Burma) it is over 5000 ft.

There are peaks here and there which are above 6000 ft high. The highest peak in the State is the *Blue Mountain* (*Phawngpuii*) which is 7100 ft high and *Mt. Lengteng* which is 7,050 ft There are several other mountains. These are *Naunaurza* (7,050 ft), *Surtlang* (6,618 ft), *Zopuitlang* (6,439 ft), *Lurhtlang* (6,350 ft). *Tantlang* (6,320 ft). *Hmuifangtlang* (6,307 ft), *Chalfilhtlang* (6,249 ft), *Ngurtlang* (6,218 ft), *Tawizo* (6,200 ft), *Lungreng* (6,107 ft) etc.

River

There are many small, deep and rugged rivers. Most of these flow either to the north or to the south by creating deep gorges in between the north-south hill ranges (*Map*-3). This happens due to the height of the hills in the middle of the State. This State has many rivers, streams, canals and swamps. Actually, Mizoram is a gifted one in water resources. In the north the river *Tlawng* (*Dhaleswari*), the *Tuirial* (*Sonai*) and the *Tuivawl* starts from the middle of the State and runs towards north to fall in the *Barak* river in Cachar district of Assam. In the south, the river *Khawthlangtuipui* (*Karnafuli*) flows towards the western border of the State from southern part to northern part and after flowing near about the middle of the border this runs towards Bangladesh. The river *Chhimtuipui* (*Koladyne* or *Kanadan*) enters inside Mizoram from Burma and it flows towards south with another river *Tulpui* so as to re-enter Burma.

The length of the river *Tlawng* is 185,15 km., *Tuirial* 117,53km., *Tuivawl* 7,45km., *Khawthlangtuipui* 128,08km., *Chhimtuipui* 138, 46km., *Tiau* 159,39km., *Tuichang* 120,7ↄkm. *Tuichawng* 107,07km., *Mat* 9,016km., *Tuipui* (*Khawchhak*) 8,694km., *Teirei* 7,884km. *Tuirini* 5,957km. *Serlui* 5,535km. All these rivers are generally fed by monsoon rain. In winter, the volume of water in the river is less and some rivers are almost dried up. The *Tlawng*, the *Tuirial*, the *Khawthlangtuipui* rivers are navigable always even in the dry season.

Lake

There are some lakes. The biggest of which is *Palak* lake situated in the south eastern corner of the *Lunglei* district. It is oval in shape, its length is about 660 yards and width about 600 yards. *Tamdil* is another lake of this State situated 40 miles away to the east of *Aizawl* in between *Saitual* and *Tuaibung* villages of Aizawl district. In this lake huge quantity of prawns and some crabs are available. *Rungdil* lake is situated near *Suangpuilawn* village of Aizawl district in the north eastern corner. It is a twin lake separated from one with another by a narrow stretch of land.

Climate

Mizoram enjoys for whole year almost a pleasant climate as it is neither very hot nor very cold. But this climate is not much healthy. During the rainy season, climate of this State is very much moisty even in the lower hilly areas enervating and malarial fevers are almost common.

The western part of the State is hotter than the eastern part. Actually the eastern part is pleasant and cool even in summer. The dry season of the State is from the month of October to March. The cold season is from November to February. It is followed by the summer season from March to May. The whole of Mizoram is under the influence of monsoon wind which is coming from the north west. Monsoon season starts from the month of June to September. The coldest month is January. The average temperature of cold season is 11'8° to 20'2°C. The hottest month is April. The average temperature of hot season is 20'38° to 29'9°C.

Generally in July-August a continuous heavy rainfall starts when life in this State becomes intolerable due to some landslide which uproots the trees, slips away some stones and soils of the hills and communication is sometimes disrupted. From the month of October to December the villages of Mizoram are filled up with damp fogs during morning and night time whereas, the mountain tops are comparatively free from the fogs. In March-April, cyclonic storm is flows from south-west to north-east direction and sweeps over the hills of Mizoram specially in Lunglei district. The monsoon effects highly to the eastern border where the maximum rainfall occurs. The northern part of the State (Aizawl district) in 1985 got less rainfall (231'2 cm.) along with the southern part (Chimtuipui district 227'5 cm.) than the middle part (Lunglei district, 374'6 cm).

The hills of Mizoram are mainly formed of shale, sandstone and sometimes limestone belonging to the tertiary age and these substances are easily decomposed by the heavy rainfall to form soil which at places causes heavy landslides during the rainy season.

Flora

Mizoram is popular in the name of *Botanist's Paradise* as varieties of vegetation grows here abundantly. Many Ayurvedic medicinal plants are also available here. The hills of Mizoram are covered with dense evergreen forest of trees, plants, bushes, creepers and grasses. Rainfall and temperature of this State is suitable for trees, plants and bamboos. Most of the flora of Mizoram resembles with that of the State of Manipur and Assam. Some of them are similar to that of Bhutan and Upper Burma. *Rhododendron*, cotton, cane, *ikra*, bamboo, grass, cactus, ferns, *rhynchostylis retusa* (*foxtail*) orchids, wild flowering plants are available here. Paddy, maize, millet, pulses, cabbage, cauliflower, sweet potato, tapioca, chillies, ladies-finger etc. grows here. Fiberless ginger is a common crop and cultivated in their garden. It is widely marketed to other neighbouring States. *Tezpat*, *Dalchini*, *Golmarich* etc. grows in the southern part of the State. Mustered, sesame, super sized potato are common cultivated crops of their garden. Bigger sized sweetest banana, papaya, pineapple are very much famous here. Not only these but sugarcane, orange, mango tea, coffee, cocoa rubber, cardamom, cashewnut etc. also grows here.

Agriculture

Mizoram is entirely hilly area excepting a few small stretches of plain surface where wet rice cultivation is practised. The clay soil of the valley is more fertile than the hilly region. Red loamed soil of Mizoram is suitable for cultivating fruit trees. Soils of this State consists of shale sandstone and occasionally of limestone.

Mizoram is deficit in foodgrains due to steepy hills all over the State. Though about 80 per cent of the population of Mizoram is engaged in agriculture still the production of foodgrains per capita is very low. This State has been depending on supplies of foodgrains from outside.

All the cultivable land is a common property of the villagers. No individual his has separate personal holdings of agriculturable land. In earlier days each village was ruled by a Chief (*Lal*). The Chief was the owner of the land of his village who was to allot land for cultivation to each family-heads of his village. At the abolition of the Chieftainship, Mizoram Government took all rights on land from them and the administration on land was occupied by the *Lushai* (*Mizo*) *Hills District Council* and the *Village Councils*.

Jhum or shifting or slash-and-burn type of cultivation is the principal method of their agriculture without using plough like Africa, New Guinea, Philippines, Borneo etc. This *jhum* cultivation is also practised in some parts of Arunachal Pradesh, Nagaland, Assam (Mikir Hills and North Cachar Hills) and Meghalaya of North East India. It varies with the geographical condition of the land. This (*jhum*) procedure is uneconomic and wasteful method. This is one of the causes of soil erosion and land slides. Thus, Government wants to bring more and more areas of land under permanent terrace cultivation in Mizoram. To maintain ecological balance of Mizoram the State Government is now alloting lands in rural areas to individual family-head on contact basis that he or his family members would utilise the alloted land for permanent cultivation and he or his family members would not take up any other land for *jhuming*.

Each year in the month of January, members of the *Mizo Village Council* used to select a suitable land within their village for *jhuming* for the year. After selecting the land a lottery is to cast among all head of the families of that village to distribute a *jhum* field among them. There is so far no size limit of this alloted *jhum* field. One could cultivate the alloted land only for one year. For next year the said procedure of allotment of land is repeated by the *Village Council* to allot fresh selected areas.

Immediately after getting the alloted *jhum* land they started to cut the jungles with *Heicha* or *Hreipui* (axe) and *chem* (dao, knife). They left these cut-out jungle trees for about two months to dry under sunlight. After that, they destroyed all these dry trees by burning. Ashes of these trees are distributed by them throughout their *jhum* field as manure which soak in the rain. Soon after distributing the ashes they hoed over lightly the soil-surface from the lower end of the *jhum* field and proceeded upward by digging shallow holes to put seeds into each hole for seedlings. High altitude, steepness of hills, water feature etc. hampers to use some land of Mizoram under cultivation.

Mizoram Agricultural Department has been giving a large scale of demonstrations regarding improved technique of farming with modern agricultural implements among the local farmers. The local cultivators have now been made aware about modern agricultural method than their primitive method of *jhum* cultivation with primitive agricultural implements. There are five "agricultural" districts in Mizoram. These are : Aizawl East, Aizawl West, Lunglei, Saiha and Kolasib. Mizoram Government has launched a *jhum* control programme at

Aiback block, the implementation of which started from 1987-88 by covering 1,994 families till 1989.

Terrace cultivation on hill slopes was introduced in Mizoram during the First Five Year Plan. Now almost all the villages which are surrounding Aizawl town have taken terrace cultivation. Co-operative agricultural farms have been organised at Punkhai, Demagiri, Borepansui, New Jaganasuri, Bedsuri etc. The *Village Councils* have now taken initiative to set-up terrace cultivation in easy gradient of slopes.

Agricultural Implements

Their agricultural implements are very simple. They have a dao (*chempong*), an axe (*Heicha*) and a hoe. Their dao also act as a big knife which has a triangular blade of 3 inches width at the end and half an inch at the handle. It has sharpness only on the broad side. This is used for clearing the jungle. The axe is about 1½ inches wide at the edge-head and its handle is made with a piece of bamboo. It is used specially for felling the trees in the *jhum* fields. The hoes closely resemble the axe. Its head is little lighter and broader than axe.

A cane made basket (*congwang*) is used by the women for carrying paddy from the field. There is another basket called *bengrit*. It is used with the help of a bamboo made strap (*namkol*) by men and women on their back to carry vegetables and also to bring drinking water within bamboo tubes or utensils. They keep paddy at home within a cane-made basket called *lo*. For winnowing paddy they use bamboo made *codal* and a wooden paddy huskar with stick called *sum-sutum*.

Sericulture

The climatic condition, moisture content in the air, topography and soil in Mizoram is advantageous to grow *mulberry*, *tasar* and other plants which are eaten by silk worms. The Government has taken steps for cultivation of these plants to keep a continuous supply of food to silk worm rearers.

Mulberry, tasar and muga silk are being produced in

Mizoram. There are sericultural centres at Zemabawk and Durtlong. At present (1985) Mizoram has 25 sericulture-farms and about 350 rearers have received grants from Mizoram Government.

Irrigation

Government is trying to make self-sufficient the agricultural production in Mizoram. The annual rainfall of Mizoram is 277'7 cm. (1985) which usually starts from June and continues upto October. The soil of Mizoram can not retain this rain water to moist its agricultural fields. Though there is a fair percentage of clay in the soil still water holding capacity of the soil is very low due to porousness of soil. During winter the top soil becomes very dry. The soil is generally acidic in nature due to the continuous washing away of alkaline top surface soil by rain water. The soil in the valley is rich alluvial.

Government has now taken several projects to irrigate the agricultural fields for the whole year through river canals. It is planned to build a dam across the *Tlong* river at Bairabi close to Cachar District of Assam. Besides generating power and providing water-way for navigation, the dam would ensure irrigation facilities on the bank of the river for permanent cultivation.

Forest

The jungle products of Mizoram is rich. There are several types of timbers, sal, bamboo, cane etc. Three types of forest is found in Mizoram. These are: tropical wet evergreen, tropical semi-evergreen and montane sub-tropical. Forest trees in the hilly areas are gradually decreasing as people are using them for their firewood, constructing materials of house etc and also for *jhum* cultivation. Many hill slopes are now completely bare of trees as *jhum* cultivation has turned them into patches of endless dust.

Forest areas of Mizoram is owned by the State Government (7,127,22 sq. km.), District Councils (1786 sq. km.) and Village Councils (7,022 sq. km.). These forest areas are divided into protected forest, reserved forest, village safety forest, wild life sanctuary and unclassified forest areas. In

1980-82, the forest areas of Mizoram was 11,971 sq. km. which was 13,860 sq. km. in 1972-75 (Table 1). Thus the forest areas has gone down in Mizoram. The large scale deforestation will cause soil erosion at an accelerated level and may lead to floods during monsoon.

TABLE 1

Forest Areas

State	Forest area in sq. km.		Change of forest areas
	1972-75	1980-82	in sq. km. (+) Increased (—) Decreased
Assam	21,055	19,796	(—) 1,259
Manipur	15,090	13,572	(—) 1,518
Meghalaya	14,390	12,458	(—) 1,932
Nagaland	8,154	8,095	(—) 0,59
Tripura	6,330	5,138	(—) 1,192
Arunachal Pradesh	51,438	58,104	(+) 6,666
Mizoram	13,860	11,971	(—) 1,889

Source : *Himalaya* : *Man and Natuve*, VIII (11), April, 1985.

Fauna

The vegetation and climate of Mizoram offers an ideal sanctuary to wild animals. Wild animals and birds are plenty all over the hilly jungles of Mizoram. It is strange as no birds now a days are seen in any locality of the State. This is perhaps due to their fear from the people. If any bird comes to the eyes of a *Mizo* it is caught at once or shot to cook. Similarly, there are no stray dogs or cats on the streets of Aizawl due to fear as those are killed to be eaten by the Mizos.

There are several sancturies. These are : *Dampa Wild Life Sanctuary* (572 sq. km.), *Ngenpui Wild Life Sanctuary* (110 sq. km.), *Blue Mountain Wild Life Sanctuary* (60 sq. km.) etc. The fauna consists of *mithun* (*Bos frontalis*) which is semi-domesticated animal. Wild elephants are found in the foot hills. Tiger, bison, buffalo, rhinoceros, barking deer, sambar, leopard, Himalayan black bear, Malay bear, wild dog, wild cat, rat, wild pig, monkey, jackal, snakes (*viper*, *python*, *cobra*, *grass-snakes*), lizards, toads, eagle, vulture, skylark, owl, crow, hornbill, jungle fowl etc. are common in Mizoram. These wild animals have been gradually lost to the cruel spear of hunters. The tribals of Mizoram eat all kinds of animals. The famous great Hornbill bird is hunted by them mainly for their decoration purpose. Some of the animals specially rats cause the damage to their crops.

Famine (Mautam and Thingtam)

There was a big famine (*mautam*) in 1860s' due to rats in Mizoram. Another big famine (*Thingtam*) was in 1880s' due to rebellion activities. Again in 1911 there was another big famine all over the State as rats came as a plague with the seeding-fruits of bamboo. In 1959, there was again a largest famine all over the State. It is observed that at the interval of 40 to 50 years Mizoram is facing famines. They call famines as *Mautam* and *Thingtam*. There is an interval of approximately 18 years in between one famine (*Mautam*) to another (*Thingtam*). Famines are mainly due to seeded bamboo fruits of two special species of bamboo trees, locally known as *Maw* and *Rawthing*. At the interval of forty to fifty years these two special species of bamboo in this State blossom and bear fruits. These fruits are delicious food of rats which acts as a strong *fertility pill* on the body of rats. As such rat-population abnormally and rapidly increase at incredibly multiplication in highest rate. Innumerable rats gather there to exhaust the bamboo fruits and consumes very much quickly all the crops of the State. Ultimately this causes widespread famine (*Mautam*) which creates a great distress to the people of Mizoram.

Geology

The rocks are mostly similar to the *Tipam* and *Surma* series of the *Lower Miocene Age*. The *Tipam* series rocks form the flanks and the *Surma* series the core. Granite is the mineral wealth of Mizoram. Thin layers of lignitic coal have also been reportedly available here. In 1963, it was reported by the Geological Survey and Planning Department that an area of coal mine has been discovered at the outer surface in the south near *Chwngte* by the side of the river *Tuichawng*. Two areas of coal mines have also been found in the north near Bairabi and at Saiphai. Methane gas have been reported to be occurring in this State. It has also been reported that salt springs are there in western, eastern and northern side of Mizoram. The soil of this State is fairly thick and almost free from boulders and gravels. It is a clayey loam with sand, silt etc. The colour of soil is like ash with a slight yellowish tint. The Geological Survey of India (North Eastern Region) has recently investigated in to some areas of Mizoram to get some more mineral wealth.

The entire area of Mizoram consists of red loam soil. It is composed of sand stone and shales of tertiary age. Marine fossils of that period have been found near Lunglei in dark grey sand stones and shales. It is reported that Dr. R.S. Patil of Geological Survey of India had cellected the mega-fossils from the calcareous grey sandstone-siltstone and the mud pellet conglomerate horizons of the Upper Bhuban Formation of Aizawl and Chhimptuipui districts. The fauna was mega invertebrates of gastropods, pelecypods, coral, echinoids, decapod crustacea. Fossil shark teeth had also been reportedly found. The invertebrate faunas have some resemblenee with the fauna of Garo Hills.

Industry

Mizoram is much behind in heavy industry in comparison to other States. Due to non-availability of coal and oil, acute shortage of electricity power and difficult hilly terrain, heavy industries could not be set up here. Mizoram Government has planned to set up industrial estates at Aizawl, Kolasib and Luangual. These places are centrally situated along the main routes.

It is reported that the *Tatas* offered technical knowledge for setting up different industries in Mizoram and for extraction of fibres and minerals. The *Birlas* also offered their knowledge and services for the production of edible oil. It is further stated that the private entrepreneurs are not much willing to set up industrial units due to lack of infrastructure. Due to absence of good communication and transport facilities and *inner line permit* system of Mizoram the outsider plain people are not much eager to set up their industries in Mizoram. Most of the items of daily needs have to be brought inside the State from Silchar (Assam) by road and as such most of the things in Mizoram are very costly.

Rural Industrial Projects has started since 1963 in Aizawl. Under this project training is being given in carpentry, bakery, *gur* making, oil extraction from seeds, blacksmithy, tailoring, embroidery, knitting, cotton ginning, spinning, bee-keeping and weaving. Mizoram Government thinks that sericulture, piggery, weaving animal husbandry, orange and pine-apple cultivation should be encouraged to the maximum production. There is much scope for forest product industries. There are cottage industries of woollen carpets, Mizo cane hats, cane baskets and furnitures. Government is now setting up one paper and paper pulp factory at Bairabi. Blacksmithy and brick making industry has been set up in small scale. Mizoram is exporting fiberless ginger, bamboo and cane products. Mizoram Government proposed in 1980 to set up a Rs. 30 lakh watch assembly unit at Aizawl in collaboration with the HMT factory of Bangalore.

Economy

The economic condition of Mizoram is not much satisfactory. They have been facing acute problems of communication and marketing their products. People have to walk 5 to 30 kms. to sell their agricultural items. Like other hill tribes of north east India, agriculture is the main occupation of the Mizos. They have practised from time immemorial the shifting (*jhum*) cultivation in the hills by destructive system of cutting down the forest trees and reducing those by burning soon after drying under sunshine. Permanent wet cultivation is also practised whenever plain suitable land is available. In the *jhum* besides paddy, maize, sesame, castor, and cotton various types of vegetables are also cultivated. Their method of cultivation is, however, primitive. For that, rice cultivation is quite low which generally depends on the timely arrival of monsoon. Hence the production is not sufficient for the rapid increase of population to meet their requirement round the year. Moreover, a considerable quantity of rice is used by every Mizo family for the purpose of brewing rice beer and the fact that a comparatively less number of Mizos take rice cultivation. For these, availability of rice for self supporting in Mizoram is not much bright and a large quantity of rice have to be import from other States to Mizoram.

Denudation of forest materials for their *jhum* cultivation has caused ecological disturbance to erose soil, land slides, less monsoon etc. As it is told earlier that Government has taken initiative to convert their procedure of *jhum* cultivation to permanent cultivation by alloting suitable land to individual rural families. The *jhumia* families with the help of Government develops their land in the form of construction of terraces and plantation of each crops and spices in individual cultivator's range, pine-apples, lemons, ginger, banana etc. are grown in plots. by them by terracing the hill slopes. They also cultivated cash crops such as black pepper, coffee, cashewnut, rubber, cardamom etc.

Weaving

Most of the Mizo women weave their own clothes. In the village a loom apparatus is in each house like the *Assamese*, the *Manipuri*, the *Tripuri* and the *Naga* people. The Mizo women are expert in weaving. The loin loomed cloths which they make are strong and last for long time. They use local cotton which grows in their *jhum* field. They generally like simple designs for their clothes. Mizo *Puanchei* (beautiful designed ladies lower garment) and *Kawrches* (a blouse with artistic designed in the border) have much demand among the outsiders specially by the Europeons and Americans. Mizo shawls are beautiful and attractive.

Basketry

Some of the Mizo men are expert basket weaver and carpenter. Bamboo and cane goods are manufactured mostly for domestic use. They have different types of baskets. Their artistic designed basket *lalpi* is strong and lasts for long time. This *lalpi* basket has a cover and it is made of two layers : upper layer and inner layer. The upper layer is made of cane and the inner layer is made of bamboo. It is used for keeping the valuables of the households.

Some of their male folk are very good brass-moulder and blacksmith. They know to make gun-locks. They rear cattle, pig, fowl etc. in their house for domestic consumption. They rarely rear these for commercial purpose.

Energy and Power

Electricity was first introduced in Mizoram in 1962 when a small diesel generator was commissioned to lit up Aizawl. In 1972, there were five diesel power stations in the State at Aizawl, Lunglei, Kolasib, Serchhip and Hnahthial. These generated electricity for the whole State. In 1977, there was a generator of 248 kw. which was commissioned at Lunglei and another 240 kw. generator at Champhai. Installed capacity of power as on April, 1985, was 80'51 mw. diesel and 1'00mw. micro hydel in Mizoram. Total 134 villages till 1985 have been electrified. In 1985, installed capacity (diesel) was highest at *Luangmual* (3520 km) thereafter at *Aizawl* (1500 kw) and *Lunglei* (1371 kw).

The Power and Electricity Department of Mizoram took-up about 48 per cent *Rural Electrification Work* to provide light to every corner of Mizoram. To improve the trans-mission and transformation of electric power, 132 kw sub--stations in *Zemabawk*, *Lunglei* and *Serchhip* are now being completed by them. This department undertook *Tuirivang* and *Khawiva* micro hydel project with 300 kw. and 1050kw. respectively. Three more projects are to be started at *Tuipui* (500 mw), *Tuisumpui* (450 mw) and *Maicham* (2000 mw). Diesel installation of 3'76 mw. have already been started. The 132kv. line from *Serchhip* to *Lunglei* has already been commissioned since 16th December, 1987. During the 7th Plan, 132kw from *Jiribam-Aizawl* and 66kw from *Vairengte Aizwal* was commissioned.

Water Supply

The Mizos do not settle near the water sources. As water sources are far away from the village, the Mizos are suffering from acute shortage of water. Sometimes the villagers had to fetch water from *doong* (water shed), river etc. about 20 km. away from their house. The people of Mizoram in towns and villages had no other alternative but to store rain water. The Government has stepped up to meet the requirement of water to people. By 1977, the Aizawl Water Supply Scheme which involved drawing water from the *Dhaleswari* river, 24 km. away from the town have been completed. At *Champhai* and *Durtlong* water supply schemes have started functioning. Some more water supply schemes in rural areas have also been commissioned. The Government of Mizoram took up active action to set more and more water supply schemes in the State to overcome water scarcity.

The Scarcity of drinking water in the hilly areas of Mizoram during dry season is being overcome with various efforts made by the Public Health Engineering Department. Till 1988, forty-five numbers of water supply schemes had been commissioned in rural villages by covering 293 villages. The major part of the greater Aizawl Water Supply Scheme is being completed by the PHE Department of Mizoram. The foundation stone of greater Lunglei Water Supply Scheme has already been laid and expected to be completed soon to start its water works.

Prehistoric Archaeoloy

The archaeological remains of this State is, so far, not much reported and it seems to be scanty. Near *Tualcheng* village, eastern part of Mizoram, there is a row of stone slabs. At Champhai, there is a monolithic tomb called *Mangkahie Lung* (*Mangkhaia's* tomb). A stone monument called Sibuta Lung is situated near Tachhip village, 14 miles south of Aizawl. Mizoram is almost unknown to the Archaeological world as there is no systematic archaeological exploration and excavation so far done by any archaeologist to know better about archaeological remains in Mizoram.

Communication

There is no railway line inside the State. Rail line to traffic, however, would be opened by June-July, 1990 at *Bairabi* just at the border of Aizawl district of Mizoram and

Cachar district of Assam on the left bank of *Tlawng* river of Mizoram. It would be 18 km. long metre gauge N.F. Railway line in between *Lalabazar* (Cachar District of Assam) to *Bairabi via Katlicherra* and *Jamira* (Cachar District of Assam). The railway line between Assam's *Lalabazar* township and *Jamira*, covering a distance of 35 km. was opened in April, 1989. Mizoram will now have a railway stretch of only 149 kms. A railway Out-Agency is there in Aizawl.

National Highway No. 54 is the only highway of this State. It runs from Silchar (Cachar District of Assam) to Aizawl with 180 km. length (*Map-4*). This highway was further extended from Aizawl to Lunglei (235 km.), Lunglei to Saiha (165 km), Lunglei to Tlabung (Demagiri, 98 km), Aizawal to Champhai (192 km). Transport is vital for the administration in Mizoram. The Mizos are now fond of *Maruti* and *Gypsy* light vehicles. These two brands are running in plenty on the streets of town and city. Not only the mobility of the people but also, the supply and distribution of essential commodities depend on transport facilities.

There are State Highways, District Roads, Inter Village Briddle Path, Jeepable and Truckable PWD and BRTF Roads. But the condition of some roads is below standard due to poor surface condition, topography etc. During Summer, owing to heavy land slides, the roads become impossible. The soil of the roads is loose and often even well kept roads get blocked. Some of the roads are too narrow to run two vehicles together. Most of the roads are steep between mountainous wall on one side and a sheer drop on the other. If one sighted a car coming from the opposite side of the narrow road, he had to go back to the nearest bend to let that vehicle to pass.

There was total 31 surface routes with an approximate total of 3933 km. length route till 1985. There is a metalled State Highway to Imphal (Manipur) through Seling and Darlong of Mizoram. There is an oldest route from *Tlabung* (*Demagiri*) to *Lunglei* which was a bridle-path before 1980. After that some cart ways was made in and around *Lunglei*, *Tlabung* and *Aizawl*. By 1942, *Silchar Aizawal* bridle path was converted to a jeepable road and by 1953 *Aizaw Lunglie* path converted to to a road. In 1972, *Tlabung* (*Demagiri*) was connected with mettled road for *Lunglei* and *Champhai* connected with *Lunglei* in 1973. All these roads are gradually improving since 1980 onwards in their width and are being thickly constructed for heavy vehicles.

There is no airline's air-route inside the State. However, Mizoram helicopter services are available in week days and flight is available in between *Aizawl-Silchar*, *Aizawl-Imphal*, *Aizawl-Guwahati*, *Aizawl-Shillong* etc. Helicopter service is also available inside the State in *Aizawl*, *Lunglei*, *Champhai*, *Zemobawk* etc. *Tuirial* Helipad is there for helicopter services. *Silchar* (*Kumbhirgram* airport, Cachar District of Assam) is the nearest aerodrome. In fact, Mizoram has very less communication with the mainstream of Indian life due to geographical isolation, fluctuating temperature, humidity, dense forest, hilly terrain, scarcity of drinking water, lack of motorable proper road, inner line permit etc. The cost of living in Mizoram is very high.

Till 1985, there were total 277 Post Offices and Sub-Post office in Mizoram. There is a medium wave Radio Station at Aizawl which provides the coverage of the whole area of the State. A T.V. transmission centre has already been set up near Aizawl town

Inner Line Permit

In 1873, a traffic regulation was made for Mizoram (Lushai Hills) by the British Government (*Bengal East Regulation No. I, Section V*) by introducing an Inner Line Permit System. According to this regulation out-siders other than tribals of Mizoram can not go without an Official Pass Certificate within this area. This Inner Line Permit thus protects the interest of both the indigenous people of Mizoram and the plain people of the other parts. On the noe aadd it prevented the plain people about encroachment on tribal land to settle there permanently and on the other hand it defended from the danger of raids and hostility by the tribals to plain areas. Not only this, this also helped to preserve the culture and custom of the local people and it supported to develop them according to their own way.

After Independence, this Inner Line system still continues to guard the religious and social practices of the tribal people of Mizoram against the possible exploitation on social, economic etc aspects as it controls the illegal travellers like money lenders, inflow of unskilled labourers, beggers, cheaters, businessminded outsiders etc to enter into their land. This protects the unique culture of the tribals from damaging effects of too-many civilized visitors of the plain area as well as visitors of the other countries. Perhaps for this reason there is almost no porter coolie in Mizoram. Lack of porter labourer is a serious problem to do hard laborious work. There are not many Mizos left to work on road construction projects or less dignitary work. The majority of them are farmers and the remaining one are the Government officials and the businessmen. As a result, Mizoram is almost bound to import labourers from other States for a specific period to do road work etc.

For Indian tourists, there is no restriction to get their Inner Line Permits from the Deputy Director of Supply and Transport, Government of Mizoram, Silchar (Assam) by paying Rupee one as a permit fee to cross the Inner Lime border to visit inside the State. Recently, the Government of India has been trying to improve their travel and civil aviation depart- For ments. that, they have now liberalised their Inner Line Permit System for Indian tourist. The State Government has a proposal to construct some more tourist lodges at different sites of Mizoram to attract the tourists to see green hills and valleys of Mizoram. There is much possibility to withdraw this Inner Line Permit System by the Government soon for Indians. This Inner Line Prohibition was modified in 1930, 1933 and 1970. The Central Government, however, agreed in 1986 with Mr. Laldenga, MNF leader not to amend or repeal the existing Inner Line Regulation without the consent of the State Government.

Literacy and Education

The total literate persons in Mizoram is 2,90,225,53 (*Census 1981*). The percentage of literates to total population is 59.50 per cent which ranks third in comparison with other States and Union Territories of India in literacy percenttage after Chandigarh and Kerala (Table 2 and 3). The Mizos had the highest literacy in India in 1951. The percentage of literates to total population is 65.09 per cent in Aizawl District, 56.89 per cent in Lunglei District and 37·07 in Chhimtuipui District.

TABLE 2

Literacy of Mizoram

Year	Population	Total No. of Literates	Percentage of Literates
1901	82,434	771	0.93
1911	91,204	3,635	4.41
1921	98,406	6,183	6.28
1931	1,24,404	13,320	10.54
1941	1,52,786	29,765	19.50
1951	1,96,202	61,093	31.13
1961	2,66,063	1,17,094	44.00
1971	3,32,390	1,78,793	53.79
1981	4,87,774	2,90,225,53	59.50

Source : *Census of India 1901 to 1981.*

During the time of British rule, the Christian Missionaries did their pioneering efforts to introduce and improve the education among the Mizo people. They had introduced Roman script for formal education. Proper atten tion for education, however, have been made in this area only after Independence and this State is showing quick progress in education. Female literacy is also progressing at a speedy rate. Mizo boys and girls are now encouraged not only to attend to their Schools and Colleges in Mizoram but also to go for higher education with Government Scholarship and voluntarily to Indian Colleges and Universities of Delhi. Bombay, Madras, Calcutta, Guwahati, Shillong, Dibrugarh etc, as well as abroad.

In 1972, a Directorate of Education and Social Welfare was set up in Mizoram to look after development of education.

TABLE 3

Literacy of India

India/State/Union Territory	Population (1981)	Total Literate	Percentage of Literates to total Popula-tien
1	2	3	4
INDIA	683,810,051	237,991,932	34.80
Uttar Pradesh	110,858,019	30,388,013	27.38
Bihar	69,823,154	18,163,410	26.01
Maharashtra	62,693,898	29,695,721	47.37
West Bengal	54,485,560	22,271,867	40.88
Andhra Pradesh	53,403,619	15,989,266	29.94
Madhya Pradesh	52,131,717	14,502,063	27.82
Tamil Nadu	48,297,456	22,111,593	45.78
Karnataka	37,43,451	14,228,947	38.41
Rajasthan	34,102,912	8,201,615	24.05
Gujarat	33,960,905	14,858,075	43.75
Orissa	26,272,054	8,964,625	34.12
Kerala	25,403,217	17,571,819	69.17
Assam *	19,902,826	—	—
Punjab	16,669,755	6,791,547	40.74
Haryana	12,850,902	4,605,649	35.84
Delhi	6,196,414	3,783,611	61.06
Jammu & Kashmir *	5,981,600	—	—
Himachal Pradesh	4,237,569	1,777,201	41.94
Tripura	2,060,189	856,688	41.58
Manipur	1,433,691	601,943	41.99
Meghalaya	1,327,874	441,077	33.22
Goa, Daman & Diu	1 082,117	604,489	55.86
Nagaland	773,281	324,700	41.99
Arunachal Pradesh	628,050	126,185	20.09
Pondichery	604,136	327,600	54.23
Mizoram	487,774	290,241	59.50
Chandigarh	450,061	291,091	64.68
Sikkim	315,682	106,780	33.83
Andaman & Nicobar Islands	188,254	96,520	51.27
Dadra & Nagar Haveli	103,677	27,578	26.60
Lakshadweep	40,237	22,018	54.72

* Projected figures

Source : Census of India 1981.

There is a District Education Officer of inspectorate circle for each district. By the end of March, 1985 there were 927 Primary Schools with 45,015 male and 41,722 female students; 490 Middle Schools with 16,515 male and 15,338 female students; 140 High Schools with 8,608 male and 6,831 female students and 12 Colleges with 3,340 male and 1,546 female students. Mizoram has got North Eastern Hill University's Mizoram Campus at Aizawl (Pachhunga University College, Aizawl). There was a proposal in 1989 that a new University in Mizoram at Aizawl would be opened soon.

Language

The colourful tribes of this region are speak *Tibeto-Burman* language in their respective tribal dialects of their own. The *Lushai* or *Dulian* or *Mipatawng* language is a *lingua franca* in Mizoram. In town area, people generally talk in English. Rarely they speak in Hindi as perhaps they dislike to entertain it. In village, neither English nor Hindi is rapoken by them. But outside the State Mizoram, they however, can manage to speak broken Hindi with Hindi speaking people in case the person do not know English.

They do not have their own scripts. For that, they are using *Roman* scripts. The Christian Missionaries were first to introduce education in this area along with the British Government and they introduced Roman scripts here. *Lushai* or *Dulian* dialects of *Tibeto-Burman* family of the *Lushai, Kuki, Mizo, Lakher* group are almost similar one with another with certain variation in intonation and accent of the land where they are living in. They have some affinities with the Manipuri (*Meithei*) language. The *Chakma* people speak a dialect which is almost similar to that of *Chittagong's* (Bangladeshi) language. The *Reangs* are almost akin to the *Chakmas*.

Chieftainship

The administration of Mizoram during the time of Britishers was run by a Superintendent (after Independence they are known as a Deputy Commissioner) with the assistance of Chiefs and Circle Interpreters. Under the 6th Schedule of the Constitution of India the Mizo District Council was set

TABLE 4

Dulian Language

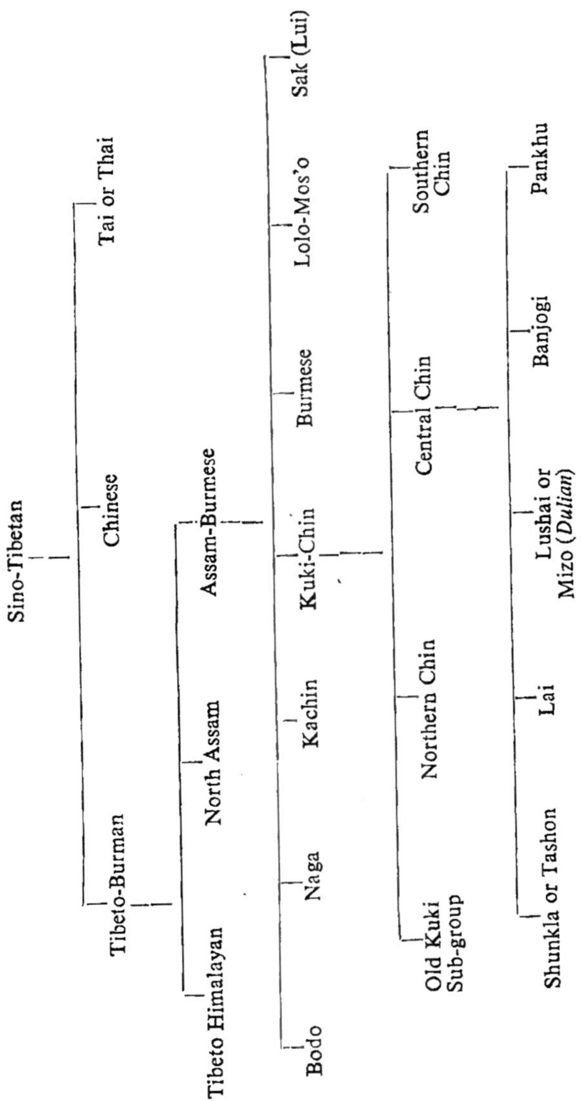

* P.K. Bandyopadhyay (1985) : 29.

up in 1952. At the recommendation of the District Council, the Chieftainship was abolished in 1955 by an Act of Assam Government when Mizoram *Lushai Hills* was an autonomous district of Assam. Thereafter, the Chief became powerless at the induction of District Councils.

Historically, it is stated that all the Lushai Chiefs are the descendents of *Thangnur* who lived in the earlier part of the 18th century at *Tlangkna*, north of *Falam* of *Chin Hills* in Burma. Due to economic hardship they moved towards western side and occupied *Lushai Hills* (Mizoram). It is reported that *Sailo* Chief established his control over north and south Lushai Hills. They drove the *Old Kuki* tribe towards northern side. These *Old Kuki* tribes had migrated to Lushai Hills before them.

Generally the youngest son of a Chief of *Sailo* family of Lusei clan had to inherit the Chiefship (known as *Lal*). This chieftainship was hereditary. He was to be a head of his clan and possessed unlimited power. He was to rule his residing main village (*Khawpui*) and other sub-villages (*Khawapers*) of his clan members under him. Brothers of a Chief could set up a new village in new sites separately under them at their own capacity and they could be a new Chief among thir own followers.

A Chief (*Lal*) had to settle most of the disputes of his main village and sub-villages. He had to appoint some elderly Mizo male residers of his village as his councillors (*Upas*) to get assistance in his administrative work. The sub-villages (*Khuwapers*) were generally placed by the Chief under the charge of his sons. The Deputy Commissioner had, however, the power to dismiss any Chief. Sometimes the Mizos had few unofficial female Chiefs (*Rains*) who had some power and importance in their village.

In Mizo society there is no high or low status. There was no individual ownership of land. Before 1952, when the Chief had power, all the land was owned by the Chief on behalf of the village community. No villager could have cultivated without any permission from their Chief. Actually their Chief had to allot the area for cultivation only at the capacity of the agriculturist on a temporary basis. He had to select the *jhum* site and decide when and where a villager could cultivate. The *Ramhuals* are the best agriculturists and they had the privilege to select the best site for cultivation. Each cultivator had to give a share of rice which he produced to their Chief and the quantity depended on the quality of *jhum* land assigned to him.

A Chief was to receive the fine imposed on the offenders. He had to receive the right fore-leg of every wild animal which was killed by his villagers. The house of a Chief was generally much bigger than the house of the common people. The villagers had to build and carry out annual repairs of the house of the Chief without any cash remuneration. In return, the Chief had to give them a big feast.

A Chief had to receive fish-tax (*ngawichhiah*), honey tax (*khuaichhiah*) etc. A Chief was to get free porters when he travelled from one place to another. A Chief had right to drive out from his village any person who had incurred his displeasure or whom he had considered as not good. A villager had his right to migrate from one area of a Chief to another if the latter one (Chief) agreed.

Besides the *Upas*, the Chief had to appoint some more village officials. They are : the *Tlangau* (village announcer) who had to announce the order of a Chief in a loud voice ; the *Thirdeng* (a village blacksmith) whose duty was to make and repair tools such as hoes, daos, axe etc ; the *Puithim* (village priest) who performed the sacrifice etc. The Chief had a separate personal priest known as *Sadawt*. The *Ramhual*, who was an unofficial important person, was to get preference of first choice of *jhum* land for a year. A Chief also had to appoint *Zalens* who was the first person to choose jhum land and he even get preference than to that of *Ramhuals*. These *Zalen* were actually a near relative of the Chief.

Slavery

In earlier days the Mizo Chiefs enjoyed in raiding the neighbouring hill territories and also plain areas to bring wealth to add as their own and to capture some person to make their slaves. A Chief was to protect his followers and offered them best livelihood. Naturally he could attract more followers in his land to absorb the smaller Chiefs and his followers under him. This system created an inter-tribal rivalries between stronger Chief and weaker Chief. As such a dispute was always there with the clan members of eastern, western and northern areas of Mizoram. It is reported that a Chief's house acted as an asylum of the offenders. If a person after committing any offence entered the house of a Chief he could get protection in lieu of his slave life (*chemsenboi*) to that Chief.

Police

During British administration in *Lushai Hills* (Mizoram), police forces was required to keep peace in the area. *Aijal* (Aizawl) Police Station was first to he established in 1896 ; Sairang Out Post was established in 1948.Later-on Mizoram Government strengthened the police department by setting Police Headquarters at Aizawl with Inspector General of Police as its head. The IGP is to get assistance from his Duputy Inspector General of Police, Superintendents of Police, Deputy Superintendents of Police etc. There is a Superintendent of Police posted in each district assisted by Deputy Superintendent of Police, Inspectors, Sub-Inspectors, Assistant Sub-Inspectors and Constables.

In 1985, altogether 18 Police Stations and Out Posts in Mizoram existed to improve the law and order situation under the charge of Sub-Inspectors. All Police Stations are set up after Independence except Aizawal Police Station. Total cases reported during 1985 at Aizawl District for offences is 483, Lunglei District 256 and Chhimtuipui District 213. The *Village Councils* exercises great influence on the social life of villagers in Mizoram.

Curfew Habitation

Outsiders would be certainly surprised when they will see the shops and business markets are closing their doors for the day at about 4 p.m. and most of the people of Mizoram are returning to their home by 5 p.m. Actually this has happened as they had faced several times *curfew* in their State in the past on several occasions and they are now gladly accustomed with night *curfew* as their daily routine. The Mizos have yet to learn to move freely in the small hours of night. By 6 p.m. most of the streets have a deserted look. By that time the Mizos are almost over their dinner.

Population

The total population of Mizoram is 4,93,757 (*Census of India 1981*) of which 2,57,239 are male and 2,36,518 are female (Table 5.) The urban population is 1, 21, 814 and rural 3,71,943. The population of Mizoram is predominantly tribal. The total tribal population is 46,1913 and the percentage was 93.54 per cent in 1981. There are many tribes and sub-tribes among them with traditional culture and languages. It is said that the Mizos look very mild but when occasion comes they can be very tough at their demand.

TABLE 5

Population of Mizoram

Name of District	Population		Total	Density of population per sq. km.
	Male	Female		
Aizawl	1,76,242	1,64,584	3,40,826	27
Lunglei	45,998	40,513	86,511	19
Chhimtuipui	34,999	31,421	66,420	17

The Mizos are inhabited in other States also such as Manipur, Tripura, Assam and Meghalaya. They also live in Calcutta and in Burma and Bangladesh. The following are the major tribes and sub-tribes of Mizoram *viz* Lakher (Mara), Lushai, Hmar, Powi (Poi), Ralte, Khiangte, Simte, Paite, Gangte, Thadou, Zou, Vaiphei, Chawnghu, Fanai, Tlanglaus, Pangs etc. They came to this area from eastern and northern part of this State and the western part (Chin Hills) of Burma. There are some sub-tribes of the Lushai and the Kuki. They are : the Chuingow, Chuihang, Zadeng etc. There are some other tribes also in Mizoram. They are : the Riang, Chakma, Mag etc, who came from *Chittagong Hill Tracts* of Bangladesh and Tripura. There are also some non-tribals like Nepali, Assamese, Bengali, Bihari who have recently settled in this state.

TABLE 6

Main Tribes

Districts	Headquarters	Main Tribes
Aizawl	Aizawl	Mizo (Lushai) Hmar, Paite, Gangte, Thadou, Zou, Ralte, Vaiphei, Simte, Kuki, Riang, Mog.
Lunglei	Linglei	Lushai, Paite, Pawi (Poi), Chakma
Chhimtuipui	Saiha	Pawi (Poi), Lakher, Chakma.

Working Population

The Mizos are very hard working people. There were 87.1 per cent in 1961 of the total population cultivator and 12.9 per cent other types of worker. In 1971 there were 87.6 per cent cultivator and 12.4 per cent other types of worker ; 44.6 per cent of the total population were male worker and 43.0 per cent female. Most of the women in the villages are helping their male folk in *jhum* fields.

Migration

The Mizos came to their present habitat from *Chin Hills* of Burma. According to their legends they originally belonged to *Sinlung* area on the bank of the river *Mekong* in south-western China. They migrated to Mizoram in different waves from *Chin Hills* in the latter part of the 18th century. This migration was forced on them by the stronger people of Burma and also, due to great famine. After migration to Mizoram *Lushai Hills*) they pushed out other earlier inhabited *Old Kuki* tribes such as the *Rangkhols*, *Baites*, *Thadous* etc. towards north of the State and the *Mizos*, the *New Kuki* tribes occupied the present Mizoram area.

Some of the Mizos have migrated to the north-eastern part of Tripura State. Similarly, some of them have Migrated to the southern part of Manipur State, North Cachar Hills and Mikir Hills of Assam State. They also migrated to the eastern range of *Chittagong* (Bangladesh) and to a part of western Burma. Several thousands of the Mizos are now settled also in Shillong and other places of Meghalaya. Thus, it is observed that they have scattered in most of the places of north-east India including in their own land Mizoram.

House Pattern

The Mizos generally build their house close to one another in an orderly manner, arranged in a part of rows, the front side of each pair facing one with another on the top of hill ridges for their defence. The village is separated by running in between a pair of rows of houses. This type of arrangement of village houses on rows running parallel to the main street are also seen in the villages of the *Apatani* in Arunachal Pradesh. Mizo villages vary in size and population. Small villages are formed with not less than thirty houses while the larger villages consists over five hundred houses. All these villages are separated from one another by several miles.

The houses are built on strongly woven splited bamboo or timber-wood platform. Each house has wooden posts and timber gates. The houses are thatched with *sunn* grassed thatched-roof. These are generally constructed with bamboo wall, bamboo floor and thatched roof. The rich families are using C.I. sheets tin roof, wooden floor, *ikra* wall plastered with mud or cement and sand. A Mizo hut is raised at about one or two feets above the ground level. The floor is made on a wooden or bamboo planks called *machan*. Each house has a single big room without any partition inside the room. One may be surprised as the tin-roofed-houses has a big sized long funnel which they use to collect rain-water from the roof to their reservers and they use that water for the whole year.

The trophies, skulls and horns of animals which they killed are proudly displayed by them in the main front portion of their house. Their room is quite spacious and its length is almost thrice than its breadth. At the middle of the room there is an earthen hearth where cooking is done. In the last portion of their room they make a raised wooden platform by the side of walls which they use as a sleeping platform for the whole of their family members. The room has two doors one at the front side and another at the back. Their houses generally does not have any window. They usually keep the domestic animals below their plank of the room.

Due to acculturation, education, high status and quick developments the Mizos are now rapidly changing their traditional house pattern of earlier days. They now construct several rooms in their houses with doors and windows with ventilations. Now there is a bamboo fencing with bamboo spikes and timber gate in their compound for the security of the house and family members. Most of them have a kitchen-garden in their house-compounds.

In old days, they had no habituation to repair their old and broken houses. When their old houses became unfit for habituation they had to build another new house for staying purpose in a new site nearby to their earlier old damaged houses and they had to leave that old house to be demolished naturally in course of time. The Mizos haye started living in a fixed dwelling house.

Zawlbuk

Zawlbuk is a dormitory for the young unmarried boys. But this has now almost vanished. In old days every village has a *zawlbuk*. This is a big house with one room. The young male bachelor of the village had to sleep here at night. This *zawlbuk* now also exist among some of the *Mizos* where it acts only as a recreation club. Young male folk are trained here on various arts and crafts, dances and musics, wrestling, behaviour, morality, ceremonial function and discipline. It is also used as a guest house of the male members of the village. Women are not allowed inside this *zawlbuk*. This dormitory system is now, however, gradually fading away due to education, spread of Christianity and acculturation.

Social Custom and Code of Conduct

The Mizos are very much disciplined people. Some excellent social custom is found among them. These are based on some good principle of self help and co-operation of one Mizo with another. This helping attitude and co-operation is almost nil among other societies This rare social customs are really appreciable which teaches a man to be kind, hospitable, unselfish, brave, equality of status and energetic habit.

As per *hnatlang* system, the Mizos contribute their labour for the welfare of their community by helping to construct inter-village paths, community halls, water points etc. According to their *tlawngaihna* or *tlawnghaimaina* system, the Mizos extend their help to a distress one as their social obligation. If a Mizo is missing, a customary search party from the village of the missing person will voluntarily go out for seven days to find out that missing person. If a Mizo dies in another village, other than his own village, his dead body is carried voluntarily by the villagers of the dead person to bring to his own village. If a Mizo is invited to a feast, he is expected to eat little food so that, others may not be deprived from that feast. If a young man meets with an old person who is carrying a heavy load, the Mizo young man is expected to immediately relieve that old one by carrying that heavy load to the destination of that old person. If a person falls sick in the village and needs shifting to a hospital which may be situated a long distance, the Mizo youth villagers will carry the sick person immediately on a stretcher on their back all the way even if it is several day's march to reach to a hospital. If a villager's house is destroyed, his co-villagers are expected to build a new one or rebuild that immediately.

To accept a reward or remuneration of such services is below their dignity. There are many other voluntary useful services among the Mizos till today.

Religion and Belief

The traditional religion of the Mizos is *Animism*. They believe in one supreme God who is the creator of every thing in this world. This supreme God is known to them as *Pathian*, a benevolent being. But *Pathian*, according to their belief, has little to do on human affairs as numerous demons and spirits (*huais*) are more powerful among the mankind than their God *Pathian*. *Huais* (spirits) are two types : good and evil. These spirits live in trees, mountains, rocks, streams and caves. The good *huais* (spirit) causes good to mankind and sometimes it is said that it acts as *Pathian*. The evil spirit (*khuavang*) causes harm to people. All types of calamities, failure of growing crops, ill health, disease, death and other misfortunes are due to evil demons (*khuavang*). They thought, their *Puithian* can (magic doctor/*bez*/sorcerer) know what particular spirit is the cause of the trouble. *Pathian* prescribes, according to the nature and magnitude of the distress, what particular sacrifice is necessary to appease the spirit. At this, a member of the clan sacrifices pigs, fowls and other domestic birds or animals whatever asked by the *Pthian*. The number and method of sacrifices varies from clan to clan.

They believed that the good person's soul after death goes to heaven (*pialral*) where they would live, in comfort and happiness as all good things are available there in plenty and the life is luxurious. The bad one are punished in the hell (*Mithikhua*) which is a village of dead person with sorrow and deserted. This site is supposed to be located in the *Rih* lake in *Chin-Hills* of Burma near *Champhai*, a border-village Mizoram. After staying in this place for sometime the bad person's soul is to get their rebirth in the lower position of life. According to their belief those who have given five big feasts and have killed an elephant, a bear, a wild boar, a wild *mithun* (bison), a king cobra they can go easily to heaven (*pialral*).

Now only few of the Mizos are *Animist*. This religion was spread sometimes before 1927. The first Presbyterian Missionary Rev. William Williams followed by Savidge and Lorrain entered into north *Lushai Hills* (Mizoram) in 1891 from Khasi Jaintia Hills. This was almost immediately after the setting up of British administration and Military Headquarters at *Aijal* (Aizawl). About 95 per cent of the Mizos are now Christian. The Missionaries are completely successful in Mizoram to spread the Christianity. Most of them are *Protestant* and some of them are *Catholic*, the *American Baptist Mission*, *Union Penticostal*, *Salvation Army*, the *North East India General Mission*, the *Presbyterian Church*. The *Roman Catholic Mission*, the *Seventh Day Adventist*, *Independent Church of India* etc. are spreading the Christianity among the Mizos. They are very keen on going to the Church for Sunday service and very rarely miss it.

The *Chakmas* are Buddhist people. They are inhabited in the south-western corner of the State along with some *Mog* and *Riang* people. The *Mogs* are Buddhist but the *Riangs* are mainly *Animist* though there are many worshippers of Hindu God and Goddess. All these people are different from the *Mizos* in language, culture and religion.

TABLE 7
Religion of Mizoram

Name of Religion	Person	Male	Female
Christian	4,13,840	2,07,485	2,06,355
Buddhist	40,429	21,073	19,356
Hindu	35,245	25,660	9,585
Muslim	2,205	1,812	393
Sikh	421	376	45
Jain	11	7	4
Others (Religious Persuasion)	1,606	826	780
Total	4,93,757	2,57,239	2,36,518

Source : Census of India 1981

Superstitions and Believes

The Mizos are superstitious race. They do not kill certain animals as they believe it is unlucky. There is no *totemism* in this superstition. They believe in witchcraft and black magic. Besides these wizards they believe in evil spirit which, according to them, is supported to have the habit to enter inside the bodies of good person to make trouble. As per their belief each person has possessed three types of spirits : *Khawhrin* general and medium type, *Thlarao* wiseness and *Thlarao* foolishness. The Mizos believe in rebirth like the *Hindus*. As it is stated earlier that they believe, the spirit of a dead person goes to *Pialral* where all good things are available in plenty. The people who are good will stay here with full of comforts and happiness. Those who are not good, they will go to *Mitthi-Khua* (which is a place of sorrow) and their spirit after staying in this place for some time returns to this earth either in the shape of a new born child or a lower ranked creature.

Festivals and Feasts

There are several types of festivals among the Mizos. Most of them are in connection with their agriculture related to season, crops and stages of their *jhum* operation. During festival, their dances and music takes main part with rice-beer *Zu* which they widely consume. There are, in connection with the plantation of crops, three types of feasts called *Chap-char Kut, Mim Kut* and *Pawl Kut*. The first one is the most important spring festival held in between the cutting of jungles and burning of *jhums* usually in the last part of February and first part of March every year. This is celebrated with great enthusiasm and splendour. The meaning of the *Chap-char Kut* is *Chap*-bamboo, tree or other jungle cut down and awaiting for burning for *jhum, Char*-felling of trees which are exposed to sun to make it dry, *kut*-festival. They believe that this festival would ensure a good harvest in their field. The *Pawl Kut* is celebrated during September to January when rice harvest is almost reaped. It is another great festival with plenty of fun-fare and feasting. This festival is mainly for the children who are dressed in their best and are fed with rice meat and boiled eggs. *Min Kut* festival is held with great fun-fare with plenty of rice-beer when maize harvest is reaped during August to September. This festival is celebrated with feasting, singing and dancing.

They have *Mithi-rop lam* (dance of the dead) feast. It is held in honour of the deceased-members of a clan by keeping the effigies of the fore-fathers of various family members of the clan who are arranging the *Mithi-rop lam* feast. The effigies are taken back soon after the dance and feast by the respective descendants.

Dance

The Mizos have their traditional dances. Their most popular dance is the *Cheraw* (bamboo dance). In this dance six girls squat on the ground holding bamboo poles which are rhythmically shifted and struck against one another. Six other girls dance-moving between the shifting bamboos. *Khual lam* is another popular dance. In this dance a group of boys with flying hand dance rhythmically with gentle turns below their own *puandum* (a special Mizo shawl) on the tunes of gongs and drum beats. There is another dance known as *Solakia*. In this dance, men and women dance rhythmically by making a big circle at the tune of drum beats.

Musical Instruments

The Mizos are fun loving people and love to sing and dance. Almost all Mizos can sing. Their favourite musical instruments are : *Daiaipong, Dalpabo, Dapi, Goseem Sheliangdah* etc. The instruments *Daiaipong* and *Dalpabo* produce different sounds with their three numbers of brass metaled discs of each sets. A bell metalled gong is called *Dapi* which produces a loud majestic sound. A common *tom-tom* (drum) they like to use in their music. *Goseem*, an iron made flute pipe is also used by them. *Sheliangdah*, (a veena) is another musical instrument. They can prepare a reed instrument by inserting reeds into a dry hollow gourd. Tunes of Mizo folk songs are alike to Naga and some other songs are sung in soft and low tones.

The Mizo younger generation is now preferring the western music and dances. Western tunes have got mixed up with the tune of their Mizo traditional songs. Their favourite musical instrument is Spanish-guitar which can be seen even in the most interior villages of Mizoram. They like to play mouth-organ, piano, tape recorder, record player, radio, T.V. etc.

Administration (Historical and Political)

There are no systematic records to trace the history of the Mizo tribes. The Mizos, however, came to Lushai Hills (Mizoram) from the Chin Hills of Shan State of Burma. During 1400 AD to 1700 AD they entered Burma from south-east Asia. It is presumed that due to famine or pressure of over population or pressure of the stronger clan the *Chins* in

Burma, they moved further west and entered inside the area of Lushai Hills in 17th to 18th century from Upper Burma under the leadership of their *Chiefs*.

Their first Chief was known to be a Lushai called *Zahmuaka* who had six sons. They formed six ruling Lushai clans : *Zadeng*, *Palian*, *Thangluah*, *Rivung*, *Rekhum* and *Sailo*. It is said that *Sailova*, the Chief, set up a tradition of *Sailo* chief. They came to rule in the northern and middle parts of the Lushai Hills (Mizoram). There was inter-tribal and inter clan feuds among them with other immigrant communities such as the *Hmars*, the *Pawis* (*Poi*) etc. The *Sailo* chief among them emerged very powerful and stronger who ruled over many villages for many years.

Most of the Chiefs had their bitterness with another Chief. They had border disputes and clashes with their neighbouring tribes. From 1840 to 1892, the Mizos continued to resist the new rulers. In 1850, a war had broken out in between the tribes of north, south, east and west of Lushai Hills (Mizoram). This war continued for few years. The Lushais made some hostility with the people of Chittagong Hill Tracts, Sylhet and Cachar. At this, in 1871-72, two British punitive columns had entered for the first time inside the Lushai Hills : one from Chittagong and another from Cachar. In 1890, the angry Lushai rebels had attacked the Britishers in Aijal and Changsil. Pi Ropuiliari resisted the British occupation of Lushai Hills during the period 1871-1893. In 1893, she was captured by the British forces. She died in 1895 in Chittagong prison. To control the Lushais, the British administrators had annexed this Lushai Hills in 1891 with India and set up their administrative and military headquarters at *Aijal* (Aizawl), The history of British administration in Lushai Hills truly begins in the year 1891 when this area was divided by them in between Assam and Bengal. Prior to 1890, there was no regular administrative set up. In 1891, the northern part of the Lushai Hills with headquarters at Aijal went to the province "Assam" while the southern part with headquarters at Lunglei was administered by the undivided province "Bengal" (at that time present day's West Bengal together with Bangladesh was called "Bengal").

Again there was a rebellion attack in 1892 by the Lushais all over the Lushai Hills. The north and the south Lushai Hills was amalgamated in 1898 and it was brought under the province "Assam". This Lushai Hills district was made a *Scheduled* district of Assam in 1901-02 with its headquarters at Aijal. A *Superintendent* (later on called as Deputy Commissioner) was placed as an *In-Charge* of this Lushai Hills district with two sub-divisions. For administrative convenience, this district was divided into 18 *Circles*. Among these, 12 and 6 *Circles* was formed for Aijal and Lunglei Sub-Divisions respectively. For each Circle there was a *Circle Interpreter* (*Dobhasi*) who acted as a Liasion Officer of the Superintendent and the village Chiefs of different tribes. These Circle Interpreters were those Lushais who were educated in the Missionary Schools. Government paid them a salary.

The village administration was left out to the "Chief" (*Lal*). This village Chief had two sets of function, one secular and village defence and the other one religious and ceremonial. A Chief was responsible for peace and prosperity of his village. A Chief had to settle all disputes in his village according to their customary laws of the land. He had to distribute the *jhum* land among his villagers for *jhuming*.

The *Chief* was to get assistance by a Council of Village elders called *Upas*. They were appointed by the Chief. Besides the *Upas*, the Chief had to appoint few village officials to get help on village administration. They were : the *tlangau* (village announcer who was to announce the orders of the Chief in a loud voice , the *thirdeng* (village blacksmith), the puithiam (village priest), the khawchhiar (village writer) etc. The British rulers had increased the number of Chiefs by taking out from other clans and allotted them some vacant land to establish their own village. This type of Chief was known as *Hnamchawm* chiefs. There were some other chiefs of the *Lakher*, the *Pawi* (*Poi*) in the southern part of Lunglei subdivision. They did not follow the *Sailo* chiefs. There was also the *Fanai* chiefs. All these chiefs followed their indigenous system of village administration. This chieftainship was hereditary. The *Sailo* chiefs were generally the member of the *Sailo* family of the Lushai clan. Similarly, the other chiefs were from their respective family and clan. The village, where the chief resided was called *Khawpui* (principal village) and the other surrounding villages which were under the rule of the chief was called *Khawapers* (sub-villages). Sometimes these sub-villages were run under the charge of chief's son. The chief was to get the best *jhum* site and *buhchhun* (free contribution of huge quantity of paddy) from each household of his village. The villagers contributed without any labour charge the biggest sized house for their chief. He was to get *Sachhiah*, share of the right fore leg of every hunts, fine which was levied for offences, tax revenue in paddy from his villagers. A chief could turn out anyone from his village whom he disliked. A villager had his right to migrate to another village if the chief of the latter village agreed to give him shelter in his village.

The Superintendent was empowered to interfere in the administration of chiefs only when the case of a villager went out beyond the control of the chief such as serious types of inter-clan dispute, criminal activity etc. The Superintendent was the official head of all Government departments in Lushai Hills. The entire power was in his hand till Lushai Hills became an autonomous district of Assam under 6th Schedule to the Constitution of India. This area was administered through certain brief and simple rules called *Rules for Administration of Justice* in Lushai Hills.

There was no political activities in Lushai Hills till the end of Second World War. The Christian Missionaries entered into the Lushai Hills in 1891. They set up Primary Schools and Hospitals. They introduced Christianity widely since 1907 onwards in this area. After that, some newly educated Christian Mizos were slowly turning against their *Chiefs* who ruled them with their iron hands. At this, the *Chiefs* had opposed to all Christian teachings as it interfered the traditional Mizo life and religion. But most of the Mizos were at that time, rapidly converting themselves into Christian.

On 3rd January 1921 the Governor-General-in-Council declared the Lushai Hills as backward tract under *Section 52 of the Government of India Act 1919*. By the *Frontier Tract Regulation No. II of 1880*, it was excluded from the operation of laws, both Criminal and Civil Procedure Code. The hill areas of Assam, at the *Simon Commission's Report (1929)*, were divided into *excluded areas* and *partial excluded areas*. Under *Section 92 of Government of India Act, 1935*, the Lushai Hills District was included in the list of *Excluded Area* within the Province of Assam from 1st April, 1937 and was adminstered by the Governor of Assam through a Superintendent. This excluded area meant that no Act of the Central or Provincial Legislature could apply to the *Lushai Hills District* without the instruction of Governor of Assam who was empowered to make regulations to keep proper law and order for this *excluded area* (the term exclu ed area does not mean that this area was outside India). Under the Rule for Administration of Justice in Lushai Hills, the Deputy Commissioner (formerly Superintendent) was the head of criminal and civil justice. He also exercised the powers of the District Civil and Session Judge. The Criminal Procedure Code applied to the district only in spirit. The Administration of Justice was conducted within less possible time and in a very simpler method. The separation of *Burma* in 1935 and formation of East Pakistan (now Bangladesh) in 1947 has created a big change in the political life of the Mizos.

Mizo Union was the first political party which was formed in Lushai Hills on 9th April, 1946. Mr. Pachhunga was the first elected President of that party. At the Independence of India in 1947, this party decided to keep *Lushai Hills* as a part of Assam and they had sent their decision to the Governor of Assam. At this, another political party known as United Mizo Freedom Organisation (UMFO) which was formed after 1947 under Mr. Lalmawia, demanded to merge Lushai Hills with *Burma*. This party got full support from the Mizo *Chiefs*. But, this party could not attract much to the Mizos and it later-on merged with the Eastern India Tribal Union (EITU) a political party of the Khasi Jaintia and Gara Hills of Assam (now Meghalaya) which desired to carve-out a separate State within Indian Union. The Mizo Union was affiliated to the *Indian National Congress*. A civil disobedience movement was launched by the Mizo Union in 1943 against the authority of the Chiefs. Soon after the *Constitution of India* came into force in 1950, the administration of Lushai Hills was brought under Council of Ministers of Assam.

The *Mizo Union* was very much popular in *Lushai Hills District of Assam* and it captured all the three allotted seats in the first general election in 1952 in the *Assam Legislative Assembly*. It had gained most of the seats in the *District Council* and *Village Councils* which were set up in 1952 to do the work on legislative and executive matter. The Chieftainship was abolished with effect from 1st April, 1955 by an act of the Government of Assam. On 3rd April, 1953, the *Pawi-Lakher Regional Council* was set up and the area of the *Pawi-Lakher* was given Autonomous administration.

At the time of the second general election in 1957, the *Mizo Union* could secure only two seats in the *Assam Assembly* while the third seat was captured by the *Eastern India Tribal Union (EITU)*. The Mizo Union however, retained its majority the *District Council* and *Village Councils*. In 1959 *Mizo National Famine Front* was formed by Mr. Laldenga for relief work when there was a serious famine in *Lushai Hills*. Mr. Laldenga was a havildar-clerk in the *Indian Army*. He was a member of the *Pawi* tribe (*Fanai*). After sometimes, he became a clerk in the *Mizo District Council*. He was dismissed from this Council in 1958 due to misappropriation. He became the President of this *Mizo Nationol Famine Front*. This Front turned itself into *Mizo National Front (MNF)* on 12th October, 1962 to establish a *Government of Sovereign. Independent, Greater Mizoram*. This MNF divided the *Lushai Hills District* (unofficially) for their own political activities into four zones. Each zone was called by them a *bung* and was kept under a self-styled *Chief Commissioner*. Under him there was self-styled *Deputy Commissioner* for sub-areas of *bung*. There was self-styled *Mizo National Army*. Some of them had surrendered afterwards to Indian Government and got their job in *2nd Battalion* of the *Assam Regiment*.

In 1960, Assam Assembly had adopted the *Assam Language Bill*. This Bill safeguarded the tribal languages only at their district level and not at the State level. The *Mizo Union* and *Eastern India Tribal Union* (*EITU*) were not satisfied.

at this *Bill* and they withdrew their three elected members from the State *Assembly of Assam*. At that time it was headed by the Chief Minister Sri Bimala Prasad Chaliha.

In the third general elections in 1962, the *Mizo Union* won two Assembly seats while the third seat went to the *Mizo Union* supported nominee of the *Eastern India Tribal Union* (*EITU*) which was associated with the *All Party Hill Leaders' Conference* (*APHLC*) of Shillong (now the capital of Meghalaya). On 24th October, 1962, both the *Mizo Union* nominees resigned from their Assembly seats at the demand of *APHLC* but, the *EITU* nominee refused to resign his seat from the Assembly. After that, two bye-elections were held in 1963 for *Aijal* and *Lunglei* constituencies and in 1964 for *Aijal East*. In 1963 bye-election, the *MNF* party raised their demand for independence of *Mizo Hills*. They won both the seats by defeating *Mizo Union* candidates with a small margin of votes and sent Mr. John F. Manliana who won from *Aijal West* and Mr. Lalmawia (*Junior*) who won from Lungliei Constituency for *Assam Assembly*. In December 1963 the *MNF* president Mr. Laldenga and vice-president Mr. Lalnunmawia were arrested while they were returning along with some other Mizo people from their visit to East Pakistan (now Bangladesh) to get arms and army training of *MNF* volunteers to fulfil the dream of *MNF* for *independent, greater Mizoram*. They were later released in February, 1964 on acceptance of their written understanding of good conduct to the Assam Chief Minister. The second bye-election of 1964 was held for *Aijal East* Constituency of the Assam Assembly as this seat was vacated at the resignation of the *EITU* member Mr. R. Thanhlira who got appointment as Chairman of the *Assam Public Service Commission*. In this bye-election Mr. Chalchhunga, the *Mizo Union* president won by a good margin of votes.

The MNF openly, therefore, forcefully collected *donations* from towns and villages for their *MNF* volunteer's arm training and procuring arms for them. A conference was held in Junary 1965 with all Mizo and near-Mizo parties of Assam, Manipur, Tripura and Mizoram at *Churachandpur* (Manipur). In October 1965, a deputation from *Mizo Union* met with the then Prime Minister, Late Shri Lal Bahadur Shastri for early constitution of a Mizoram State. At this, Late H.V. Pataskar (the then Chairman of the Hill Areas' Commission) under *Nehru Plan* of Autonomy came to examine the *Mizo Union's* demand. But the *Mizo Union* had boycotted this *Pataskar Commission* while *MNF* met Mr. Pataskar to submit their *Memorandum* in which they had demanded *sovereign and independent Mizoram.*

Actually Assam Government did not plan suitably for Mizo Hills District to improve and develop the area. This deprivation made the Mizo people unhappy and some of them felt that this neglectness was a bad bargain for the Mizos to continue as a part of India. Dissatisfaction with Assam Government was very high when the tragic famine of 1959 descended upon them while miser planned policy and *Assam Language Bill (1960)* was adopted. Their anger thus burst out into open rebellion activities. The *MNF* had started an armed uprising on 28th February 1966 by declaring *Independence.* They jumped and attacked different towns in Mizo Hills District, raided treasuries, tried to take over the administration, disrupted communications and attempted to drive out non-Mizos from this district. For this disturbance, army was called out in Mizo Hills District on 3rd March, 1966. The army controlled first Aijal and thereafter Lunglei Subdivisions within a week. On 2nd March, 1966, the Assam Government declared the Mizo Hills District as a *disturbed area* for six months under *Armed Force's (Assam and Manipur) Special Power Act, 1958.* By an extra ordinary *Gazettee Notification* published on 6th March 1966 the Government of India declared the *MNF* as unlawful organisation.

During the Indo-Pak war of 1965, Mr. Laldenga was under a great pressure from his party volunteers (rebels) to start trouble in Mizo Hills District. But he could not do so as he was not fully prepared. Mr. Laldenga, therefore, on 1st March 1966 formed a self styled underground *shadow government* and named it *Mizoram Sarkar* with the following office bearers which was secretly announced :

President : David Laldenga
Vice President : Lalnunmawia
Home Minister : Sainghaka
Finance Minister : C. Lalkhawliana
Defence Minister : R. Zamawia.
Foreign Minister : Lalhmingthanga
Information Minister ; Ngurkunga
Chief Justice : John F. Manliana

In December 1965 and January 1966, the MNF had organised a massive fund collecting drive. Contributions were taken by-force from the people. On 22nd June 1966, three delegates of the *Mizo Union* met the then Prime Minister Late Mrs. Indira Gandhi in New Delhi for Statehood. of Mizoram within India.

The 4th general elections of 1967 in Mizo Hills District for the three seats of the Assam Assembly was boycotted by the *Mizo Union* on the ground that there was no peace and normalcy due to insurgency by the rebels of this district. Mr. A. Thanglura, a *Congress* candidate for Aijal West seats was however declared elected as unopposed. In 1968, there was bye-election to the Legislative Assembly for *Aijal East* and *Lunglei* constituencies. It was very difficult for Security forces to deal with the MNF rebels and even to differentiate the underground and the overground Mizos. It was also difficult for the Government to provide security to all the villagers. The Mizos were living scattered which was an advantage to the insurgents. Thus, Government introduced grouping of villages on voluntary and compulsry basis to isolate the *MNF* rebels from the overground Mizos and to develop the economic condition of Mizo Hills District. There were four categories of groupings : *Progressive and Protected Villages* (*PPV*), *New Group Centres* (*NGC*), *Voluntary Group Centres* (*VGC*) and *Extended Loop Area* (*ELA*). About 75 per cent population was effected by these grouping. The order for grouping was issued out by the *Defence of India Rules* (*DIR*) 1962. According to this, about fifty thousand population from 106 villages were resettled in 18 *Group Centres* along Silchar-Aijal-Lunglei, the main road, from Aijal to Lunglei. The first phase of grouping was started on 4th

January, 1967. The Mizo villagers were forced-out of their ancestral dwelling old houses at a very short notice which created a lot of sufferings, torture, atrocities, loss of properties and compelled them to live in a larger village of *Group Centres*.

Immediately after the villagers had vacated, all the houses therein were destroyed as per Defence of India's rule and order. Due to night curfew the villagers had to report every evening to the authority of their Group Centres. The average population in a centre was 2,500 to 7000. Each centre was under an Administrative Officer who got assistance from Extension Officers for development work. A *Group Centre* had Schools, Doctors, Pharmacies Co-operatives Civil Supplies, Godown etc. At the time of shifting they got free ration for more than a year starting from early part of 1967 to June 1968 and rehabilitation grant of Rs. 400 to Rs. 500 only for each family. Free agricultural seeds and implements were also given to them. Cultivable land near their *Group Centres* was alloted by the Government. Assam Government came out with an ordinance known as the *Assam Maintenance of Public Order* (AMPO) 1968. This continued grouping of villages in Mizoram.

The second phase of grouping was made for New Group Centre (NGC) in north, west and east of Northern Mizoram at the order of the District Magistrate in 1969. About 55,000 of population from 185 old villages were grouped into 39 *New Group Centres* under 6 section on Tripura border, East Pakistan (now Bangladesh) border, Lunglei-Demagiri road Lunglei-Lawngtlai road, Selling-Champhai road, Darlawn-Khawbung-North Vanlaiphai-Serchhip road.

The third phase of grouping was made for *Voluntary Group Centres* (*VGC*) in 1968-69 and formally in 1970. Total of 110 villages were grouped into 26 Centres. The fourth phase of grouping was made for *Extended Loop Area* (*ELA*). Total about 63 villages weie grouped into 17 *Group Centres.* The Mizos were, however, fed up with this grouping and regrouping of villages. They challenged the laws in the High Court, Gauhati (Guwahati) which issued a stay-order to the State Government (Assam). Thus, groupings were withdrawn.

In November 1966, Assam Government decided to bring the Mizo Hills District and Cachar District under one administrative unit under a Commissioner-in-Charge. This decision was taken due to geographical isolation of Mizo Hills District from the capital of Assam Shillong (now it is the capital of Meghalaya) and for difficult communication links with the rest of the State especially during monsoon time. But, sporadic disturbances still continued in Mizo Hills District till 1970. Indian army had, however, successfully smashed the key links of the rebellian activities. About 3,500 rebels were either killed or captured since August 1968 and nearly 2,500 rebels surrendered to the Assam Government till amnesty was offered. In January 1969 about 200 rebels made hostility with two *Central Reserve Police* (*CRP*) units. On 15th August 1971, Assam Government repeated its amnesty offer. At this, some rebels including 17 leading members of *MNF* surrendered to the authority. Among them, there was self-styled "Foreign Minister", "Finance Minister and "Education Minister" of the underground so-called "Government of Sovereign, Independent Mizoram".

The Government of India took a decision in 1971 to convert this Mizo Hills District into a *Union Territory* which was agreed by the political leaders of this land. As per *North Eastern Area Re-organisation* (*Amendment*) *Act of 1971* (*Act No. 81 of 1971*) this area became an *Union Territory* on 21st January, 1972 and was named *Mizoram*. According to the Act the *North Eastern Council* (NEC) was formed to co-ordinate the development and security in the area of North East India. The office of *NEC* was established at Shillong (Meghalaya) in 1972. The said Act allotted one seat in *Lok Sabha* and one seat in *Rajya Sabha* for Mizoram. *Article No. 239 of the Constitution of India* was amended to make Mizo Hills District as one of the *Union Territories* to have a local legislature with a Council of Ministers. The Legislature of the *Union Territory* comprised total thirty elected and three nomited members. Of them, 21 were in *Aizawl* District, five in *Lunglei*, four in *Saiha*. The total number of registered voters was 1,57, 007. It got fully autonomous status with a new Lt. Governor as head of the administration of this territory.

Mizoram's capital was formed at *Aizawl.* This territory was started with three districts, nine Sub-Divisions, three autonomous *Hill District Councils,* six Towns, twenty-three Police-Stations, three hundred one Village Councils and twenty Community Development Blocks.

TABLE 8

District of Mizoram

Districts	Area in Sq.	Population	Density of Population per sq. km.
Aizawl	12,581	3,40,826	27
Lunglei	4,536	86,511	19
Chhimtuipui	3,957	66,420	17

Source : Population Census 1981.

The first election of the Legislative Assembly was held in April 1972 and 73 per cent votes were polled. *Mizo Union* won 21 seats out of 30 in the Mizoram Assembly. Thus, the first popular Ministry was formed by the *Mizo Union* on 3rd May 1972 with 4 Cabinet Ministers and 1 Deputy Minister. Mr. Chalchhunga became the Chief Minister. In that election fourteen leading ex-rebels also sought votes but they could not win. Immediately after the formation of the Mizoram Legislative Assembly in 1972, the old District Council was dissolved. In the area of the *Pawi (Poi)-Lakher Regional Council* three separate new *District Councils* was set up for the *Pawi (Poi),* the *Lakher (Mara)* and the *Chakmas.* But insurgency by the MNF rebels was still continuing in Mizoram. On 10th March, 1974, Lt. Governor S.P. Mukherjee and his security guard were attacked by the *MNF* rebels while he was travelling on *Aizawl-Silchar* road. Lt. Governor's leg was injured in that attack. For this, on 8th September 1974 this territory was declared as disturbed area.

Mizo rebels issued *Quit Mizoram Notice* to non-Mizos by giving a deadline of 31st December, 1974. Nothing happened after the *Quit Mizoram Notice* which seemed to them to have been ignored by the non-Mizos. The rebels were perhaps setting out to implement it on a very important one so that it would catch the public eye. On 13th January, 1975, two rebel gunmen dressed in Police Uniform entered in broad day light inside the Conference Room of the Police headquarters in Aizawl where at that time a Conference was going on with three senior Police Officers. They sprayed bullet on them and shot dead the top ranked Police Officers of that room. The victims were Mr. G.S. Arya IGP, Mr. C.B. Sewa DIG and Mr. U.S.P.K. Panchapagesad SP (CID) of Aizawl. They died on the spot. In view of increasing report of cruelty and violence, the order under Armed Forces (Special Power) Act was extended for another six months to help the civil authorities. On 26th June 1975, *Emergency* was declared for whole country of India by the President of India. An *Agreement* was made by the Government of India with the MNF on 1st July 1976 that MNF would give up the violence activities in Mizoram. The *Emergency* was lifted on 22nd March 1977 soon after the results of the 6th General Election of India was announced.

Brig. T. Sailo of *People's Conferencc* installed a five member Ministry on 2nd June, 1978. But this ministry hardly functioned for five months due to withdrawl of the support of 8 MLAs and resignation of the Speaker. After that, President's rule was imposed in Mizoram on 11th November, 1978. The mid-term election to the Legislative Assembly was held on 24th and 27th April 1979. The 3rd popular Mizoram ministry was formed on 8th May, 1979 by Brig. T. Sailo. at the victory of *Peoples Conference (A)* with five ministers. The 7th *Lok Sabha* election was held in January 1980. Dr. Rathuama, *Steering Committee* won the seat. In the middle of May 1980, insurgency again started in Mizoram. Then Central Government decided to start talk with the MNF leader Mr. Laldenga and suspended all operation by the security forces in Mizoram from the midnight of July 31st August 1, 1980 as Mr. Laldenga agreed to stop insurgency from that day. Mr. Laldenga left Delhi on 21st April, 1982 as the last round of talk between the MNF leaders and Government of India broke due to shifting stand of Mr. Laldenga as well as differences on different issues with the Central Government (such as special status for Mizoram, full-flazed Statehood and abolition of the provision of the 6th Schedule for Mizoram).

The fourth election to the Legislative Assembly was held on 15th April, 1984. Under the leadership of Mr. Lalthanhawla (*Congress-I*) the 4th ministry was formed in Mizoram on 5th May 1984. In this election Congress-I secured 20 seats out of 30. Three nominated persons were also of Congress-I. Thus, the total strength of Congress-I was 23 (elected/nominated) in the Assembly. Mr. Laldenga was called back to Delhi from London on 29th October, 1984 for a series of peace talk which was started from 17th December, 1984. The eighth Lok Sabha election to Mizoram parliamentary constituency was held on 24th December, 1985. Mr. Lalthanwle of Congress-I without any contest was elected. Chief Minister Mr. Lalthanhawla Congress-I stepped down in favour of Mr. Laldenga at the instruction from Congress-I high command of Delhi on 21st August 1986 and he become a Deputy Chief Minister of Mr. Laldenga Ministry according to the Accord which was signed by the MNF and Central Government on 30th June 1986. This accord indicated that the outlawed *MNF* would be a full-fledged political party in Mizoram and the insurgency activities of MNF would be called off and lay down their arms and ammunitions.

The aspiration of Statehood was generated among the people of Mizoram with a logic that if Nagaland could be given Statehood, why Mizoram can not get it. At the strong demand, Mizoram Statehood, the *53rd Constitution Amendment Bill, 1986* was passed by the parliament by absolute majority of votes on 7th August, 1986. The President of India also agreed on Mizoram Statehood Bill, 1986 on 14th August, 1986. At this, Mizoram became the 23rd *State* of India on 20th February, 1987.

Fifth election of Mizoram Assembly was held on 16th February, 1987. In that, *MNF* led by Mr. Laldenga got 24 seats out of 40, *Congress-I* led by Mr. Lalthanhawla got 13 seats and *Peoples Conference* led by Brig. T. Sailo got 3 seats. Thus, Mr. Laldenga formed his new ministry. Afterwards there was a split in the ruling MNF. Nine MNF MLA withdrew their support to Mr. Laldenga and formed

MNF (D). This happened on 29 August, 1988 and Mr. Laldenga's ministry was brought to minority in the Mizoram Assembly. Ultimately Mizoram Assembly was dissolved by the President of India on 7th September 1988 and President's Rule was imposed in Mizoram. Both the houses of Parliament (Lok Sabha and Rajya Sabha) had approved on 2nd November, 1988 about President's Rule.

Sixth election of Mizoram Assembly was held on 21st January, 1989 for 40 seats. A coalition two-tier Ministry headed by Mr. Lalthanhawla, *Congress-I* formed his ministry on 24th January, 1989 following the decisive victory of *Congress-I* and *MNF (D)* alliance and is scontinuing.

On 24th November 1989, ninth Lok Sabha election was held and Mr. C. Silvers Congress-I won the seat by defeating his rival *MNF* candidate. On September 26, 1990, Brig. T. Sailo's party merged with Janata party.

District Council, Regional Council and Village Council

In 1950 when the Constitution of India came into force the administration of Lushai Hills District (Mizoram) was brought under the Ministers of Assam. On 25th April, 1952 *Autonomous Mizo District Council* with executive and legislative powers for managing the matters about the Mizo tribes under *Constitutional Article No. 244 (2) of the Schedule* on the basis of the first general election for the *Council* was. Constituted. Total seat was 24 and term was 5 years. Eighteen were elected from the parliamentary constituencies of Lushai Hills District (Mizoram) and six were nominated by the Assam Government on the advice of the Chief Executive member. The nominated seats were for the government. The District Council was responsible for the following main function :

1. *Executive* (i.e. private disputes in-between two persons and public disputes for a whole village).
2. *Administrative* (i.e. allotment, occupation and use of land ; forest ; regulation about *jhum* ; establishment of *Village Council* and *Town Committee* ; inheritance of property ; marriage and custom, and,
3. *Judicial* (i.e. murder, theft, divorce etc).

District Council was to establish primary schools, dispensaries, markets, cattle ponds, ferries, fisheries, roads and water-ways. It was to levy taxes on profession, trade, sales of goods and controlled the trading by the non-tribals. *District Council* was to minimise the tribal problems and to engage on developmental work in Mizoram.

On 23rd April 1953, *Pawi-Lakher Autonomous Regional Council* was set up under *Article No. 275 (II)* of the 6th Schedule of the Constitution with elected members and was given *Autonomous* administration in *Pawi-Lakher* area. The function of the *Regional Council* was almost same as those of the *Mizo District Council*. Only the exception was that it did not control primary education of their area.

The second and third term of the *District Council* was held in 1957 and 1962. Due to insurgency the fourth term was held on 24th April, 1970 instead of the year 1967. The *Mizo District Council* was abolished in April 1972 when Mizoram became an *Union Territory*. *Section 20B of the 6th Schedule* to the Constitution was amended in 1971 to incorporate North Eastern area (reorganisation) Act 1971 and the Union Territories (Amendment) Act 1971. A Notification (No. CCMP 3/72/70/77-1 dated 2nd April, 1972) was issued for the *Pawi (Poi)-Lakher Autonomous Region* by a administrator of Mizoram to reorganise this *Regional Council* for the *Pawi* the *Lakhers* and the *Chakmas*. Thus *Pawi autonomous region*, *Lakher autonomous region* and the *Chakma autonomous region* were formed under *Section 4 (1) of Pawi-Lakher Autonomous Region (Reorganisation) Order, 1972* with 6 members to each of these to develop tribal customs, culture and dialects (vide, *Mizoram Gazette*, vol. I, Part I, Aizawl, dated 21st 1972 pages 1-2). *Under Notification No. LDD/8/72/53* dated 29th April 1972 (vide *Mizoram Gazette*, Aizawl, 5th May 1972) these three *Regional Councils* were upgraded to three District Councils and the first election was held for these in June 1973. The *District Councils* of this State have got more power at the latest *Amendment* to the 6th Schedule of the Constitution of India in 1988. The *Chakma*, *Pawi* and *Lakher District Councils* are functioning smoothly by providing the rights and privileges of the minorities to preserve and protect their life and culture. Autonomous Council for *Hman* tribes is to be formed very soon.

There are two tier administration by the *District Council* and the *Regional Council.* Both these Councils. have their own Court for trial of civil and criminal cases of the tribes of their respective area. As the Chieftanship was abolished, the statutory *Village Council* took the place of the *Chiefs.* The *Village Council* had been set up in every village for local administration either under *District Council* or *Regional Council.* The *Village Council* was constituted with *Lal* or *Chief.* The *Upas* (elderly men of the village) help the Chief (*Lal*). The Chief and the *Upas* constituted the *Village Council.* The Chief (*Lal*) preside over the *Council.* All types of ordinary disputes in between the people is to discussed and settled by the *Village Council* which acts as a village court. They used to settle minor disputes as per their customary law of their land. There were total 390 inhabited villages in Aizawl District, 161 in Lunglei District and 170 in Chimtuipui District out of total 400, 163 and 173 villages respectively till 1981.

The Chairman and the Deputy Chairman are elected by the elected members from them of the *District Council.* They acted like Speaker and Deputy Speaker of the *District Council.* The Chairman is to call for Council meetings and he is to preside over that. In absence of the Chairman the Deputy Chairman is to perform this duty. Like this, the *Regional Council* have a Chief Executive and Deputy Chief Executive and four other executive members to function as a legislature. The District Council have a Chief Executive member and a few other executive members who are collectively responsible to the *Council.* They are to function as a legislature. The *Regional Council* are to protect the tribals from exploitations and allow them to have autonomous administration.

Games and Sports

They like all types of modern and indigenous games and sports. They are efficient hunter and wrestler. Most of them are fond of fresh meat. For that, they cleverly trap their games. Sometimes long lines of rough fencings are kept by them in jungles. Thesc fencing have small openings at some intervals. Through these openings they catch peasants, jungle-fowls etc. which comes to these fences and try to run away along this till an opening is found out and ultimately they get snared. They kill porcupines with their bamboo spears. They trap tigers under a platform of heavy logs. They are not fond of community hunting. Muzzle loading guns are used by them to kill wild cats, deers etc. They are good fishermen and they catch fish with fishing rods, fishing baskets, traps, spears etc.

Young boys and girls are fond of modern sports and they are participating in different competition of Inter-State and national sports and games. Some of them know wrestling, judo, karate etc. The Education Directorate is giving them training for Scouts and Guides, physical education and sports. Recently Mizo team has climbed the *Mount, Bhagirathi-II* in 1989.

Weapons

Most of the Mizos are brave and good fighter. Their main weapons are *kawlnam* (Burmese *dao*) (dagger), spear, bow, arrow and sometimes they use poisonous bamboo-flint locked muskets, knife etc. A *dao* and a shield are the constant companion of a *Lushai* fighter. Their spears are not superior weapon which is about 4 feet 6 inches long with iron blades and spikes at the other end of the shaft. It is reported that they came to use gun and gun-powder since 1840. Some of them know *guerilla* warfare and also the art of trench.

During Lushai expedition in 1871-72, General Brownlow was wounded due to the Lushai fighters. In 1891, Captain Brown the first Political Officer of North Lushai Hills died due to the Lushai fighters. They are very brave and strong.

Head Hunting

The Mizos are very expert warrior. They would not spare anybody from taking revenge for any harm or insult to them.

They are expert to use modern arm and ammunitions. Before the spread of Christianity among them, they were reported as head hunters. In old days a warrior after killing his enemy generally brought the head portion to his home to show it to others to get glory for his heroism. But, this head hunting was an uncommon practice among the Mizos and this is now totally extinct.

Health

The Mizos are healthy people. But the State Mizoram is not a healthy place. There is scarcity of drinking water. The female members of each house have to collect water by going down from steepy hills for thousand feets or more to fetch water from local pits and ponds to draw water in their big bamboo tubes. Generally water of these pits and ponds are the cause of intestinal diseases. Malaria, asthma, intestinal and skin diseases are common among the Mizo people. Chicken Pox, tuberculosis, pneumonia, pertuasis, diptheria, dysentery, tetanous are also found among them. Many of them have little sense of hygiene as they with contagious diseases freely mix with others. Mizoram Government has already taken proper attention about their health care. Government has set up hospitals and subsidiary health centres. Health Department of Mizoram has made a great achievement in various National Health Progrommes like Public Health, Family Welfare, Leprosy control and Malaria eradication programme.

Mizo boys of six or seven years old generally starts smoking. They are very much fond of smoking and are causing their ill-health as nicotine of tobacco-smokers transforms into gas or stream and a smallest percentage of nicotin which enters through the mouth may cause a great harm to health. If the smoker does not inhale, a smallest fraction of nicotine may enter into blood and it creates a danger for the disease of cancer to the smoker's body. Some of the Mizo women are also smoker. It is said by the recent researchers that smoking by women could result in spontaneous abortion, still birth and low weight of the issue.

Liquor, Drugs, etc

It is said that a Mizo can not live without liquor. Most of them are liquor lover. Indigenous rice-beer *Zae* is popular among them. This home-made *Zu* plays an important item in their life and culture. It is an essential item for religious ceremonies, festivals and social functions. It is a drink for young and old, ladies and gents.

The ex-*MNF* Ministry in 1987-88 cancelled the ban on foreign liquor. At that time maximum number of the Mizos were intoxicated with bottle of foreign wine. For this, the powerful Church of Mizoram was not satisfied at the revoked ban and ultimately Church had led to the downfall of the *MNF* ministry. Present *Congress-I* and *MNF (D)* alliance ministry has reimposed the ban on wine soon after assuming their office after the downfall of *MNF* (Laldenga) Ministry.

Thailand, Burma and Laos constituted a region for producing opium. Heroin is reported to be smuggled into India especially through Mizoram and Manipur from Indo-Burma border, Mizoram's 404 km. long border with Burma has become the new narcotic gateway to India. Thus, there has been increase in consumption in Mizoram. *Ganja, Charas*, Nicotine-juice, LSD, Herion, Opium, Mandrax etc. are widely popular among the younger generation. People of Mizoram are now worried about these social menace which are almost easily available in Mizoram. Government of Mizoram and the Church leaders are trying to prevent these in the State. During the last few years a number cf *Homes* have been set up to help the poor and rehabilitating drug addicts.

It is seen that the Mizo men, women and children are all smoker of *vailos* (local cigarettes). Mizo men are using a pipe which is made of special type of bamboo. The women are using a smaller sized *hukah* (smoking apparatus). They are carrying this *hukah* even when they go out for their *jhum* field. Mizo women are also using a tobacco smoking pipe called *Tuibah*.

They do not have the habit of chewing arecanut with lime and betel leaves. It is their exceptional habit in comparison with the other tribes and castes of North Eastern India of the *Khasis, Garos, Jaintias, Assamese, Manipuries, Nagas, Tri-Puris, Arunachalese* etc.

Food and Drink

Rice is their main food which is taken either in ordinary boiled form plain rice or with meat and boiled vegetables along with chillies. The Mizos are consume all kind of animals such as white-bellied mouse, owl, dog, pegion, monkey, tiger, elephant, bear, *mithun* (*Bos frontalis*), beef, pork, chicken, mutton, etc. Practically they have no taboo on any food. They, however, do not eat cat as they dislike to eat this. Smoked elephant's flesh is their favourite and delicate food. Many of them dislike to eat snakes and bats. They like both fresh and dried fish to eat. Generally they prefer to eat boiled meat and boiled vegetables than preparing a fry or prolonged-cooked one. Some of them preserve meat in the way of dry fish. Generally they smoke the flesh of meat and then try like dry-fish and keep for months together. They like *sallad* to eat with their every day food. They prefer boiled mustered leaves to eat which is their common food-items for most of the days along with their boiled rice. They do not eat much fruits. However, they like to eat pineapple which grows in large quantity in Mizoram.

In old days they disliked to drink milk. During those days they used to drink tea without milk. But now they have changed and gradually this attitude is disappearing. They now drink milk and eat milk-made items. Tea is their popular drink with cakes and sweets.

Physical Features of the Tribe

The tribes of Mizoram belong to Tibeto—Burmese group of Indo-Mongoloid people. The Mizo male are medium to above medium statured people with mesocephalic to brachycephalic head. They are almost like the *Manipuri* in physignomy and have much resemblance with the *Khasis* of Meghalaya with typical Mongolian features of flat face, strong and stoutly muscular built body with highly developed calves. Their complexion is brown varying from dark to light brown. The women are generally medium to short statured people. Their face is generally round, the cheek bone is high, broad and prominent, eyes are small and almond shaped, nose is flat *platyrxhine* with wide nostrils. Like most of the tribal people of North Eastern region men have very little hair on their face. The Mizo ladies are better looking. They generally leave their hair loose and sometimes tie them into a knot at the back. Their fashion varies from village to village. The educated ladies now prefer to cut their hair in the style of Western countries.

Dress and Ornaments

Modern young men and women have almost rejected the dress and ornaments of their ancestors. In town area they prefer the European dress and modern cloth. They are using knitted woollen jackets, trousers, shirt, coat, tie and shoe. They are using woollen blankets. The people of Mizoram are now changing very rapidly due to spread of education and Christianity. Their women have generally struck to their native costume. Some of them are, however, now using modern dresses of shirt-pant, skirt, mini, midi etc. with high heeled shoes.

Some Mizo men in their town house have started now to use *pyjama* and *gengi*. They are, however, using *derchen* (loin-cloth) at home which they tie round their waist to ankle to cover lower part of the body which seems to be a *lungi*. Some are using their different types of turban such as *Dercop, Pan-dom, Panmongbom, Thangnanpon* etc. with or without *Tuhpah* (a cotton made ornaments for beautification). A waist band (*chombom*) is used by them to carry money. In old days they wore a single plain cloth of about 7 feet long and 5 feet wide which they wrapped around their whole body. Before that, men had to put a coat which was to reach below their waist and fastened at their throat. It was a single cloth. In old days men used *Khisangs* (a costly beads) on their earlobes and sometimes very small wooden or bone studs in their ear lobes. Men kept, during those days, long hair on their shoulder by tieing in a knot. Modern Mizo men do not use any kind of ornaments and they dress their hair regularly by cutting out like other people.

Modern Mizo ladies are using a handloomed big and thick cloth which they tie round their waist to ankle to cover the lower part of their body. It is beautifully designed and multi-coloured garment called *poan* or *puanchei* and they put it like *lungi* in the style of the *Burmese*. They are also using a decorated skirt called *Khamtang*. It is said that the Mizo skirts normally takes much time to weave, almost a year. For upper part of their body they put home-made jacket-type of blouse with or without collar and pockets. It seems to ba a small sized shirt. This is called *Kawrchei*. Sometimes they are using a colourful scarf called *Pon-dom* or *Punggaisan*. In old days the Mizo women had used a loin-cloth (*Nishan*) which was a big plain cloth. Before that, in long past, women had to wear a coat and cloth like their gents and in addition a short dark blue *petticoat*. The ladies are using necklaces which called *Phisong*, *Pathi*, *Khimo*, *Khivamvui* etc., silver made ear-ring (*Dieicam*), lead made armlet (*Hah*) and brass made bracelets (*Chonbhang*). The costly and popular ornaments are ambar necklaces and cornellian beads. These are inherited from father to son through several generation.

The Mizo women leave their long hair loose or tie them into knot at the back. But modern women now cut their hair small in Western style. Some of them dressed their hair with pigs fat. They are using all types of cosmetics. Tattooing is absent. But in old days, it is said, they marked circles which indicated a record of love affairs.

Marriage

They are patrilineal, patrilocal and patriarchal people. Their marriages are of three types. These are : negotiation ; service and rarely elopment. Marriage is considered *legal* soon after the formal marriage ceremony. Mizo tribe has a number of clans. All these clans are not fully *exogamous*. Marriage between member of same clan is generally discouraged but it is not prohibited. Thus marriage between member of the same clan is possible.

Mizo boys and girls can mix freely with one another. In

the evening the bachelors often go-round courting the maidens which is called *nula-rim* system (i.e. *dating* with the lover). Actually, marriage is performed only when a boy falls in love with a girl. Marriage is generally settled through negotiation of bride price and usually it is performed through courtship. Boys get married within the age group of 18 to 25 years and girls 16 to 22 years. Each clan has a fixed bride price. The boy who desires to marry a girl, whom he choose by himself, must pay the bride price. Father or nearest male relative of the bride will get the bride-price. Bridegroom has to pay some subsidiary prices other than this bride-price to the members of the bride-side. The negotiation of marriage is to start in between girl's side and boy's side when the girl indicates her willingness to marry the boy whom she love and if her parent approve that particular boy. Members from groom's house first approach to girl's house to know their willingness. Then a lengthy discussion is involved regarding negotiation of bride price on money and materials. The groom's side generally tries to low-down the amount of the bride-price and the bride's side takes the opposite position to increase it. This discussion step by step continues and sometimes for a year or years together. They consider it as a good omen not to come to a settlement of agreement quickly. This traditional marriage ceremony takes place soon after the negotiation of bride-price is over. The marriage *date* is generally fixed by the parent of the groom at the approval of the parent of the girl. In old days according their custom marriage was celebrated outside their Church. At present most of the marriage is solemnised inside their Church and after that parent of the bride offers a big feast by inviting people of the area, relatives and people of the bridegroom. On the night of the wedding day the bride is to go to her newly married groom's house with some escorts of her girl-friends by making a small procession. In old days, the young folk was to harass this type of procession by pelting dirty water on them and on arrival to groom's house, the bride had to be received with warm welcome by the parent of the groom along with local people whosoever present in the house of the groom. This visit to grooms house now generally happens in noon time on the wedding day so that, marriage could be performed on that night itself. The following morning the bride returns to her parent's house and spend the day there itself. On the following night the bride is taken back at night time to groom's house where she would be resided with her husband for good.

The boy, whose parent can not pay the bride-price and subsidiary prices, has to serve in the house of his would-be father-in-law for a period varying from one to three years. During this time he has to stay with his would-be in-laws and work as a member of that family. In this case cohabitation is not prohibited.

Marriage by elopment is not lacking. In this, there is no restriction of intermarriage among different groups of the Mizo tribes. Cohabitation is not permitted till the girl is fully grown-up. Unmarried girl have maximum liberty and pre-marital relations are not uncommon. If a girl becomes pregnant before her marriage, the father of the girl is entitled to get suitable damages and the claim by the girl is backed by the village elders. If the boy agrees to marry that girl, his parents have to pay nothing more than the usual bride-price. In their society this type of affairs is not a matter to talk about. This is perhaps due to their broad minded society which believes suitable amendment can wash away the wrongs.

Child marriage is not in vogue. *Monogamy* is normally practised by them. *Polygamy* is, however, seen among few rich people of the *Thadou* and *Vaiphei*. Now a days there is no restriction for inter-tribal marriage. *Polyandry* is never allowed. Marriage between parallel first cousin is prohibited. Cross-cousin marriage is a popular choice among them. Widow remarriage is permissible. The younger brother of a husband can marry the widow of his elder brother (*Levirate*) but the elder brother can not marry the widow of his younger brother.

A widow may or may not stay in her husband's house after the death of her husband. But it is customary to remain in the house of her dead-husband for at least three months till the lamentation ceremony (*Thlahual*) is over. If during the first three months time she has made any sexual intercourse with anybody she is liable to pay the full penalty imposed on her for commitment of adultery exactly in the same manner as if her husband was alive. A man who has lost his wife is not allowed to remarry within three years of his wife is death.

The elder sons generally goes out from their parent's house after marriage and forms a new family in their own separate house. The youngest son who is to inherit the property of his father is expected to stay with his parents to look after them during their old age time.

Divorce

Divorce is allowed. The bond of matrimony among them is very loose. Divorce is very simple and it does not require to go to the Court etc. If divorce is wanted by a wife she is to refund the bride-price to her husband. If it is sought by a husband for the reason other than barrenness, adultery, sickness of incurable diseases, he is to pay some fine to the village elders and to his wife. This fine is settled after discussion by the parties concerned. A divorced wife is allowed to go by leaving her all children with her husband except the suckling one and she is entitled to get some amount from her divorced husband to maintain that infant suckling issue. If a couple do not get-on they can separate by mutual consent or if the husband does not like his wife he can send her back to her parent's house for good.

Position of Women

Tribal women of this region are holding a high position. They are maintaining same status with their gents. They are co-operated to their men folk in office-work, bazar, house-hold work etc. A large number of young Mizo women are serving at Secretariat and also, in other departments. Among them some are Administrator. Stenographer, Teachers of School-College-Univerity and some are doing some clerical works. Some of them are now controlling vehicular traffic by standing on the road with their full dressed uniform of Home Guard. They work with their men in the agricultural field and plays an important role in agricultural activities. The main function of women is to collect woods for cooking, bringing water from water sources within their bamboo pipes, washing the clothe, making the garments, ginning-weaving-sewing works, pounding of rice, cooking and managing the children at home. Like the *Khasis* and *Jaintias*, the tea-stalls are managed by the Mizo women. Tea- girls' are serving tea in some tea stalls. Some of them are selling betel leaf and betel nut in their way-side temporary shops.

The married women have almost no right in the property of her father. All the movable and immovable property of her dead father is inherited only by her brothers. A widow can not get any property of her husband except her own cash, ornaments, clothes and weaving apparatus which she got from her father at the time of her marriage. These she can take back whenever she desire to live alone other than with her parent or remarry. Property which belongs to an unmarried daughter generally goes to her brother after her death. If a married woman dies without having any son then her brother is to inherit that (if her father is dead) otherwise, father again inherits that property which he gave at the time of her marriage.

Customary Law of Inheritance

As it is stated earlier that father's property is generally inherited by sons. In some Mizo tribe and sub-tribes either the youngest or eldest son is to inherit all the property of his dead father and he is compelled to look after the widowed mother by staying in the house of his father. The other sons and daughter generally have no claim on the property of their father. In some Mizo tribes, property is equally inherited by all the sons. Among some of the tribes only the eldest son is to get lion share of his father's property as he has to maintain his widowed mother and the remaining portion of the share is equally distributed among other sons.

If a man dies by leaving behind his minor children, younger or elder brother of the dead person has to look after the property and also, family of the dead brother till the sons are grown up. When the minor sons became mature he has to hand-over the property of his dead brother to them. If a man dies without having any son, his property is inherited by his nearest male relative but not by the daughters of the dead person.

Birth Rule

They consider more children for better living. They generally welcome a male child. The mother after the birth of her child can not go to spring nor she can wash her child in cold water till two fowls is not sacrificed. Seven days after the birth of a son the house hold spirit is to to appeased by offering a chicken and seven packets of rice with vegetables. These are hung under the edge of a roof. In case of a daughter, it is observed after five days. After performing this, the baby could be brought out of the room under the sky.

Parents of a new born baby is to give two feast at the birth of a child. The first feast is two days after the birth and the second one is after nine days. There are other ceremonies and sacrifices related with the birth of a child and it varies from clan to clan. If the baby is a boy then his parent is to present a cloth to his maternal uncle and if girl then to her maternal aunt.

Name Giving Ceremony

The most important ceremony in connection of birth of a child is the name giving ceremony which they perform either after two or nine days after the birth. It variel from clan to clan. Among some people they give name to a new born baby immediately after the birth.

The maternal uncle of a new born child is to occupy an important place on birth ceremony. Generally he is to give a name to the baby. If the first issue is a daughter then part-name of her paternal grand mother is added to her name. Similarly, part name of the maternal grand father is added to the name of the second son. If the second issue is a girl then part name of her maternal grand mother is added to the name of that girl child. The other children generally gets names after any friend of their father. But, at present, they are not following much all these rules. The name giving ceremony is performed by offering a feast to village elders by the parent of a baby.

Disposal of Dead

They bury the dead one. The news of a death is sent through the available relatives and friends. The dead body is given a bath and thereafter dressed up with best and fine clothe and fastened to a bamboo frame in a sitting position by keeping the legs fully in stretched position. If the dead person is a male, his weapons *dao* and spear are kept beside him. All these are to be observe and it is called *Ral.* If the dead person is a woman, the *Ral* is observed by keeping the dead one in a sleeping position instead of sitting. A pig, goat and dog is sacrificed and the flesh of these are cooked to arrange a big feast in the house of the dead person among the visiting friends, neighbours and relatives. It is their custom to serve drinks and foods to each and every body those who comes to condole with the members of the dead one. This custom they are still following. The Mizos come to pay their homage to the dead person in the shape of money and other gifts.

They also offer drinks and food (meat) to the dead body. They think the spirit of the animals, which they sacrifice for the said feast, are to accompany the dead person to *Mithikhua* (dead person's village). Some of them believe that without this killing of animals the dead person's spirit can not find out the way to take rest and the spirit of these dead animals are leading the spirit of a dead person to *Mithikhua.* Some other believe that the dead person is to walk a long distance other than this earth. So he will get strength from these drink and food (meat) for his way to reach and so on.

They bury the dead one in a common burial ground. Sometimes the relatives erect a memorial stone for the dead person. If anyone dies abnormally on water, people would pay him a great honour to bury his dead body. This is perhaps due to scarcity of water in Mizoram and they believe such death is a lucky matter. On the other hand if any one dies by falling down from a tree people generally dishonour him to bury by fastening a cloth in his neck. This is perhaps due to full thick green forest and trees in Mizoram and they believe such death is a bad-luck.

TWO

BRIEF DESCRIPTION OF THE DISTRICTS

Mizoram, the 23rd State of India, is divided into three districts. These are : Aizawl District, Lunglei District and Chimtuipui District. Previously Mizoram was known as *Lushai Hills* District of Assam and was divided into Aijal Sub-Division and Lungleh Sub-Division. It became an Union Territory on 21st January, 1972. On 1st September, 1972, Mizoram was divided into three districts as mentioned above. The Lungleh Sub-Division was bifurcated to form Lunglei District and Chimtuipui District and Aijal Sub-Division was upgraded to Aizawl District. On 20th February, 1987, Mizoram became a *State*. Its southern part during the time of undivided India was administered by undivided Province *Bengal* and the northern part by the province *Assam*. In 1898, the southern and northern parts of Mizoram (*Lushai Hills*) was joined together and was brought under "Assam". From 1901-02 onwards this area was made a *Scheduled* District of Assam. Its separation from Burma in 1935 and the partition of India in 1947 had effected a significant change in Geographical boundary which caused an economical, political and social changes among the life of the Mizos.

Aizawl District

This district was, long back known as North Lushai Hills

Sub-Division and thereafter it was known as Aijal Sub-Division and later-on Aizawl District. This district is situated in the northern part of Mizoram. It is bounded in its south with Lunglei District, south-west with Bangladesh, north-west with North Tripura District of Tripura, north with Cachar District of Assam, north-east with Churachandpur District of Manipur and east with Tiddim-area of Burma.

Aizawl District is mainly the home of the *Lushai*, *Paite*, *Hmar*, *Thadou*, *Kuki* tribes. Aizawl town is the capital of Mizoram and headquarters' of Aizawl District. Aizawl is a hilly town, situated at about 1,132 meters above the sea level. The area of this District is 10,127,47 sq. km. The total population is 3,40,826. The male population is 1,76,242 and female 1, 64, 584. The density of population per square kilometre is 27 and percentage of literacy is 65'09 per cent (*Census or India 1981*).

The available mineral products of this District is almost nil. No big industries have so far been set up here. Cotton grows here in plenty. Small scale industries like tailoring, furniture workshop, knitting industry, printing press, blacksmithy are set up here. Trade like carpentry, maize crusher, tailoring has developed here.

Aizawl District is a beautiful and developed one than other two remaining Districts. There are several motorable routes and Aizawl town is connected with most of the town and big village of this State. This District has four Sub-Divisions. They are : Mamit, Aizawl (Sadar), Kolasib and Champhai. There are total twelve Community Development Blocks (CDB) in Aizawl District. These are : Lokicherra, W. Phaileng, Reiek, Thingdawl, Darlawn, Tlangnuam, Aibawk, Serchhip, Thingsulthliah, Ngopa, Khawzawl, E. Lungdar.

In Aizawl District total 8 Colleges, 103 High Schools, 255 Middle Schools, 562 Primary Schools have been set up till April, 1985. At present one University has been setup in Aizawl town known as Pachhunga University College. Previously it was under North Eastern Hill University (NEHU), Shillong. There are several Cooperative Societies such as industrial, livestock, fishery, handloom, farming, lamps canteen etc.

Important places of this District are : Aizawl, Tamdil,

Bairabi, Vairengte, Kolasib, Bung, Paikhai Champhai, Vantawng etc.

1. Aizawl, the capital town, means fruit garden because, in their language *Ai*=fruit,, *zawl*=garden. It is connected by the Satellite Station for STD telephone facility. A TV Transmission centre is being set up here in addition to the relay TV Station. A Radio Station is situated here. *Vayudoot* air-services are available here in between Calcutta-Aizawl-Silchar-Aizawl-Calcutta. Daily helicopter services are available in between Silchar-Aizawl, Aizawl-Lunglei, Aizawl-Zemabawk Helipad, Aizawl-Champhai, Aizawl-Imphal, Aizawl Guwahati-Aizawl-Shillong etc. Aizawl town is 180 km. far from Silchar (Assam). National Highway No. 54 passes through this town from Silchar (Assam). Daily road transport services are there from Shillong (Meghalaya)-Silchar-Aizawl. State Transport Delux Buses generally takes 8 (eight) hours and light vehicles 6 (six) hours journey to reach Aizawl from Silchar.

The origin of Aizawl as a habitation may be said from 1890 when Mr. Dolly of the *Assam Police* arrived here with 400 men of *Silchar Military Police Battalion* under Col. Skinner to attack the *Chief* Lianphunga for raiding the *Chittagong Hill Tracts.*

Aizawl town is always busy with political, cultural and commercial activities. It has mild refreshing fanned breeze always with enjoyable temperature throughout the year. Approximate temperature is 19°C to 29°C in Summer, 11°C to 21 C in winter and approximate average rainfall is 231' 2 cm. (in 1985) which generally starts from May to September.

The traffic points are generally controlled here and signalled by the girl-cops with full dressed Home Guard's uniform. A hillock called *Laipuitlang* (seat of a cannon) is found here which projects like a big pillar and it seems to control over the northern part of the capital Aizawl. Scarcity of water is there. Drinking water of Aizawl is not much safe and good for health.

Bara Bazar and New Market are situated in the heart of the capital and they are the largest place for shopping.

Daily labourer *Coolee* is almost nil in this capital. *Hally Tila*, at the highest place of northern edge of Aizawl town and *Khatlo Bazar* (*Shivaji Tila*) at the south look beautiful and some rare orchids are available here. Bigger sized banana and papaya are produced here very much and are available in almost every shop in Aizawl town. Foreign dresses are largely available here.

Each locality of Aizawl has its own Church. Mizo men, women and children are very keen about going to Church for Sunday service and rarely miss it. Muslim mosque is there in Bara Bazar area. Temples of worship of Hindu God and Goddess is situated in Zodin Square. There is a State Museum in Aizawl town, Cultural Sub-Centre, Mini Zoo etc. Rare species of Asiatic fauna including sun-bear is present here in the jungle. Aizawl's centenary has already been celebrated here at Aizawl on 26th February to 28th February, 1990. It is said that first bazar at Aizawl was opened in 1910 by Mr. H.W.C. Cole, the then Superintendent of Lushai Hills. The Aizawl fort was set up by Mr. R.B. McCabe, the first Superintendent of the Lushai Hills.

(2) *Tamdil*, a site, is situated at the eastern part of Aizawl district. It has a natural lake situated in the heart of a forest. It is 60 km. far from the capital Aizawl and 10 km. from the beautiful tourist resort of *Saitual* village. A village path leads to *Tamdil* from *Saitual*.

(3) *Bairabi*, a place, is situated in the north-west border of Mizoram and Assam. Railway roots upto *Bairabi* is the only railway link in Mizoram. *Dhaleswari* river passe near to this site. A dam site is there in *Bairabi* for hydro-electric project.

(4) *Vairengte* is the gateway of Mizoram situated in the northern most place. National Highway No. 54 passes through this to connect Silchar (Assam) and Kolasib (Mizoram). A checkpost is there in Vairengte to verify the *Inner Line Permit* of each passenger.

(5) *Kolasib* is 95 km. far from Vairengte. It is the middle of the way of Aizawl-Silchar road. Most of the vehicles stop here for lunch break which runs towards Silchar and Aizawl.

(6) *Bung* is 15 km. far from Aizawl. It is a nice picnic spot. A dak-bunglow building is available here to stay.

(7) *Paikhai* is about 16 km. far from Aizawl and it is a place situated in the southern part of Aizawl. A metalled road is there upto Milriat village and thereafter village path leads upto Paikhai. This site is an isolated beautiful picnic spot. A dak-bunglow is available here to stay.

(8) Champhai is a hilly town of 1,678 metres above the sea level. It is situated near Burma border. Champhai is about 192 km, far from the capital Aizawl. Beauty of this hilly area attracts the tourists.

(9) Vantawng is the highest and most beautiful water fall in Mizoram. It falls to the river *Vauva* from a height of 750ft. It is about 145 km. far from the capital Aizawl (*via Sarchhip* the midpoint between Aizawl and Lunglei of National Highway No. 54). It is 5 km. far from the hill station *Thenzawl.*

(10) *Phawngpui* (Blue Mountain) is the highest mountain in Mizoram. It is 7,100 ft. (2,157 metre) above the sea level. There is a natural garden of rhododendron. It is skirted with natural beauty.

Lunglei District

This district is situated in between Aizawl and Chhimtuipui districts of Mizoram. It is bounded in the north with Aizawl district, south with Chhimtuipui district, west with Bangladesh and east with Burma. The present Lunglei District was formed in September, 1972.

Lunglei district is mainly the home of the *Lushai, Pawi* (*Poi*), and *Chakma*, Lunglei town is the headquarters of this district. It is a hilly town situated at 1,222 metres above the sea level. The area of this district is 4,538,00 sq. km. The total population is 86,511. The male population is 45,998 and female 40,513. The density of population per square kilometre is 19 and percentage of literacy is 56.89 (*Census of India 1981*). Rainfall is maximum in this district than other two districts. In 1985, the total rainfall was 374.6 cm. (147.1 inch) here.

The availability of mineral products in this district is almost nil. No big industries have so far been set-up here. Mizoram

Government is now taking all possible steps to develop this district. Many families have chosen industrial venture for their livelihood. Cotton grows here in plenty. Small industries such as sewing, knitting, carpentry, blacksmithy, cobler work etc. are set up here. Industrial growth centre amounting to two lakh have been set up at *Pukpui* village council area in 100 acres of land in 1986-87. Craft training centre at *Haulawng* and *Cherhlun* are set up in 1986-87 and expected to be functioning soon.

A total of 2 Colleges, 21 High Schools, 76 Middle Schools, 185 Primary Schoo s have been set-up in Lunglei District till April, 1985. There are several Cooperative Societies, such as industrial, livestock, fishery, handloom, farming, marketing, consumer, lamps, canteen, etc. There are 9 Agricultural Circles and 1346,50 acres of land have been recognised for dry terrace land till 1986. There are 6 Power Stations. Total 38 villages have already been electrified of 3021703 KwH power generated per year till 1985.

There are several motorable routes and Lunglei town is connected with most of the town and big villages of this State. This district has two Sub-Division. These are : *Tlabung* and *Lunglei.* There are four Community Development Blocks namely : W. Bunghmun, Lungsen, Lunglei and Hnahthial. Important places of this district are Lunglei, Tlabung, Lungsen etc. Lunglei is 235 km far from Aizawl. National Highway No. 54 passes through this town. It is a hilly area with natural beauty of flowers and pine trees etc. Tlabung (Demagiri) is situated near the border of Bangladesh. It is 98 km. far from Lunglei and 320 km. from Aizawl (via Lunglei). Lungsen is a small village. It is 68 km. far from Lunglei.

Chhimtuipui District

This district is situated in the southern most part of Mizoram State. The eastern and southern part of this district is surrounded by Burma, the western part is with Chittagong Hill Tracts of Bangladesh and northern part is with Lunglei district of Mizoram.

Chhimtuipui District is mainly the home of the *Lakher, Pawi* (*Poi*) and *Chakma* people. Saiha town is the headquarters of this district. It is a hilly town of 1,225 metre above the sea level. The area of this district is 3957 sq. km. Total rural area is 3904 sq.km. and 53 sq.km is the urban area. Total inhabited village is 170 and only one town was inhabited till 1985. The total population is 66,420. The male population is 34, 999 and female 21,421. The density of population per square kilometre is 17 and percentage of literacy is 37.07 (*Census of India 1981*). Male literates are 15593 (84.55 per cent) and female 9028 (25.73 per cent).

Availability of mineral products of this district is not much. Granite is available here. No big industries have so far been set up here. Government is now taking all the steps to develop this district. Small industries like handloom, carpentry, tailoring, bakery, press and binding of books etc. are set up here.

There are several firms such as poultry, pig, goat, sheep, cattle, buffalo, mithun etc. There is a fish firm of 345 village fish pond. Total number of Colleges is 2, High Schools 16, Middle Schools 63, Primary Schools 180 till 1985. Total 13 villages have been electrified and electricity installed capacity was 708 kw. till 1985.

There was 3 Sub-Divisions : Saiha, Lawngtlai and Chawngte. This Chhimtuipui district has 4 Community Development Blocks. These are : Chawngte, Lawngtlai, Sangau and Tuipang. Saiha is the headquarters, of this district It is an important place as administrative activities are set up here. Many mettled roads have connected Saiha with rest of the town and big villages of Mizoram. These are : Saiha-Lunglei (165 km.) Saiha-Tuipang (75 km.) etc. National Highway No. 54 runs upto Saiha. There are all-weathered several State roads. *Kaladan/Talpui/Khawchhak* is a big river which runs towards south to enter Burma through the middle of this district. *Sertui* and *Tulohong* rivers also pass through this district to run towards south. *Tuipang*, a big village is situated in the eastern part of this district. Tongkolawing is a village in the southern part and *Parva* village is situated in the south eastern part of this distriet. *Vaseitlang* is also a big village.

TABLE 9

Districts, Sub-Divisions, Blocks and Towns

Districts, and Headquarters (Total Villages)	Sub-Divisions	Blocks	Towns
1	2	3	4
1. Aizawl Hqs. Aizawl (Total 393 villages)	Mamit, Aizawl (Sadar) Kolasib, Champhai.	Lokicherra, W. Phaileng, Reiek, Thingdawl, Darlawn, Tlangnuam, Aibawk, Serchhip, Thingsulthliah, Ngopa, Khawzawl. E. Lungdar.	Aizawl, Kolasib, Serchhip, Champhai,
2. Lunglei Hq.s Lunglei (Total 161 villages)	Tlabung. Lunglei	W. Bunghmun, Lungsen, Lunglei, Hnahthial.	Lunglei.
3. Chhimtuipui Hqs. Saiha (Total 170 villages	Saiha, Lawngtlai, Chawngte.	Chawngte, Lawngtlai, Sangau, Tuipang.	Saiha

Source : Census of India 1981 : Mizoram.

THREE

BRIEF DESCRIPTION OF THE TRIBES

According to the Mizo legends they are the same people as the *Chins* of Burma. They believe that their ancestors were brought into this world by a big stone which is known as *Chhinglung* meaning "covering rock of a hole in the earth". They believe that *Chhinglung* stopped its process of producing tribes soon after the *Raltes* had come over to this earth because, the *Raltes* bragged too much. At this, *Chhinglung* got angry and disliked to producc any more human beings. Besides this belief some other stories are there about origin of the Mizos.

There is no recorded history about the date of their migration to Mizoram. Perhaps *Chhinglung* is the present place called *Sinlung* in *Chin* bordering *Shan* State. It is believed that they have immigrated into Lushai Hills (Mizoram) within 17th to 18th century from hill tracts of Upper Burma bordering Lushai Hills (Mizoram) in between the *Run* and the *Tiau* rivers. It is said that in about 1780, due to pressure from other strong tribes or so in Burma, the *Sailo* families with their followers migrated to Lushai Hills (Mizoram) from south to north direction through the Chindwin valley and Chin Hills and entered to Lushai Hills, North Cachar Hills (Assam), Manipur, Tripura and Chittagong Hill tracts (Bangladesh). They drove the earlier tribes such as the *Hrangkhwals*, *Baites*, *Thado*, etc. towards northern part who so ever migrated to Lushai Hills before them. But they could not eject all the earlier tribes. Thus, they absorbed with them few earlier tribes and collectively all these tribes and sub-tribes are called as the *Kukis* who have their distinct customs, manners, practices etc. The Sailos had united internal position along with their *Lushei* clan in the year about 1810 and occupied most of the areas in between *Champhai* and *Demagiri* of Lushai Hills and borders of Cachar (Assam) and Sylhet (Bangladesh). The history of the Lushais in the early 19th century was the history of endless disputes of the *Sailo* family. According to E.A. Gait, the Lushais made their appearance in Lushai Hills about the year 1840. It is said that many akins of the Lushais (Mizos) are still serving in BAF (Burma Armed Forces).

Mizo is a generic term which includes all the *Lushais* and akin tribes. In earliest days the Mizos were known as the Lushai. Racially they are of Mongoloid origin and they belong to Tibeto-Burman linguistic group. There are total 15 classified Scheduled Tribes along with the other tribes, sub-tribes and immigrant people of Mizoram.

Chakma

The Chakmas, the South-Eastern Asian people, are the *Arakanese* immigrants. There is some controversy about their actual original place of inhabitation. According to their historical evidence they were inhabited in the southern hill tracts of Chittagong (Bangladesh) which extended along the *Matamuri* river. This hill tract is continuous to the hills of *Arakan* or *Arakan Yoma* in Burma. However, most of the Chakmas are migrants to Mizoram from *Chittagong Hill Tracts.* They are now inhabited in south-western part of Mizoram ; Kailasahar, Amarpur, Sabroom and Dharmanagar areas of Tripura and East and West Kameng and Tawang districts of Arunachal Pradesh and Nowgong district of Assam. But most of them are inhabited in the central part of *Chittagong Hill Tracts* of Bangladesh.

The Chakmas are economically, culturally, socially and politically most backward tribe and they totally different from the tribes of the *Lushai, Pawi (Poi) Lakher, Kuki* etc. of Mizoram. The Chakmas are Buddhist. They worship Buddha and also some Gods and Goddesses of Hindu deity such as mother

Laksmi (Malakshminima), Ganga river (Gangamana) etc. and their traditional deities.

According to their religion they are divided into four divisions. These are : (a) *Bhikku,* (b) *Rouli* (c) *Ojha,* and (d) *Gankuli.* The Bhikkus are the orthodox monk or Buddha. The Roulis are the village-priest to perform customary rites of their religion. The Ojhas (Sorcerer) are to drive away the evil spirits by propitiating them. The Gankulis are the singer of narrative and sentimental songs by going round from village to village and gives religious small advices among the ordinary people. They have some customs which seems to be similar to that of *Animists.*

The Chakma tribes is divided into 35 clan or sects (*goza*) which are sub-divided into Sub-clans (gustis). They cannot marry within the same *gusti.* They are *monogamous* people. Some of their *gozas* are : Bengsa, Dame, Tunya, Borbo, Mulimia, Malima, Tauja, Barua, Koda, Buma, Kurchya, Kadua, Wuangsa, etc. There is no marriage restriction or professional distinction among the *gozas.* Marriage is generally held by negotiation. Child marriage is not practised among them. About 55 years ago the age of marriage was 16 to 17 years in case of male and 12 to 13 years in case of the females. Now the age of marriage have increased by 3 to 4 years more. Free mixing among the boys and girls are not allowed. Bride price is there, cash and materials are to be paid by the groom's father to bride's father. But, the materials like ornaments, utensils etc. are taken with the bride to groom's house. Widow remarriage and divorce are allowed.

The Chakma men wear mill-made *dhoti,* shirt, genji etc. Sometimes, they are using their *dhoti* like a *lungi* of Burmese style at their home. Their women wear two pieces of hand-woven clothe with bigger sized blouse. Ornaments is used only by the women and those are similar to that of the Bengalee women. In leisure time women weave their clothe. Long ago, the Chakmas were semi—nomadic people. The eldest son is to inherit the property of his dead father.

They have Buddhist temples and Schools. Their village councils have the members of elders. They have their Chief who is a leader or *sardar* (*Dewan*). He is to settle generally the communal disputes, petty theft and minor offences of the Chakmas. Social disputes and minor criminal cases are to settled by the person whom they call *Karbari* who is an elected honorary member (unanimously) by the villagers. They have also *Khijayas* and *Talukdars* to run their village administration. In general, the social discipline of the Chakmas are very hard. In case of major offences the offender is externed from the village. For minor offences fine is levied to the offender.

They prefer to have their villages by the side of a river. Their food habits are comparable to those of the *Khamtis* of Arunachal Pradesh. They are *Hinayana* Buddhists. But, they eat fowl's meat and fish if those are killed by others.

They speak a corrupted form of Bengali language the dialect of which is an admixture of Assamese, Bengalee, Chittagong-Bengalee and also Burmese group of languages. Long ago their dialect was written in Burmese way. *Jhum* cultivation is their main source of livelihood. At present some of them are opting for agriculture through plough cultivation on a permanent basis. Some educated Chakmas are now holding Government jobs and doing their trades and business.

The Chakmas cremate the dead. A Buddhist *Rouli* recite *mantras* at the time of cremation. The ashes are immersed in a river. Sons shaves off their hair. After seven days sons perform *sradha* (purification) ceremony.

Gangte

They are inhabited in the north eastern part of Aizawl district of Mizoram. Many of them are residing in Churachandpur district of Manipur. Some are residing in Meghalaya. They are *Kuki-Chin* group of tribe. They have two clans. These are, *Thangjom* and *Thanglun.* These are divided into number of sub-clans. Their clan is *endogamous* but sub-clans are *exogamous.* Marriage with mother's brother's daughter is preferred by them. Two types of marriages are there. These are marriage by negotiation and elopement. Marriage with father's sister's daughter is, however, not encouraged.

Most of their houses are constructed on plain surface with wood and bamboo. Gents wear a traditional head gear (*Tukpa*), tailor-made pant and shirt. Female wear blouse and skirt. They also wear their traditional clothe ***Panbe*** and ***Ponab***, the lower and upper garment respectively. In leisure time women weave cotton shawl and loin clothe at their home for their own use. They have their village headman *(Khullakpa)*. The Gangtes cultivate mainly paddy and pineapple. They bury their dead near their house. They do not have any common burial ground.

Hmar

They are inhabited mainly in the northern part of Aizawl district of Mizoram. Many of them are residing in Churachandpur district of Manipur. Some of them are living in Assam and Tripura. They are *Old Kuki* group of tribe.

The name *Hmar* was given by the Lushai people of Mizoram. The word *Hmar* means "north" in Lushai language. This word is to denote them as immigrants into Mizoram from Manipur side. Their dialects have some close similarities with the Mizo people. Some believe that they have migrated from *Sinlung* of Central China. Some other believe that they migrated to the north of *Champhai* river from *Tai* or *Shan* land and finally settled in Mizoram and Manipur Hills. However, some of them have been settled in Cachar and North Cachar Hills of Assam and also in Tripura. In the past they were nominated nomadic in habit to search for better cultivable *jhum* land.

They claim that historically and culturally they are different from other tribes of Mizoram. They have a distinct language. They are highly literate people and have their own literary society which has been started in 1921. Their first text book came out in 1944 which was published in *Hmar* language but written in *Roman* scripts.

They have 24 clans and 211 sub-clans. They prefer clan *exogamy*. Four types of marriages are there. These are marriage by service, elopement, entrusion and arrangement or negotiation. *Monogamy* is their ideal form of marriage. Their *Khuonglawm*, *Lunglak* and *Sesun* festivals have much similarities with the *Shan* people of Burma. They have *Rong* (Kingship), *Lal* (*Chiefship*), *Siehmong* (Village Council) and *Sier*

(Dormitory). Their *chiefship* is hereditary and occupied by only the male descendant of the *Chief.*

The *Hamr* people are generally short to medium in stature, strong and muscular in appearance, face is broad and round, cheek bone is high, eyes are small, nose flat and short, skin colour varies from dark brown to light yellow. Their youngest son generally inherits the house of his father as he is supposed to lookafter his parents even after his marriage and he does not build his separate house after his marriage.

They practise *jhum* (shifting) cultivation and plant pineapple. Their houses are built on stilts. The floor of a house is raised from the ground at about 1 ft to 3 ft high. Their houses are about 24 ft × 20 ft in size and made with wood, bamboo and thatches. Most of them are now Christian. In town area men wear tailor-made pant, shirt, bushirt, tie etc. and the female wear blouse with skirt, frock etc. Traditional dress for men is *hrenpereng*, a short loin cloth of about 5 ft long and 2 ft width and, for women *tharlaizawm*, a loin cloth of about 6 ft long and 3½ ft width. Unmarried girls wear another type of cloth called *townlopuon*.

They bury their dead.

Kuki

The *Kukis* are not a single group of people. The term *Kuki* is a generic word which covers a number of tribes, subtribes and clans of common characters. This term denotes to the *Zoumi* people. This *Kuki* word is a derogatory term which are given perhaps by the Bengalees long back. This vague term *Kuki* is applied by the plain people. The Manipuris called them *Kongjai*. The Lushais called them *Dzo* or *Zho*.

The Kukis are scattered all over the State Mizoram specially towards the northern part of Aizawl district. They are also inhabited in Manipur, Tripura, Nagaland, North Cachar Cachar district of Assam, Khasi and Jaintia Hills districts of Meghalaya and *Chin Hills* of Burma.

According to their legends the Kukis originally belonged to a place called *Sinlung* on the bank of the river Mekong in south-western part of China. Due to some natural calamities, famine and nomadic habit they migrated to *Shan* country. They migrated again towards *Chin Hills*, *Irrawadi Valley* and *Chindwin* of Burma. In search of more fertile land, they gradually migrated to Mizo Hills, Manipur, Tripura and Assam. This habit of migration has now been checked and settled permanently.

They were head-hunters in earlier days. The Kukis belong to the Mongoloid family and, linguistically they belong to Tibeto Burman group. The principal Kuki clans are: Biete. Changsen (Jansen), Thadou, Khelma, Rangkol or Bangkol, Sakachep, Vaiphei. Linthang, Thaugin, Lurhim and Hmar. At the end of the eighteenth century, the *Rangkhols* and the *Bietes*, either under pressure from the stronger clans like the *Changsen* (*Jansen*) and the *Thadou* or due to their migratory habit moved across the plain areas of Cachar and settled in North Cachar Hills. They are known as *Old Kuki* group of tribes. Later on the *Changsen* (*Jansen*) and the *Thadou* were compelled to migrate to seek new shelter towards north by leaving their earlier inhabited place of Mizoram. They migrated in the middle of nineteenth century and are known as *New Kuki* group of tribe. This classification of *Old* and *New Kuki* groups does not have any significance. This denotes only the "time" elements against them.

They have hereditary village *Chief* who has some power. Their traditional religion is *animism*. At present, most of the Kukis are Christian. Some of them follows their traditional religion. Physically the Kukis are strong and stout. They are short to medium in stature. Height of men is generally 5 ft to 5½ ft and women 4½ ft to 5 ft. Their legs are muscular. Their complexion is dark. Both male and female have long hair. Men tie their hair with a bun to keep at the back of the shoulder and women tie their hair above their head like the *Apatani* women of Arunachal Pradesh. But now the male does not like to keep their hair long. They cut their hair small and dress it in modern style. Traditionally the Kukis men and women both wore a cloth wrapped round their waist and hung it upto ankle. Long back tattooing system was there on their body. The pattern of this was a small black coloured circle on their forearm, usually in their left hand. Previously men used small plugs or rings by piercing their ear-lobes.

They prefer to live on hill top. The Kuki villages have a a cluster of houses and are closely constructed. Their houses are built on wooden or bamboo platform. Timber is used for very big houses. Their rooms are quite spacious. Their domestic animals are kept below the *machans*. In the middle of their room there is an earthen hearth. Their rooms have two doors, one at the front side and other at the back. Their rooms does not have any window. The educated people are now constructing their houses with several rooms, doors, windows and ventilations. Long ago, the Kukis had no habit of repairing their houses. When it was unfit for habitation they built a new house in a new site.

Their main traditional occupation is *jhum* cultivation and hunting. Their economic condition is good. Cane and bamboo products are manufactured for domestic use. Women are expert weaver. Few men are very good carpenter and blacksmither.

Their clans are not fully *exogamous*. Marriage within the same clan is discouraged but not prohibited. There is no restriction of inter-marriage among different tribes of Kuki group. Marriage is generally of two types : negotiation and love-marriage. Adultery and incest is almost nil. Divorce is allowed at the consent of the community and the person who prays for divorce, he or she is to pay compensation to the opposite party and a communal feast. Widow remarriage is possible. Younger brother is to marry the widow of his elder brother (*levirate*) but the elder brother can not marry the widow of his younger brother. *Polygamy* is found among some rich people but he can not marry a fourth one if the other three wives are alive. They generally carry a netted bag with steel pipe, tobacco etc. Pipes are smoked by both men and women.

They are expert in archery and using spears. They are fond of meat. *Zu* (rice beer) is their favourite drink. They believe in life after death and rebirth. They bury their dead.

Lakher (Mara)

The Lushais gave them the name Lakher. This is because a Lushai person saw the first Lakher women plucking cotton (*la*=cotton, *kher*=to pluck). But they called themselves *Mara* or *Tlongsai.* However, they are inhabited in the southern part of the Chhimtuipui district of Mizoram. They are immigrants from *Chin Hills.* Some of them are still inhabited in *Chin Hills* of *Haka* sub-division of Burma.

The Lakhers have a distinct pattern of belief, custom and tradition which has somehow some similarity with the *Fijian* and the *Indonesian.* Their *Mara* language is different from the *Mizo* language. Most of them are Christian. The Lakher men wear a shirt and a loin cloth and women wear a dark blue coloured petticoat type of cloth having embroidry on its border, a short blouse or skirt and a red with black striped cloth (*puan*). The Lakher men generally wear a turban on their head. Men prefer to keep their hair long and they tie it above the forehead. Traditionally a boy can not cut his hair after his age of nine. Women keep their hair long and fix it with hair pins. Women wear ornaments of cowrie, conch-shells, beads and old coins. They wear a belt around their waist to belly. However, some of the Lakhers are now preferring modern European dresses and hair style.

The Lakhers includes in their composition of the *Indonesian* race. Externally they have accepted more or less the *Kuki* culture and internally at heart they have somehow accepted the *Naga* culture. The Lakher men are well built and have good physique. The women are taller than the *Lushai* and the *Kuki* women. They have a light brown complexion and are darker than the *Lushais.* They have a broad nose, high cheek bones and Mongoloid eyes.

The *Pawi-Lakher Regional Council* was set up in 1953 and the *Pawi-Lakher* area was given autonomous administration. Their *Chief* had full control over his village. But this *Chieftainship* was abolished in 1955 by an Act of Government of Assam. The *Regional Council* has its own court for trial of the area.

The Lakher culture is neither *Kuki* nor *Naga* but in-between these two culture. Their main agricultural products are rice, millet, maize, tobacco, ginger, bean and arum. They pull up paddy plants with roots when it is ripe and not cut-out by sickles.

The eldest son inherits a lion share of the property of his father. If there is no son, a brother of the deceased inherits his property. Women can not inherit any property of her father or husband. Daughters get only when her brothers gives her. The younger brothers get a small share.

The Lakher women are hard working. Marriage is generally arranged by the parents. Bride price among them is high and it varies on clans. Child marriage is most common among them. Inter-clan marriage is permissible. But the ruling clans can marry only amongst themselves or with higher clan. Divorce is almost nil. They are somehow conservative type and prefers to follow their old customs and traditions. They have three main clans *viz.* Hlychho Choza (the ruling clan), Khaila Nohro (higher clan) and Azyu Tlapi (commoner).

The Lakhers do not have any guest house and *Zawlbuk* (bachelor's dormitory). They believe that illness and bad luck is due to *Khazangpa* (evil spirit). The Lakhers have their traditional dance and these are common among the Mizos and the Pawis.

The Lakher male, female, old and young are all habituated to smoke. They have been growing tobacco in their *jhums*. The smoking pipe of men and women are different. Female's smoking pipe passes through a container of nicotine mixed preserved water and they carry with them even while they are travelling. This indigenous small apparatus with seems to be a small *Hucca*. Men smoke directly from their pipe. But now some of the Lakhers prefers to smoke cigarettes made by themselves by rolling with home-grown tobacco in cut pieces of thin papers. The drinking habit is fairly common among them.

They bury their dead.

Lushai (Mizo)

They are inhabited mainly in the districts of Aizawl and Lunglei. Some are inhabited in the northern part of Chhimtuipui district of Mizoram. Few are residing in Chandel and

Senapati districts of Manipur, Khasi Hills district of Meghalaya and Cachar district of Assam.

The *Kacharis* use the word *Lushai* as a derogatory term. The terms the *Mizo* and the *Lushai* are used synonymously. The word *Mizo* is recently adopted which ueans "Hillman" in *Zoumi* language. The word *Lushai* is presumed to have derived from *Luchhai*.

They belong to the Mongolian race of *Chin-Kuki* group. The *Malay* and the *Burmese* elements are present more or less in the Lushai's dress and culture. The Lushais came to Mizoram from *Chin Hills* of Burma. Till the year 1870 they were known as the *Kuki*. Since 1871 it was replaced by the term the *Lushai*. From 1950 this term has been changed by the generic term the *Mizo* in wider sense.

In their village they live in thatched and bamboo made huts on hill tops. Their villages vary in size according to their population and one village is separated with another by several miles. In their society none is high or low in status. There is no individual ownership of cultivable land. Most of the land is owned by their *Chief* who takes advices from *Upas* (Councillors). Marriage with mother's brother's daughter is preferred but the marriage with the father's sister's daughter is possible but not liked.

The Lushais are fast giving up their old customs and have adopted western pattern of life. The boys and girls are mixing freely. The boys get married in between 18 to 25 years of their age and girls 16 to 22 years. There is a bride price which is to be paid by the groom. Divorce is common. After separation for five years one can remarry. Men prefers to wear western dress. They wear trouser and shirt even in the interior villages. They use cane and bamboo made hat which seems to be a cricket-cap. They also use some other types of hats. Women have generally stuck to their native costume but some of them are now using all kinds of modern dresses of skirts, frocks, mini-midi etc. Generally they wear a beautiful cloth called *Puonchei* which they tie round their waist to ankle to hang to cover the lower part of the body. Another cloth, called *Kawrcchi* they wear with artistic designed blouse to cover their upper part. Women generally keep their hair long. Their valuable ornaments are amber necklaces and cornelian beads.

The Lushai male, female and children are smoker. The smoking pipes of men and women are different. The village men and women generally carry with them an artistically designed and hand-woven side bag to carry tobacco pipe and other items.

Lushai or *Dulian* is their dialect. *English* is a common language among the educated youth. Their staple food is rice with boiled vegetable with sufficient quantity of chillie. Tea is popular among them. They like cakes and sweets. Beef and pork are delicious food. They domesticate pig, fowl, cow etc. In liesure time men make handicrafts with bamboo and cane and women keep themselves busy in their handloom work. Youngest son inherits all the moveable and immoveable properties. The Mizo District Council has passed an *Inheritance Act* in 1956 which has now been accepted by most of the Lushai people. Their social customs are examplary to all. Under the system of *hnatlang*, *tlawmngaiha* etc. the Lushai villagers are expected to contribute their labour for the welfare of their community and people. The *Lushai*, the *Pawi* and the *Lakhers* have traditional bamboo dance (*Cheraw*) in common. At present young Lushai men and women prefer the western music and dance.

Mizo

The term *Mizo* is coined to identify all the tribes, sub-tribes who are of the same origin having social and cultural affinities. The *Lushai* Hills which was named after one of the main tribes called *Lushai* was changed to *Mizo* Hills in 1954. Many people belonging to the main tribe have identified themselves as *Mizos* and *Lushai* dialect has since been accepted as the *Mizo* language. In all aspects the Mizos are same with that of the *Lushais*.

Mog

The Mogs are found in western border of Aizawl district of Mizoram. Majority of them are residing in southern part of Tripura and Chittagong Hills of Bangladesh. Their dialect is akin to Arakanese. According to Grierson, *Mog* language belongs to Assam-Burmese group of *Tibeto Chinese* family.

They have there own language and own scripts. They are Buddhist in religion. They also worship Hindu deities like mother Ganga, Kali etc. They have their headman and village council. They select their headman whom they call *Bonaraug* (*Choudhury* or *Tahsildar*). This election is made on the basis of wealth and social status of the elected person.

They live in the plains. They have large dormitory for boys. Girls are allowed in this dormitory but they are not allowed to stay at night. Men wear a loin cloth *dhoti* in the style of the Burmese, a *genji* and a head gear which is a small piece of cloth. The head gear they usually put is like an *Assamese* youth. Women wear two pieces of clothe to cover upper and lower part of their body which seems to be *mekhala* of an *Assamese* and *fanek* of a *Meithei-Manipuri*. They wear blouse with *orna* type of breast cover. Sometimes they put head-gear which covers upto their forehead. Women are using gold bangles, ear-rings, necklace etc.

They have two endogamous divisions. Their clan *Palamsa* is sub-divided into two exogamous sub-clans. They have three types of marriages. These are by negotiation, by service and by love-marriage. Widow re-marriage and divorce is permissible. They cremate their dead after performing funeral rites. Seven days after the death they observe *Atman* with the help of their priest. A feast is given to the priest and others. The eldest son gets half of the property of his father and the remaining half is equally divided among the other sons. Similarly, eldest daughter gets half of the share of her mother's ornaments and the rest is equally divided among other daughters.

Paite

They are inhabited in the north eastern and central part of Aizawl district of Mizoram. Some of them also inhabited the middle part of Lunglei district. Many of them are residing in *Churachandpur* district of Manipur, Tripura and *Chin* State of Burma.

The Paites are considered to be an *Old Kuki* group. Previously all of them were *animist* and followed tribal religion. Now most of them have converted to Christianty. They speak *Paite* dialects which belongs to the *Tibeto Burman* family of *Kuki Chin* group. The Paite have certain divisions. *Dapzan Paite, Bukpi Paite, Lausan Paite, Thaute Patte* etc. The *Dapzan Paite* are inhabited in between *Tiau* and *Run* river. All these Paite have some similarities with the Lushai people of Mizoram. They are socially, politically, economically and educationally an advanced tribe. They formed *Paite National Council* in 1949. The first village of the Paite is said to have been set up at *Chimnuai*, near *Tiddim.*

Their dresses resemble to that of the *Lushai* people. Women dress is more colourful than the dresses of men. Women wear blouse or jacket and a garment which is colourful and decorated cloth tied round their waist to ankle like the *Lushai* lady. But they do not wear huge ivory ear ring like them. Men prefers to wear modern European dresses.

They do not have guest house. The youth of the village generally sleep in the verandah of their *Chief.* They have hereditary village Headman. There is Village Council with some elders. There was dormitory (*Haam*) for the unmarried youth which has now almost disappeared.

Rice is their main food. They practise *jhum* (shifting) cultivation. They are short to medium statured and skin colour varies from dark brown to light yellow. Two types of marriages are there *viz.* marriage by negotiation and marriage by choice. There is a peculiarity about marriage among them. This is because a young Paite boy is to cohabit with his future wife for a period of three years. If no child is born or she does not become pregnant the couple is to be separated. If within that period the woman becomes pregnant the marriage is to be completed and bride price is payed only after the birth of the baby. There is very rare case of inter-marriage them. The son of a *Chief* is supposed to marry his first cousin.

The eldest son generally inherits the house of his father as he is supposed to look after his parent. They bury their dead.

Pawi (*Poi*)

They are inhabited in the south and south-eastern part of Mizoram. They are immigrants from the *Chin* Hills of Burma. The *Pawi* call themselves *Lai* which is commonly known as *Chins* in the *Chin* Hills district of Burma. The *Pawi* and the *Chin* are the same people. The Pawis speak the *Lai* language at home and *Mizo* (*Dulian*) language in Schools etc. and with the other tribals.

The *Pawis* and the *Lushais* have similar custom and ways of life. But the *Pawi* are more conservative and less westernised than the *Lushais*. Among the Pawis the following clans are most common. These are : *Chinzah, Hlawnchhing, Bawitlung, Zathang, Hniahm, Khenglawt, Satheng* and *Mualching.* The sub-clans are *Tlanglan, Bawm* and *pang.* Inter-marriage with the *Mizos* and the *Lakhers* are mostly common.

They prefer maize and millet. They do not grow much rice. Men have long hair tied in a knot on the head. Women have also long hair. Women wear a lot of ornaments around their neck, arms, ear and ankle. But now the modern youth are not keeping their hair long and they prefer western dresses and style.

Among the Pawis, the eldest son inherits the property of his father. The Pawi men generally keep their hair long and tie those as a bun above their forehead. In 1953 the 12 membered Regional Council gave them autonomy of village administration. Education among them had spread slowly than the Lakhers and the Lushais.

They bury their dead.

Ralte

They are mainly inhabited in Aizawl district of Mizoram. Some of them are also inhabited in Manipur. They speak a dialect which is different from the *Lushai* or *Dulian* language. In their custom they differ slightly from the tribes the *Lakher*, *Lushai* and the *Pawi*. They have headman. Their dress is similar to that of the *Lushai* people. Most of the Raltes are talkative and quarrelsome people. They bury their dead outside their village,

Riang

They are resided in *Mayanithlang*, in the western part of the Aizawl District of Mizoram. They migrated from *Shan* State of Burma. They belong to the *Mongoloid* racial group and their dialect has been classified as to the *Austro Asiatic* group of *Tibeto-Burman* family. Their dialect is their own and it is known as *Polong-O.* This Riang dialect is also known as *Riang.*

They are agriculturist. They practised *jhum* cultivation like the *Lushais, Kukis, Lakhers, Pawis* etc. There are two groups of the Riang population. These are : *Meska* or *Mechka* and *Maisoi* or *Malchhui*. These are divided into several sub-groups (*dafa*). Each of these sub-groups have their elected Chief called *Rai* and *Sardar* (*Kachak* or *Kanchan*). They used to settle the minor cases of their village.

Men wear hand made loin cloth *dhoti* and a piece of wrapper, shirt and genji. Men sometimes put their head gear which is a piece of a small cloth. Women wear a long piece of cloth called *Rignai* or *Pachhra* which they wrap around their waist and it is hangs down to cover upto their lower part. Another cloth called *Riah* they wear to cover the upper part of their body.

Riang women like silver ornaments. They wear silver-coined necklace (*Rangbatang*) and other necklaces, silver ear rings, silver armlets and big sized silver bracelets.

They are endogamous tribe. They do not marry outside their tribal community. There are two types of marriages. There are love marriage (*Halakchhai*) and negotiated (*Halakch-ham*). Parallel cousin marriage is most common. Cross-cousin marriage is rare among them. Child marriage is not allowed. Divorce is permitted. They have match-maker (*Ghatak/ Andra*) through whom marriage is arranged.

Their houses are built on the top of hills and on a high bamboo platform called *Tong.* The walls are made with split bamboo. The roof of their house are hempen globed. They call their settlement area as *Parah* and have named that *parah* at the name of their *Sardar.*

They are fond of rice beer. Their religion is animism. They also worship Hindu gods and goddesses like Vishnu, Kali,

Laksmi etc. Their important religious festivals are Ker, Ganga Puja etc and their important deity is *Matai Katar* (*Sib-Durga*).

They cremate their dead.

Simte

They are *Kuki* group of people. They are inhabited in the northern part of the Aizawl district of Mizoram. They are thinly populated in this State. Most of them are inhabited in Churachandpur District of Manipur.

Thado

In old days they were inhabited in southern and middle part of Mizoram. But the Lushais after their coming to Mizoram, in old days, pushed them out towards northern region of the Aizawl district of Mizoram. They have less population in Mizoram. They are thickly populated in *Senapati* and Churachandpur district of Manipur. They are also inhabited in some parts of Nagaland ; *Cachar* district of Assam and *Upper Chindwin* district of Burma. They have more or less assimilated with the *Hmare*, *Bietes* and the *Lushais*.

They speak their own dialect *Thado*. Linguistically they belong to the *Tibeto Burman* family, racially they belong to the *Mongoloid* family. Among them bride-price is there. They prefer marriage with mother's brother's daughter but never with father's sister's daughter. It is customary for them that a brother takes as his wife the deceased brother's widowed wife although he may be already a married one.

Rice is their staple food. They practise *jhum* cultivation. They have their village *Chief* who occupy his post on hereditary basis. Among them, land is mainly owned by the Chief who gives it on rental basis to the villagers. They dibble seeds into small holes made by hoe (*tucha*). They do not sow seeds by broadcast way. They are economically developed tribe.

They bury their dead.

Viaphei

They are mainly inhabited in north eastern part of Aizawl

district. They are also inhabited in Churachandpur and Senapati districts of Manipur and North Cachar Hills of Assam.

They are *Old Kuki* tribe and belong to the *Indo Mongoloid* group. It is said that, they had migrated to Manipur from *Chin Hills* of Burma. They have their own dialect *Vaiphei*. This dialect has some similarities with the *Lushai* language. Most of them were animist and followed their tribal religion. Now most of them have converted to Christianty.

They have twelve exogamous clans. Two types of marriages are there *viz.* marriage by negotiation and self-arranged marriage. Rule of exogamy is not strictly followed by them. Bride price is there. They are monogamous and prefer nuclear family. A rich man may take any number of wives but they hardly take a fourth wife if the other three are alive. They have their Village *Chief* (*Housa*). The Village *Chief* takes the responsibility to look after the village administration with the help of village elders. They have also village *Darbar* (*Inpi*).

Rice is their staple food. They practise *jhum* (shifting) cultivation. They have their traditional dress and ornaments. But the gents of younger generation likes to wear modern European tailored dress of shirt, pant, tie etc. They formed the *Vaiphei League* in 1952 and it was renamed as the *Vaiphei National Organisation* in 1960 to look after the interest of the *Vaiphei* tribes. They formed the *Vaiphei Working Committee* in around 1942.

They bury their dead.

Zou

The *Zou* is an ethnic group of united Zoumi. They are inhabited in the northern part of the Aizawl district of Mizoram. They are thinly populated in Mizoram. They are mainly inhabited in Churachandpur Chan-del Districts of Mani pur. The *Zou* is believed to be the progenilor of the *Zoumi*.

They are *Kuki-Chin* group of people. According to the *Paite* the *Zau* are the northern *Chin* people who were inhabited in *Chin Hills* of Burma and identified them as *Tiddim-Chin*

They have some similarities with the *Paite* people. A clan of *Zou* is called *Baite* who came out from the *Zou* people to get their separate identity. The *Baite* people are mainly inhabited in *Churachandpur* and *Chandel* districts of Manipur and also in Burma. They give their identification as the *Naga* group of people.

Zou clan is exogamous but they do not strictly follow this. Marriage is performed by negotiation or by cho ice. Rice is [their their staple food. They practise *jhu*m (shift ing) cultivation.

They bury their dead

PART II

FULL BIBLIOGRAPHY OF MIZORAM AND THE TRIBES

A

1. Abbi, B.L. (*Ed*) 1984 : *North East Region : Problems and Prospects of Development*. Chandigarh, Centre for Research in Rural & Industrial Development, 361 p.

2. Acharyyay, N.N., 1984 : Modernisation of Mizoram. *Proceedings North East India Historical Association*, No 5:219-34.

3. Acharya, S.K., 1974 : Agriculture in Meghalaya, Mizoram and Mikir and Cachar Hills. *Artha Vigyana*, March, 50-76.

4. Adampur, 1862 : *A Report on Adampur Massacre*, (The Mizos ransacked on 22nd January, 1862 three villages of Sylhet district).

5. Adams, P.F. : *Confidential Notes on Local Self Government among the Hill People*. Shillong.

6. —— 1945 : *Some notes on Policy for the Hill Tribes of Assam*, Shillong.

7. Agarwal, A.K., 1983 : Land ownership system in the Hill areas of the North East Region and its effect on development of agriculture. *Social Research*. 3(1) 32-9.

8. —— 1988 : Industrialisation in Mizoram : Need and Problem. *Khadigramodyog*, 34 (12), Sept., 523-33.

9. —— 1989 : Rural development programmes in Mizoram. Proceedings of a Seminar on *Perspective, Issues and Experiences of Rural Development in North East India*, held on 26-27 May 1989 by N-EICSSR, Shillong, 1-11 (*mimeo.*)

10. Agarwala, Prahlad 1987 : Letters, Mizoram Poll. *Amrita Bazar Patrika*, March 3 : 6 (col. 3-4).

11. Agnihotri, Malti, 1977 : A Mizo (Lushai) folktale : Liandova and his brother. *Folklore* (Calcutta), 18(2), Feb. 44-53.

12. —— 1980 : Kungawrhi, A Mizo (Lushai) folktale. *Folklore*, 21 (2), Feb., 44-51.

13. Agnihotri, S.K. (Tr), 1976 : Nang Sen Pung ; A Mizo folklore. *Folklore*. 17(4), April, 129-30.

14. Agro Economic Research Centre n.d. : *Mizos : Shifting Cultivation*. Jorhat, Agro Economic Research Centre. (It is an *unpublished* Report of the year 1965).

15. : *Rural life in Assam Hills*. Jorhat, A.E.R.C.

16. —— 1963 : *Survey of the village Hmunpui* (*Mizoram*). Jorhat, A.E.R.C.

17. —— 1973 : *The economics of shifting cultivation in North East India* (*Ad hoc study no. 22*). Jorhat, A.E.R.C.

18. Ahluwalia, B.K. *and* Shashi, Ahluwalia (*Comp.*), 1986 : *Social and Economic development in Northeast India.* Delhi, Gian Publishing House, 200p.

19. Allen, B.C., 1902 : *Census of India 1901, Vol. IV Assam, part I, Report.* Shillong, Assam Secretariat Printing Office. (*Reprinted* in two volumes in November 1984 by Manas Publications, Delhi).

20. ———, 1905-1915 : *Assam District Gazetteers, vol. II, IX, X* and *Supplement to vol. X.* Calcutta, Baptist Mission Press (New edition, 1905) ; Delhi, Gian Publications (*Reprinted,* 1980).

21. ———, 1905 : *The Lushai Hills District Gazetteers : Assam Districts Gazetteers.* vol. III. Calcutta, Printed at the City Press.

22. ———, 1906 : *Assam District Gazett, vol. X : Khasi and Jaintia Hills, Gara Hills and Lushai Hills.* Allahabad, Printed at the Pioneer Press.

23. Allen, B.C., *et al* 1979 : *Gazetteers of Bengal and North East India.* Delhi, Mittal Publications (*Reprinted*), 663p.

24. Allen, B.C., 1980 : *Gazetteer of the Khasi and Jaintia Hilla, Garo Hills, Lushai Hills.* Delhi Gian Publications (*Reprinted*).

25. *Amrita Bazar Patrika,* 1972 : Mizoram. *Amrita Bazar Patrika, Supplement page,* January 21.

26. ———, 1974 : Troubles in Mizoram. *Amrita Bazar Patrika,* November 20 and November 21.

27. ———, 1983 : Demand to Save Chakmas from Victimisation. *Amrita Bazar Patrika,* October, 5.

28. *Amrita Bazar Patrika*, 1985 : New land use policy in Mizoram. *Amrita Bazar Patrika*, February 21 : 3.

29. ———, 1985 : Jhum system to go in Mizoram. *Amrita Bazar Patrika*, April 23, Tuesday : 7.

30. ———, 1985 : Mizoram. *Amrita Bazar Patrika*, April 22 : 7.

31. ———. 1985 : Mizoram Forest Department making good work, *Amrita Bazar Patrika*, June 16 : 5.

32. ———, 1895 : Mizo talks in difficulties : Laldenga. *Amrita Bazar Patrika*, November 22, Friday : 1.

33. ———, 1986 : Talk with Laldenga to be resumed soon. *Amrita Bazar Patrika*March 10 : 12 (col. 5-6).

34. ———, 1986 : Laldenga hopes for early accord, *Amrita Bazar Patrika*, March 16 : 1 (col. 5-6).

35. ———, 1986 : TNV-MNF truck : Delhi in touch with Tripura *Am. Baz. Pat.*, April 9 : 1 (2-3).

36. ———, 1987 : Mizoram election on February 16. *Am. Baz. Pat.* January 13 : 12 (1-2).

37. ———, 1987 : Editorial : Laldenga or Lalthanhawla ? *Am. Baz. Pat.*, January 15 : 6 (1-2).

38. ———, 1987 : Mizoram Assembly poll on February 16. *Am. Baz. Pat.*, January 18 : 4 (7-8).

39. ———, 1987 : Ramyo's secret meeting with Laldenga. *Am. Baz. Pat.*, January 18 : 5 (3).

40. ———, 1987 : Mizoram Congress mobilises re-

sources for poll campaign. *Am. Baz. Pat.*, February 6 : 7 (2-3).

41. *Amrit Bazar Patrika*, 1987 : Gorkha team meets Sangma. *Am. Baz. Pat.*, Feb. 13 : 3 (1). [*Mizoram Gorkha Sangh*].

42. ———, 1987 : Mizoram goes to the polls today. *Am. Baz. Pat.*, Feb. 16 : 1 (3-6) and 12 (6-8).

43. ———, 1987 : Four more States to be put on Rail map. *Am. Baz. Pat.*, Feb. 19 : 3 (1-3).

44. ———, 1987 : MNF secures absolute majority. *Am. Baz. Pat.* Feb. 19 : 1 (7-8) and 12 (7-8).

45. ———, 1987 : Editorial : MNF wins in Mizoram. *Am. Baz. Pat.*, Feb. 19 : 6 (1-2).

46. ———, 1987 : Mizoram, Arunachal attain Statehood. *Am. Baz. Pat.*, Feb. 21 : 1 (7-8) and 12 (5)

47. ———, 1987 : Burmese troops kill 640 rebels in Shan. *Am. Baz. Pat.*, March 3 : 5 (6).

48. ———, 1987 : Tension in Mizoram. *Am. Baz. Pat.*, March 4 : 5 (1-2).

49. ———, 1987 : Editorial : Bloodshed in Mizoram. *Am. Baz. Pat.*, March 5 : 6 (1-2).

50. ———, 1987 : Dhaka impeding return of Chakmas. *Am. Baz. Pat.*, March 6 : 7 (5-8).

51. ———, 1987 : Move to close down *Jhums*. *Am. Baz. Pat.*, March 9 : 3 (1-2).

52. ———, 1987 : Editorial : Another Chakma massacre. *Am. Baz. Pat.*, March 11 : 6 (1-2).

53. ———, 1987 : Anti-Defection Bill may be adop-

ted in Mizoram. *Am. Baz. Pat.*, March 20 : 3 (6).

54. *Amrit Bazar Patrika*, 1987 : Pragmatism of MNF apt to be eye opener. *Am. Baz. Pat.*, March 21 : 3 (6).

55. ———, 1987 : Plan to expand coffee cultivation in N-E area. *Am. Baz. Pat.*, March 21 : 5 (2-3).

56. ———, 1987 : Scheme to replace jhum cultivation in Mizoram. *Am. Baz. Pat.*, March 24 : 3 (3).

57. ———, 1987 : MNF has to work hard said by Mr. Laldenga. *Am. Baz. Pat.*, March 25 : 7 (1-4).

58. ———, 1987 : "No debacle for Cong-I" (said by Mr. Lalthanwala). *Am. Baz. Pat.*, March 25 : 7 (5-7).

59. ———, 1987 : MNF extends full support to Laldenga. *Am. Baz. Pat..* April 3 : (1-3).

60. ———, 1987 : Editorial : The return of Chakmas. *Am. Baz. Pat.*, April 6 : 6 (1-2).

61. ———, 1987 : Laldenga confirms election promises to people. *Am. Baz. Pat.*, April 10 : 3 (6).

62. ———, 1987 : High level team for defusing Mizoram-Assam dispute. *Am. Baz. Pat.*, April 10 : 3 (3).

63. ———, 1987 : Mizoram to have permanent cultivation. *Am. Baz. Pat.*, April 10 : 3 (3).

64. ———, 1987 : Move for NE tribals' united struggle. *Am. Baz. Pat.*, April 11 : 3 (1-2).

65. *Amrita Bazar Patrika*, 1987 : Chakmas fleeing to India to escape death. *Am. Baz. Pat.*, April 13 : 8 (4-5).

66. ———, 1987 : Geological investigations may open new economic avenues in N-E States. *Am. Baz. Pat.*, April 15 : 8 (2-3).

67. ———, 1987 : Rare Mizoram orchids face extinction. *Am. Baz. Pat.*, April 19 : 5 (3-4).

68. ———, 1987 : Saikia's plea for more 'Ahmadnagar experiments'. *Am. Baz. Pat.*, April 19 : 3 (5.6).

69. ———, 1987 : NE Regional Parties' Forum plagued with differences. *Am. Baz. Pat.*, April 28 : 3 (1-3).

70. ———, 1987 : Editorial: Vote for status quo. *Am. Baz. Pat.*, April 29 : 6 (1-2).

71. ———, 1987 : Safe corridor for smugglers. *Am. Baz. Pat.*, May 3 : 3 (5).

72. ———, 1987 : A complete metamorphosis. *Am. Baz. Pat.*, May 8 : 3 (1-3).

73. ———, 1987 : Code of conduct for MLAs soon : Corruption of Mizo State staff a big problem. *Am. Baz. Pat.*, May 8 : 3 (1-3).

74. —=—, 1989 : Mizoram : Golden Triangle, new drug route to India. *Am. Baz. Pat.*, April 7 : 7 (1-3).

75. ———1987 : Indira housing project in Mizoram. *Am. Baz. Pat.*, May 8 : 3 (1-3).

76. ———, 1987 : High Court, PSC for Mizoram soon, *Am. Baz. Pat.*, May 10 : 3 (4-5).

77. ———, 1987 : Three N E States to ban sale of salt. *Am. Baz. Pat.*, May 15 : 3 (4).

78. *Amrita Bazar Patrika*, 1987 : Jungle turns into a land of peace. *Am. Baz. Pat.*, May 17 : 7 (6).

79. ———, 1987 : Anti-drunkar squad for Mizoram. *Am. Baz. Pat.*, May 21 : 3 (1-2).

80. ———, 1987 : Centre approves a High Court for Mizoram. *Am. Baz. Pat.* May 24 : 5 (1-2).

81. ———, 1987 : Liquor, drugs seized in Mizoram. *Am. Baz. Pat.*, May 26 : 3 (3).

82. ———, 1987 : Drug traffickers' move to spoil youths in N-E region. *Am. Baz. Pat.*, April 26 : 3 (4-5).

83. ———, 1987 : Mizoram to buy rice from Burma. *Am. Baz. Pat.*, June 4 : 8 (3).

84. ———, 1997 : Three N-E States to be on Rail map by 1990. *Am. Baz. Pat.*, June 17 : 3 (1-3).

85. ———, 1987 : National Highway No. 54 by 1990. *Am. Baz. Pat.*, July 23 : 5 (6).

86. ———, 1988 : Editorial : Right step in Mizoram. *Am. Baz. Pat.*, Sept. 8 : 6 (1-2).

87. ———, 1989 : Manipur, Mizoram, Arunachal to come on Railway map. *Am. Baz. Pat.*, March 13 : 7 (5).

88. ———, 1989 : Mizoram's efforts towards economic independence. *Am. Baz. Pat.*, April 1 : 7 (2-5).

89. ———, 1989 : Poll scenario in the North East election 1989. *Am Baz. Pat.*, Nov. 21 : 8 (1-5).

90. ———, 1990 : Burmese troops seize bases of Karen rebels. *Am. Baz. Pat.*, Feb. 4 : 7 (2-4).

91. *Amrita Bazar Patrika*, 1990 : Foundation stone of Mizoram House laid. *Am. Baz. Pat.*, Feb. 10 : 3 (5-6).

92. ———, 1990 : Editorial : Laldenga advises Mann. *Am. Baz. Pat.*, Feb. 18 : 6 (1-2).

93. ———, 1990 ; Trafficking of Burmese heroin through China. *Am. Baz. Pat.*, April 3 : 5 (1-4).

94. ———, 1990 ; Plight of Burmese on the eve of elections. *Am. Baz. Pat.*, April 28 : 5 (1-3).

95. ———, 1990 : N-E States plan to boost tourism. *Am. Baz. Pat.*, June 26 : 5 (2-4).

96. ———, 1990 : Chakma Ditorial : DPs creating law and order problem. *Am. Baz. Pat.*, July 7 : 5(1).

97. ———, 1990 : Editorial : of two rebels. *Am. Baz. Pat.*, July 11 : 6 (1-2).

98. ———, 1990 : Laldenga to be buried near War Memorial *Am. Baz. Pat.*, July 14 : 5(1-3).

99. Anderson, J.D., 1885 : *A short list of words of the Hill Tippera language with their English equivalents ; also of words of the language spoken by Lushais of the Sylhet frontier.* Shillong, Assam Secretariat Press, 13p.

100. Anderson, H., 1913 : *Report of a visit to the South Lushai Missions of the B M S.* London, B.M.S, : 33-6.

101. Anonymous, 1872 : Tipera and Chittagong Kukis. *Indian Antiquary*, vol. 1 : 225-26.

102. ———, 1892-1993 : *Routes in the Chin-Lushai tract.* Simla, Govt. Central Printing Office, 163p.

103. Anonymous, 1893 : *Military Report of the Chin Lushai country*. Simla, Govt. Press, 112+liip..

104. ———, 1894 : Tod und Jenseits bei den Luschais. *Mitt, Geog. Ges. Jena.*, 13 : 30-1.

105. ———, 1899 : *Mi-zo Zir Tir Na Bu, a Lushai Primer* (*in Lushai* dialect). Shillong, 10 p.

106. Aram, M., 1974 : *Peace in Nagaland*, New Delhi, Arnold Heniman Publishers (India).

107. Archives, 1913 : *Report of a visit to the South Lushai Mission*. London, Baptist Missionary Society Archives.

108. ———, 1913 : *Slavery on British Territory*: *Assam & Burma*. Aberystwyth Wales, Calvinistic Methodist Archives or National Library of Wales.

109. ———, 1936 : *Proceedings of the Home Department 1909 to 1936*. New Delhi, National Archives of India.

110. Assam Govt., 1900 : *Records of Assam Govt. 1814 to 1900*, Shillong.

111. ———, 1954 : *The Assam : Lushai Hills District Act* (Acquisition of *Chiefs* rights). Gauhati, Assam Govt.

112. ———, 1959 : *Report of the Committee appointed to examine the measures required to be undertaken for the rehabilitation of the people living in the borders of Mizo district adjoining East Pakistan*, Shillong, Tribal Areas Deptt., Govt. of Assam : 4-7, 15-6, 18-9.

113. Assam Govt., 1963 : *Report on the Second Round Socio-Economic Survey in Mizo Hills.* Shillong, Assam Govt.

114. Assam Proceedings, 1890-91 : *Assam Proceedings.* Shillong, Record Office, Govt. of Assam. (It refered many sporadic tribal raids, demarcation of the boundary between Chittagong Hill Tracts and Lushai Hills, demarcation of the boundary between Chin Hills and the Lushai Hills, the rising of the Western Lushai Hills Expedition of 1891 and so on).

115. Assam Secretariat 1890 : Political and Judicials. *A Military Proceedings*, August, nos. 68-152.

116. ———, 1890 : Political and Judicial. *A Foreign Proceedings*, August, Nos. 1-46.

117. ———, 1894 : *Gazetteer's of North Lushai Hills.* Shillong, Assam Secretariat Press.

118. ———, 1905 : *Assam Secretariat, Home-B, July nos. 1601-16*, 6 *Education*, Shillong, Govt. of Assam.

119. ———, 1926 : *Assam Secretariat, Pol.-B, September, nos. 491-94, 14-Education.* Shillong, Govt of Assam.

120. ———, 1915 : *Assam District Gazetters, vols. 1-5* Shillong, Assam Secretariat Press.

121. Assam Tribune, 1970 : The Mizos. *The Assam Tribune* (Gauhati), October 2

122. ———, 1979 : Tripura village burnt down by Mizo insurgent. *The Assam Tribune*, March 22.

123. ———, 1985 : Mizoram CM's talk with Church leaders. *The Assam Tribune*, July 11 : 4

124. Assam Tribune, 1985 : Mizoram sanctuary boundary demarcated. *The Assam Tribune*, July 26 : 4.

125. ———, 1985 : Mizo ultimatum (Editorial column). *The Assam Tribune*, Nov. 30 : 4 (col. 1-2).

126. ———, 1986 : Editorial Towards Mizo Accord. *The Assam Tribune*, Feb. 25 : 4 (1-2).

127. ———, 1986 : Peaceful condition in Mizoram stressed. *The Assam Tribune*, March 11 : 1 (6-8) & 8 (5).

128. ———, 1986 : Mizo peace talks from March 15. *The Assam Tribune*, March 14 : 4 (1-2).

129. ———, 1986 : NEC to implement 30 schemes in Mizoram. *The Assam Tribune*, March 17 : 7(3-5).

130. ———, 1986 : Mizo problem in decisive stage. *The Assam Tribune*, March 19 ; 1 (1-3).

131. ———, 1986 : Book Review : Folklore in its entirety *Kuki Life And Lore*—Tarun Goswami, North Cachar Hills District Council, Halflong, Assam, India, Rs. 210 $ 16, p. 648. *The Assam Tribune*, March 30 : 4 (col. 7-8).

132. ———, 1986 : Laldenga's Aides leave for Delhi. *The Assam Tribune*, April 1 : 1 (col. 3).

133. ———, 1986 : Editorial : Out look for Mizoram. *The Assam Tribune*, April, 3 : 4 (col. 1-2).

134. ———, 1986 : Urgent accord on Mizoram urged. *The Assam Tribune*, April 13 : 4 (3-4).

135. Assam Tribune, 1986 : Disturbed areas belt on Indo-Burma border. *The Assam Tribune*, April 15 : 6 (5).

136. ———, 1987 : Laldenga Ministry to take oath today : PM Inaugurates Statehood. *The Assam Tribune*, Feb. 20 ; 1(1-3).

137. ———, 1987 : Editorial ; MNF Victory. *The Assam Tribune*, Eeb. 20 ; 4 (1-2).

138. ———, 1987 : Aizawl may face acute shortage of drinking water, *The Assam Tribune*, Feb. 20 ; 4 (7-8).

139. ———, 1989 ; Mizoram Statchood Day 20th February. *The Assam Tribune*, Feb. 20 ; 6 (1-8).

140. ———, 1989 ; Mizoram industrial policy approved. *The Assam Tribune*, March 10 : 4 (7-8).

141. ———, 1989 ; Water supply in Mizoram. *The Assam Tribune*, March 20 : 7(5).

142. ———, 1989 ; Hmar bandh call. *The Assam Tribune*, March 24 ; 8 (5).

143. ———, 1989 ; Lalthanhawla ministry faces opposition campaign. *The Assam Tribune*, March 25 : 5(3-5).

144. ———, 1989 : Mizo delegation for 'Panchyati Raj' meet. *The Assam Tribune*, April 1 ; 3 (5).

145. ———, 1989 ; Mizoram's efforts towards economic independence. *The Assam Tribune*, April 2, 3 (3-5).

146. ———, 1989 : Mizoram Cigarette factory. *The Assam Tribune*, April 4 ; (3(4).

147 ———, 1989 ; Mizoram : A Narcotic Gateway *The Assam Tribune*, April 7 ; 5 (3-5).

148. Assam Tribune, 1989 : Mizoram launches scheme to end jhuming. *The Assam Tribune*, June 24 : 5 (4-5).

149. ———, 1989 ; Rubber cultivation picking up in N-E. *The Assam Tribune*, June 24, 5(5-6).

150. ———, 1989 ; Manipur : Govt. not to allow HPC to set up base. *The Assam Tribune*, June 24 : 3 (4) (i.e. Hmar People Convention).

151. ———, 1989 : Laldenga not to jo'in Cong (I) *The Assam Tribune*, June 29 : 1 (8).

152. ———, 1989 ; New Regional Party formed in Mizoram. *The Assam Tribune*, July 14 : 5 (1)

153. ———, 1989 : Mizo team climb Mt. Bhagirati II *The Assam Tribune*, July 14 ; 8(1).

154. ———, 1989 : Mizoram Election Manifesto case. *The Assam Tribune*, September 28, : 6(3).

155. ———, 1989 : MNF appeals to defer L.S. Polls in Mizoram. *The Assam Tribune*, Oct. 29 : 3(1-3).

156. ———, 1989 ; Mizos in Tripura call for poll boycott, *The Assam Tribune*, Nov. 2 ; 5(3).

157. ———, 1989 ; Sailo's party recognised by N.F. *The Assam Tribune*, Nov. 11, 1(1-3) & 8 (6).

158. ———, 1989 : The spreading tentacles of the dring menace. *The Assam Tribune*, Sunday Reading, Nov. 19, I(1-8).

159. ———, 1989 ; Electioneering in Mizoram *The Assam Tribune*, Nov. 21, 5(2).

160. Assam Tribune, 1989 : Spiritual revival in Mizoram. *The Assam Tribune*, Nov. 21, 7(1-2).

161. ———, 1989 : Mizoram will become self-sufficient in foodgrains. *The Assam Tribune*, Dec. 22 : 3(2-4),

162. ———, 1990 : 47 Candidates for Mizoram Council Poll. *The Assam Tribune*, January 31 ; 3 (6).

163. ———, 1990 : Rs. 125 Crs. for Mizoram's Annual Plan. *The Assam Tribune*, Feb. 8 : 3 (3).

164. ———, 1990 ; Hmar activist killed. *The Assam Tribune*, February 13 (6(6).

165. ———, 1990 ; Dismissal of Mizoram Govt. demanded. *The Assam Tribune*, February 22 : (1-3).

166. ———, 1999 : Mizoram State Day from Feb. 26. *The Assam Tribune*, Feb. 22 : 3 (4).

167. ———, 1990 : Permanent Bench of Gauhati HC at Aizawl. soon. *The Assam Tribune*, March 7 : 1(8).

168. ———, 1990 : Budget session of Mizoram Assembly begins. *The Assam Tribune*, March 17 : 7 (6-8).

169. ———. 1990 : Non-tribal trading act to be referred to Centre. *The Assam Tribune*, March 18, 8(3).

170. ———. 1990 : Deficit budgets for Mizoram, Tripura. *The Assam Tribune*, March 20, 1(1-4), 8(6-7).

171. ———. 1990 : Seminar on Agrarian situation in North East. *The Assam Tribune*, March 24, 7(3)

172. ———. 1990 : Mizoram Newsletter : Privilege motion against newspaper editor.

The Assam Tribune, March 24, 5(4-5).

173. Assam Tribune, 1990 : Burmese army personnel attack villagers, one hurt. *The Assam Tribune*, March 30, 8(5).

174. ———, 1990 : One lakh floating population in Mizoram. *The Assam Tribune*, March 31 : 3(6).

175. ———, 1990 : MLA suspended for threatening Mizoram speaker. *The Assam Tribune*, April 6 : 8(5).

176. ———, 1990 : Heroin trade : 10 years RI to Burmese national. *The Assam Tribune*, May 7 : 3(3).

177. ———, 1990 : Mizoram democratic party suffers major jat. *The Assam Tribune*, May 10 : 6(3).

178. ———, 1990 : Stress on development of handloom. *The Assam Tribune*, May 17 : 5(8).

179. ———, 1990 : Night curfew in Mizoram village. *The Assam Tribune*, June 14 : 1(1).

180. ———, 1990 : Permanent HC Bench in Mizoram opened. *The Assam Tribune*, July 6 : 1 (4-5).

181. ———, 1990 : Laldenga dead. *The Assam Tribune*, July 8, : 1 (5-6) and 6(4).

182. ———, 1990 : Laldenga : A leader of insurgency. *The Assam Tribune*, July 8 : 6(6-7).

183. ———, 1990 : Demand for full-fledged HC in Mizoram. *The Assam Tribune*, July 9 : 3 (1-2).

184. ———, 1990 : State funeral to Laldenga on July 12. *The Assam Tribune*, July 10 : 1 (8),

185. Assam Tribune, 1990 : JD activities unauthorised : Fernandes. *The Assam Tribune*, July 17 : 6 (6).

186. Assembly Library 1971 : *Proceedings of the Mizo District Council in the 68th session held at the Council Chamber.*

187. Asthana, A.N. (*Ed*) 1910 : *Proceedings of a worshop on Agricultural Research in North Eastern Hills Region* : *I C A R.* Shillong, Director ICAR Research Complex for NEH Region.

188. Athparia, R.P. 1985 : Hmar : Tribal Identity. *Social Research* (Shillong), 5 (2-3), April-Sept. : 14-22.

189. Auva, C.V.L. 1981 : *Religious beliefs and customs among the Mizos before the advent of Christianity. Unpublished* D.Phil degree (under Prof. M.K. Kutty, Head, Deptt. of Philosophy). Gauhati University.

B

190. Badgley, W.F. 1873 : The Lushais. *Indian Antiquery*, 2 : 363-66.

191. ———, 1873 : The Lushai expedition, from reports of the Surveyors. *Proc. Roy. Geog. Soc.*, 17 : 42-55.

192. Baines, Athelstane 1976 : *Ethnography* (*Castes and Tribes*, Delhi, Concept Pub. Com. (*Reprinted* 1st Pub. in India in 1912) : 133-34, 134-35.

193. Balfour, E.G. 1976 : *Encyclopaedia Asiatica*. Delhi, Cosmo Publications (*Reprinted*).

194. Bandyopadhyay, P.K. 1980 : Pattern of authority and influence in the Mizo society : A note. (*Proceedings* of a Seminar on the *Tribes of North East India*, held in Sept. 22-24 by NEICSSR with S.H.T.C., Shillong). Calcutta, Firma KLM (P) Ltd (1984), (*Ed.*) by S. Karotemprel.

195. Bandyopadhyay, P.K, 1981 : Land Relations and Land Use pattern : The Mizo Dimension. (Proceedings of a Seminar on *Land and Land Relations in the Hills of North East India*, held on 28-30 mouth by NEICSSR, Shillong), Delhi. Peoples Pub. House (1987), (Eds.) by B.B. Dutta Karna, N.N.

196. ———, 1982 : Folk Expression of Mizos : An Overview. (Proceedings of a Seminar on *Folklore in North East India*, held on 17-18 November by NEICSSR, Shillong). New Delhi, Omsons Pub. (1985), (Ed.) by Soumen Sen.

197. ———, 1982 : Press in North Eastern Region : A Review. *Yojana*, 26 (14-15), August 16-31 and 55-7.

198. ———, 1983 : Election Scene in Mizoram : A Note. Proceedings of a Seminar on *Electoral Politics in North East India*, held on 14-15 December by NEICSSR, Shillong (Ed.) by P.S. Datta.

199. ———, 1984 : A Note on Authority and Influence of the Mizo. (*In*) *The Tribes of North East India*, (Ed.) by S. Karotemprel. Calcutta, Forma KLM Pvt. Ltd : 422-28.

200. ———, 1985 : *Leadership among the Mizos : An emerging dimension*. Delhi, B.R. Publishing Corporation, 296 p.

201. ———, 1986 : Election Scene in Mizoram : A Note. (*In*) *Electoral Politics in North East India*, (*Ed.*) by P.S.

Dutta, New Delhi, Omsons Publications : 167-75.

202. Bandopadhyay, S.B., 1901 : *The Kukis.*

203. Banerjee, A.C., 1944 : *Annexation of Burma.* Calcutta.

204. ———, 1946 : *The Eastern Frontier of British India.* Calcutta.

205. Banerjie, Indranil 1986 : Mizoram : Quest for Peace. *India Today*, July 31 : 26-9.

206. Baptist Church, 1930: *General Secretary's Report, June, 1980.* Gauhati, Council of Baptist Churches in North East India (*For Private Circulation*).

207. Baptist Missionary Society, 1913 : *Report of a Visit to the South Lushai Mission.* London, BMS. Indian Secretary.

208. Barbe, M. 1845 : Some account of the Hill Tribes in the Interior of the District of Chittagong (in a Letter to the Secretary of the Asiatic Society of Bengal, Calcutta). *Jour. of the Asiatic Society of Bengal*, Vol. 14 pt. I : 380-91.

209. Bardaloi, G.C. *etal.*, 1923 : Notes on Certain Frontier Tribes. (*In*) *Census of India 1921, vol. III, Assam, pt. I-Report, Appendix-B.* Shillong, Govt. Press : 10-6.

210. Bardoloi, Gopal, 1986 : *Economy of North East India : A Statewise Analysis.* Gauhati, LBS Publications.

211. Bareh, Hamlet, 1967: Patterns of Economic Enterprises in the Hill areas of North East India. (*In*) *A Common Perspective for North East India*, (Eds.) by

R. Mitra and B. Das Gupta, Calcutta, Pannalal Das Gupta : 923-31.

212. Baresh, Meyer, 1967 : The Concept of a '*Tribe*' in East Pakistan: The Case of the *Chakma* of the Chittagong Hill Tracts. (*In*) *Abstracts of American Anthropological Association, 66th Aannual Meeting*.

213. Barkataki, S (Ed.), 1969 : *Tribes of Assam*, New Delhi, National Book Trust (India) : 71-4, 81-98, 99-107, 107-10, 136-42, 142-51, 152-53.

214. ———, (*Comp*), 1982 : *Tribal Folk-tales of Assam* (*Hills*). Gauhati, Publication Board, Assam (*Reprint* of 1970 edition) 1-42, 44-82, 83-102, 182-83.

214. Barnard, J.T.O, 1930 : The Frontier of Burma. *Jour. of Roy. Cen. As. Sec.*, XVII.

216. Barooah, S.R., 1990 : Letters to the Editor : Railways in NE Region. *The Assam Tribune*, Feb. 17 : 4(3-4 .

217. Barpujari, H.K, 1963 : *Assam in the Days of the Company*. Gauhati, Spectrum Publications.

218. ———, 1970 : *Problems of Hill Tribes of North East Frontier, a Critical Analysis of the Problems and Policies Towards the Hill Tribes of the Frontier*. Gauhati, Lawyers' Book Stall, 275 p.

219. ———, 1981 : *Problems of the Hill Tribes, vol. III*. Gauhati, Spectrum Publications.

220. Barthakur, D.N., 1985 : Development of Human Resources for Agriculture and Allied Sectors

in the North East Hill Region (*In*) *Planning in North East India*, (*Ed.*) by K. Alam. New Delhi, Omsons Publications : 33-46.

221. Barthakur, M., 1985 : Formation of Planning and Development Strategies for North East India, the Land of Seven Sister. (*In*) *Planning in North East India*, (*Ed.*) by K. Alam New Delhi, Omsons Pub. : 260-67.

222. Baruah, Hem, 1956 : *The Red River and Blue Hills*. Gauhati, Lawyer's Book Stall.

223. Barua, P.C., 1983 : Appropriate Technology for North East Regional Development. *Productivity News*, 21 (7) : 21-4.

224. ———, 1990 : *Development Planning of North East India : Agricultural, Economic, Environmental, Financial Industrial, Manpower and Rural.* Delhi, Mittal Publications.

225. Baruah, Sanjib, 1986 : Immigration, Ethnic Conflict and Political Turmoil : Assam, 1979-1985. *Asian Survey*, 26 (11), Nov. : 1184-1206.

226. ———, 1989 : Minority Policy in the North East : Achievements and Dangers. *Economic and Political Weekly*, XXIV (37), Sept. 16 : 2087-91

227. Baruah, Seema, 1974 : Enchanting Mizoram. *North Eastern Affairs*, 3(1), April-June: 59-62.

228. Barua, S.N., 1977 : Patkai and its Natural Environment. *Arunachal News*, 5(9), Jan.-Feb. : 18-22.

229. ———, 1990 : *Tribes of Indo-Burma Border*, Delhi, Mittal Publications.

230. Basu, A., 1978 : *Report on Shifting Cultivation on Mizoram and Tripura.* Report Submitted to Anthropological Survey of India, Shillong. (*Unpublished*).

231. Basu Arati, 1981 : *Report on Mizoram.* Proceedings of a Seminar Held in Calcutta by Anthropological Survey of India, 26 p.

232. Basu, Pravash Chandra, 1931 : The Social and Religious Ceremonies of the Chakmas. *Jour. and Proceedings of the Asiatic Society of Bengal*, New Series, 27(2) : 213-23.

233. Baveja, J.D., 1970 : *The Land Where Bamboo Flowers.* Gauhati Assam Publication Board, 84 p.

234. ———, 1982 : *New Horizons of North East*, Gauhati, Western Book Depot : 38-42, 114, 119, 120.

235. ———, 1985 : Mizo Mind Ready for Era of Peace. *Patriot*, January 17.

236. Baviskar, B.S., 1975 : Tribes and Nation Building in the North East. *Vanyajati*, XXIII (2-3), April-July : 16-7.

237. Bawichhuaka, H.K. ; Chalchhunga and Pahlira, C., 1966 : *Memorandum to the Prime Minister, Mrs. Gandhi on June 22. 1966.* Aizawl, Mizo Union.

238. Bayfield, G.T., 1873 : Narrative of a Journey from Ava to the Frontiers of Assam and Back, Performed Between December 1836 and May 1837 Under the Orders of Col. Burney. . . . Simla. *Selection of Papers.*

239. Bernot, L. and : Chittagong Hill Tribes. (*In*)

Denise, Bernot, : 1957 *Pakistan : Society and Culture,* (*Ed.*) by Stanley Maron. New Haven, (Conn: Human Relations Area Files), Yale University: 46-61.

240. ———, 1958 : *Les Khyangs des collines due.* Paris, Pion Publisher.

241. Bessaignet, P., 1958 ; *Tribesmen of the Chittagong Hill Tracts* (*Publication No 1*). Dacca, Asiatic Society of Pakistan.

242. Bez Baruah, R.N., 1982 : Anti-Jhuming measures in the North East. *Himalaya* : *Man and Nature,* 5 (8), Jan. ; 13-4.

243. Bhadra, Gautam, 1975 : The Kuki uprising (1917-1919): Its Causes and Nature. *Man in India,* 55(1), Jan.-March : 10-56.

244. Bhadra, R.K., 1974 : Indian Tribes and Their Modernization. [*Vanyajati,* XXII (2), April 40-9.

245. ———, 1975 : Indian Tribes and Their Modernization. *The North Eastern Research Bulletin* VI, Summer : 41-50.

246. Bhagabati, A.C, 1988 : Tribal Transformation in Assam and North East India : An Appraisal of Emerging Ideological Dimensions. (Presidential Address, Section of Anthropology and Archaeology). Pune, *Indian Science Congress, 75th Session.*

247. Bhat, Sudhakar, 1975 : *The Challenge of the North East.* Bombay, Popular Prakashan 62-77.

248. Bhatnagar, Pramod, 1981 : *Zoramthangi* : *Daughter of the hills,* Delhi, Vikrant Press, 199 p.

249. Bhattacharjee, Anil, : Tripura : Mizos Demand Regional

1990 Council. *Amrita Bazar Patrika*, May 16 : 7(2).

250. Bhattacharjee, A.K. : *Evolution of Nagaland*. Calcutta; The Book Trust.

251. Bhattacharjee, K.K., 1983 : *North East India : Political and Administrative History*. New Delhi, Cosmo Publications : 7, 40, 88, 89, 90, 95, 97, 105, 222.

252. Bhattacharyya, N.N, 1989 : Viability of the States of North East India. *Jour. NEICSSR*, 13(1) April : 1-6.

53. Bhattacharjee, P.R. : Regional Planning for North East India. *Current Biography*, 641 : 232-41.

254. Bhattacharjee, R., 1983 : Hmar tribe : Their society and Some of its Aspects. *Proceedings of North East India Historical Associations*, No. 4 : 79-88.

255. Bhattacharjee, S.K. 1 85 : Paite of Mizoram. Proceedings of a Workshop-Seminar on National Project *People of India*, December 6, 1985, 2nd Session, Shillong, Anthropological Survey of India (*Mimeo*).

256. ———, 1987 : Hmar of Mizoram. Proceedings of a Workshop-Seminar on National Project *People of India*, May 24, 1987, Shilliong, Anthro. Surv. of India (*Mimeo*).

257. Bhattacharya, S.S., 1969 : The Mizo Wareor. *Folklore*, X(8), Aug. : 305-08.

258. Bhikkhu, Pragya Joyoti, 1989 : Letter to the Editor : Facilities for Chakma. *Shillong Times*, Aug. 21 2(3-4).

259. Bhuyan, S.K., 1949 : *Early British Relations with Assam*.

Gauhati, Deptt. Historical and Antiqua.

260. Bhuyan, S.K. 1949 : *Anglo-Assamese Relations (1771-1826)*. Gauhati, Deptt. Historical and Antiquarian Studies in Assam.

261. ———, 1983 : *A History of Assam 1682-1826 A.D. (Tungkhungia Buranji)*. Delhi, B.R. Publishing Corporation (*Reprint*, 1st Published in c. 1932).

262. Biakchhawna, 1972 : Regionalism in Mizo Politics. *Aizawl Times*, Oct. 7.

263. Biswas, Suhas K., 1963 : The Trait of Making Earthenwares in the Mizo District and its Cultural Evolution in Assam. *Bulletin Anth. Surv. of India* 12 (1-2).

264. Biswas, S.K, 1976 : Cropping Pattern Potentialities. Proceedings of a Seminar on *Strategy for Planned Economic Development of Mizoram*, July (*Mimeo*).

265. Blockman, H., 1872 : Koch Bihar and Assam. *Jour. of Asiatic Society of Bengal*, XLI, pt. I, No. I-V : 94.

266. Bora, A.K., 1985 : Problems and Prospects of Better Utilization of Land in the Hills of North East India, (*In*) *Land Use Pattern in North East India* (*Ed.*) by B.B. Dutta. Ludhiana, Gagan Publishers : 41-54.

267. Borah, Aswhini Kr., 1989 : Input of Modern Technology for Rural Development in North East India : A Case Study. Proceedings of a Seminar on *Perspective, Issues and Experiences of Rural*

Development in North East India held on 26-27 May by NEICSSR, Shillong, 7p (*Mimeo*).

268. Borah, K.C., 1987 : A Note on Agriculture and Plantation in Mizoram. *North East Quarterly* (Gauhati), 2(4), Nov. Dec. : 16-28.

269. Bora, P.K., 1975 : Soil Fertility and Fertiliser use Pattern in Assam, Meghalaya and Mizoram. *Jour. of North Eastern Council* (Shillong), Aug. : 38-49.

270. Borthakur, D.N. *et al.*, 1978 : Shifting Cultivation in North Eastern Region. (*In*) *Resources Development and Environment in the Himalayan Region*. Deptt. of Science and Technology, Govt. of India : 330-42).

271. Borthakur, I.K., 1977 : Jhuming and its Consequences. *Yojona*, XXI (1).

272. Bose, J.K., 1936 : Unknown Tribes of the Shan States. *Science and Culture* (Calcutta), August.

273. ———, 1980 : *Glimpses of Tribal life in North East India.* Calcutta, H.M, Roy for Institute of Social Research and Applied Anthropology : 10-4, 14-7, 17-8, 19, 20, 21, 22.

274. Bose, Nirmal Kumar 1967 : National Seminar on Hill People. *Man in India*, 47(1), Jan.-March : 1-7.

275. ———, 1970 : Inaugural Address, (*In*) *Research Programmes of Cultural Anthropology and Allied Discipline*, (*Ed.*) by Surajit Chandra Sinha, Anth. Surv. of India, Calcutta.

276. ———,1971 : *Tribal Life in India*. New Delhi, National Book Trust (India).

277. Bose, Nirmal Kumar, 1972 : *Some Indian Tribes.* New Delhi, National Book Trust (India).

278. Bose, Saradindu, 1967 : *Carrying Capacity of Land Under Shifting Cultivation.* Calcutta, Asiatic Society, 155 p.

279. Bose, Saradindu and Vaskar Saha (*Eds.*), 1982 : *Population Data Regarding Forestry Communities Practising Shifting Cultivation (Report for India, 1980).* New Delhi, Inspector General of Forests, Ministry of Agriculture : 25-7.

280. Bose, Saradindu ; S. Ghatak and Behra, R.K., 1982 : Shifting Cultivation in India, (*In*) *Economies of the Tribes and their Transformation* (*Ed.*) by K.S. Singh. New Delhi, Concept Pub. Com. : 216-25.

281. Boyd, Major, 1881 and 1883 : *Deputy Commissioner's Report for 1881-82. Proceedings of a Meeting* with Commissioner in April and May 1881 and June 1883.

282. Bright, W., 1957 : Alternations in Lushai. *Indian Linguistics, Bagchi Memorial Vol.*

283. Browne, H.A., 1884 : Account of the Chins of the District of Thayetmyo : Extract from the Statistical and Historical Account of that District. (*In*) *Customary Law of the Chin Tribes* by Py. Maung Thet. Rangoon, Govt. Press : 1-15 (*Appendix*).

284 B., H. R., 1889 : *The Lushais, 1873 to 1889.* Shillong, Govt. Press.

285. Brown, R., 1871 : *Account of Manipur and the Hill Territory (1873).* Calcutta: Supdt., Govt. Printing, *Reprinted* by Sanskaran Prakashan, Delhi in 1975 and it entitled, *Statistical Account of Manipur* : 47-53

286. Bruner, E.M., 1959 : Kinship Organization Among the Urban Batak of Sumatra. *Trans. N.Y. Acad. Sci.*, Series II, vol. 22 (2) : 118-25.

287. Buckland, C.E., 1901 : *Bengal Under Lieutenant Governors, vol. I (Gray)*. Calcutta, Govt. Press.

288. Burling, R., 1957 : Lushai Phonemics. *Indian Linguistics, Taraporewala volume.*

289.———, 1959 : Proto Bodo. *Language*, 35, July-Sept. : 433-53.

290. ———, 1967 : Tribesmen and Lowlanders of Assam. (*In*) *Southeast Asian Tribes, Minorities and Nations, vol. I*, (*Ed.*) by Peter Kunstadler. Princeton New Jersey, Princeton University Press : 215-29.

291. Burma Gazetteer, 1910 : *Burma Gazetteer : Northern Arakan District.* Rangoon, Govt. Press.

292. Butler, J., 1855 : *Travels and Adventures in Assam.* London, Smith Eider : 80-101.

293. ———, 1873 : A Rough Comparative Vocabulary of Some of the Dialects Spoken in the Naga Hills District. *Jour. Roy. Asiatic Soc. of Bengal*, 42, pt. 1, Appendix : ii xxix.

294. ———, 1978 : *Travels and Adventures in the Province of Assam. Reprinted* by Vivek Pub. Com., Delhi).

C

295. Calvinistic Methodist Archives, 1913 : Calvinistic Methodist Archives or National Library of Wales, Abrerystwyth Wales. *Slavery in British Territory*, Assam and Burma.

296. Cambridge University, 1970 : *Buddhism and Spirit Cult in North Eastern Thailand.* (Unpublished) Ph. D. Dissertation of Cambridge University, U.K.

297. Campbell, A., 1874 : The Looshais (Chittagong). *Jour. of the Royal Anthropological Institute*, 3 : 57-64.

298. Campbell, George, 1874 : *Specimens of Languages of India Including Those of the Aboriginal Tribes of Bengal, the Central Provinces and the Eastern Frontier.* Calcutta, Govt. Printing Press ; 204-.7, 220-36.

299. Cantlie, Keith, 1949 : Forward. (*In*) *Lushai Chrysalis* by A.G. McCall. London, Luzac and Co.,

300. Carey, B.S. and H.N. Tuck, 1896 : *The Chin Hills : A History of the people, our Dealings with them their Customs and Manners and a Gazetteer of their Country, vol. I and II.* Rangoon, Supdt., Govt. Printing (Burma).

301. ———, 1983 : *The Chin Hills.* Delhi, Cultural Publishing House (*Reprinted*).

302. Cariapp, A.C., 1974 : Mizo Hostiles Activity. *Hindu,* April 27 : 6.

303. Carrapiett, W.J.S., 1929 : *The Kachin Tribes of Burma.* Rangoon, Govt. Press.

304. Carter, Rev. H.W. (Ed), 1945 : *Mizoram Baptist Kohhran Chanchin.* Lunglei (*Revised and enlargged* by Rev. H.S. Luhia in 1981) (in Mizo).

305. Carvan, 1971 : Amnesty to the Mizos. *Carvan,* Oct. 1.

306. Census, 1961 : *Census of India 1961, vol. I, pt. II-C (ii) : Language Table.* Delhi, Manager of Publications.

307. ———, 1961 : *Census of India 1961 : Village Survey, Assam : Durtlang ; Jawngtlai.*

308. ———, 1965 ; *Census of India 1961 ; District Census Handbook Mizo District, Assam.* Delhi, Manager of Publictions.

309. ———, 1965 : *Census of India 1961, vol. III, Assam, pt. V-A : Scheduled Tribes and Scheduled Castes (Reprinted from old Census Reports and Special Tables),* by E.H. Pakyntein.

310. Central Gazetteer, : *The Gazetteer of India, Indian*

Union, vol. I : *Country and People.* Delhi. Publication Division.

311. Centre for Adult, 1990 : Proceedings of a Seminar on *Mizo Freedom Fighter* : *Role of Pi Ropuiliani in the Freedom Struggle of Mizoram*, Held on 6-7-1990 Organised by C.A.C.E., Shillong of N.E.H.U.

312. Chakrabarti, S.B. 1989 : Antyodaya : The Revised Strategy for Rural Development : Some Perspectives. Proceedings of a Seminar on *Perspective, Issues and Experiences of Rural Development in North East India*, held on 26-27 May organised by NEICSSR Shillong (*Mimeo*.) 11p.

313. Chakravarty, B.C., 1958 : *British Relation with the Hill Tribes of Assam.* Calcutta, Firma K.L. Mukhopadhya, (*Reprinted* in 1964) : 47-82.

314. Chakravartty, D.N., 1986 : Planning in North Eastern Region. *The Assam Tribune*, January 26, (*Republic Day Supplement*) : 8 (6-8) and 10 (1-4).

315. Challiana, P., 1978 : *Pi Pu Nun.* Aizawl, The Trio Book House.

316. Chaltuahkhuma, 1981 : *Political History of Mizoram.* Aizawl, L.B. Press.

317. Chambers, O.A., 1889 : *Hand Book of the Lushai Hills.* Calcutta, Intelligence Branch, Govt. Printing Press, 94p.

318. ———, 1893 : *Report on the Chittagong Column, Chin Lushai Expedition of 1889-90.* Simla, Govt. Central Printing Office, 235p.

319. Chanakya, 1974 : Impact of Regional Parties in Nagaland and Manipur. *The Assam Tribune*, March 6.

320. Chanda, Arup, 1988 : The Fleeing Burmese : Sanctuary in India. *The Statesman*, December 10, *Saturday Magazine*, 1(1-8) 4(1-4).

321. ———, 1989 : Election 1989 ; And Now, the 'Christian Card' in N.-E. ? *The Statesman*, November 19 : 1(2-7).

322. Chandra Vimal, 1964 : The Constitutional Safeguards and Privileges Accorded to the Tribes. *Vanyajati*, XII (4), October : 161-72.

23. Chapman and Clark, 1968 : Mizo Miracle. Madras, *Christian Literature Service* : 13-4.

324. Chari, R.B., 1973 : *Census of India 1971, Series-II Pt.-I of 1975, Scheduled Castes and Scheduled Tribes.* Delhi, Manager of Publications.

325. Chatterji, Neera, 1975 : *The Mizo Chief and his Administration.* Aizawl, Tribal Research Institute, Govt. of Mizoram, 22p.

326. ———, 1975 : *Zawlbuk as a Social Institute in the Mizo Society.* Aizawl, T.R.I., Govt. of Mizoram, 35p.

327. ———, 1975 : *Status of Women in the Earlier Mizo Society.* Aizawl, Tribal Reseasch Institute, 2p.

328. ———, 1975 : *The Pride of Mizoram.* Aizawl, T.R.I., Govt. of Mizoram.

329. ———, 1975 : *Monoliths and Landmarks of Mizoram.* Aizawl, T.R.I., Govt. of Mizoram.

330. Chattopadhyay, K.P., 1953 : Tribal Education. *Man in India*, 33(1), Jan.-March, 1-18.

331. ———, 1953 : A Short Note on Cultivation Among Tribal Folk in India (Assam). *Vanyajat* : 2 (4).

332. Chattopadhyaya, Kamaladevi, 1978 : *Tribalism in India*. New Delhi, Vikas Pub. House, 224-40.

333. Chattopadhyay, Suhas, 1969 : *The English and the Lushais (1844-1904)*. Gauhati University, Ph. D. Thesis (*Unpub.*)

334. ———, 1984 : Sukpilala's Sunad: An interesting Event in the History of Anglo-Lushai Relationship. *Proceedings of North Eastern India Historical Association* (Aizawl), no. 5: 101-06.

335. ———, 1985 : Role of the Raja of Tripura and the English in Capturing the Mizo Chief Lalchukha. *Proceedings of NEIHA* (Agartala), no. 6: 197-200.

336. ———, 1985 : *Mizoram Under the British Rule*. Delhi, Mittal Publications, 225p.

337. ———, 1986 : Account of Rani Banaitangi : A Lushai "Chieftainess". *Proceedings of NEIHA* (Pasighat), no. 7: 171-72.

338. ———, 1988 : Early History of the Mizos. *Proceedings of NEIHA*, (Guahati) no. 9: 101-05.

339. ———, 1990 *Mizoram Encyclopaedia (3 vols)*. Delhi, Mittal Publications (*in Press*).

340. Chatterji, Suniti : *Kirata-Jana-Krti : The Indo*

Kumar, 1951 *Mongoloids*. Calcutta, *Royal Asiatic Society of Bengal.*

341. Chaturvedi, M.D. and: *A Study in Shifting Cultivation of*
B N. Uppal, 1953 *Assam*, (*Ed.*) by Prem Nath. New Delhi, Indian Council for Agricultural Research, 22p.

342. Chaube, S.K., 1968 : Dimensions of Assam Hills Problem. *Mainstream*, December 7.

343. ———, 1968 : What was wrong with the Sixth Schedule ? *The Assam Tribune*, December 12.

344. ———, 1968 : British Contribution to the Hills Problem. *The Assam Tribune*, November 20.

345. ———, 1969 : Assam Hills Problem, Historical Background. *Mainstream*, Feb. 15

346. ———, 1969 : Early British Policy on the North Eastern India. *The Assam Tribune*, May 5.

347. ———, 1971 : Tradition and Modernisation in in the Assam Hills. *Indian Journal of Political Science*, January-March.

348. ———, 1972 : Constitutional Evolution of Mizoram. *Amrita Bazar Patrika*, (*Mizoram Supplement*), January 21.

349. ———, 1973 : *Hill Politics in North East India*, Bombay, Orient Longman, 35, 57, 114, 118, 160-71.

350. ———, 1978 : Rani Gaidiliu: Profile of a Tribal Woman Leader. (*In*) *Tribal Women in India* (*Ed.*) by Committee.

Calcutta, Indian Anthropological Society : 32-8.

351. ———, 1982 : Nation Building and Politics in the North East Indian Hills. (*In*) *Tribal Movements in India, vol. I* (*Ed.*) by K.S. Singh. New Delhi, Manohar Publications: 27-37.

352. ———, 1984 : The Sixth Lok Sabha Elections in the Hill States of North East India. *Political Science Review*, 18 (2), April-June: 105-20.

353. ———, 1985 : *Electoral Politics in North East India.* Madras, University Press (India).

354. Chaudhury, Achyut Charan, : *Srihatter Itibritta, vol, I and II.* Calcutta.

355. Chaudhury, Kalyan, 1974 Nagas and Mizos. *Frontier*, January 5: 5-8.

356. Chaudhuri, K.C, 1988 : Uniting the Mizos: Fear of Cross-Border Agitation. *The Statesman*, July 2.

357. Choudhuri, Rabijit, 1989 : Mizos in Tripura, Press for Autonomous Council. *Shillong Times*, March 10: 3 (1-4).

358. ———, 1989 : MNF to Join National Front. *Shillong Times*, March 11: 1 (3-6).

359. Choudhury, Rabindra Kr. 1989 : Rural Poverty in North East India : Its Absolute and Relative Magnitude. Proceedings of a Seminar on *Perspective, Issues and Experiences of Rural Develop-*

ment in North East India, held on 26-27 May, organised by NEIC-SSR, Shillong (*Mimeo*.): 1-12.

360. Chawngliana, Kenneth, 1978 : *Impact of Christianity in Mizo Social Structure*. Poone, Poona University, (*Unpublished*) Ph. D. Thesis

361. Chawngthan, Pari, 1988 : *Western Impact on Society in Mizoram*. (*Unpublished*) Dissertation for M. Phil (History Deptt.), NEHU, Shillong under Dr. S. N. Rao.

362. Chawnvunga : n.p. : *Mizo Tribal Religion: A Historical Approach*. Ph. D. Thesis (*in Progress*), History Deptt., NEHU, Shillong under Dr. M.S. Sangma.

363. Ch. Chhunga, 1970 : Mizoram Bids Farewell to Arms. *North Eastern Affairs*, Annual.

364. ———, 1972 *Welcome Speech of the Chief Minister, Ch. Chhunga on the Inauguration of the Union Terriory on 21st January, 1972.* Aizawal, Directorate of Information & Public Relations (*Pamphlets*)

365. ———. 1972 : *Text of the Speech of the Chief Minister on the Occasion of Inauguration of Lnnglei District, September, 1972*. Aizawl, Govt. of Mizoram.

366. ———, 1972 : *Inauguration of the Union Territory on 21st January, 1972*. Aizawl, DIPR.

367. Ch. Chhunga; Suprawnga and Bawichhuaka, H.K., 1970 : *Memorandum to Prime Minister of India on 15-12-1970.* (It is published in *Mizo Unrest* by B. B, Goswami, Jaipur, Aalekh Publishers in 1979).

368. Chib, Sukhdev Singh, 1984 : *Caste, Tribe and Culture of India, vol. VIII, North Eastern India.* New Delhi, Ess Ess Publications. 384 p.

369. ———, 1977 : *This Beautiful India : Union Territories of India.* New Delhi. Light & Life Publishers: 108-19.

370 . Chief Secretary, : *Government of Mizoram : Official Hand Book on Mizoram, vol. I and II.* Aizawl, Issued by the Chief Secretary to the Govt. of Mizoram.

371. Chin Special, 1948 : *Act XLIX of 1948 of the Parliament of the Union of Burma, as Amended by Act IX of 1957, the Chin Special Division Act (Extension of Laws, Amendment).* Rangoon, Govt. Press.

372 Chinza, L., 1966 : *A Few Memoranda from the Pawi-Lakher people from South Mizo District.* Aizawl.

373. Chinzah, Lalchunga, 1967 : *The Pawi-Lakher People of Mizo District* Aizawl, P L. Regional Council.

374. Chinzah, L., : *The Case for the Mizos.* Lunglei, Pawi District Council.

375. ———, 1970 : *For their Redemption.* Lunglei, Pub. by author.

376. Chinzah, L. : *Laitlang*. Lunglei, Pawi District Council.

377. Chopra, Pran, 1964 : *On an Indian Border*. Delhi, Asia Pub. House.

378. Choudhury, P.C., 1959 *The History of Civilisation of the People of Assam to the Twelfth Century A.D.* Gauhati, Deptt. of Historical & Antiquarian Studies in Assam.

379. Christian Peace Mission, 1966-67 : *Letter Addressed to the President of the MNF Underground Govt. for Bringing Peace in Mizoram, Dated 17-4-1966 and 18-5-1967*

380. Christian Peace Committee, 1969 : *Letter to B.C. Carriappa, Commissioner of Cachar and Mizo Districts, dated 1-3-1969 and 21-6-1969.* Aijal, Christian Peace Committee.

381. Clark, Mary Mead, 1978 : *A Corner in India.* Gauhati (*Reprinted*).

382. Clow, Andrew, 1945 : *The Future Government of the Assam Tribal People.* Shillong, Assam Govt.

383. Cole, H.W.G., 1912 : Ethnographical Notes : The Lushais (*In*) *Census of India 1911, vol. III, Assam.* Shillong, Assam Secretariat Press, 137-41.

384. Command Paper, 1947 Burma Frontier Areas, Committee of Enquiry. *Parliamentary Command Paper No.* 7138 June.

385. Commissioner of Cachar, 1969 : *Christian Peace Committee, Letter to B.C. Carriappa, dated 1-3-1969.*

Silchar, Commissioner of Cachar and Mizo Districts.

386. Commissioner of Cachar 1969 : *Christian Peace Committee, Letter to B.C. Carriappa, dated 21-6-1969.* Aijal, Commissioner of Cachar and Mizo District.

387. Constituent Assembly: 1947 *North East Frontier (Assam) Tribal and Excluded Areas Sub-Committee, vol. II (Evidence), pt. I, Lushai, North Cacher, Garo, Mikir and Naga Hills.* Delhi, Constituent Assembly of India, 204 p.

388. Cook, C., 1968 : Mizo and Naga Problems. *Eastern World* (London), 22 (5-6), May-June, 18-9.

389. Cormack, M.L., 1960 : *She Who Rides a Peacock Indian Students and Social Change.* Bombay, Asia Pub. House,

390. Crawford, C.G., 1984 : *Hand Book of Kuki Custom (Comps.)* by W. Shaw, B.C. Gasper and L.L. Peters. Imphal, Directorate for Development of Tribals and Backward Classes, Govt. of Manipur, 22 p. (*Reprinted*) (1st published in 1927).

391. Crace, J.M. et al 1935 : Notes on Some Assam Hill Tribes (*In*) *Census of India, vol. I, India, pt. III B. Ethnographic Notes* (*Ed.*) by J.H. Hutton. Simla, Govt. of India Press.

392. Crosthwaite. Charles, : 1912 *The Pacification of Burma.* London.

393, Cumming, R.C.R. *et at*, 1923 : Notes on Certain Frontier Tribes, (*In*) *Census of India 1921, vol. III, Assam, pt. I-Report, Appendex-B.* Shillong, Govt. Press: 10.6.

D

394. Dalton, E.T., 1845 : Report of his visit to the Hills in the Neighbourhood of the Soobanshri River. *Jour. of the Asiatic Society of Bengal*, XIV, pt. I,

395. ———, 1872 : *Descriptive Ethnology of Bengal*. Calcutta, Supdt. of Govt. Printing Press, 44-8 (*Reprinted* in 1960 by Indian Studies Past and Present, Calcutta). Also, (*In*) *Nagas in the Nineteenth Century*, (Ed.) by Verrier Elwin, Bombay, Oxford University Press (1969).

396. ———, 1973 : *Tribal History of Eastern India*. Delhi, Cosmo Publictions (*Reprited*, earlier title was *Descriptive Ethnology of Bengal*).

397. Damant, G.H., 1875 : The North Cachar Hills and their Inhabitation. *Calcutta Review*, LXI: 97-9.

398. Damant, G.H., 1876 : *Report on a Tour in the North Cachar Hills*.

399. ———, 1880 : Notes on the Locality and Population of the Tribes Dwelling Between the Brahmaputra and Ningthi River. *Jour. of Royal Anthropological Society*, XII : 228-31, 237-39, 252-55.

400. Danda, Ajit K., 1988 : Ethnicity in a Pluri-cultural Society. *Jour. Indian Anth. Soc.*, 23 (1), March: 36-8.

401. Das, Arunava, 1988 : Mizoram Today. *Amrita Bazar Patrika, Sunday Magazine*, December 18: 15 (1-3), 18 (1-3) 19 (1-3).

402. ———, 1988 : Highland Charm. *Amrita Baz. Pat., Sunday Magazine*, Dec. 18: 17 (2) 18 (1-2).

403. Das Bhuban, M., 1960: *Ethnic Affinities of the Rabha*, Gauhati, Gauhati University, Deptt. of Publication : 69-71.

404. Das. B.M., 1977 : Inheritance of Cerumen Type and its Importance in Population Studies. *Man in India*, 57 (4), Oct.: 305-12.

405. Das, Jogesh, 1972 : *Folklore of Assam* (*Folklore of Indian Series*). New Delhi, National Book Trust (India), 4,5,6,18.20.

406. Das, M M., 1978 : Customary Law of the Lusei Society of Mizoram. (Paper presented in the All India Seminar on *Customary Law. Unpublish-*

ed), Anthropological Survery of India, Calcutta.

407. Das, N.C., 1984 : Problems of Marketing of Handloom Products in North Eastern Region with Special Reference to Assam, *(In) Marketing in North East India*, (*Ed.*) by J.B. Ganguly, Delhi, Omsons Publications: 119-31.

408. Das, N.K., 1983 : Agrarian Situation in the Hills of North East India. *Social Mirror*, 1: 1-17.

409 ———, 1989, : *Ethnic Identity, Ethnicity and Socia Stratification in North East India* New Delhi, Inter-India Publications: 87, 156-57,211,266,267-68.

410. Das, N.K. and D.P. Mukherjee, 1976 : The Mizo Political Movement. Proceedings of a Seminar on *Contemporary Tribal Movements*, Organised by Anth. Survey of India, Calcutta.

411. Das, R.K., 1979 : Some Aspects of Changing Social Relations : A Study of a Thadou Village. *Jour. of Social Research*, XXII (1), March: 35-41.

412. Das, S., 1969 : The Lesser Known Tribes of South Lushai Hills, (*In*) *Tribes of Assam*. (*Ed*,) by S. Barkataki. New Delh National Book Trust (India): 99-110,

413. Das, S.J., 1972 : The Mizos as I Know Them, *Amrita Baz. Pat.*, (*Mizoraml Suppliment*), January 21.

414. Das, S.M., 1967 : A Brief Scheme for Formation of Hill States, (*In*) *A Common Perspective for North East India*, (*Eds.*) by R. Mitra and B. Das Gupta. Calcutta, Pannalal Das Gupta: 138-40.

415· Das, S.T. 1980 : *The People of the Eastern Himalayas*. Delhi, Sagar Publications.

416. ———, 1986 : *Tribal Life of North Eastern India*, Delhi, Gian Publishing House.

417. ———, 1987 : *Life Style, Indian Tribes, Locational, Practice*. Delhi, Gian Publishing House, 65-132,198-221.

418. Das, T.C., 1934 : Social Organisation of the Purum Kukis. *21st Indian Science Congress*, Bombay.

419. ———, 1936 : The Economic Adjustments of Kuki Tribes. *23rd Indian Science Congress*, Indore.

420. ———, 1937 : Some notes on the Economic and Agricultural Life of a Little Known Tribe on the Eastern Frontier of India. *Anthoropos*, 32: 440-49.

421. Das Gupta, K.R., 1983 : Need for Agricultural Resource Planning in the North East Region with a View to Boosting Agricultural Production. *Social Research, Jour. of the Institute of Social Research* (Shillong), 3 (3-4), July-December : 13-22.

422. Das Gupta, Malabika, 1982 : Re-establishment of Evacuated Villages in Mizoram. *Jour. NEICSSR*, VI II, Oct., 14-6.

423. Das Gupta, Malabika, 1986 : North East, Regional Imbalances and Seventh Plan. *Economic and Political Weekly,* March 29: 528-29.

424. ———, 1986 : Greater Mizoram Issue and Tripura. *Economic and Political Weekly,* Sept. 13: 1629-30.

425. Datta, K.N., n.p. : *A Handbook of Old Records of the Assam Secretariat.* Shillong, Assam Secretariat. (Unpublished).

426. Datta, K.P. 1985 : Mizo Perspective. *Link,* 27 (28), Feb. 17, 23-5.

427. Datta, Parthasarathi, 1981 : Future of the Past: A Few Words on Land Ownership Pattern in Mizoram in Anticipation. (Proceedings of a Seminar on *Land and Land Relations in the Hills of North East India,* May 28-30, organised by NEICSSR, Shillong.) (*In*) *Land and Land Relations in the Hills of North East India, (Ed.)* by B.B. Dutta. Delhi, Peoples Pub. House.

428. Datta, S.K., 1977 : Hill Politics of North East: Regionalism to the Force. *The New Horizon* (Aizawl), vol. I.

429. Datta Ray, B. (*Ed.*) 1978 : *Social and Economic Profile of North East India.* Delhi, B.R. Pub. Cor.

430. ———, 1982 : Operation and Implementation of the Sixth Schedule in North East India: An Appraisal. *Proceedings of North East India History*

Association. (Imphal), no. 3: 229-46.

431. Davis A.W., (*Comp*.) 1894 : *Gazetteer of the North Lushai Hills, Compiled Under the Order of the Chief Commissioner of Assam.* Shillong, Assam Secretariat Printing Office, 55p.

432. Deori Omem, 1984 : North East : A Perspective, (*In*) *North east Regions, Problem and Prospects of Development*, (*Ed*). by B.L. Abbi. Chandigarh, Centre for Research in Rural and Industrial Developments: 181-89.

433. Deptt. of Historical : *Kachari Buranji*, Gauhati, Deptt. of Historical and Antiquarian Studies, Govt. of Assam.

434. Deutch Yvonne, 1984 : *The Illustrated Encyclopaedia of Mankind*, vol. 3. New York, Marshall Cavendish: 370.

435. Dev, Bimal J. and Dilip K. Lahiri, 1983 : *Lushai Customs and Ceremonies.* Delhi, Mittal Publications, 172p

436. Devi, Anima 1958 : Specimens of Meiti Proverbs. *Indian Folklore*, vol. 1, no. 3, 63-74.

437. ———, 1958 : The Proverbial Lore of the Gangtes. *Indian Folklore*, 1 (4),, Oct-Dec.: 73-80.

438. Dev Barma, Thakur Jitendra Mohan, 1958 : Origin of Tripura and its People. *Vanyajati*, 6 (3), July, 108-16, (about *Kukis*).

439. Dev Shastri, Dharma, 1960 : Asam ke Mizo Jel Men (*in Hindi*). *Vanyajati* 8 (2), April: 81-4.

440. Dev Varman, S.B.K. n.p. : *The Tribes of Tripura.* Agartala, Director of Tribal Research: 1-3, 4-7, 11-2, 15-6, 20-22, 25-6.

441. ———, 1986 : *The Tribes of Tripura: A Dissertation.* Agartala, Directorate of Research (*2nd Edition*) : 13-7, 18-21, 27-9, 30-1, 34.8.

442. Dewan, Biraj Mohan, 1969 : *Chakma Jatir Etibritto* (*in Bengali*) New Rangamati (Bangladesh), Hill Chittagong.

443. Dewan, Vijay, Kumar 1976 : *North Eastern Region Local Acts of Assam, Nagaland, Manipur, Tripura, Mizoram* and *Arunachal Pradesh, Vols. I-VIII.* Allahabad, Orient Law House.

444. Dey, Tushar Kanti 1980 : *Life and Socio-Economic Conditions of the Lushai-Kuki Tribes 1850 1914.* (Unpublished) Ph. D. Thesis, Gauhati University.

445. Dibrugarh University 1975 : Seminar on *Sociological Perspective on North Eastern India and the Second Annual Conference of the North East India* (*Sociological Association*). Dibrugarh University, Deptt. of Sociology (March 10, 11, 12,1975).

446 Dihingia Homeswar, 1980 : *Assam's Struggle Against British Rule* (*1826-1863*). New Delhi Asian Publications Service, 160p.

447. Director of Informa. 1977 : Supplement of Mizoram by Directorate of Information and Public Relation, *North Eastern Spectrum*, 1 (6): 37-44.

448. District Council, 1969 : *Brochure on the Mizo District Council, Aizawl*, 1969. Aizawl. District Council, District Records Office, (Unpublished).

449. District Gazetteer, 1915 : *District Gazetteer, pt. II, table III, Suplement to the Vol. X*. Shillong. Govt. Press: 8p.

450. Dixon, Roland B. 1922 : The Khasi and the Racial History of Assam. *Man in India*, 2 (12), March-June : 1-11.

451. Dodwell, H.H., : *The Cambridge History of India*, vols V and VI.

452. Dokhuma, James (*Ed.*), 1975 : *Zoram Kohhran Tualto Chanchinte (in Mizo*). Aizawal.

453. Downs, F.S., 1971 : *The Mighty Works of God*. Gauhati.

454. ———, 1971 : *A Brief History of Council of Baptist Churches in North East India*. Gauhati.

455. Downs, Frederick S, 1983 : *Christianity in North East India*. Delhi, Indian Society for Promoting Christian Knowledge: 14-5.

456. ———, 1987 : Historiographical Issues in the Study of the History of Christianity in North East India. *Proceedings of North East India History Association* (Kohima), no. 8: 315-22.

457. Dube, Leela, 1974 : Sociology of Kinship : A Trend Report. (*In*) *A Survey of Research in Sociology and Social Anthr-*

opology, Vol. II by ICSSR. Bombay, Popular Prakashan, 233-376 (scatteredly menti oned).

458. Dube, S.C. (*Ed.*), 1977 : *Tribal Heritage of India, vol. I: Ethnicity, Identity and Interaction.* New Delhi : Vikas Publishing House.

459. Dube, S.M., 1975 : North East India: A Sociological Perspective. Proceedings of a Seminar on *Sociological Perspective on North East India and the 2nd Annual Conference of the NEI Sociological Association, Dibrugarh University, Deptt. of Sociology,* 10, 11, 12, March, 1975.

460. Dun, E.W., 1886 : *Gazetteer of Manipur.* Calcutta, Supdt. of Govt. Printing, India. 32-6, (Reprinted by Vivek Publishing House, Delhi in 1975).

461. Dunbar, G., 1915 : Tribes of Brahmaputra Valley. *Jour. of Royal Society, Arts* (London), LXIII.

462. Dutta, Birendranath (*Ed.*) 1985 : Focus on Folklore of North East India, 1983-'84 and 1984-'85 of part I and part II. gauhati *Assam Academy Review*: 1-84 and 1-78 respectively.

463. Dutta, B.B., (*Ed.*), 1986 : *Land Use Pattern in North East India.* Ludhiana, Gagan Publishers

464. Dutta, K.N., 1969 : Manipur Rebellion and Rising of the Eastern Lushais, (*In*) *Land*

marks of Freedom Struggle in Assam, by K.N. Dutta. Gauhati, Lawyers Book Stall.

465. Dutta, P.S. 1988 : *Shifting Cultivation of North East, A case for Reassessment*. Proceedings of a Seminar of IASSI, Nov. 1-3, New Delhi (*Mimeo*.)

466. Dutt, Shosee Chunder, 1984 : *The Wild Tribes of India*. New Delhi, Cosmo Publications (*Reprinted*, 1st Pub. in 1884): 156-63

467. Dutta, S.K., 1974 : Resentment Over Mizo Union Congress Merger. *The Times of India* (Delhi), April 27.

468. ———, 1974 : Mizoram Remains Unsettled, An Alienated People. *The Times of India*, May 30.

469. ———, 1976 : The Rescal in Tribal Folklore. *North Eastern Spectrum*, I (1), July : 23-6.

470. ———, 1977 : Hill Politics of North East: Regionalism to the Force. *New Horizon* (Aizawal), July-Sept.

471. Duwara, Thaneswer, 1990 *Uttar Cachar Paharar Lok Sanskriti (in Assamese)*. gauhati, Assam Pub. Board.

E

472. Eales, H.L, 1892 : *Tamgthas or Kukis. Census of 1981, Imperial series, vol. IX : Burma Report.* Rangoon, Govt. Press, 200p.

473. East, C.J., 1873 : *An Account of the Proceedings of the Chittagong Column of the Lushai Expeditionary Forces (1871-1872).*

474. Ecologist 1971 : The Tribes of Assam. *The Ecologist* (Wadebridgc, England), 1(17), Nov.

475. ———, 1975 : The Mizos. *The Ecologist* VI (5) June.

476. E.I.A., 1971 : Naga and Mizo Nationals, *Eastern India*, Association, VII, July.

477. Economic and Political Weekly, 1978 : Mizoram : The Laldenga Factor. *Economic* and *Political Weekly*, XIII (19), May 13 : 786

478, Economic and Political Weekly, 1978 : Mizoram : The Relevance of Laldenga. *Economic and Political Weekly*, XIII (42), Oct 21 : 1750.

479. ———, 1979 : Mizoram : Political Failure. *Economic and Political Weekly*, XIV (26), June : 1066-67.

480. ———, 1979 : Mizoram : Fiction and Fact. *Economic and Political Weekly*, XIV(34), August : 1443-44.

481. ———, 1980 : Mizoram : Forced Urbanisation. *Economic and Political Weekly*, XV (36) Sept. 5 : 1439.

482. ———, 1981 : Mizoram : Hard Bargaining. *Economic and Political Weekly*, XVI (30), July 25 : 1219.

483. Economics and Statistics, 1976 : Mizoram : Statistical Handbook. Aizawl, Govt. of Mizoram, Deptt. of Economic & Statistics, 300p.

484. Eid, A.S., 1893 : *Chin-Lushai Land.* Calcutta.

485. Elles, E.R., 1893 : *Military Report on the Chin Lushai Country.* Shimla, Govt. Press, 16p.

486. Elly, E.D., 1978 : *Military Report on the Chin.* Aizawal, TRI Mizoram (Reprinted)

487. Elwin, V. 1961 : *Nagaland*, Shillong, P. Dutta for the Researh Department, Adviser's Secretariat, 108p.

488. ——— ,(*Ed*), 1969 : *The Nagas in the Nineteenth Century*, Bombay Oxford University Press, 650p.

489. Embree, J.F. and W.L. Thomas (Jr.), 1950 : *Ethnic Groups of Northern nad Southern Asia.* New Haven, Yale University, Southeastern Asian Studies.

490. Espee, 1977 : Mizo Dance and Music : Manipuri Dance ; Films for Children. *North Eastern Spectrum,* II (2) August : 37-9.

F

491. Fischer, Cecil E.C., 1978 : *The Elora of the Lushai, Hills.* Aizawl, TRI Mizoram (*Reprinted*).

492. Fisher, Capt., 1840 : Memoir of Sylhet, Cachar and the Adjacent Districts. *J.A.S.B.*, IX : 836-37.

493. Fraser, P., 1913 : Slavery on British Territory : Assam and Burma. Carnarvan.

494. Fried Morton H., 1968 : On the Concept of Tribe and Tribal Society. (*In*) *Essays on the Problems of Tribe*, (*Ed.*) by June Helm. Washington, American Ethnological Society.

495. Friedman, Jonathan, 1985 : Post-structuralism and the New Moon. *Ethnos*, 50(I-II) : 123-33, (*Kachin-Chin*).

496. Fryer, G.E.. 1875 : On the Khyeng People of Sandowary Arakan. *J.A.S.B.*, pt. I.

497. Fuller, Bamyld, 1929 : Forward. (*In*) *History of Assam Rifles*, by L.W. Shakespear. London, Macmillan (*Reprinted* in 1981 by Spectrum Publications, Gauhati),

498. Furer, Haimendorf, C. von, 1936 : *Custom is King*. London.

499. ———, 1938 : Through the Unexplored Mountains of the Assam-Burma Border. *Geographical Journal*, 91 : 201-19.

500. ———, 1980 : *A Himalayan Tribe : From Cattle to Cash*. Sahibabad, Vikas Publishing House : 173, 217.

501. ———, 1982 : *Tribes of India : The Struggle for Survival*. New York, Oxford University Press (*1st Indian Impression* from Oxford University Press, New Delhi in 1985): 313-22.

G

502. G.A.L.T., 1885 : *Supplementary Report on the North East Frontier of India, Notes on the Lushai Tribes*. Simla, Govt. Press.

503. Gage, A.T., 1901 : A Botanical Tour in the South Lushai Hills. *Records of the Botanical Survey of India, vol. I, no. 13*. Calcutta, Office of the Superintendent of Government Printing (India). (*Reprinted* in 1978 by TRI, Aizawal).

504. Gait, E.A., 1892 : Kuki-Lushai (*In*) *Census of India 1891, vol. I, Assam, Report*, Shillong, Govt. Press : 251-54.

505. ———, 1902 : *Census of India 1901, vol. VI : The Lower Provinces of Bengal and their Feudatories, pt. I, Report*. Calcutta Govt. Press : 420-21.

506. gait, E.A., 1926 : *History of Assam*. Calcutta, Thacker Spink, 366p (*Reprinted* in 1963 from Calcutta by Thacker Spink which was Revised and Enlarged by B.K. Barua and H.V.S. Murthv (3rd Revised edition) 449p and Again Reprinted in 1981 from Gauhati by L.B.S. Pub.)

507. Gandhi, Indira, 1972 : *Inauguration of the Mizoram Union Territory in Aizawl, 21st January, 1972.* (*Pamphlet*). Aizawl, Directorate of Information and Public Relations, Mizoram : 1-3.

508. ———, 1972 : *Speech by Mrs. Indira Gandhi, P.M. of India on the inauguration of the Mizoram Union Territory dated 21-1-1972.* Aizaw (*Pamphlet*).

509. Gangte, L.S., 1986 : Who are We ? (*In*) *In search of Identity*, (Eds.) by H. Kamkhenthang *et al.* Imphal, Kuki Chin Baptist Union : 42-51.

510. ———, ? : *Zomi Polity*. Imphal, Pub. by Author.

511. Ganguli, P. *and* D.C. Bhowmic, 1985 : Urbanisation in North East India: Its Implications for Planning. (*In*) *Planning in North East India*, (Ed) by K. Alam. New Delhi, Omsons Pubs. 253-59.

512. Ganguly, J. *and* P.S. Datta, 1982 : A Note on the Pattern of Land Ownership in Mizoram. *North East Quarterly*, 1(1), August. 78-84.

513. Gazettee, 1972 : *The Mizoram Gazettee, vol. I, pt.1* Aizawl, Govt. of Mizoram, April 21 : 1-2 and May 5.

514. Gaugin, T., 1980 : *Discovery of Zoland.* Churachandpur (Manipur) Pub. by Author.

515. Ghatak I.B., 1945-46 : Ethnology of India. *The Quarterly Jour. of the Mythic Society* (Bangalore), 36 (1) : 24-5.

516. Ghosh, A.K., 1979 : Tribal Development. *Himalaya : Man and Nature*, 2 (8), January, 18-24.

517. Ghosh Bhabani, 1971 : Future of Democracy and Regional Autonomy. *Mainstream*, 9 (21), January 23.

518. Ghosh, Biswanath, 1987 : Laldenga Pacing an Uphill Task. *Amrita Bazar Patrika*, May 7 : 8 (6-8).

519. ———, 1987 : Industrial Policy for Mizoram Formulated. *Amrita Bazar Patrika*, May 8 : 7 (1-6).

520. ———, 1987 : MNF Members do not Want to Take Up Arms Again. *Amrita Bazar Patrika*, May 10 : 7 (1-6).

521. Ghosh, Brijit *et al.*, 1956 : *Development Plans for Falam, Haka and Tiddim : Northern Chin Hills*, Rangoon, The National Housing, Town and Country Development Board.

522. Ghosh, Santanu, 1979: Mizo Insurgency : Is There Any End of Tunnel ? *Hindusthan Standard*, August 31.

523. Ghosh, Santanu, 1986 : Mizoram : After the accord. *Sunday*, Sept. 14 : 34-5.

524. Ghosh, S.C., 1909 : Chakma Jati. Calcutta, *Bangya Sahitya Parishad (series 24)*.

525. Ghosh, S.K., 1980 : *Echoes from North Eastern India*. New Delhi, S. Chand.

526. Ghosh, Sujit K., 1988 : Lushai Expedition and Haricharan Sarma : A Native Bengalee of Cachar. *Proceedings of North East India History Association*, (guahati), no. 9 : 159-64.

527. Ghosh, S.K. *and* Prabha Chopra, 1980 : *Echoes from North Eastern India*. New Delhi, S. Chand : 103-09.

528. Ghurya, G.S., 1980 : *The Burning Cauldron of North East India*. Bombay, Popular Prakashan.

529. Giles, A.R., 1907 : *Whilom Raiders*, Allahabad, Govt. Press.

530. Ginzatuang, V., 1972: *Zomi Inkuan Laibu*. Rangoon, 2p.

531. Gogoi, J.K., 1976 : *Identification of Backward Districts of Assam, Meghalaya and Mizoram : An Inter Temporal Analysis*. Delhi, (*Unpublished*). M. Phil Dissertation, Jawaharlal Nehru University, 92p.

532. Gohain, Bikash Chandra, 1977 : *Human Sacrifice and Head Hunting in North Eastern India*. Gauhati, Lawyer's Book Stall, 102p.

533. Gohain, D., 1972 : Field Research in Tribal Areas : Experience in North East India.

(*In*) *Socio Economic Research in Tribal Areas*, (Ed.) by P.C. Goswami. Jorhat, Agro Economic Research Centre : 62-7.

534. Goswami, Binod Behari, 1959 : The Aijal Market—Mizo District. *Modern Review*, February.

535. ———, 1959 : *Demographic Problem in the Lushai Hills. Assam Anthropological Association* (Gauhati), August.

536. ———, 1959 : Population Pressure in Lushai Hills. *Vanyajati*, 7 (4). Oct. : 130-35.

537. ———, 1960 : System of Bride Price in the Lusha Tribe. *Jour. of Social Research*, 3(1) March : 44-7.

538. ———, 1960 : Heavenly Bodies and the Lushai. *Folklore*, 1 (2), March-April : 113-16.

539. ———, 1960 : Kinship System of the Lushai. *Bulletin of Anth. Surv. of India*, IX(2), July : 81-8.

540. ———, 1962 : Mizo Laws of Inheritance. *Bulletin of the Deptt. of Tribal Cultural and Folklore Research* (Gauhati).

541. ———, 1963 : A Note on the Lushai Family. *Eastern Anthropologist*, 16 (3), Sept-Dec. : 201-06.

542. Goswami, B.B., 1966 : Spirit Possession in a Hill Tribe of Assam. (*In*) *Proceedings of the Summer School in Anthropology*,

Darjeeling, (Ed.) by N.C. Choudhary. Calcutta, Anth. Surv. of India (*Mimeo.*).

543. Goswami, B,B,, 1970 : Relationship Between Family Size and Agriculture in a Hill Region of Assam. *Tribe* (Udaipur), VII(3).

544. ———, 1972 ; The Tribes of Assam : A Few Comments on Their Social and Cultural Ties with Non-tribes. (*In*) *Tribal Situation in India*, (Ed.) by K. Suresh Singh. Simla, Indian Institute of Advance Studies.

545. ———, 1973 : The Tribes of North East India : A Few Comments on Their Social and Cultural Ties with the Non-tribes. *The North Eastern Research Bulletin* (Dibrugarh), IV, Summer : 41-8.

546. ———, 1974 : Structural Phenomenon of Kinship with Regard to the Lushai (Mizo). (*In*) *Tribe Caste and Peasantry*, (Eds.) by K.S. Mathur and B.C. Agrawal. Lucknow, Ethnographic and Folk Culture Society : 40-7.

547. ———, 1974 : A few Propositions for the Study of Tribes in North Eastern Region of India. *North Eastern Affairs*, 2 (4), Jan.-March : 31-2.

548. ———, 1975 ; Out-group From the Point of View of In-group. *Man in India*, 55 (4), Oct.-Dec. : 326-38.

549. ———, 1975 : The study of the Concept of '*Vai*' in Mizoram.

550. Goswami, B.B., 1975 : A Brief Note on Salvage Ethnology in North East India. (*In*) *International Committee on Urgent Anthropological & Ethnological Research Bulletin*, (Vienna), 17.

551. ———, 1976 : *The Mizo Unrest : A Study in Politicisation of Culture.* Ph. D. Thesis of Gauhati University, Anth. Deptt.

552. ———, 1977 : A Plea for Drawing the Profiles of the Hill Towns of North East India. *Jour. of NEICSSR* (Shillong), 1 (1), April : 7-8.

553. ———, 1977 : Social and Political Institutions of the Mizo. Proceedings of a Seminar on *Social and Political Institutions of the Hill People of North East India*, Organised by NEICSSR, Shillong and Sponsored in Collaboration with Anthropological Survey of India, Calcutta. (Published by Anth. Surv. of India).

554. ———, 1978 : Violence and Adaptability, (*In*) *Cultural and Biological Adaptability of Man with Special Reference to North East India*, (Eds.) by A.C. Bhagabati and R.K. Kar (This is also, *Bulletin of Anthropology Deptt., Dibrugarh University vol. 6, 1977*), Dibrugarh, Dibrugarh University : 16-23.

555. ———, 1978 : Tribe to Peasant, Not Caste: Some Comments on the Mizo Situation.

Eastern Anth., 31 (3) July-Sept. : 259-68.

556. Goswami, B.B., 1978 : Out-Group from the Point of View of the In-Group. (*In*) *North East India : A Sociological Study*, Ed. by S.M. Dubey, Delhi, Concept Publishing Company : 99-110.

557. ———, 1978 : Mizoram Today. *Col.* III, no. 1. Oct.

558. ———, 1979 : Mizoram. *Highlander* (Kohima, Nagaland), March 29-June 7.

559. ———, 1979 : By Product of Christianity on the Hill Tribesmen of North-East India. *RE*: *Review of Ethnology* (Wien, West Germany), 7 (1-9) : 42-6.

560. ———, 1979 : *Mizo Unrest.* Jaipur, Aalekh Publishers.

561. ———, 1980 : Perspective on Cultural Changes Among the Mizos. (*In*) *Eastern Himalayas : A Study on Anthropology and Tribalism*, Eds. by T.C. Sharma and D.N. Majumdar. New Delhi, Cosmo Publications : 76-85.

562. ———, 1981 : A Preliminary Note on Speech Distribution of the Lakher. *Man in India*, 61 (3), Sept. : 289-302.

563. ———, 1982 : Relationship Between Family Size and Shifting cultivation in Mizoram. *Jour NEICSSR* (Shillong) VI (1), April: 26-8.

564. Goswami, B.B., 1983 : Cultural Adaptability of Violence *Human Science* (Calcutta), 32 (4), December: 237-47.

565. ———, 1989 : Socio-Economic Development in Mizoram : A Few General Comments. Proceedings of a Seminar on *Structures of Socio-Economic under Development and Exploita-Tian in North East India* Held on 27-28 Feb. 1989 Organised by Sacred Heart College, Shillong (*Mimeo*).

566. ———, ? : *Seven Types of Bride Price Among the Lushai Tribe of Assam*. (Discussed.)

567. ———, 1968 : Lushai Explanation on Ascriptive Alliance. *Proceedings of All India Sociological Conference* (*Delhi*), *Panel 4*.

568. Goswami, B.B. *and* D.P. Mukherjee 1982 : The Mizo Political Movement. (*In*) *Tribal Movement in India*, vol. I, (Ed.) by K.S. Singh. New Delhi, Manohar Publications: 129-50.

569. Goswami, M.C. *and* : H. Kamkhenthang, 1972 Mother's Brother in Paite Society. *Man in India*, 52 (1).

570. ———, 1974 : Uterine Brothers and Sisters (Laizom) Among the Paite. *Jour University of Gauhati*, XX-XXII.

571. ———, 1974 : A Paite Dwelling House. *Bulletin Deptt. of Anth., Gauhati University*, vol. 3.

572. Goswami, P.C., 1963 : *The Economic Development of Assam.* Bombay, Asia Publishing House.

573. ———(Ed.), 1969 : *Rural Life in Assam Hills (Village Survey Reports on Kanther Teiang, Mawtnum, Hmunpui and Banshidua).* Jorhat, Agro. Economic Research Centre.

574. ———(Ed.), 1972 : *Socio-Economic Research in Tribal Areas.* Jorhat, Agro. Eco. Research Centre, 130p.

575. ———, 1973 : *Status Paper on Shifting Cultivation and Soil Conservation in North Eastern India.* Gauhati, Director of Soil Conservation.

576. Goswami, Praphulladatta, 1982 : *Essays on the Folklore and Culture of North Eastern India.* Gauhati, Spectrum Publications.

577. ———, 1985 : Foreword. (*In*) *Kuki Liki Life and Lore by* Tarum Goswami. Haflong, North Cachar Hills District Council: i-iv.

578. Goswami, Tarun, 1985 : *Kuki Life and Lore.* Halflong, (Assam), North Cachar Hills District Council: 580p.

579. Gougin, T., 1947-48 : *The Zou Custom Book.* Churachandpur, Published by the Author, Zomi Press.

580. ———, 1972 : *Discovery of Zomi Resurgence.* Churachandpur, Pub. by the Author, Zomi Press (This has been *reprinted* in 1983).

581. Gougin, T., 1980 : *The Discovery of Zo Land*. Churachandpur, Pub. by the Author, Printed at Zomi Press: 120p.

582. ———, 1984 : *History of Zomi*. Churachandpur, Pub. by the Author at Zomi Press (Manipur): 248p.

583. Gougin, T. and S.K. Samte ? : *Memorandum Submitted to His Excellency V.V. Giri, the President of India by the Zomi National Congress*. (In) *Discovery of Zo Land* by T. Gougin (1980). Churachandpur, Pub. by T. Gougin (Author), 121 (i)-122: (ii).

584. Government of Assam, 1889-1904 : *Administration Reports on North Lushai Hills (1890-1998)*. Shillong, Govt, of Assam.

585. ———, 1890-1998 : *Administrative Reports on Lushai Hills*. Shillong, Govt. of Assam.

586. ———,1966 : *Pamphlet No. AGP (I & P) No. 8/66 dated 22-4-1966*. Shillong, Directorate of Information and Public Relations, Govt. of Assam..

587. Government of Bengal, 1897 : *Administrative Reports on South Lushai Hills (1890-'97)*. (In) *Diaries of the Superintendent of South Lushai Hills District*. Calcutta, Govt. of Bengal.

588. Government of Burma, 1907 : *Administrative Reports on Chin Hills (1890-1907)*. Rangoon, Govt. of Burma.

589. Government of India : *Lushai Expeditionary Despatches*
1872 *[1871-'72]*. Simla, Govt. of India Gazette.

590. ———, 1949 : *Constituent, Assembly of India (Official Report), vol. IX.* New Delhi, Lok Sabha Secretariat, Govt. of India.

591. ———, 1951 : *The Fifth Schedule, Section 26 (2), Amendments to the Constitution (Scheduled Tribes) Order (Union Territories), 1958, Part-II, Mizoram*.

592. ———, 1965-66 : *Report of the Commission on the Hill Areas of Assam*. New Delhi.

593. ———, 1966 : *Extraordinary Gazettee, Part-II. dated 6-3-1966.* Delhi, Govt. of India.

594. Government of Mizoram, 1976 : *The Mizoram Gazettes 1972-'76.* Aizawl, Govt. of Mizoram.

595. ———, 1981 : *Report on Socio-Economic Review, 1979-'80.* Aizawl, Govt. of Mizoram, Statistics & Economics Deptt.

596. Governor in Council, 1933 : *Inner Line or Boundary Line of 1933 (Orders by the Governor in Council). (In) Church & Political Upheaval in Mizoram* by John Vanlal Hluna. Aizawl, Mizo History Association (1985), 157-62.

597. Grant-Brown, G.E.R., 1911 : *Burma Gazetteer, Upper Chindwin District, vol. A*. Rangoon, Suptd.

of Govt. Printing & Stationary (*Reprinted* in 1960).

598. Grierson, George A, (Ed.) 1909 : *Linguistic Survey of India, Vol. III, Part-I, Kuki-Chin and Burma Groups*. Calcutta, Supt. of Govt. Printing (*Reprinted* in 1967 by Motilal Banarsidas, Delhi).

599. ———, (Ed.), 1986 : *Languages of North-Eastern India. 2 Vols.* Delhi, Gian Publishing House (*Reprinted*).

600. Griffiths, W., 1847 : *Travels in Assam, Burma, Bhutan, Afganistan and Neighbouring Countries*. Calcutta, Bishop's College Press (*Reprinted* in 1984).

601. Guha, A., 1973 : Geography Behind History : An Introduction to Socio-Economic Study of North East India, *North Eastern Affairs* (Shillong), 2 (1).

602. Guha, Amalendu, 1985 : Forward. (*In*) *Mizoram Under the British Rule* by Suhas Chatterjee. Delhi, Mittal Publications: iii-iv.

603. Guhs, K., 1960 : Tribal Handicrafts in India. *Vanyajati*, VIII (3), July: 117-23.

604. Guha, Seema, 1986 : Mizo Accord and the Congress. *Times of India*, July 21.

605. Guha Thakurta S.N., 1986 : *Tripura*. Delhi, National Book Trust (India), 23,25,33,35,103,104,

606. Gupta, K.M., 1980 : Mizoram mein Shanti Sthapana in Hindi. *Himalaya : Man and Nature*, 3 (8-9), Jan.-Feb., 25.

607. Guptara, Prabhu S., 1975 : Unrest in Mizoram. (*In*) *Light of Life* (*All India Monthly Magazine of Christian Witness*, 17 (9), July.

608. Gurudev, S., 1973 : Aspirations and Realities in Mizoram. *The Statesman* (Calcutta), June 9.

609. ———, 1988 : Laldenga's Revivalist Slogans Disturbing. *The Statesman*, May 10 : 14 (3-6).

H

610. Haksar, Nandita, 1985 : A Case Study. *Seminar* (New Delhi), 308, April, 14-7.

611. Hall, D.G.E., 1955 : *History of South East Asia.* New York, St. Martins' Press.

612. Hamilton, F., 1814 : *An Account of Assam.* London. (This book Edited by S.K. Bhuyan in 1940 and Published from Gauhati, Deptt. of Historical & Antiquarian Studies, Govt. of Assam, 104p.)

613. Handbook, 1973 : *Official Handbook of the Government of Mizoram, vol. 2..* Aizawl.

614. Hanson, Ola, 1913 : *The Kachins.* Rangoon, American Baptist Mission Press.

615. Haokip, Hawlngam *et al* (*Eds.*), 1986 : *In Search of Identity.* Imphal, Kuki Chin Baptist Union, 66p.

616. Harvey, G.E., 1925 : *History of Burma*. London.

617. Hasan, Amir ? : *Tribal Administration in India*. New Delhi, B.R. Pub. Cor.

618. Hau, Vum Ko ? : *Profile of a Burmese Frontier Man*. Rangoon, Pub. by the Author.

619. Hawla, V. (*Ed.*) 1969 : *Zoram Hmar Chan Zosapte Chanchin* (*In Mizo*). Aizawl, Synod Book Room, 52p.

620. Hawla, V., 1983 : *Rawngbawltu Kal Tate* (*In Mizo*). Aizawl, Synod Publication Board.

621. Hazarika, Susmita, 1990 . Assam-Burma Tie in Ahom Rule. *The Assam Tribune*, June 10 : 4 (3-6) 5 (4-5).

622. Head, W.R., 1917 : *Handbook on Haka Chin Custom*. Rangoon, Govt. Press (*Reprinted* in 1949).

623. Heine-Geldern, Robert von, 1917 : Kopfjagd und Menschenopfer in Assam und Birma und Ihre Ausstrahlungen nach Vorderindien. *Mitteilungen der Anthropologischen Gesellschaft* (Wien), 47, 1-165. (*In French*).

624. Helme, C.J, 1932 : The Effect on the Lushais of Contacts with Civilization. (*In*) *Census of India 1931, vol. III, Assam*. Calcutta, Govt. of India, Central Publication Branch. (*Part I, Report, Appendix A2, p. V.*)

625. Hendersen, Eugenie J.A., 1948 ; Notes on the Syllable Structure of Lushai. *Bul. Sch. Or. and Afr. Studies*, 12: 713-25.

626. Henry, Yule, 1855 : *A Narrative of the Mission to the Court of Ava in 1855*. Kuala Lumper, Oxford Publications, 265p.

627. Hesselmeyers, C.H. ? : The Hill Tribes of the Northern Frontier of Assam. *Jour. of Asiatic Society of Bengal*, XXXVII.

628. Hezlett, J., 1961 : *Letter from J. Hezlett, Supdt. of Lushai Hills, 12th May, 1916 to the Commissioner, Surma Valley and Hill Districts, Silchar (Ar. No. 203G)*.

629. Highlander, 1979 : Mizoram. *Highlander (Kohima)*, vol. II, No. ?69, dated 6.3.1979.

630. Hill, L.G., 1962-'63 ; *An Ethnographic Survey of the Kuki Chin Speaking People of the Burma Border*. Oxford University, Dissertation (*Unpublished*).

631. Himalaya, 1976 : Rail Link to Mizoram soon. *Himalaya*, 5 (3), March, 12.

632. ———, 1976 : Developing Mizoram. *Himalaya*, 5 (3), March, 12.

633. ———, 1977 : *Mizoram Himalaya: Man & Nature*, 1 (3), August, (-9.

634. ———. 1979 : Editorial : Work for Peace in Mizoram. *Himalaya : Man & Nature*, 3, August, 1.

635. ———, 1979 : Mizoram. *Himalaya : Man & Nature*, 3 (5), October, 12.

636. Hinalaya, 1979 : Visit to Mizoram and Other News. *Himalaya* : *Man & Nature*, 3 (7), December, 19.

637. Hinda, Khoda, 1989 : Letter to the Editor: Chakma's Problems in Arunachal. *Shillong Times*, October 17: 2 (3-4).

638. Hindu, 1971 : Mizo Demand for Full Statehood. *Hindu* (Madras), July 22.

639. Hindustan Times 1971 : New deal for the Mizos. *Hindustan Times*, July 17.

640. ———, 1989 : Mizoram CM Flays Laldenga. *Hindustan Times*, Dec. 12 : 10 (4-5).

641. ———, 1990 : New Rail Links in North East. *Hindustan Times*, January 2 : 9 1-3).

642. ———, 1990 : Laldenga Plea to Mann. *Hindustan Times*, Feb. 14: 9 (4).

643. ———, 1990 : Burma Rebels Seek India's Help. *Hindustan Times*, March, 14:2(4-5).

644. ———, 1990 : Mizo CM Blames Chin Extremists. *Hindustan Times*, May 2 : 10 (7-8).

645. ———, 1990 : Neck Cancer Cases High in N-E Hills. *Hindustan Times*, May 20: 6 (3).

646. ———, 1990 : Permanent Bench of Guwahati H.C. Set Up. *Hindustan Times*, July 6 : 7 (4-5).

647. ———, 1990 Leaders Pay Tributes. *Hindustan Times*, July 9:10 (5).

648. ———, 1990 : Editorial, Laldenga. *Hindustan Times*, July 9, 11 (1-2).

649. ———, 1990 : Man Who Lived for the Mizoram Cause. *Hindustan Times*, July 10:7 (1-2).

650. ———, 1990 : Zoramthanga Adhoc MNF President. *Hindustan Times*, July 10: 9 (7-8).

651. ———, 1990 : Leaders Pay Tributes to Laldenga, *Hindustan Times*, July 12: 10 (8).

652. Hluna, J.V., n.p. : *Collection of MNF Documents*. (*Unpublished* Typed Materials).

653. ———, ? : *Kan Pastorte* (*Collection of the Biographies of Pastors in Mizoram*). Aizawl, (*Unpublished, in Mizo*).

654. ———, 1970 : *Chanchin Tha Chu Ka Zahpui Silova* (*Drama Based on True Story*). Shillong, Mizo Church Youth Fellowship (*Mimeo, in Mizo*).

655. ———, 1983 : *A Search for Mizo Identity*. Aizawl, Pub. by the Author.

656. ———, 1985 : *Church & Political Upheaval in Mizoram*. Aizawl, Mizo History Association.

657. ———, 1985 : Mizo Problems Leading to Insurgency. *Proceedings of North East India Association* (NEHU, Shillong). No. 6: 442-49.

658. Hluna J, V., 1986 : Role of Missionaries in Mizoram Education. *Proceedings of NEIHA*, (Pasighat), No 7: 283-90.

659. ———, 1987 : Peace in Mizoram : A Study of the Contributions of the Churches. *Proceedings of NEIHA*, (*Kohima*), No. 8: 497-509.

660. ———, 1988 : Female Education in Mizoram. *Proceedings of NEIHA*, (Guwahati), No. 9: 304-09.

661. ———, 1989 : Role of Church in Mizoram Assembly Election 1989. *Proceedings of NEIHA, Xth Annual Session*, (Shillong), Oct. 12-14, 1989 (*Mimeo.*)

662. Hlychho, Zakhu 1971 : *Memorandum to Commissioner of Cachar & Mizo District*, July *19, 1971.*

663. Hminga, C.L., 1963 : *Christianity and the Lushai People*. Manchester (U.K.), Manchester University (*Unpublished*) M.A. Dissertation.

664. ———, 1976 : *The Life and Witness of the Church in Mizoram*. (*Unpublished*)D.Miss. Theological Seminary, U.S.A.

665. ———, 1978 : *Mizoram Chhim Biala Thawk Tawh B.M.S.* (*in Mizo*). Lunglei, Missionary-te Chanchin, 7p.

666. Hmingliani, 1986 : Mizo Hmeichhe Din Hmun. (*In*) *Mizo Hmeichhe Tangrual Souvenior* (Aizawl), 11p.

667. Hobbs, C., 1956 : The Chins. (*In*) *Burma*, (Ed.) by F.N. Trager, (*Subcontractor's Monograph HRAF-37. N.Y.U. 2*). New Haven, Conn, Human Relations Area Files, Yale University 3 vols.: 721-77.

668. Hodgson, Brian Houghton, 1857 : Comparative Vocabulary of the Several Dialects of the Kirantee Language. *Jour. of the Asiatic of Bengal*, vol. 26: 350-71.

669. Hodson, G.F., 1962 : Sino-Assam Frontier. *The China Quarterly*, October-December.

670. Hodson, T.C., 1905 : *Thado Grammar*. Shillong, Eastern Bengal & Assam Secretariat Printing Office.

671. ———, 1909 : Notes. (*In*) *Folktales of the Lushais and their Neighbours* by J. Shakespear. *Folk Lore* (London), vol. 20: 338-420.

672. ———, 1915 : Lushais. (*In*) *Encyclopaedia of Religion & Ethics*, vol. 8. (Ed.) by James Hastings. Edinburg, T.& T. Clark: 197-98. (*Reprinted* in 1921 from London).

673. ———, 1921 : The Doctrine of Rebirth in Various Areas in India. *Man in India*, 1 (2), June: 1-17.

674. , 1921 : Three Marriage. *Man in India*, 1 (3), Sept.: 202-21.

675. Houghton, B., 1892 : *Essay on the Language of the South Chins and its Affinities*. Rangoon, Govt. Press.

676. Houghton, Bernard, 1893 : A Folk Tale of the Lushais : The Story of Kungori. *Indian Antiquary*, 22 : 78-80.

677. ———, 1895 : Kami Vocabularies (i.e. *Jour. Royal Asiatic Society* : 111-38 (i.e. *Kami* are *Chine Lushai* Group of Tibeto Burman Family).

678. ———, 1896 : Outlines of Tibeto-Burman Linguistic Palaeontology. *Jour. Royal Asiatic Society of Great Britain and Ireland*: 23-55.

679. Hrangthiaua and Lal Chunginunga, 1978 : *Mizo Chanchin*, Aizawl, Lalrinliana & Sons, 55p.

680. Hrangtawna, Tlau and Bualchhuak 1986 : *History of Tlau Hnam (In Mizo)*, Champhai, Kahrawt Veng, 19p.

681. Hughes, H.G. , 1876-77 : *Administration Report on the Hill Tracts of Arakan*. Rangoon, Govt. Press.

682. ———1881 : *The Hill Tracts of Arakan*. Rangoon.

683. Hunter, W.W., 1876 : *A Statistical Account of Bengal, vol. VI, Chittagong Hill Tracts, Chittagong, Noakhali, Tipperah, Hill Tipperah*. London, Trubner & Co. (*Reprinted* in 1973 by D.K; Pubg. House).

684. ———,1879 : *Statistical Account of Assam, vol. II*. London, Trubner & Co., 186-88, 384-87 (*Reprinted* by B.R. Pubg. Cor., Delhi).

685. ———,1886 : *Imperial Gazetteer of India*, (*vol. X*). London: 150-51.

686. Hunter, W.W., 1973 : *A Statistical Account of Bengal, vol. VI.* Delhi, D.K. Pubg. House (*Reprinted*), 59-65.

687. ———, 1975 : *A Statistical Account of Assam, vol. II.* Delhi, B.R. Pubg. Cor. *Reprinted*).

688. Hutchinson, R.H.S., 1897 : *Vocabulary of the Lushai Language.* Calcutta, Bengal Secretariat Press, 22p.

689. ———, 1909 : *Chittagong Hill Tracts.* London (*Reprinted* by Vikas Publishing Company, Delhi in 1978), 108p.

690. Hutton, J.H., 1922 : Indian Ethnology in Current Periodical Literature. A New Type of Snare Known Both to the Sema Nagas Who Call it *Akwegen* and the Thado Kuki Who Call it *Toupel*. *Man in India*, II (3), Sept., 172.

691. ———, 1922 : Thado-Kuki Terms of Relationship. *Man in India*, vol. 2 (1-2), March-June. 93-6, 108-110.

692. ———, 1922 : A New Type of Snare Known Both to the Sema Nagas and the Thado-Kukis. *Man*, July.

693. ———, 1924 : *Kukis* (Thado) *Man*, vol. 24, Article No. 77: 104.

694. ———, 1924 : Some Astronomical Beliefs in Assam. *Folk Lore* (London), XXXVI (II), June: 113-31.

695. Hutton, J.H., 1924 : Occurrence of the Blow-gun in Assam. *Man*, XXIV (VIII): 77.

696. ———, 1931 : Wild Man in Assam. *J.A.S.B.*, XXVII (2).

697. ———. 1932 : Races of Further Asia. *Man in India*, XII (1), Jan.-March: 1-18.

698. ———, 1932 : Cynotherapy. *Man in India*. XII (2-3), April-Sept: 69-72. (Thado, Lushai, Chin, Kuki),

699. ———, 1932 : Metempsychosis. *Man in India*, XII (2-3), April-Sept, 73-6. (Lushai).

700. ———, 1932 : An Introduction and Supplementary Notes. (*The Lakhers* by N.E. Parry. London, Macmillan Company (*Reprined* by Firma KLM Private Ltd. Calcutta on Behalf of Tribal Research Institute, Aizawl in 1976): ix-xvi.

801. ———, 1941 : Presidential Address. *Flok Lore* (London), Lii, June: 83-100. (Karen People).

702. ———, 1951 : Kuki, Chakma. (*In*) *Caste in India*. Bombay, Oxford University Press: 277, 283 (*Glossary*).

703. ———, (Ed.) 1969 : Head Hunting. *Encyclopaedia Britanica, vol. II.*

704. Hutton, J.H., 1929 : Introduction, Notes, Appendices, Illustrations and Index. (*In*) *Notes on the Thadou Kukis* by William Shaw. Shillong, Govt. Press (Published on Behalf of the Govt. of Assam.)

I

705. Illustrated Weekly, 1980 : Mizoram. *Illustrated Weekly.*

706. Imperial Gazetteer, 1908 : *Imperial Gazetteer of India : Eastern Bengal and Assam (Provincial Series).* Oxford, Horace Hart, Printer to the University : 392-416, 456-68.

707. Inderjit, 1973 : Focus on Nagaland and North Eastern Region. *The Assam Tribune*, Sept. 10.

708. ———, 1985 : Mizoram : Need for Caution. *The Assam Tribune*, August 31 : 4-5.

709. India, 1954 : *Census of India 1951, Paper no. I, Language.* New Delhi, Government of India Press.

710. India Abroad, 1989 : Burma Tribals Ask Merger. *India Abrood*, (New York), March 3.

711. Indian Council, of Social Science Research, 1972 : *A Survey of Research in Sociology and Social Anthropology, vol. III.* Bombay, Popular Prakashan : 32, 51, 52-3, 55.

712. Indian Government, 1966 : *Report on the Commissioner on the Hill Areas of Assam, 1965-66.* New Delhi, Ministry of Home Affairs, Indian Govt.

713. India Today, 1978 : Trouble in the Hills (Insurgency). *India Today*, June 16-30.

714. ———, 1979 : The North East Tribal Awakening (Report). *India Today*, December 16-31.

715. ———, 1989 : Mizoram : Rejecting the Rebel. *India Today*, Feb. 15 : 23.

716. Information and Public Relations, : *Mizoram News Magazine*, August. Aizawl, Information and Public Relation, Govt. of Mizoram.

717. ———, 1985 : *Mizoram Today : A Quarterly Journal.* Aizawl. I. and P. R. Govt. of Mizoram.

718. Iyer, L. A. Krishna *and* L.K. Bala Ratnam, 1961 : *Anthropology in India.* Bombay, Bharatiya Vidya Bhavan : 51, 138.

J

719. Jacob, C.van Leur, 1955 : *Indonesian Trade and Society : Essays in Asian Social and Economic History.* The Hague, Van Hoeve : 56-7.

720. Jafri, S.S.A., 1980 : Industrial Classification and Hierarchical Order of Towns in the N-E Region of India. *Jour. NEICSSR* (Shillong), IV (II), Oct. : 19-25

721. Jain, T.C., 1973 : Mizoram : A Society Without Inhabitation. *Social Welfare*, 20 (2), May : 7-8.

722. Jam Khothang T. *and* H., Kamkhenthang, 1975 : An Introduction to the Language and Culture of the Paite (Tedim Chin). A Symposium on the *Culture of the Hill People of Manipur.* Imphal, Manipur State Kala Akademy.

723. Jenkins, F., 1942 : *Selection of Papers Regarding the Hill Tracts Between Assam and Burma and on the Upper Brahmaputra*. Calcutta, Govt. Printing Press.

724. ———, 1980 : An Account of the Assam Tribes, (In) *Report on the Province of Assam*, (Ed.) by A.J. Maffatt Mills. Delhi, Gian Publishing House (*Reprint* of 1854).

725. Jha, Prem Shankar, : Assam the Aliention of the Tribes. *Week End Review* (New Delhi), vol. II(2), (Edited by S.Mulgaokar, Published by *Hindustan Times Ltd*.].

726. Jha, S.D., 1985 : A Perspective View of Appropriate Technology with Respect to N.E. Region. (*In*) *Planning in North East India*, (*Ed.*) by K. Alam. New Delhi, Omsons Publications : 288-96.

727. Jit, Amar, 1990 : Burma : Karen Insurgency continues. *The Assam Tribune*, June 26 : 4 (7-8).

728. John, Austen, 1967 : Beginning of Christian Work in the Hill Areas of North East India Region. (*In*) *A Common Perspective for North East India*, (*Eds.*) by R. Mitra *and* B. Das Gupta. Calcutta, Pannalal Das Gupta : 243-48.

729. John, Austen, 1967 : Scme Observations on the Hill, Tribal Students on North Eastern Region. (*In*) *A Common Perspective for North East India*, (*Eds.*) by R.Mitra *and* B. Das Gupta. Calcutta, Pannala Das Gupta : 249-55

730. Johnstone, J., 1896 : *My Experiences in Manipur and the Naga Hills.* London, Sampson Low, Marston and Co. : 25-7.

731. Johri, Sitaram, 1933 : *Where India, China and Burma Meet.* Calcutta, Thacker Spink and Co.

732. ———, 1967 : Integrated Study of the Hill Men of Assam (*In*) *A Common Perspective for North East India*, (*Eds.*) by R.Mitra *and* B.Das Gupta. Calcutta, Pannalal Das Gupta : 180-90.

733. Jones, David E. *and* Edwin, Rowlands, 1903 : *Lushai English Primers.* Mizo Leh Sap Tawng Hma-bu Welsh Presbytarian Mission, North Lushai Hills.

734. Jordan, M., 1958-59 : L'animisme des Chins. *Bulletin de la societe des Missions Etrangeres de Paris* (Hong Kong).

735. Journal Asiatic Society, 1933 : A Note on the Thado Kuki Belief About the Were-lioness. *Jour. of Asiatic Society of Bombay for 1932.*

736. Journal Asiatic Society, 1933 : On a Thado Kuki Accumulation Droll. *Jour. of Asiatic Society of Bombay for 1932.*

737. Jugantar, 1986 : Brihat Mizoramer Dabi Pradhanmantri Mamen Ni (*in Bengali*). *Jugantar* (Calcutta), July 13 : 1 (7-8).

K

738. Kabui, Gangmumei, 1989 : Tribes in North East India in Historical Perspective : The Emerging Pattern and the Perspective for the Future. *Vanyajati*, XXXVII (4), Oct. : 12-9.

739. Kakati, Satis Ch., : Greater Mizoram Demand. *The Assam Tribune*, July 13 : 3 (3-6).

740. ———, 1981 : Tangle in Mizoram : The Many Faces of Mr.Laldenga. *The Statesman*, Oct. 14 : 8.

741. Kamkhenthang, H. : A Collection of Paite Proverbial Sayings. *Paite Paunak* (Imphal).

742. ———, 1976 : The Paite. *Manipur State Kala Akademi Quarterly Journal*, II (1) : 7-13.

743. Kamkhenthang, H., 1984 : A Note on the Religious Belief of the Northern Chin (Zoumi). (*In*) *The Tribes of Northeast India*, (*Ed.*) by Sebastian Karotemprel. Calcutta, Firma K.L.M. Pvt. Ltd. (For Sacred Heart Theological College, Shillong) : 114-23.

744. ———, 1990 : Christianity vis-a-vis Tribal Religion in Manipur. Proceedings of a Seminar on *Religion in Tribal Areas in North East India*, Sponsored by NEICSSR, Shillong, held on 16-17 February 1990. (*Mimeo.*)

745. ———, 1990 : Identity Crises Among the Tribes of Manipur, (*In*) *Nationality, Ethnicity and Cultural Identity in North East India*, (*Ed.*) by B.Pakem. New Delhi, Omsons Publications : 275-90.

746. Kamkhenthang, H. *et al* (*Eds.*), 1986 : *In Search of Identity*. Imphal, Kuki Chin Baptist Union, 66 p.

747. Kapthianga, J. *and* Dosanga, 1972 : *Pamphlet No. 1 of the M.L.P. Headquarters*. Aizawl, Issued by the President and General Secratary (*Unpub.*)

748. Kapthuama, R., 1971 : Mithun in Mizo Culture and Economy. *Pines* (Shillong), 1(1), March :99-101.

749. Kar, Kalyan, 1979 : Mizoram's Potential Yet to be Tapped. *Economic Times*. Sept. 1.

750. Kar, R.K., 1990 : The Peoples of North East India : An Appraisal. *Vanyajati*, 38(1), Jan. : 11-9.

751. Kauffmann, H.E., 1938 : Die Fallen der Thadou-Kuki in Assam. *Zeitschrift fur Ethnologie*, 70, Jahrgang : 1-18.

752. ———, 1941 : Die Spiele der Thadou-Kuki in Assam. *Zeitschrift fur Ethnologie*, 73 : 40-71.

753. Kaushal, Swaraj, 1990 : Laldenga was Proud of Being an Indian. *Hindustan Times*, July 9 : 10 (6-8).

754. Keys, Charles F., 1977 : The Golden Penninsula. (*In*) *Culture and Adoption in Mainland, Southeast Asia*, 115p.

755. Khathing, D., 1984 : Science Education in the North East. (*In*) *Northeast Region : Problems and Prospects of Development*, (*Ed.*) by B.L.Abbi. Chandigarh, Centre for Research in Rural and Industrial Development : 249-56.

756. Khawtinkhuma *and* Vanthuama, 1947 : Mizo Memorandum. (*In*) *The Mizo Dilemma* by Amit Kumar Nag. Silchar, Tribal Mirror Publications (1984) : 82-9

757. ———, 1947 : Mizo Union Memorandum. (*in*) *Church and Political Upheaval in Mizoram*, by John Vanal Hluna. Aizawl, Mizo History Association (1985) : 166-75.

758. Khupzathang, 1973 : *Zo Suanh Khangthu Simna Laibu* (Genealogy of the *Zo* (*Chin*) race of Burma). Prague, 267p.

759. Khupzago, Pasian Thabu, 1984 : *South East Asia*. Aizawl. 1p. Regarding Kukis in Three Nations with 2,000,000).

760. Kiautuma, H. K., : *Pawi Lakher Chanchin*. Lunglei, Pawi Lakher Regional Council.

761. Kiautuma, H.K. and Saidenga, Elis, : *Mizo Labour Party* (*Pamphlet*). (*In Mizo*) (Regarding its Origin and Aims.) Lunglei, Mizo Labour Party ; (*Unpub.*).

762. Kipgen, K.H., 1982 : *The Thadou Kukis : A Brief Account of History and Culture*. Motbung (Manipur), Pub. by the Author.

763. Kirsch, A.T., 1967 : *Phu Thai Religious Syncretism*. Ph.D. Dissertation, Harvard University (U.K.)

764. Konow, Sten, 1903-09 : *Tibeto-Burman Family*. Calcutta, Supdt. of Govt. Printing (India).

765. Kriesel, Melvin E. (*Jr.*), 1976 : Kuki Disturbances in Tripura in 1860-61 : Notes. *Social Scientist* 4(9), April : 60-5.

766. Krishner, Frank, 1989 : Interview with A.H.Scott Lyngdoh : India will not get Weaker if Regional Parties get Stronger. *Shillong Times*, March 12 : 2. 1-5, 4 (5-6)-

767. Kristian Thalai Pawi, 1979 : *Silver Jubilee* (*1954-1979*) *Souvenir*. Aizawl, Central K.T.P. Committee, 89p.

768. ———, 1979 : *Handbook*, Aizawl, Central K.T.P. Committee.

769. ———, 1980 : *Report of 1979-89 : General Cenference of K.T.P., Aizawl.*

770. ———, 1980 : *Personal Evengelism*. Aizawl, K.T.P. Committee,

771. Kuki National Assembly, 1969 : *Kuki National Assembly Annual Meeting Resolution*, (Held on 10-11 October, 1969).

772. Kumar, Arun, 1990 : Rebel--Drug Nexus Threatens N-E. *Hindustan Times*, May 4: 10 (7-3).

773. Kumar, B.B. *and* Thotkhosei, 1974 : *Hindi-Kuki-English Dictionary*. Kohima, Nagaland Bhasa Parishad.

774. Kumar, Krishan, 1965 ; The Changing Lushai Society. *Quest* (Bombay), 45 : 37-47.

775. Kundu, N.N., 1985 : Gangte, Hmar and Darlong Communities of Mizoram. Proceedings of a Workshop-Seminar on National Project *People of India*, December 6, 1985, 2nd Session, Shillong, Anthropological Survey of India, (*Mimeo.*)

776. ———, 1987 : Vaiphei of Mizoram. Proceedings of a Workshop-Seminar on National Project *People of India*, May 24, 1987, Shillong, Anthropological Survey of India (*Mimeo.*)

777. Kunstadler. Peter (*Ed.*), 1967 : *South East Asian Tribes, Minorities and Nations, vol. I.* Princeton (N.J.), Princeton University Press : 205.

778. Kushal, S., 1990 : Mizos Exhorted to Work Hard. *The Assam Tribune*, February 20 : 1 (5).

L

779. Lahiri, R.M., 1954 : *Annexation of Assam*. Calcutta, General Printers & Publishers, 250p.

780. Lahiri, T.B., 1989 : Strategy for Rural Development in North East India. Proceedings of a Seminar on *Perspective, Issues and Experiences of Rural Development in North East India*, Organised by NEICSSR, Shillong, held on 26-27 May, 1989 ; 11p. (*Mimeo*).

781. Lalauva, R., 1982 : *Mizo Kohhran Hnuhma*, (*In Mizo*). Aizawl, Maranaha Press, 135p.

782. Lalbiakliana, 1979 : *Mizoram Zirna Chanchin* (i.e. Social Education of Mizoram). Aizawl, Pub. by Author.

783. Lalchunga, Chinzah 1967 : *The Pawi-Lakher People of Mizo District*. Lunglei Pawl-Lakher Regional Council.

784. Lal Dena ? : *Political Development in the Hill : A Rapid Survey in Colonial Perspective.* Imphal, J.N.U Centre.

785. ———, 1977 : *Social and Political Institutions of the Hmars.*

786. ———. 1978 ; Patterns of Leadership in a Changing Hmar Society. (*In*) *Cultural and Biological Adaptability of Man with Special Reference to North East India,* (*Eds*) by A.C. Bhagabati *and* R.K. Kar (This is also, *Bulletin Deptt. of Anthropology, Dibrugarh University, vol. 6, 1977*). Dibrugarh, Dibrugarh University, Deptt. of Anth. : 86-95.

787. ———, 1982 : Colonialism and the Study of Christian Missions in North East India (with Special Reference to Manipur). *Proceedings of North East India History Association* (Imphal) No. 3 : 131-36.

788. ———, 1988 : *Christian Missions and Colonialism A Study of Missionary Movement in N-E India with Particular Reference to Manipur and Lushai Hills (1894-1947).* Shillong, Vendrame Institute, 131p.

789. Laldenga, 1968 : *Zalenna Thuchah.* Aizawl, MNF Hqrs. (*in Mizo*).

790. ———, 1973 : *Mizoram Marches Towards Freedom* (*Pamphlet*). Aizawl, M.N.F. Hqrs.

791. Laldenga, 1978 : English Translation of the Tape Recorded Speech of Laldenga which was sent by him from Delhi to Mizoram in the Third Week of April, 1978, Through Hrangdawla, General Secretary, M.J.P. (*In The Mizo Dilemma*, by Amit Kumar Nag. Silchar, Tribal Mirror (1984). 73-81.

792. Laldenga *et al*: n.d. : MNF Declaration of Independence, (*In*) *Church & Political Upheaval in Mizoram*, by John Vanlal Hluna. Aizawl, Mizo History Association (1985) : 183-88.

793. Laldenga and Lianzuala, 1965 : MNF Memorandum (October 30, 1965). (*In*) *Church & Political Upheaval in Mizoram*, by John Vanlal Hluna. Aizawl, Mizo History Association (1985) : 176-82.

794. Lalhmingthanga (*Ed.*) 1972 : *Problems of Peace Making in Mizoram*. Aizawl, MNF Hqrs.

795. ———, ? : Ex-Foreign Minister of Underground Government, *Exodus Politics* (A Booklet, *in Mizo*).

796. Lalhmuaka, 1981 : *Zoram Zirna Lam Chhinchhiahna*. (*In Mizo*). Aizawl, Tribal Research Institute.

797. ———, (*Ed.*) 1981 ; *The Records of Zoram Education*. Aizawl.

798. Lalkhama 1984 : 'Nula-Rim' : Mizo Customary Practice of Courting Girls. *M.N.M.*, 1, August:. 18-21.

799. Lalkunga, C. 1979 : *History of Mizo Education.* Aizawl, Hnamte Press, 6p.

800. Lalmachhuana, 1980 ; Some Aspects of Mizoram Economy and Prospects of Development. (*In*) *Tribal Economy of North Eastern Region* (*Ed.*) by T. Mathew. Gauhati Spectrum Publications.

801. Lalnunmawia, 1988 : *The Welsh Presbyterian Mission in Lushai Hills, 1891-1953. (Unpuplished)* Dissertation of M. Phil, History Deptt., NEHU, Shillong under Dr. M.S. Sangma.

802. Lalremsiama, F., 1988 : *The Traditional Political Institutions of the Luseis. (Unpublished)* Dissertation of M. Phil, History Deptt., NEHU, Shillong under Dr. M.S. Sangma.

803. ———, n.p. ; *The Traditional Social and Political Institutions of the Mizos.* Ph. D. Thesis, History Deptt., NEHU, Shillong.

804. Lalrimawia, 1980 ; Anglo Lushai Relations (1850-90) *Proceedings of North Indian History Association,* (Shillong), Vol. I, (*Ed.*) by Jayanta Bhusan Bhattacharjee (1981). Shillong, NEI History Association, Deptt. of History, NEHU : 45-50.

805. ———, 1981 : Pre-Historic and Historic Migration of the Mizos. *Proceedings of NEIHA*, vol. 2. (Dibrugarh), North East India History Association, Dibrugarh University : 23-33.

806. ———, 1982 : Pawi Custom in Lushai Hills. *Social Research*, 4 : 6-11.

807. ———, 1982 : Lushai Chiefs under British Rule. *Proeeedings of NEIHA*, vol. 3, (Imphal), North East India History Association, Manipur University: 137-46.

808. ———, 1982 : Settlement Pattern of the Hmars in North East India. *Proceedings of NEIHA*, vol. 3. (Imphal) *op. cit*: 41-52.

809. ———, 1982 : *Lushai Hills Administrative Development, 1890-1947*. Guwahati, Gauhati University, Ph. D. Thesis (*Unpublished*).

810. ———, 1983 : Brief Survey of the Administrative Development in Lushai Hills (1890-1947). *Proceedings of NEIHA*, vol. 4, (Barapani)., North East India History Association Union Christian College : 139-44.

811. ———, 1984 ; Missionaries and Education in Mizoram. *Proceedings of NEIHA*, Vol. 5, (Aizawl), Pa Chhunga University : 135-39.

812. ———, 1985 : Lushai Rising 1893-95. *Proceedings of NEIHA*, vol. 6. (Agartala), North East India History Association : 255-60.

813. Lalrimmawia : *The Welsh Presbyterian Mission in Lushai Hills, 1891-1953*. (*Unpublished*) M. Phil Dissertation of History Deptt. North Eastern Hill University, Shillong.

814. Lalrinawma (n.p.) : *The Mizo Union : Social Background of Mizo Politics, 1935-1972.*

Ph. D. Thesis, History Deptt ; N.E.H.U., Shillong, under Dr. Imdad Hussian (*Unpublished*)

815. Lalruanga, 1982 : Hero of Mizo Folktales. Proceedings of a Seminar on *Folklore in North East India,* Held on 17-18 November, 1982, organised by NEICSSR, Shillong. (*In*) *Folklore in North East India,* (*Ed.*) by Soumen Sen. New Delhi, Omsons Publications (1985) : 191-94.

816. ———, 1985 : *A Study of Mizo Folk Literature.* (*Unpublished*) Ph. D. Thesis, Deptt. of Folklore, Gauhati University.

817. ———, 1985 : Hero of Mizo Folktales. (*In*) *Folkore in North East India,* (*Ed.*) by Soumen Sen. New Delhi, Omsons Pubs : 191-94.

811. Lalsangpuia, H.S. 1988 : *Frontier Policy under Lord Mayo with Special Reference to the Lushais in the N.E. Frontier.* (*Unpublished*) Dissertation of M. Phil. History Deptt., N.E.H.U., Shillong, under Dr. Imdad Hussain.

819. Lalsuaka, 1982 : *Mizo Huntawng,* (*In Mizo*). Aizawl, Pub. by the Author .

820. Lalthamaia, 1976 : Window on Mizoram. *North Eastern Review,* November.

821. Lalthangliana, 1967 : *Letter to Stanley Nichols Roy, General Secretary, APHLC, No. 20(1)EA/66 dated Aizawl, the 13th*

March. 1967 by MNF Foreign Secretary (*Underground*).

822. Lalthangliana, B., 1975 : *History of Mizo in Burma*. Mandalay (Burma), History Deptt. Arts and Science University, 7p.

823. ———, 1977 : *History of Mizo in Burma*. Aizawl, Zawlbuk Agencies.

824. ———, 1977 : Mizo. *Mizoram Today*, vol. II. Aizawl, Director of Information & Public Relations.

825. Lalungmuana, 1989 : *Themes and Techniques of Mizo Fiction*. (*Unpublished*) Ph. D. Dissertation, Khasi Deptt., North Eastern Hill University, Shillong .

826. Lalthankungi, 1985 : *A Study of Education and Dynamics of Tribal Development ; A Case Study of Kawrthah Village in Mizoram* (*Unpublished*) M.A. Dissertation, Deptt. of Education, N.E.H.U., Shillong.

827. Lassen, Christian, 1867 : *Indische Alterthumskunde*. Leipzig, L.A. Kittler.

828. Latter, T., 1846 : A Note on Some Hill Tribes on the Kolodyne River. *Jour. Asiatic Society of Bengal*, No. 169.

829. Law Research Institute, : *Mizo Customary Laws and Practices*. Gauhati, The Law Research Institute, Eastern Region Gauhati High Court (*Mimeo*).

830. Leach, E.R. 1946 : *Cultural Change with Special Reference to the Hill Tribes of Burma and Assam* London University, Ph D. Dissertation.

831. Leach, E.R., 1954 : *Political Systems of Highland Burma. A Study of Kachin Social Structure.* Cambridge, Harvard University Press, 324p.

832. ———, 1957 : Aspects of Bride Wealth and Marriage Stability Among the Kachin and Lakher. *Man*, 57. Article No. 59, April.

833. ———, 1960 : Descent, Filiation and Affinity. *Man*, January, Article No. 6.

834. ———, 1961 : The Frontiers of Burma. *Comparative Studies in Society and History*, (The Hague), 3(1) : 49 68.

835 ———, 1961 : Asymmetric Marriage Rules, Status, Difference and Direct Reciprocity. *Southwest Journal of Anthropology*, 17(4) : 343-51.

836. ———, 1961 : Aspects of Bride Wealth and Marriage Stability Among the Kachin and Lakher. (*In*) *Rethink ing Anthropology*, by E.R. Leach London, University of London, The Athlone Press : 114-23.

837. ———, 1963 : Alliance and Descent Among the Lakher : A Reconsideration. *Ethnos*, 28(2-4) : 237-49.

838. Lees, Nassau, 1865 : *Memorondum of a Tour through the Tea District of Eastern Bengal.*

839. Lehman, F.K., 1959 : *Some Anthropological Parameters of a Civilization : The Ecology and Evolution of India's High Culture.* (*Unpublished*) Doctoral Thesis,

Deptt. of Anthropology, Columbia University, New York.

840. Lehman, F.K., 1959 : Haka Chin : Syllabic Junetune and the Problem of the Mono Syllabic Languages. *Proceedings of the 4th Annual National Conference on Linguistics of the Linguistic Circle*, New York, May 9, 1959.

841. ———,1962 : On Certain Unconsidered Aspects of Double Descent Systems. *Man*, 62 (214), 130-34.

842. ———, 1963 : *The Structure of Chin Society: A Tribal People of Burma Adopted to a Non-western Civilizations.* Illinois, Studies in Anthropology, No. 1, Urbana I.U. University of Illionis Press, 244p. (*Reprinted* in 1980 by T.R.I., Aizawl).

843. ———, 1967 : Ethnic Categories in Burma and the Theory of Social System. (*In*) *South East Asian Tribes, Minorities and Nations, vol. I,* (*Ed.*) by P. Kunstadler. Princeton University Press, Princeton, New Jersey,

844. ———, 1979 : Review of Lalthangliana'a Book *History of Mizo in Burma, Thu Leh Hla* (Aizawl), September, 1979.

845. Levi-Strauss, Claude 1951 : Miscellaneous Notes on the Kuki of the Chittagong Hill Tracts, Pakistan, *Man*, vol. 51, no. 284.

846. Lewin, T.H., 1869 : *The Hill Tracts of Chittagong and Dwellers Therein*. Calcutta, Bengal Printing Company.

847. ———, 1870 : *Wild Races of South Eastern India*. London, W.H. Allen & Co. (*Reprinted*) by Firma KLM Pvt. Ltd on Behalf of Tribal Research Institute, Aizawl, Mizoram in 1978).

848. ———, 1874 : *Progressive Colloquial Exercises in the Lushai Dialect of the Dzo or Kuki Language*. Calcutta, Central Press. (*Reprinted*) in 1984 by TRI, Aizawl).

849. ———, 1885 : *A Fly on the Wheel*. London, W.H. Allen, 466p. (*Reprinted*) in 1977 by Firma KLM Pvt. Ltd on Behalf of T.R.I., Aizawl, 318p.

850. ———, 1890 : *Progressive Exercises in Lushai Grammar*. London,

851. ———, 1896 : *Hill Tracts of Chittagong and the Dwellers Therein*. Calcutta, Bengali Press, 98p.

852. ———, : *A Dictionary of Lushai words*. London.

853. ———, 1943 : An Anthology of Marriage Sermons: Chakma of Chittagong. *Man in India*, 23 (2) , 106-110.

854. Liangkhaia (Ed.) 1948 : *Mizo Chanchin*, (*in Mizo*). Aijal, Hmingliana & Sons (*Reprinted* in 1976 from Aizawl).

855. ———, (Ed.) 1951 : *History of Lushai*. Aizawl, Hmingliana & Sons.

856. Liangkhaia, (Ed.), 1976 : *Mizo Chanchīn*, (*in Mizo*). Aijal, Hmingliana & Sons.

857. ———, (Ed.) 1979 : The Impact of Christianity on Mizo Society. *Mizoram Today.* IV (1).

858. Liankhohau T., 1990 : *Social, Cultural, Economic and Religious Life of a Transformed Community. A Study of the Paite Tribe.* Delhi, Mittal Publications (*In Press*) .

859. Lian Kim, R. 1953-54 : *Some Chin Folk Tales.* Rangoon, Hill Chin Students' Union's Annual Magazine, 4p.

860. Lian, Nok Swan, 1968 : *Mangkam Sinna, English-Tiddim Chin. Translation & Composition.* Lanvakhua, Ton Thang, 95p.

861. Lianzuala and Laldenga, 1965 : Memorandum Submitted to the Prime Minister of India by the Mizo National Front, General Headquarters, Aizawl, Mizoram on the 30th October, 1965. (*In*) *Church & Political Upheaval in Mizoram*, by John Vanlal Hluna. Aizawl, Mizo History Association (1985), 176-82.

862. Lianzuala, S., 1966 : *Pamphlet.* Secretary, Ministry of Information, Broadcasting and Publicity (MNF), Govt. of Mizoram, (*Published in June*).

863. Library, Indian Office, 1938 : *Note of His Excellency, the Viceroy on Excluded Areas 1938.* London, Indian Office Library (*Unpublished*).

864. Library, Indian Office, 1941 : *Note on the Future of the Excluded Areas of Assam, 1941*. London, Indian Office Library (*Unpublished*).

865. Lloyd, G.T., 1923 : *Census of India 1921, Assam, pt. II, Tables*. Simla, Govt. Press

866. Lloyd, J.M., 1955 : *On Every High Hills*. Liverpool, Foreign Mission Office : 36-8.

867. Loeffler, L.G., 1959 : Die Khyang der Chittagong Hill Tracts. *Z. Ethn.*, Band 84 : 257-69 .

868. ———, 1960 : Patrilateral Lineation in Transition : The Kinship System of the Lakher (Mara), Arakan. *Ethnos* 119-50.

869. Logan, J.R., 1848 : Customs Common to the Hill Tribes Bordering on Assam and Those of the Indian Archipelago. *Jour. of the Indian Archipelago and Eastern Asia*, 2 : 229-36.

870. ———, 1858 : The West Himalaic or Tibetan Tribes of Assam, Burma and Pegu. *Jour. of the Indian Archipelago and Eastern Asia*, 2 : 68-114.

871. Lorrain, J.H., 1934 : Some Important Questions and their Answer. (*In*) *Leadership Among the Mizos*, by P.K. Bandyopadhyay. Delhi, B.R. Publishing Corporation (1985) : 262-66.

872. ———, 1940 *Dictionary of the Lushai Language*. Calcutta, Royal Asiatic Society of Bengal (*Reprinted* by

the Asiatic Society, Calcutta in 1975).

873. Lorrain, J. Herbert and W. Fred Savidge, 1898 : *A Grammar and Dictionary of the Lushai Language (Dulian Dialect)*. Shillong, Assam Secretariat Printing Office, 346p. (*Reprinted* by Firma KLM Pvt. Ltd. Calcutta in 1976 for Tribal Research Institute of Mizoram, Aizawl and also, by Cultural Pub. House, Delhi in 1984, 352p.)

874. ———, 1900 : Lorrain und Savidge Beideh Luschais in Assam. *Globus*, 77 : 163-67.

875. Lorrain, James Herbert, 1940 : *Dictionary of the Lushai Language*. Calcutta, Royal Asiatic Society of Bengal, (*Bibliotheca Indica, Work No. 261*). [*Reprinted* in 1975 by Asiatic Society, Calcutta].

876. Lorrain, Reginald A., 1913 : *Five Years in Unknown Jungles for God and Empire*. London, Lakher Pioneer Mission.

877. ———, 1917 : *Mara Chutuana Nata A Reina Chabu : A Mara or Lakher Primer and Reader*. Calcutta, Baptist Press.

878. ———, 1925 : *Marapenaw English Rei Chabu*: *English for the Lakher Tribesmen*. Calcutta, Baptist Press.

879. ———, 1951 : *Grammar and Dictionary of the Lakher or Mara language*. Gauhati, Govt. of Assam, Dept. of Historical nd Antiquarian Studies.

880. Lowis, C.C., 1910 : *The Tribes of Burma ; Ethnographical Survey of India (Burma, No. 4)*. Rangoon, Govt. Press. (*Reprinted* in 1919 and 1949).

881. Ltoyd, G., 1923 : *Report on the Census of Assam (Notes on Kuki and Lushai Tribes)*. Shillong, Govt. Press.

882. Luaia, H.S., : *Mizoram Baptist*. Aizawl, Kohhran Chanchin.

883. Luaia, H.S. ; N.I.L.Kalte and Zairema, 1967 : *Letter Dated 18-5-1967 (Addressed to the President)* Aizawl, Govt. of Mizoram.

884. Luce, G.H., 1959 : Chin Hills Linguistic Tour. *Jour. of Burma Research Society*, 42 (1) : 19-31.

885. ———, 1959 : Old Kyaukse and Coming of the Burmans. *Jour. of Burma Research Society*, 42 (1) : 75-109

886. Lunghnema, V.,1977 : *Hmar Genealogy*. Imphal, 5p.

887. Lunglei District Congress Committee, 1973 : *Resolution No. 1, Merge of Mizo Union with Congress*. Lunglei, District Congress Committee During October.

M

888. Mackenzie, A., 1884 : *History of the Relations of the Govt. with the Hill Tribes of the North East Frontier of Bengal.* Calcutta Home Deptt. Press, 586p.

889. ———, 1869 : *Memorandum on the North-East Frontier of Bengal.* Calcutta, Bengal Secretariat Press.

890. ———, 1979 : *The North East Frontier of India.* Delhi, Mittal Publications (*Reprinted* ; 1st Published in 1884 entitled *History of the Relations of the Govt. with the Hill Tribes of the North East Frontier of Bengal.* This has been reprinted 2nd time in 1981 by Mittal Pub., Delhi).

881. Macrae, J., 1801 : Account of the Kookies Luacts. *Asiatic Researches,* 7 (6) : 183-98.

892. Madan, T.N. and Sarana, Gopala, 1962 : *Indian Anthropology : Essays in Memory of D.N. Majumdar (Sr.)*

Bombay, Asia Publishing House : 330.

893. Mahajan, V.S., 1988 : *Economic Development of Border States of India.* New Delhi, Deep and Deep Pub.

894. ——— (*Ed.*), 1988 : *Emerging Pattern of North Eastern Economy.* New Delhi, Deep and Deep Publications.

895. ———, 1990 : Constraints in Agricultural Development in North East with Special Reference to Mizorm Experience. Proceedings of a Seminor on *Constraints of Agricultural Development in North East India,* July, 2-3, Organised by NEICSSR, Shillong, 7p. (*Mimeo*).

896. Mahanta, Chitra, 1962 : *Mizo* (*In Assamese*). (*In*) *Asomar Janajati,* (*Ed.*) by Pramod Chandra Bhattacharya. Jorhat, Asam Sahitya Sabha : 141-54.

897. Mahapatra, L.K., 1968 : Social Movements Among Tribes of Eastern India. *Sociologous* (Berlin), 18.

898. ———, 1988 : Ecology and Economy of Swidden Cultivation in India. *Proceedings of a Seminar of* : *I A S S I,* November 1-3, New Delhi (*Mimeo.*)

899; Mahapatra, R.Das, 1958 : A Lushai Lullaby. *Social Welfare,* 5 (7), October : 17.

900. Mainstream, 1979 : Forebodings in Aizawl. *Mainstream,* XVII (42), June 16:7.

901. Maira, Biswapati, 1977 : Winning Over the Mizos. *Hindustan Standard*, July 27.

902. Majumdar, D.N. (*Sr.*), 1944 : *The Fortunes of Primitive Tribes.* Bombay [Asia Publishing House : 210 (*Kuki*).

903. ———, 1954 : *Races and Culture of India.* Bombay, Asia Publishing House : 68-73 (*Kuki*).

904. ———, ? : Assam Ke Kuki Log (*In Hindi*). *Hindi Vishwa Bharati*, Vol. I : 439-47.

905. Majumdar, D.N. (*Sr.*) *and* Madan, T.N.. 1956 : *An Introduction to Social Anthropology.* Bombay, Asia Publishing House : 83, 84, 87, 93, 94, 95, 109, 120, 251, 253.

9C6 Majumdar, D.N. (*Jr.*), 1980 : North East India : A Profile. (*In*) *Eastern Himalayas : A Study on Anthropology and Tribalism*, (*Eds.*) by T.C. Sharma and D.N. Majumdar. New Delhi, Cosmo Publications : 23-62.

907. ———, 1982 : An Appraisal of the Tribal Situation in North East. (*In*) *India's North East*, (*Ed.*) by Pankaj Thakur. Tinsukia, Prakash Publishing House : 126-42.

9C8. ———, 1984 : Foreword. (*In*) *Leadership Among the Mizos : An Emerging Dimension*, by PK. Bandyopadhyay, Delhi, B.R. Publishing Corporation : Vii-IX.

909 Majumdar, Pantha Pradip, 1990 : North East ; Wither Sporting Talent (Sports) *The Assam Tri-*

bune, (*Sunday Reading*), April 29 : II (1-8).

910. Majumdar, R.L., 1962 : *History of the Freedom Movement in India*, vol. I. Calcutta.

911. Malhotra, R., 1985 : Tribal Groups in India : Their Problems and Development. *Vanyajati*, 33(2), April : 9-17.

912. Malleson. G.B. (*Ed.*)1857 : *Kape and Malleson's History of Indian Mutiny, vol. I-IV.* (*Ed*). by G.B.Malleson, London.

913. Malsawmdawngliana n.p. : *British Colonialism in Mizoram.* Ph.D. Thesis (*in Progress*) History Deptt., NEHU, Shillong under Dr. J B.Bhattacharjee.

914. Mangrai, 1965 : Mangrai's Reproduction of Pemberton's *Account on Shan* (*Pong Chronicles.* (*In*) *The Shan States and British Annexation, Appendix-III.* New York : XX, 108-16.

915. Man in India, 1925 : Indian Ethnology in Current Periodical Literature [Regarding the Occurrence of the Blow-gun in Assam by Dr. J.H.Hutten in "*Man*" for July, 1924. He is Inclined to Regard the Thado-Kuki Blow Gun of Bamboo Cut Off]. *Man in India*, V (1-2). March-June, : 161.

916. ———, 1937 : Notices of Books : The Advancement of Sciences London, British Association, 1937, pp. 264, 3s. 6d. *Man in India*, XVII (4), Oct.-Dec. : 263-64 (about Kuki).

917. ———, 1948 : Notes and Queries: Advisory Council for Lushai Hills. *Man in India*, XXVIII (3), Sept. : 181-82.

918. Mann, K., 1989 : Polygamy and Status of Women : Case of Tribal North East India. *Man and Life*, 15 (3-4), July-Dec. : 171-82.

919. Mara Freedom Party, 1965 : *Memorandum to Shri Pataskar, Chairman of Commission for Hill Areas of Assam from Mara Freedom Party*, June, 1965, 20p.

920. Marjorie, Sykes : *Mizo Miracle*. Madras, Christian Literature Society, 85p.

921. Masani, M.R., 1965 : Nagaland Problem : A Constructive Approach. *Times of India*, February 19 : 1.

922. Mathew, George, 1989 : Education for Integrated Tribal Development : A Case Study of Dynamics of Development of Kawrthah village in Mizoram. Proceedings of a Seminar on *Perspective, Issues and Experiences of Rural Development in North East India*, held on 26-27 May, 1989, Organised by NEICSSR, 10p. (*Mimeo.*)

923. Mathew, K.M. (*Ed.*), 1983 : *Manorama Year Book, 1983*. Kerala, Manorama Publishing House : 696-99.

924. Mathew, T. (*Ed.*) 1983 : *North Eastern Hill Regions of India : Problems and Prospects of Development*. New Delhi, Agricola Publications.

925. Mathew, Uzunnalil, 1975 : Christianity and Education in North East India. (*In*) *Report and Proceedings of a Seminar on Sociological Perspective on North East and, the Second Annual Conference of the North East India Social Association*, Dibrugarh, 10-12 March, 1975, Dibrugarh University.

926. Mathur, K.S., 1972 : Tribe in India : A Problem of of Identificaltion and Integration. (*In*) *Tribal Situation in India : Proceedings of a Seminar*, (*Ed.*) by K. Suresh Singh. Simla, Indian Institute of Advanced Study : 457-61.

927. ———, 1969 : Tribal Identity. *Eastern Anthropologist*. XXII (2), May August : 135-39.

928. Mawisr, J.H.,1905 : *The History of the Welsh Calvinistic Methodist Foreign Mission to the End of the Year 1904*. London, Welsh Mission : 227-33.

929. McCall, Anthony G., 1941-42 : A Cottage Industry in Assam. *Geog. Magazine*, 14 : 42-7.

930. McCall, A.G., 1949 : *Lushai Chrysalis* (with a Foreword by Keith Cantlize). London, Luzac and Co., 320p. *Reprinted* by Firma K.L.M. Pvt. Ltd., Calcutta in 1977 on Behalf of the Tribal Research Institute, Mizoram, Aizawl).

931. ———, 1980 : *The Lushai Hills District Cover (1931-43)*. Aizawl, Tribal Resea-

rch Institute (Mizoram) (*Reprinted*).

932. McCosh, J., 1836 : Account of the Mountain Tribes on the Extreme N.E. Frontier of Bengal. *Jour. of the Asiatic Society of Bengal*, 5 : 193-208.

933. McClain, 1974 : *Kehhran Chanchin.* Aizawl, UPC Hqrs (*In Mizo*).

934. Mc Culloch, W., 1859 : Accoun of the Valley of Munnipore and of the Hill Tribes : With a Comparative Vocabulary of the Munnipore and Other Languages. *Selections from the Records of the Government of India, No. 27.* Calcutta, Govt. Press 55-64 (*Appendix-II and vocabulary,* xi to xliii.)

935. McRae, John, 1801 : Account of the Kookies or Lunctas. *Asiatic Researches*, VII (vi).

936. Mc Swiney, J., 1912 : Assam. (*In*) *Census of India 1911, vol. III, pt. II.* Shillong, Assam, Secretariat Printing Office : 129 133.

937. Medhi, Surendra, Nath , 1990 : Article 244A should be Omitted. *The Assam Tribune*, August 31 : 4 (3-6), 7 (1).

938. Meerworth, A.M., 1919 : *Indian Museum* (*Calcutta*) *Ethnographical Gallery Guide Book, No. 2 : The Andamanese, Nicobarese and Hill Tribes of Assam.* Calcutta, Govt. Printing Press, India.

939. ———, 1981 : *The Andamanese, Nicobarese and Hill Tribes of Assam.* Gauhati,

Spectrum Publications *Reprinted*, 1st Pub. in 1919),

940. Mehra, Preeti, 1990 : Water Quality in the North East. *Science Today 2001*, 24 (3), April ; 28-40.

941. Mehrotra, R., 1976 : Problems of Rapid Economic growth of Mizoram: Proceedings of a Seminar on *Strategy for Planned Economic Development of of Mizoram*, held during 29-31 July in Aizawl (*Mimeo*).

942. Memorandum, 1947 : *First Memorandum of the Mizo Union with Three Points Demand Submitted to the Sub-Committee in Aizawl.*

943. ———, 1954 : *Memorandum of the United Mizo Freedom Organisation, Submitted to the Secretary, State Reorganization Commission, New Delhi, May, 28, 1954.*

944. ———, 1965 : *Memorandum Submitted to the Prime Minister of India by the Mizo National Front, General Headquarters. Aizawl, Mizoram dated October 30, 1965.*

945. ———, 1969 : *Memorandum Submitted to the Prime Minister, Mrs. Gandhi by H.K. Bawichhuaka, Chalchhunga and C. Pahlira on June 22, 1966.*

946. ———, 1971 : *Memorandum of the Pawi-Lakher Autonomous Regional Council for Making Provision to Create Three Autonomous District Councils for*

Powi Lakher, Chakma under the Separate Legislative Body. (It was submitted to the Prime Minister of India, August, 1971).

947. Mendus, E. Lewis 1956 : *The Diary of a Jungle Missionary.* Liverpool, Mission Press.

948. ———, 1968 : *A Jungle Diary.* Liverpool, Foreign Mission Office.

949. Middleton, J. and D. Tait (Eds.) 1958, : *Tribes without rulers.* London, Routledge and Kegan Paul.

950. Miglani, Sanjeev 1988 : The Battle continues in the North-East. *The Statesman* (Calcutta), Saturday Magazine: 1(1-8), 2(4-8).

951. Military Report, 1893 : Chin-Lushai Country. Dehradun, *Military Report* : 36-7, 41-2.

952. ———, 1908 : Assam. Dehra Dun, *Military Report.*

953. ———, 1930 : *Military Report on Proceedings and Assam District, vol. III.* Simla, Govt. of India Press.

954. Mills, A.J. Maffatt (Ed.), 1854 : *Report on the Province of Assam.* Calcutta, Calcutta Gazettee Office, 54+clxxviii, Appendix (*Reprinted* by Gian Publications, Delhi, 1980).

955. Mills, J.P. : *A Note on the Future of the Hill Tribes of Assam and the Adjoining Hills in Self Governing India* (*Secret* .

956. ———, 1926 : Assam-Burma Frontier. *Geographical Journal*, 67 : 289-301.

957. Mills, J.P., 1935 Kuki. (Notes on a tour in the Chhitagong Hill Tract in 1926). (*In*) *Census of India, vol I : India Part-III : Ethnographical* (*Ed.*) by J.H. Hutton. Simla, Govt. Press : 121.

958. ———, 1928 : The Hill Tribes of Assam, IV : The Kuki Clans. *Assam Review*, I (IV), June : 9-11.

959. ———, 1930 : Notes on a Absolete Kuki Oetal vessel and fire making by men and women of the Old Kuki clan of Cachar. *Man*, 30(1) : 1-2.

960. Mills, J.P. and A.H. Fletcher, 1935 : Notes on the Biete Kukis. (In) *Census of India 1931, vol.* I : *India, Part III : Ethognraphical* (*Ed.*) by J.H. Hutton. Simla, Govt. Press. 133.

961. ———, 1935 : Notes on the Khelma Kukis. (In) *Census of India 1931, op. cit.*, : 133-34.

962. Mill. J.P. *et al*, 1935 : Notes on Some Assam Hill Tribes. (In) *Census of India 1931, op. cit.* : 126-46.

963. Ministry of Home Affairs, 1966 : *Report of the Commission on the Hill Area of Assam, 1965-'66* Delhi, Ministry of Home Affairs, Govt. of India, 4p. (About Mizo District Council).

964. Mishra, R., 1972 : Autonomous Councils of Mizoram. *Amrita Bazar Patrika*, January 21 [Mizoram Supplement].

955. Misra, Sudhakar 1979 : Mizoram ki Yek Ghalak (In *Hindi*). *Vanyajati*, XXVII (1), January : 17-9.

966. Mishra, Udayan, 1978 : The Naga National Question. *Economic and Political Weekly*, XIII(14), April 8 : 618-24.

967. ———, 1988 : *North East India : Quest for Identity*. Delhi, Omsons Publications, 155p.

968. Mitra, A., 1964 : *Census of India 1961, vol. I, India, pt. I-C (iii), Language Tables*. Delhi, Manager of Publications. Cxcii-Cxcv.

969. Mitra, P.N., 1936 : Blood Groups of the Angami Naga and Lushai Tribes. *Indian Journal of Medical Research*, 23 : 685-86.

970. Mitra, R. *and* B. Das Gupta (Eds.), 1967 : *A Common Perspective for North East India*. Calcutta, Pannalal Das Gupta.

971. Mitra, S.C., 1932 : On a Thado Kuki Accumulation Droll of a man. *Journal of Anthropological Society of Bombay*, vol. 15 (40) : 105-11.

972. ———, 1932 : A Note on the Thado-Kuki Belief About the War-lioness. *Jour. of the Anth. Society of Bombay*, 15(40) : 124-28.

973. Mitra, Sevati, 1976 : Growth, Distribution and Occupational Pattern of Tribal Population of India. *Journal of the Indian Anth. Society*, 11(3), Nov.: 257-72.

974. Mittal Publications, 1984 : *Report on the Administration of North East India* (*1921-22*) Delhi Mittal Publications (*Reprinted* ; original title was *Report on the Administration of Assam for the Year 1921-22* : *46-9*.

975. Mizo District Council, 1956 : *Zoram Hriattirna* (*An Official Organ of the Mizo Dist. Council Aijal*).

976. ———, 1957 : *Mizo Hnam Dan* (*Mizo Customary Law*) [*in Mizo*]. Aizawl, The Mizo District Council : 8-9.

977. ———, 1968 : *Zoram Hariattirna* (*in Mizo*). District Information Fortnightly. Aizawl, Mizo Dist. Council.

978. ———, (*Comp.*) : *The Collection of the Mizo District Council Acts, Regulations and Rules*, Aizawl, Mizo Dist. Council: 128-29.

979. ———, : *Brochure on the Mizo District Council*. Aizawl, Mizo District Council.

980. Mizo Leh, 1903 : Mizo. *Mizo leh vai chanchin lehkhabu*, Sept, : 1-2. (*in Mizo*).

981. Mizdeh, 1903 : Mizo Leh vai chanchin Lekhabu (*in Mizo*) *Leekha*, XII, Oct. : 3-4.

982. Mizo National Front, 1965 : *Memorandum of the National Front, General Headquarter, Aizawl*. (Submitted to the Prime Minister of India on 30th October).

983. ———, 1971 : M *N F white paper, 1971*. Aizawl, M.N.F. (*Mimeo.*)

984. Mizo National Front : *Engvangin Age M.N.F. a Lo Phir* (Why did M.N.F. Divide) [*A Booklet in Mizo*). Aizawl, M.N.F. Returnees Rehabilitation Association Committee, 1p.

985. ———, : *Mizoram is for Mizo People* (*Pamphlet in English*). Aizawl, Publicity Deptt. of M. N. F, Underground Govt. (Mizoram).

986. MNM, 1984 : Mizo Festivals and Dances. Mizo *National Magazine*, August 1, : 56-9.

987. M.Z.P., 1975 : *Chanchinbu : A Monthly Journal of the Mizo Students Association* (*In Mizo*). Aizawl, M.Z.P.

988. M.S P. (M.S, Prabhakara), 1990 : In the Thick of it. *Frontline* (Madras), May 12-25 : 33-41.

989. Mizo Synod, 1977 : *Presbyterian Kohhran Khawmpuri Thurel Pawlmawh Lakkhawm*. Aizawl, Syond Press (In *Mizo*).

990. Mizo Union, 1947 : *The First Memorandum of the Mizo Union with Three Points demands submitted to be Sub-Committee. Aizawl*

991. ———, 1947 : *The Mizo Union's Memorandum dated 23.4. 1947*.

992. ———, ? : *Mizo Union Tum Dan Mizo* (Aims and Objects of Mizo Union). Aizawl, Mizo Union Headquarters (In *Mizo*).

993. ———, 1971 : *Memorandum dated 17.7.1971*. Aizawl, Mizo Union Youth Wing.

994. Mizo Union, ? : *Brief History of the Mizo Union Party*. Aizawl, Mizo Union (*Unpublished*).

995. Moerman, M., 1968 : Being Lue : Uses and Abuses of Ethnic Identification. (In) *Essays on the Problem of Tribe*. (*Ed.*) by June Helm. Seattle, American Ethnological Society.

996. Marvis, J.H. 1910 : *The History of the Welsh Calvinistic Methodist Foreign Mission to the End of the Year 1904*. "*The Lushai Hills*." London, Welsh Mission : 227-33.

997. Mukherjee, Deba Prasad, 1965 : Anthropological observations on to Print Patterns Among the hill tribes of North East India. *Z. Morph. Anthrop.*, 56 : 217-31.

998. Mukherjee, Deba Prasad *and* Sima Mukherjee, 1965 : A Study of Foot Contour Among the Sema of Naga Hills and the Lushai of Mizo Hills. *Man*, 65 : 154-55.

999. Mukherjee, D.P. ; Sima Mukherjee *and* Pathak, R.D., 1976 : A Micro-Demography of Social Change Cmong the Mizo Population of Shillong. *North Eastern Research Bulletin*, 7 : 14-7.

1000. Mukherjee, D.P. *and* N.K. Das, 1976 : The Mizo Political Movement. Proceedings of a Seminar on *Contemporary Tribal Movements in India*, held in Calcutta by Anthropological Survcy of India. (This was Published in 1982 by Manohar Publications, Delhi which Edited by K.S. Singh).

1001. Mukherjee, D.P. ; P.Gupta *and* Das, N.K., 1982 : The Zeliangrong or Haomei Movement. (*In*) *Tribal Movement in India*, (*Ed.*) by K.S. Singh. New Delhi, Manohar Publications : 67-95.

1002. Mukherjee, Dilip, 1975 : Terrorism in Mizoram : Need for Measured Response. *The Times of India*, January 1.

1003. ———, 1976 : Peace Returns to Mizoram : End of a Prolonged Insurgency. *The Times of India*, July 5.

1004. Mukherjee, Kalyan, 1990 : Cry, Freedom : Looking Back. *The Illustrated Weekly of India*, July 22-28 : 76-77 (i.e. *Interview with M.N.F's Laldenga in 1984*).

1005. Mukherji, Ranjit, 1974 : Problems of Shifting Cultivation. *North Eastern Affairs* (Shillong), 3(1), April-June : 47-54 and 57.

1006. Mullan, C.S., 1932 : Kuki (In) *Census of India 1931, vol. III : Assam Part-I : Report.* Calcutta, Govt. of India, Central Publications Branch 174.

N

1007. Naba Bharat Times, 1989 : Mizoram Meon Mantrimandal ne Shapth Lee. (*in Hindi*). *Naba Bharat Times* (Delhi), January 26 : 1 (1-2).

1008. Nag, Amit Kumar, 1957 : The Mizo Tribes. *March of India* (Delhi), 9 (7), August : 31-3.

1009. ———, 1966 : Unfulfilled Aspirations of Mizos. *Janata* (Bombay), XXI (1), January.

1010. ———, 1967 : The Society in Transition in the Mizo District. (*In*) *A Common Perspective for North East India*, (*Eds.*) by Rathin Mitra *and* B. Das Gupta Calcutta, Pannalal Das Gupta : 80-90.

1011. Nag, Amit Kumar, 1968 : *The Mizo Society in Transition : A Study of Trends.*

1012. ———, 1970-71 : On the Political Structure of North East India. *Jaurnal of Assam Political Science Association.*

1013. ———, 1972 : The Ups and Downs of Mizo politics. *North Eastern Affairs* (Shillong), (1), January-March : 17-21.

1014. ———, 1974 : Economic Compulsions of Mizoram. *North Eastern Affairs,* 2(4). Jan. Uary—March : 63-66 and 70.

1015. ———, 1977 : Mizoram : A Plea for an Appropriate Development Strategy. *North Eastern Spectrum* (Gauhati), 1(2), (1976-'77) : 15-8.

1016. ———, 1983 : Mizoram. *Amrita Bazar Patrika,* June 30.

1017. ———, 1984 : *The Mizo Dilemma.* Silchar (Assam), Tribal Mirror Publications, 92p.

1018. ———, 1987 : Laldenga Shows Signs of Frmness. *Amrita Bazar Patrika,* March 20 : 5(1-4).

1019. ———, 1990 : Chittagong Tribals' Distress yet to get Proper Attention. *Amrita Bazar Patrika,* July 27 : 5(1-6).

1020. ———, 1990 : Aizawl Completes 100 years. *Amrita Bazar Patrika,* July 29 : 5(7-8).

1021. Nag, Amit Kumar, 1990 : From 'Kuki' Identity to 'Mizo' : A Long Journey. *Amrita Bazar Patrika*, August 23 : 7(1-5).

1022. ———, 1990 : Mizoram C.M. Praises Centre for Rs. 125 cr. Allocation. *Amrita Bazar Patrika*, August 31 : 5(3-5).

1023. Nag, B.C., 1966 : Der Stamm der Mizo. *Indo-Asia* (Stutgurt), 3 : 248-52.

1024. Nag, Chittaranjan 1974 : *Impact of Christianity on the Life of the Mizos : A Study of their Social Philosophy*. (*Unpublished*). Ph. D. Thesis, Gauhati University.

1025. Nagaland Bhasha Parishad, 1973 : *Hindi Kuki English Dictionary*. Kohima, Nagaland Bhasha Parishad, 86p.

1026. ———, 1978 : *Kuki Folk Tales*. Kohima, Nagaland Bha. Pari, 64p.

1027. ———, 1977 : *Paite Hindi Self Teacher*. Kohima, Nagaland Bha. Pari., 72p.

1028. ———, 1977 : *Hmar Hindi Self Teacher*. Kohima, N.B.P., 56p.

1029. ———, 1975 : *Mizo Hindi Self Teacher*. Kohima, N.B.P., 63p.

1030. ———, 1976 : *Hindi Chakma Vocabulary*' Kohima, N.B.P., 16p.

1031. ———, 1975 : *Hindi Riang Vocabulary*. Kohima, N.B.P., 28 p.

1032. ———, 1975 : *Hindi Vaiphei Vocabulary*. Kohima, N.B.P., 28p.

1033. Nagaland Bhasha Parishad, 1975 : *Hindi Zou Vocabulary.* Kohima, N.B.P., 27p.

1034. ———, 1974 : *Hindi Gangte English Vocabulary.* Kohima, N.B.P., 28p.

1035. ———, 1975 : *Hindi Hmar Dictionary.* Kohima, N.B.P., 120p.

1936. ———, 1975 : *Hindi Paite Dictionary.* Kohima, N.B.P., 128p.

1037. ———, 1974 : *Hindi Mizo Dictionary.* Kohima, N.B.P., 119p.

1038. ———, 1973 : *Hindi Kuki English Dictionary.* Kohima, N.B.P., 86p.

1039. ———, 1974 : *Outline Grammar of Kuki.* Kohima, N.B.P., 16p.

1040. ———, 1978 : *Kuki Folk Tales.* Kohima, N.B.P., 64p.

1041. ———, 1979 : *Paite Folk Tales.* Kohima, N.B.P., 66p.

1042. Narain, Iqbal 1986 : Foreword. (*In*) *Government and Politics in Mizoram* by R.N. Prasad. New Delhi Northern Book Centre (1987) : vii-ix.

1043. Natarajan, Nalini, 1970 : Mizos : Social Institutional and Practices, *Social Welfare,* 16(2), March : 32.

1044. ———, 1973 : The Chakma. *North Eastern Affairs,* vol. 2.

1045. Natarajan, R. 1967 : *Speech of R. Natarajan, IAS, Deputy Commissioner, Mizoram*

District, Aizawl, at the Ceremonial Function on the Republic Day, the 26th January, 1967.

1046. Nath, Lal Mohan, 1982 : Social Work in Tripura-Mizo Border Hill Area. *Himalaya : Man and Nature* (Delhi), 6(7), Dec. : 11.

1047. Nath, Surendra, 1978 : A Few Impressions of Mizoram. *Mizoram Today,* III(J) : 1-3.

1048. National Archives, 1911 : *Foreign Department Proceedings, 1894 to 1911.* National Archives of India, Delhi (*Unpublished*).

1049. National Council of Agriculture, 1973 : *Background Paper on Shifting Cultivation. National Council of Agriculture, Document No. 8D/NCA/DOC/7, Nov. 6, 1973* (*Mimeo*).

1050. National Institute, 1990 : Proceedings of a Seminar on *Agrarian Structure and Land Relations in North Eastern Region,* Organised by the National Institute of Rural Development, North Eastern Regional Centre, Guwahati.

1051. Nayak, Chhaya-kanta, 1990 : Chakma Refugees Face Uncertain Future. *The Assam Tribune,* Feb. 26 : 4(7-8).

1052. Negi, A.S., 1989 : Burma's Students go to Jungles. *Amrita Bazar Patrika,* Nov. 6 : 6 (3-6).

1053. Negi, Balbir Singh, 1979-80 : *Human Geography : An Ecological Approach.* Meerut, Kedar Nath Ram Nath : 364-66

1054. Neufvile, John Bryan, 1828 : On the Geography and Population of Assam. *Asiatick Researches*, 16 : 331-52 (*Reprinted* in 1855 in Selections from the Records of the Bengal Government, No. 23. Calcutta.)

1055. Nevill, G.A. *et al.*, 1923 : Notes on Certain Frontier Tribes. (*In*) *Census of India 1621, vol. III, Assam, pt. I, Report, Appendix B.* Shillong, Govt. Press : 10-6.

1056. Newland, 1894 : *The Image of War or Service in Chin Hills.* Calcutta, Thacker Spink & Co.

1057. Newport, G.O., 1894 : Tod and Jenseits bei den Luschais. *Mitteilungeu der Geographischen Gesellschaft Jena*, 13 : 30-1.

1058. News, 1988 : Megafossils from Bhuban Formation of Mizoram. *News : Geological Survey of India* (Shillong), 7 : 11.

1059. Ngurkunga : *Political Diary of Ngurkuna, MNF Minister in Charge (Publicity).* (*Unpublished* typed Mss.).

1060. Nibedon, Nirmal 1980 : *Mizoram : The Dagger Brigade.* New Delhi, Lancers Publications, 269p.

1061. ———, 1981 : *North East India : The Ethnic Explosion.* New Delhi, Lancers Publications.

1062. Noorani, A.G. 1986 ; Constitution and Mizoram Accord. *Rajasthan Patrika.* July 26.

1963. North Eastern : Editorial : Trouble in Mizoram.

Affairs, 1974 *North Eastern Affairs*, 3(1), April-June : 7-8.

1054. NEICSSR, 1986 : Questions of Nationalities, Ethnicity aud Cultural Identity in the Context of North-East India. Proceedings of a Seminar on *Questions of Nationalities, Ethnicity and Cultural Identity in the Context of North-East India*, held during December 5-6, 1986, organised by NEICSSR, Shillong. (This has Been published in 1990, the book is entitled *Nationality, Ethnicity and Cultural Identity in North East India*, (*Ed.*) by B. Pakem. New Delhi, Omsons Publications, 388p.)

1065. ———, 1989 : Proceedings of a Seminar on *Perspective, Issues and Experieences of Rural Development in North East India*, Organised by NEICSSR. Shillong, Held on 26-27 May, 1989.

1066. North Eastern Spectrum 1976 : Mizoram : A Plea for an Appropriate Development Strategy. *North Eastern Spectrum*, 1(2), August : 15-8.

1067. ———, 1976 : Mizoram : Newsletter. *North Eastern Spectrum*, 1(3-4), Septculer Oct ober 65-7 and 1(7), January : 59.

1068. ———, 1976 : Mizoram : On the Road to Progress.. *North East. Spectrum*, 1(6), Dec. : 39-44.

1069. North Eastern Spectrum, 1976 : Book Review : Enchanted Frontiers by Nari Rustamji. Calcutta,

Oxford University, Press. *North Eastern Spectrum* vol. 1 : 83-4.

1070. Nunthara, C., 1974 : MNF holds Key to Political Stability. *Economic and Political Weekly*, IX(50), December 14.

1071. ———, 1986 : *Impact of the Introduction of Grouping of Villages in Mizoram.* Delhi, 125p.

O

1072. O'Callaghan, T.P.M. *et. al*, 1923 : Notes on Certain Frontier Tribes. (*In*) *Census of India 1921, vol. III, Assam, Pt. I, Report, Appendix-B.* Shillong, Govt. Press : 10-6.

1073. O'Donel, J.H. 1863 : Notes on the Tribes of the Eastern Frontier no, I and II. *Journal of the Asiatic Society of Bengal*, 32 : 400-07,

1074. Oriental Watchman : Editorial : Built Their Own Road. 1951 *The Oriental Watchman and Herald of Health* (Poona), March.

P

1075. Pachpore, Virag, 1986 : Insurgency in North East India : The Church Connection. *Organiser*, August 24 : 13-4.

1076. Pahlira, C. : *On Grouping of Mizoram Villages*. Aizawl, Secretary, Mizo Union.

1077. ———, 1968 : *A Paper on Talk Between the MNF and the Mizo Union*. Aizawl, General Secretary, Mizo Union, (June, 1968).

1078. ———. 1968 : Mizo Hills in the Indian Union. *Tribal Mirror* (Silchar), VI(1).

1079. Paite National Council, 1960 : *Re-Unification of the Chin People (Memorandum submitted by the*

Paite National Council for Reunification of the Chins of India, Burma and Pakistan under one Country to the Prime Minister, Govt. of India, New Delhi). Churachandpur, The Paite National Council : 1,4, 10, 14-15,20 & 24.

1080. Pakem, B., 1981 : The Changing Power Structure of the political Institution of Chieftainship in Mizoram. *Jour. of NEICSSR* (Shillong), V(II), October : 1-5.

1081. ——, 1982 : Book Review : *Mizo Unrest, A Study in Politicization of Culture* by B.B. Goswami, Aalekh Publishers. Jaipur, 1979. pp. 220, Rs. 55/- *Jour. of NEICSSR* (Shillong), VI (I), April : 39-40

1082. ——, 1984 : The Biates. (*In*) *The Tribes of North East India*, (*Ed.*) by S. Karotemprel. Calcutta, Firma K.L.M. Pvt. Ltd. : 267-94.

1083. ——, 1989 : Polity Formation in Pre-Colonial Biate Chieftaincy. *Proceedings of North East India Historical Association* (Shillong), Xth Session, Oct. ober 12-14 (Mimeo).

1084. ——, (Ed.) 1990 : *Nationality, Ethnicity and Culturalf Identity in North East India*. New Delhi, Omson Publication.

1085. Pakyntein, E.H. (*Ed.*) 1965 : *Census of India 1961, vol. III, Assam, pt. V-A : Scheduled Tribes and Scheduled Castes (Reprints from Old Census Reports and*

Special Tables). Delhi, Manager of Publications (1964), 148p.

1086. Pakyntein, E.H. 1965 : *Census of India 1961, Vol. III, Assam, pt. V-A, Scheduled Tribes and Scheduled Castes : Reprints from Old Census Reports and Special Tables.* Delhi, Manager of Publications, 428p. (1881 1921).

1087. ———, 1965 : *Mizo Hills District Census Handbook : Census of India 1961.* Shillong, Assam Govt.

1088. ———, 1966 : *A Monograph on Lawngtlai (Lungleh P.S., Mizo Hills District) : Census of India 1961, vol. III, Assam, Pt. VI, Village Survey Monograph No. 18.* Delhi, Manager of Publications.

1089. ———, 1968 : *Census of India 1961 : Assam Village Survey Monograph, Durtlang (Aizawl Police Station, Mizo Hills District.* Delhi, Manager of Publications, 48p.

1090. Palhira. C., 1970 : Mizo Hills in the Indian Union. *Tribal Mirror*, VI.

1091. Pande, K.C., 1973 : Problem of National Integration and Nehru : The Case of an Unrealised Objective. *Political Science Review*, 12, Januery-June.

1092. Pandit, C.S., 1969 : Naga and Mizo Problem. *Indian Express*, Septorber. 14 : 6.

1093. Pari, Chawngthan, 1973 : *Western Impact on Society in Mizoram.* (*Unpublished*) M. Phil Thesis of North Eastern Hill University, Shillong.

1094. Parry, N.E. 1928 : *A Monograph on Lushai Customs and Ceremonies.* Shillong, Assam Govt. Press (*Reprinted* by Firma KLM Pvt. Ltd. Calcutta in 1976, on behalf of Tribal Research Institute. Aizawl, 130p.)

1095. ———, 1931 : On the Flowering of Bamboos. *Jour. of the Bombay National History Society*, XXXIV(4),

1096. ———, 1931 : Notes on the Lushais. (*In*) *Census of India 1931, Assam, Vol. 3, pt. I, Appendix-B*. Shillong, Govt. Press : X-Xv.

1097. ———, 1932 : *The Lakhers*, (with an "*Introduction*" *and* "*Supplementary Notes* by J.H. Hutton) London, Macmillan Co., 640p. *Reprinted* in 1976 by T.R.I., Aizawl).

1098. ———, 1943 : Four Lakher songs. *Man in India*, 23(1), January : 6-7.

1099. Parry, N.E. *et al*, 1935 : Notes on Some Assam Hill Tribes. (*In*) *Census of India vol. I, Pt.III-B, India, Ethnographic Notes*, (Ed.) by J.H. Hutton. Simla, Govt. Press : 126-469.

1100. Pathak, R.D., 1977 : *Ethno-psychological Study of Abilities and Interests Patterns of Mizo Students of Shillong*. (*Unpublished*) Report, Anthropological Survey of India (Calcutta).

1101. Pathak, R.D., 1978 : Conceptual Analysis of Lushai Language in the Context of Hindi Teaching. Proceedings of a Seminar on Hindi Teaching in the Context of *Languages of North Eastern Region*, Organised by the Central Institute of Hindi, Shillong.

1102. ———, 1978 : Identification of the Groom Preferences of the Psychologically Identical and Socio-metrically Preferred Mizo Adolescent Girls. *Proceedings of Xth I.C.A.E.S.*, New Delhi.

1103. ———, 1979 : Intelligence and interest Among Mizo students of Shillorg : Ar Study in Ethno-Psychology. *Bulletin : Anthropological Survey of India*, 28(1-2) : 1-20.

1104. ———, 1983 : Bridegroom Preferences of the Psychologically Identical and Socio-metrically Preferred Mizo Girls. *Human Science*, 32(3), Sept. 169-79.

1105. Pathak, R.D. *and* D.K. Mishra, 1978 ; Hindi and Lushai Bhasaao ka Tulanatmak Adhyayan. Proceedings of a Seminar on *Purvanchal ki Bhasaao ke Sandarbh Mei Hindi Sikhan*, Organised by Central Institute of Hindi (Shillong).

1106. Patranabis, T.R., 1975 : Roots of Rebellion in Mizoram. *Organiser*, Feb.ruary 15 : 6-11.

1107. Pattanayak, Dipankar, 1987 : Letters to the Editor : Mizoram Poll. *Amrita Bazar Patrika*, March 3 : 6(3-4).

1108. Paul, Gemini, 1955 : The Lushais. *Vanyajati*, III(4), Oct. : 158-64.

1109. ———, 1957 : Anthropology and Tribal Administration. *Vanyajati*, V(1), January : 4-11.

1110. Paul, M.C., 1983 : Colonialism and Tribal Movements in India. *Hill Geographer*, 1(1-2) : 32-41 (1982).

1111. Pautu, Sanghmingthanga H., 1982 : Mizoram, Separatist Poloitics. (*Unpublished*) M. Phil Dissertation, North Eastern Hill University, Shillong, 62p.

1112. Pawai District Council ? : *Autonomous District Council.* Lunglei, Pawi Dist. Council.

1113. ———, : *Road to Pawi.* Lunglei, Pawai Dist. Council.

1114. Pawi-Lakher Regional Council (Comp.) ? : *The Collection of the Pawi-Lakher Regional Council Acts, Rules and Regulations.* Lunglei, Pawi-Lakher Regional Council.

1115. Pemberton, R.B., 1959 : *The Eastern Frontier of India.* Delhi, Mittal Publications.

1116. Peters, L.L., 1884 : *Lushai Hills District Cover.* Simla, Supdt. of Lushai Hills.

1117. ———, 1947 : Proceedings of a Meeting of the Accredited Leaders of Lushai Political Parties, held at Aijal on 14-8-1947 (*Memo No. 6926. 76G of 21.8.*'47). Published in *The Mizo Dilemma* by Amit Kumar Nag. Silchar, Tribal Mirror Publications (1984) : 90-92. It has also published in *Churches & Political U P Heaval in Mizoram*, by John

Vanlal Hluna. Aizawl, Mizo History Association (1985) : 163-65.

1118. Phayre, Lt. 1841 : Account of Arakan. *Jour. of Asiatic Society of Bengal, No. 117.*

1119. Phayre, Arthur, 1883 : *History of Burma including Burma Proper, Pegu, Taungu, Tenasserim and Arakan.* Edinburg and London, Ballantyne, Hanson & Co.

1120. Phookan, Surenram 1988 : One Year of Mizoram's Statehood. *The Assam Tribune*, February 20 : 4(3-6).

1121. Phukan, J.N. (Ed.) 1986 : Professor Dibakar Goswami Commemoration Volume. *Jour. of the Assam Research Society (Kamarupa Anusandhan Samiti, Gawahati)*, XXVIII(1984-'85).

1122. Planning and Development, 1973 : *Mizoram Draft Fifth Fve Year Plan, 1974-1979*, August, Vol. I. Aizawl, Planning and Development Department, Govt. of Mizoram.

1123. Piscitee, Teegyi 1974 : We are the Zomis. *Chin Magazine* (1973-'74) [Burma, University of Rangoon].

1124. Playne, Somerset, 1917 : *Bengal, Behar and Orissa.* London, Foreign & Colonial, 767p.

1125. Poonte, B., 1972 : *Brochure on the Mizo District.* Aizawl, Tribal Research Institute, 10p.

1126. Porter, A.E., 1933 : *Census of India 1931, Vol. V : Begnal and Sikkim, Pt. I : Report*

Calcutta, Govt. Press : 476, 519-20.

1127. Poster, Challiana, 1978 : *Pil Pu Nua.* (*In Mizo*). Aizawl, The Trio Book House.

1128. Prabhakara, M.S., 1983 : North Eastern Identity. *Hindu*, Nov. 18.

1129. Prasad, R.N., 1973 : Evolution of Party Politics in Mizoram. *Political Science Review (Quarterly)* : *Journal of the Deptt. of Pol. Sc.*, (University of Rajasthan, Jaipur), 12(3-4) : 209-10.

1130. ———, 1973 : Evolution of Party Politics in Mizoram, *North Eastern Affairs*, 2(1), April-June (Annual) : 47-56.

1131. ———, 1974 : The Sixth Schedule to the constitution. An Analysis, *North Eastern Affairs*, 3(2-3), July-Dec. : 29-34.

1132. ———, 1977 : Role of Community Development Blocks via-a-vis Agricultural Production in Mizoram. *North Eastern Spectrum*, 1(8-10): 25-7.

1133. ———, 1979 Important Features of the Sixth Schedule to the Indian Constitution. An Analysis, *Jour. of Political Studies* (Jullundur), XII, Feb. ruany 41-2

1134. ———, 1983 *Political Evolution of Mizoram (1947-1972)*. Muzaffarpur. Ph, D. Thesis Deptt. of Political Science, Bihar University.

1135. ———, 1984 The Political Institution of the Lakher Chieftainship in Mizoram.

Jour. NEICSSR (Shillong), '(2), Oct. : 24-9

1136. ———. 1987 *Government and Politics in Mizoram (1947-1986)*. New Delhi, Northern Book Centre. 367p.

1137. Prasad, R.N. et al 1988 Shifting Sultivation and Land degradation. Proceedings of a Seminar on *Review and Reprisal of Shifting Cultivation in North East India* held on 13-14 May. (*Mimeo*).

1138. Prasad, R.N. *and* A.K. Agarwal, 1990 : *Political and Economic Development in Mizoram*. Delhi, Mittal Publication (*in Press*).

1139. Prim, S., 1975 : *The Vaiphei Tribe*. Churachandpur (Manipur), L. & R. Printing Press.

1140. Prime Minister, 1986 : Steps Soon to Take : Mizo Insurgency. *Times of India*, March 10 : 1(1-3).

1141. Proceedings, 1947 : Proceedings of the Meeting of Lushai Leaders held at Aijal on 14-8-1947 (Memo. *No. 6927. 76G of 21.8.'47*).

1142. Proceedings, 1971 : *Proceedings of the Mizo District Council the 68th Session held at the Council Chamber (14-4-1971) in Assembly Library*.

1143. Publications Division, 1972 : *Mizoram (State of Our Union)*. New Delhi Publications Divisions (2nd Edition Published in 1979).

1144. Publicity Depart- : *MNF Booklet White Paper*

ment (*Sawrkar Thupuan*) Aizawl, Publicity Deptt,, Govt. of Mizoram, 2p.

1145. ———, : *Mizoram is for Mizo People* (*Pamphlet in English*). Aizawl, Publicity Deptt., MNF Underground Govt., (Mizoram).

1146. Pudaite, Rochunga 1963 : *The Education of the Hmar People.* Calcutta, Navana Printing Works Pvt. Ltd.

1147. Pugh, B.M 1967 : Social and Cultural Changes in the Hill Areas of North East India. (*In*) *A Common Perspective for North East India* (*Eds*) by Rathin Mitra *and* B. Das Gupta. Calcutta, Pannalal Das Gupta - 41-3.

1148. ———, 1967 : Politics in the Hill Areas of North East India. (*In*) *A Common Perspective for North East India,* (*Eds.*) by Raithin Mitra *and* B. Das Gupta. Calcutta, Pannalal Das Gupta : 173-75.

1149. ———, 1967 : Christianity and the Tribes of North East India. (*In*) *A Common Perspective for North East India,* (*Eds*.) by Rahin Mitra *and* B. Das Gupt a. Calcutta, Pannalal Das Gupta : 240-42.

1150. Purbanchal Prahari, 1989 : Mizoram : Lalthanhawla ki Prarthana High Court Dwara Namanjur (Dharmik adhar par chunab Prachar). *Purbanchal Prahari,* Nov. 11 , 2(4-5) (*in Hindi*).

1151. ———, 1990 : Purbottar ke sabhi Rajyon ke Liye Dhara 370 ki Mang. *Pur Pra.*, May 4 : 3(4-5) (*in Hindi*).

1152. ———, 1990 : Mizoram: Democratic Party Janata Dal Men shamil. *Pur. Pra.*, June 7: 1(4-5) (*in Hindi*).

1153. ———, 1990 : Mizoram ke Masiha Laldenga Nahi Rahe. *Pur. Pra.*, July 8 : 1(2-4) (*in Hindi*).

1154. ———, 1990 : Mizo Reta Laldenga. *Pur. Pra.*, July 9 : 4(1-2) (*in Hindi*).

1155. Purkayastha, Rakhal *and* A.B. Chakraborty, 1989 : Book Review : *Emerging Pattern of North Eastern Economy*, (*Ed.*) by V.S. Mahajan. New Delhi, Deep & Deep Publications. *Jour. of NEICSSR* (Shillong), 13(1), April : 56-60.

R

1156. Rajan, K.R. Sundar, 1987 : Relief at Laldenga's Win. *Amrita Bazar Patrika*, Feb. 25: 6(3-6).

1157. Ramachandran, S. *and* K.M. Vidyaranyulu, 1977 : The Socio Economic Impact of New Roads in Mizoram. *North Eastern Spectrum* 1(7), January : 17-20.

1158. Ramadhyani R.K., 1958 : The New Naga Unit. *The Assam Tribune*, Feb. 16 and 23: 4.

1159. Ramakrishnan, P.S. *et al.*, 1981 : Slash and Burn Agriculture in North Eastern India. (*In*) *Fire Regimes and Ecosystem Properties*, (*Eds.*) by H.A. Mooney, T.M. Bonnicksen, N.L. Christensen, J.B. Loten and W.A. Reiners, Honolulu, Hawaii. Forest Service, General Technical Report No. 26 : 570-87.

1160. Ramamani, V.S., 1988 : *Tribal Economy : Problems and Prospects*. Allahabad, Chugh Publications.

1161. Rangasami, Amritha, 1978 : Mizoram : Tragedy of Our Own Making. *Economic and Political Weekly*, XIII (15), April : 653-62.

1162. Rao, C. Narayana 1984 : Crisis in Mizoram. (*In*) *Northeast Region : Problems and Prospects of Development* (*Ed*) by B.L. Abbi. Chandigarh, Centre for Research in Rural and Industrial Development : 240-48.

1163. Rao, P.V. 1988 : *Institutional Famework for Tribal Development*. New Delhi, Inter India Publications.

1164. Rao, V. Venkata : Assam State Politics 1947-1967. *Jour. of Gauhati University* (Gauhati), XXI (1), Arts. 17-23

1165. ———, 1970 : Assam State Politics from 1947 to 1967. *Jour, of Gauhati University* XXIII(1), Arts.

1166. ———, 1975 : North East India : Problems and Prospects. *Indian Journal of Political Science*, January-March.

1167. ———, 1975 : Sociology of Mizo Politics. *Proceedings of a Seminar, Deptt. of Sociology, Dibrugarh University, Assam (March 12).*

1168. ———, 1976 : *A Century of Tribal Politics in North East India, 1874-1974*. New Delhi, S. Chand and Company : 202, 232, 319, 462, 494, 538.

1169. Rao V. Venkata, 1978 : The Sociology of Mizo Politics. (*In*) *North East India : A Sociological Study*, (*Ed.*) by S.M.Dubey. Delhi, Concept Publishing Company : 215-32.

1170. ———, 1979 : Slavery in North East India. Proceedings of a Seminar on the *History and Culture of North East India*, held on 26-28 April, 1979 in History Deptt., North Eastern Hill University, Shillong : 13-8 (*Mimeo.*)

1171. Rao, V.Venkata *and* Niru Hazarika, 1983 : *A Century of Government and Politics in North East India.* New Delhi, S.Chand. (*2nd enlarged edition*, having more information about Mizoram).

1172. Rao, N. Venkata, 1989 : Trends in Consumption and Poverty in Rural North Eastern India. Proceedings of a Semin ar on *Perspective, Issue and Experiences of Rural Development in North East India* held on 26-27 May, Organised by NEICSSR, Shillong : 6p. (*Mimeo.*)

1173. Raw La, Maran, 1967 : Towards a basis for understanding the Minorities in Burma : The Kachin Example. (*In*) *South East Asian Tribes, Minorities and Nations, vol. I,* (*Ed.*) by Peter Kunstadler. Princeton, New Jersey, Princeton University.

1174. Rawlins, John, 1892 : On the Manners, Religion and laws of cucis or mountaineers of Tipra. *Asiatic Researches* II (xii).

1175. Ray, Animesh, 1982 : *Mizoram : Dynamic of Change.* Calcutta, Pearl Publishers, 286p.

1176. Ray, A.K., 1988 : Issue of Mizo Integration. *Jour. NEICSSR*, 12 (2). Oct. : 45-8.

1177. Ray, Ashok Kumar, 1990 : *Authority and Ligitimacy : A Study of the Thadou Kukis in Manipur.* Delhi, Mittal Publications (*in Press*).

1178. Ray, Sukumar, 1967 : Music of the Hill People of North Eastern India (*In*) *A Common Perspective for North East India* (*Eds.*) by Rathin Mitra *and* B.Das Gupta. Calcutta, Pannalal Das Gupta : 29-40

1179, Read, D. ; H.Moutray *and* R.C. Roy, 1921 : Folklore and the Folklore Society. *Man in India*, 1(2), June : 40-7.

1180. Regional Council, 1971 : *Memorandum* (for Making Provision to Create Three Autonomus District Councils for Pawi, Lakher and Chakma Under the Separate Legislative Body) *to the Prime Minister of India, August, 1971* by Pawi Lakher Autonomous Regional Council.

1181. Reid, A.S., 1893 : *Chin Lushai land. including a description of the various expeditions in the Chin Lushai Hills, and the final annexation of the country.* Calcutta, Thacker and Spink, 235p. (*Reprinted*) by Firma K.L.M. Pvt. Ltd. Calcutta in 1976 on behalf of Tribal Research Institute, Aizawl).

1182. Reid, Robert, 1942 : *History of the Frontier Areas*

Bordering on Assam From 1883-1941. Shillong, Assam Govt. Press (*Rerinted* by Firma K L.M. Pvt. Ltd., Calcutta in 1978 on Behalf Tribal Research Institute, Aizawl and also *Reprinted* by Eastern Publishing House, Delhi in 1983, 303p.)

1183. ———, 1944 : Assam. *Jour. of the Royal Society of Arts*, 92 : 241-47.

1184. ———, 1944 : India's North East Frontier. *Royal Central Asian Journal*, 31 : 165-74.

1185. ———, 1944 : The Excluded Areas of Assam. *Geographical Journal*, 103 : 18-9.

1186. ———, 1966 : *Years of change in Bengal and Assam*. London, Ernest Benn Ltd. : 90, 101, 111-12, 116-17, 138, 139.

1187. Rema, C.Lal, 1967 : Communication Between the Hills and the Plains. (*In*) *A Common Perspective for North East India*, (*Eds.*) by Rathin Mitra *and* B.Das Gupta. Calcutta, Pannalal Das Gupta: 209-12.

1188. Remkunga, : *Mizo Pipute Khawsakdan Tlangpui*. Aizawl, Pub. by author. (*in Mizo*).

1189. Rengsi, V.R., 1988 : *Pre-Colonial Technology in Mizoram*. (*Unpublished*) Dissertation of M. Phill (History Deptt.), North Eastern Hill University under Dr.J.B.Bhattacharjee.

1190. ———, n.p. : *Reconstruction of Mizo History : A Technological Perspective* Ph. D. Thesis (*in Progress*), History Deptt., NEHU under Dr. Imdad Hussain.

1191. Report, 1948 : *Constituent Assembly Debates, 4th Nov., eubcr 1948, vol. vii Report of the North East Frontier* (*Assam*), Tribal and Excluded Areas Sub-Committee, 102p.

1192. ———, 1963 : *Report on the Second Round Socio-Economic Survey in Mizo Hills*. Shillong, Govt. of Assam.

1193. ———, 1965-'66 : *Report of the Potaskar Commission on the Hill Areas of Assam.* Delhi, Govt. Publications.

1194. ———, 1966 : *Report of the Committee Appointed by the Governor of Assam to Examine the Fnancial Conditions etc. of each District Regional Council.* Shillong, Govt. of Assam.

1195. ———, 1974 : *Statistical Handbook : Mizoram,* (*Report*). Aizawl, Govt. of Mizoram.

1196. ———, : Report of North East Frontier. *Assam Tribal and Excluded Areas Sub-Committee*, II, pt. I : 26.

1197. Report, 1978 : The Laldenga Factor. *Economic and Political Weekly*, XII (10), May 13.

1198. Riebeck, E., 1885 : *The Chittagong Hill Tribes* (*translated by* A.W.Keane).

1199. Risley, H.H., 1891 : Chakma, Tsakma, Tsak, Thak. (*In*) *Tribes and Castes of Bengal* by H.H.Risley. Calcutta, Govt. Press : 168-76.

1200. ———, 1903 : Seriations of the Mongoloid type : Chakma, Lepcha and Kasia and Summary of Measurement. (*In*) *Census of India 1901, vol. I : India, pt. I : Report, Enthographic Appendices*. Calcutta, Govt. Publications : 31-5.

1201. Rizvi, S.H.M., 1985 : Hmar of Manipur. Proceedings of a Work shop-Seminar on National Project *People of India*, December 7, 1985, 1st Session, Shillong, Anthropological Survey of India (*Mimeo.*)

1202. ———, 1988 : Study of Consanguinity Among Hmars of Manipur. (*In*) *Man : Current Anthropological and Archaeological Perspectives, vol. I* (*Ed.*)by K.L. Bhowmik. New Delhi Inter-India Publications : 251-58.

1203. Rizvi, S.H.M. *and* Shibani Roy, 1990 : *Customary Law of North East India.* Delhi, B.R. Publications.

1204. Roberts, Lord, : *Forty One years in India.* London.

1205. Robinson W., 1841 : *A Descriptive Account of Assam to which is Added a Rhort Account of the Negihbouring tribes.* London Ostell and Lepage Co, 421 p. *Reprinted* in 1975 by Sanskaran Prakashan, Delhi : also, (*In*) *Nagas in the Nineteenth Century*

(Ed.) by Verrier Elwin. Bombay, Oxford University Press (1969).

1206. Ropeca, 1977 : The uestions in North Eastern Region. *Ropeca* (Shillong), I (5), Sept. euber : 25.7.

1207. Rowney, H.B., 1882 *The Wild Tribes of India*. London Thos. De La Rue & Co. : 179-87. *Reprinted* by B.R. Publications. Delhi in 1974 ; also, (*In*) *Nagas In the Nineteenth Century*, (*Ed*) by Verrier Elwin. Bombay. Oxford University Press in 1969.

1208. Roy, Ashok Kumar,: 1983 Kuki National Assembly and Electoral Politics in Manipur Hills. Proceedings of a Seminar on *Electoral Politics*, NEICSSR Shillong, held on 14-15 Dec., 5 p. (*Mimeo*.)

1209. ———, 1989 : *Legitimacy and Authority : A Study of the Thadou Kukis in Manipur*. Delhi, Renaissance Publishing House.

1210. ———, 1982 : Thadou Folklore. Proceedings of of a Seminar on *Folklore in North East India* Organised by NEICSSR, Shillong on Nov. 17-18. (*Mimeo*.)

1211. Roy, Ashok Kumar,: 1985 Thadou Folklore. (*In*) *Folklore in North East India*, (*Ed*.) by Soumen Sen. New Delhi, Omsons Publications.

1212. ———, 1986 : Kuki National Assembly and Electoral Politics in Manipur

Hills. (*In*) *Electoral Politics in North East India*, (*Ed.*) by P.S. Dutta. New Delhi, Omsons Publications : 67-70.

1213. ———, 1990 : Development in North East : An Alternative Future in the National Seminar on *Preparing North East India for 2000 A.D.* Organised by C.E.D.R., New Delhi during 29-31 January, 1990 at Imphal.

1214. ———, 1990 : Forest Management : Past and Present. Proceedings of a Seminar on *Environmental Appraisal an Management in North East India* organised by the Deptt. of Earth Science, Manipur University during 15-16 April, 1990.

1215. Roy, Jyotirmoy, 1958 *History of Manipur*. Calcutta, Firma K.L. Mukhopadhyay, 190p. (*Reprinted* by East Light Book House, Calcutta in 1973, 213p.)

1216. Roy, Khiren, 1974 : Politics of Merger in Mizoram. *The Assam Tribune*, Feb. suavy 3.

1217. ———, 1974 : Abortive Peace Talks in Mizoram. *The Assam Tribune*, April 25.

1218 ———, 1990 : Tribal Politics in North East : Viewpoint. *The Assam Tribuna*, January 20 : 4(3-6) and 6 (4).

1219. Roy, Ramesh Ch. 1936 : Notes on the Chawte Kuki clan. *Man in India*, XVI (2-3), April-Sept-eubr135:55.

1220. Roy, Rati Ranjan, Laldenga on Punjab Peace Mission.

1990 *Amrita Bazar Patrika*, March 22 : 7 (1.2).

1221. Roy Burman, B.K., (*Ed*) n.d. : *A Preliminary Appraisal of the Scheduled Tribes of India*, New Delhi, Office of the Registrar General, India : 228-29, 273 (*Mimeo*.)

1222. ———, 1967 : Hillmen of North East India and tensions of Socio-Economic Deveopment. (*In*) *A Common Perspective for North East India*, (*Eds.*)

by Rathin Mitra and B. Das Gupta. Calcutta, Pannalal Das Gupta : 117-28,

1223. ———, 1969 : Some Dimensions of Transforma-Tion of Tribal Society in India. *Vanyajati*, XVII(1), January : 1-4, 17-8.

1224. ———, 1970 : *Demographic and Socio-Economic Profiles of the Hill Areas of North East India : Census of India 1961.* Delhi, Manager of Publications.

1225. ———, 1972 : Integrated Area Approach to the Problems of the Hill Tribes of North East India. (*In*) *Tribal Situation in India : Proceedings of a Seminar*. (*Ed.*) by K. Suresh Singh. Simla. Indian Institute of Advaned Study : 72-97.

1226. ———, 1980 : Rapid Appraisal of the Critical issues Relating to the Scheuled Tribes and Tribes and Scheduled Castes, (*In*) *Eastern Himalayas : A Study on Anthro-*

pology and *Tribalism* (*Eds.,*) by T.C. Sharma *and* D.N. Majumdar. New Delhi, Cosmo Publications : 11-22.

1227. Roy Burman, B.K.,: 1984 Issues in the North East : An Appraisal. (*In*) *Northeast Region : Problems and Prospects of Development* (*Ed.*) by B.L. Abbi Chandigarh, Centre for Research in Rural & Industrial Development : 174-80.

1228. ———, 1988 : Shifting Cultivation in India : An Overview. *Mainstream*, Noveuhr. 26

1229. ———, 1988 : Shifting Cultivation : A Closer look. *Proceedings of a Seminar of Indian Association of Social Science Institutions, Nov.* eober *1-3, New Delhi* (*Mimeo*).

1230. ———, 1989 : Problems and Prospects of Tribal Development in North-East-India. *Economic and Political Weekly*, 24(13), April 1 : 693-97.

1231. Roy Burman, J.J., 1982 : Social Dimensions of Changes in Land use Pattern in Mizoram. *Vanyajati*, XXX(4), Oct. : 9-12.

1232. Roy Burman, J.J., 1990 : Shifting Cultivation: An Aspect of Tribal exploitation. *Indian Jour. of Social Work* (Bombay), LI(1), January : 57-73.

1233. Roychoudhury, P., 1986 : *The North East : Roots of Insurgency*. Calcutta, Firma K.L.M. Pvt. Ltd.

1234. Ruhemann, : The relationship terms of some

Barbara 1948 Hill Tribes of Burma and Assam. *South Western Journal of Anthropology*., 4 : 155-98.

1235. Rustomji, Nari 1971 : *Enchanted Frontiers : Sikkim, Bhutan and India's North East Frontier*. Bombay, Oxford University Press, 333p.

1236. ———, 1983 : *Imperilled Frontiers*. Delhi, Oxford University Press.

1237. ———, (*Ed.*) 1990 : *Verrier Elwin : Philanthropologist, Selected Writings*. Bombay, Oxford University Press.

S

1238. Sage Publications, 1989 : *State Elections in India, 1952-'85, vol. 3, the East and North east (including Sikkim).* New Delhi, Sage Publicatiohs, 702p.

1239. Saha, Manik, 1989 : Letters to the Editor : Jhum Cultivation. *The Assam Tribune,* May 29 : 4 (3-4).

1240. Saha N. *and* M.Barkataky, 1968 : *Hmnupi : A Socio Economic Survey of a Mizo Village in Assam.* Jorhat, Agro Economic Research Centre (*Mimeo.*)

1241. Saha, Niranjan *and* Murulidhar Barkataky, 1969 : Hmunpui (A Mizo village). (*In*) *Rural Life in Assam Hills : Case Rtudies of Four Villages.* Jorhat, Agro Economic Research Centre : 235-94.

1336. Shaw, W. 1928 : Notes on the Thadou Kukis. *Proc. Roy. As. Soc. Beng.*, (*N.S.*), Vol. 24, Appendix-H : 159-62.

1337. Shillong Times 1984 : North Eastern Affairs : Chakmas Get Hell in Mizoram Border. *The Shillong Times*, July 14 : 2.

1338. ———, 1986 : Editorial : Mizo Talks in Final Round. *The Shillong Times*, March 15 : 2(1-2).

1339. ———, 1986 : Editorial : Stagrant Mizo Talks. *Shillong Times*, May 24 : 2(1-2).

1340. ———, 1987 : Election Bell Rings in Mizoram. *Shillong Times*, January 17 : 1(1-2).

1341. ———, 1987 : Editorial : The Chakma Problem. *Shillong Times*, January 17 : 2(1-2).

1342. ———, 1988 : Uncertainty Looms Large Over Mizoram, *Shillong Times*, Sept. 2 : 1(2-3).

1343. ———, 1989 : North East is not a Haven for Drugs Peddlers. *Shillong Times*, March 18 : 5(1-4), 6(4).

1344. ———, 1989 : Lalthanhawla Refutes Poll Rigging Allegation. *Shillong Times*, April 15 : 2(5-6), 3(4).

1345. ———, 1989 : Editorial : Jhuming Reconsidered. *Shillong Times*, June 2 : 2(1-2).

1346. ———, 1989 : Mizo Mountaineers Felicitated. *Shillong Times*, June 15 : 4(2).

1347. ———, 1989 : NH 44 to be Converted into 4 Way Lane. *Shillong Times*, July 14 : 1(1).

1251. Sailo, L.F., 1972 : Circumstances Leading to the Reorganisation of Mizoram. Proceedings of a Seminar on *Reorganisation of North East India*, held in 1972 at Union Christian College, Barapani, Shillong. (*Mimeo.*)

1252. Sailo, Thenphunga, 1974 : Letters to the Editor : Human Rights Committee, Mizoram. *North Eastern Affairs*, 3 (1), April-June : 4.

1253. ———, 1968 : *Village Grouping : A Misguided Cenceal (A Pamphlet)*.

1254. Sailo, T., 1974 : *Memorandum submitted to the Prime Minister of India*. Aizawl, (October).

1255. ———, 1980 : Problem of the North East : A Fresh Look. *Himalaya : Man and Nature*, 4 (6), Nov. : 7-8.

1256. ———, 1981 : *Speeches and Writings*. Aizawl, Directorate of Information and Public Relations.

1257. ———, 1988 : *Customary Laws of the Luseis*. (*Unpublished*) Dissertation for M.Phil, History Deptt., NEHU, Shillong, under Dr. M.S.Sangma.

1258. Sanajaoba, Naorem (*Ed.*) 1990 : *Manipur : Treaties and Documents (1110-1971)*, (two volumes). Delhi, Mittal Publications (*in Press.*)

1259. Sandys, E.F., 1917 : Indian Nobility (Tripura). (*In*) *Bengal, Assam, Behar and Orissa* (*Comp.*) by Somerset Playne. London, Foreign and Colonial.

Times, Oct. 16 : 2(1). [Meghalaya : *Chakma*].

1359. ———. 1989 : Editorial : Failure of an Experiment. *Shillong Times*, Oct. 17 : 2(1-2).

1360. ———, 1989 : Jampui Mizos Plan their Own self Government. *Shillong Times*, Dec. 29 : 3(1-2) [Tripura : *Mizo*].

1361. ———, 1990 : I' Card for all Border States. *Shillong Times*, Feb. 6 : 1(4).

1362. ———, 1990 : NE Cultural Meet at Aizawl. *Shillong Times*, Feb. 8 : 3(1-2).

1363. ———, 1990 : Centre Defends Appointment of Mizoram Governor. *Shillong Times*. Feb. 13 : 1(1).

1364. ———, 1990 : Editorial : New Governors *Shillong* Feb. 13: 2(1-2).

1365. ———, 1990 : Capt. Sangma's Appeal to Hmars for Abjuring Violence. *Shillong Times*, Feb. 16 : 3 (1-2) [Meghalaya : *Hmars*].

1366. ———, 1990 : Jampui Mizos up in Arms. *Shillong Times* April 25 : 3 (1-3) [Tripura : *Mizo*].

1367. ———, 1990 : Editorial : The Hmar Case. *Shillong Times*, May 1 : 2 (1-2).

1368. ———, 1990 : Editorial : Forest Cover on Decline. *Shillong Times*, June 16 : 2 (1-2).

1369. ———, 1990 : NE States to Formulate Joint Tourism Development Plan. *Shillong Times*, June 26 : 3 (1-2).

1267. Sangliana, Z.D. 1970 : Mizo Democratic Party. *Zoramthupuan* (Mizo Daily from Aizawl), Feb. suary 28, 1970,

1268. Sanglura, A., 1978 : The Impact of Christianity on the Mizo Culture, Politics and Society. *Mizoram Today* : III (I) : 19-20.

1269. Saprawangana, Ch., 1939 : *Letter : Addressed to Mr. L.L. Peters, Supdt Lushai Hills dated 13th July 1939, London.* (It is available in the Office of the Deputy Commissioner, Mizo Hills, Aizawl).

1270. Saprawnga, Ch., n.p. : *Mizo Political Thought. (Unpublished Mss.)*

1271. ———, 1967 : Factors Contributing to the Mizo Problem. *Tribal Mirror* (Karimganj), III.

1272. Saraf, Samarendra, 1969 : Tribal Unrest : An Urgent Research problem. *Bulletin of the Cultural Research Institute* (Calcutta), VIII (1-2) : 32-7.

1273. Sarin, S., 1975 : Tackling Mizo Problem (Editorial). *North Eastern Affairs*, 3 (4), January-March : 7-8.

1274. Sarin, Vik, 1980 : *India's North East in Flames.* New Delhi, Vikas Publishing House : 141-66.

1275. Sarkar, J.N., 1944 : *History of Bengal*, vol. II. Dacca.

1276. Sarkar, S.S., Usha Deka *and* Agarwal, K.K., 1955 : Brachycephaly in India. *Man in India*, 35 (4), Oct.-Dec. : 257-73

1382. ———, 1990 : Editorial : End of a Romantic Career. *Shillong Times*, July 18 ; 2 (1-2).

1383. ———, 1990 ; Rokamlova Elected Speaker of Mizoram Assembly, *Shillong Times*, July 18 : 3(2).

1384. Sbrikant, L.M., 1961 : Tribal Welfare Under Panchayati Raj. *Vanyajati*, IX (4), Oct. : 136-44.

1385. Shukla, B.P., 1980 : *What Ails India's North East ?* New Delhi, Suruchi Sahitya,

1386. Shukla, S.P. and A.K. Agarwal, 1983 : The Magnitude of the Problem of Agricultural Labour in the N.E. Region. *Jour. NEICSSR*, 7 (1), April : 34-8.

1387. Shwe Mang Ling, 1960 : Haka Hram Thawkehnak. *Hill Chin Students' Union's Annual Magazine* (Rangoon), Haka Section : 21-4.

1388. Siama, V.L. (*Ed.*), 1975 : *Mizo History*. Aizawl, Lalrinliana and Sons. 65p.

1389. Singh, Ajay, 1986 : Laldenga story. *Hindustan Times* August 31.

1390. Singh, B.P., 1987 : *The Problems of Change : A Study of North East India*. Delhi, Oxford University Press.

1391. Singh, G.P., 1990 : *The Kiratas in Ancient India*. Delhi, Gian Publishing House.

1392. Singh. Jhaljit, 1962 : *History of Wampur*. Imphal, O.K.Store, (1965), 67p.

1393. Singh, Jogendra P., : Levels of Human Resources in

North East India. *Weed Research*, 24 : 138-42.

1286. Scott, J. *and* J.P. Hardiman, 1900 : *Gazetteer of Upper Burma and the Shan States, vol. I, pt. I* Rangoon: 437 p.

1287. Seletthanga, 1978 : *Pi Pu Lenlai*. Aizawl, Lianchhungi Book Store, 25p. (*in Mizo*).

1288. Seminar, 1990 : The North East. *Seminar* (New Delhi), No. 366, February, 67p.

1289. Sen, Debasis, 1984 : Early History of the Lushai with a special reference to Lushai Chiefs. *Social Research* (Shillong), 4 (3-4), July-Dec. 13-7.

1290. ———, 1989 : A British Expedition against Burmese tribes : Pre-Assam Administrative phase. *Proceedings of North East India History Association* (*Shilloug*), *Xth Annual Session, October 12-14*, (*Mimeo*).

1291. Sen, Jyoti, 1978 : Status of women among the Tribes, (*In*) *Tribal Women in India* by Committee. Calcutta, Indian Anthropological Society : 26-31.

1292. Sen, Sipra, 1985 : *The Tribes of Meghalaya*. Delhi Mittal Publications.

1293. ———, 1986 : *Arunachal Pradesh and The Tribes*. Delhi, Gian Publication.

1294. ———, 1987 : *Tribes of Nagaland*. Delhi, Mittal Publications.

1295. ———, 1991 : *Tribes And Castes of Manipur*. Delhi, Mittal Publications.

1296. Sen, Soumen (*Ed.*) 1985 : *Floklore in North East India*. Delhi, Omsons Publications.

1297. Sen, Sumanta 1985 : 'Shanti Sena' to be revived (MNF Treaty), *Times of India*, November 8 : 1.

1298. Sen, S.N. 1957 : *Eighteen Fifty Seven*. Delhi, pub. by author.

1299. Sengupta, Anil Kumar, 1966 : Some important legends of the Hmars. *Folklore*, 7(4) : 123-30.

1300. ———, 1969 : Lushai-Kuki Clans : Re-Examined. *Eastern Anthropologist*, 22(3), Sept.-Dec. : 349-58.

1301. Sengupta, N.N. 1985 : Walango of Mizoram. Proceedings of a workshop-Seminar on National Project '*People of India*', December 6, 1985, 2nd Session, Shillong, Anthropological Survey of India (*Mimeo.*)

1302. ———, 1986 : Pawi/Poi of Mizoram. Proceedings of a workshop-Seminar on National Project "*People of India*" December 6, 1985, 2nd Session, Shillong, Anthropological Survey of India (*Mimeo*).

1303. Sen Gupta, P. 1970 : *Census of India, pt. IX, Census Atlas*. Delhi, Manager of Publications.

1304. Sengupta, S. 1972 : Village study as a tool of study in tribai areas. (*In*) *Socio-Economic Research in Tribal Areas*, (*Ed.*) by P.C. Goswami. Jorhat, Agro Economic Research Centre : 106-111.

1305. Serto, Romeo *et al.* (*Eds.*) 1986 : *In search of Identity.* Imphal Kuki Chin Baptist Union, 66p.

1306, Shafer, R. 1952 : Phonetick der alt-Kuki-Mundaten. *Zeitchrift der Duetschen Morgenlandischen Gosellshaft wies baden*, vol. 102 : 262-79.

1307. ——, 1955 : The Sino-Tibetan Languages. *Word*, 11(1) : 94-111.

1308. Shaha, Brojo Nath, 1884 : *A Grammar of the Lushai Language, to which are appended a few illustrations of the Zau of Lushai popular songs and translations from Aesop's fables.* Calcutta, Bengal Secretariat Press, 94p.

1309. Shah, S.A., 1979 : Lesser known dimensions of forest productivity and production. *Himalaya : Man and Nature*, 3(5), Oct. : 33-7.

310. Shakespear, J. 1895 : Lusheis and the Land They Live In. *Jour. of the Royal Socity of Arts*, 43, Jan. : 167-88.

1311. ——, 1898 : *Mizo leh vai then thu* (*folk tales*). Shillong Assam Secretariat Printing Office, 32p.

1312. ——, 1898 : Note on some tribal and family names employed in speaking of the inhabitants of the Lushai Hills. *Jour. of Roy. As Soc. Bengal*, 67, pt. 3 : 116-17.

1313. ——, 1903 : The Lushai. (*In*) *Census of India 1901, vol, I, India, Ethnographic*

Appendices. Simla, Govt, Press, 229p.

1314. ———. 1903 : Notes on the Lushais. (*In*) *Census of India 1901, vol. IV, Assam.* Calcutta, Supdt, Govt. Printing : 145-51 (*Part-I, Report*).

1315. ———, 1909 : Folk-tales of the Lushais and their Neighbours. *Folklore,* R 20(4)-338-420 (Illustrated, with "*Notes*" by T.C. Hodson)

1316. ———, 1909 : The Kuki-Lushai Clans (Manipur and Chittagong). *Jour. of the Royal Anthropological Institute* 39 : 371-85.

1317. ———, 1912 : *The Lushai Kuki Clans.* London, Macmillan & Co., 250p. (*Reprinted* by Firma L.K. Mukhopadhyay, Calcutta on behalf of Tribal Research Institute, Aizawl in 1976 in Part I and Part II separately).

1318. ———, 1912 : Customs at death among the Manipuris and cognate clans. *Folk-Lore,* XXIII(IV).

1319. ———, 1929 : Lushai Reminiscences. *Assam Review,* October, (1928), Jan.-July. (1929).

1320. ———, 1939 : The Making of Aijal : Letter from Lt. Col. J. Shakespear (13th July 1939, London), (*In*) *Church & Political Upheaval in Mizoram* by John Vanlal Hluna. Aizawl, Mizo History Association (1985) 142-56.

1321. ———, 1939 : *Letter Addressed to Mr. L.L. Peter Supdt. Lushai Hills, dated 13th July 1939*. (It is available in the Office of the Deputy Commissioner, Aizawl District, Mizoram).

1322. ——— 1975, : *The Lnshai Kuki Clans, Pt. I, and Pt. II*. Aizawl, Tribal Research Institute (*Reprinted*). *Reprinted* Again in 1983 by Cultural Pub. House, Delhi, 250p.]

1323. ———, 1976 : *A Short Account of Kuki Lushai Tribes*. Calcutta, Firma K.L.M. Pvt. Ltd. on Behalf of Tribal Research Institute, Aizawl (*Reprinted*).

1324. ———, 1980 : *Collections on Some Interesting Correspondences on Mizoram*. Calcutta, Firma K.L.M. Pvt. Ltd. Published on Behalf of Tribal Research Inst., Aizawl.

1325. Shakespear, L.W. 1906 : *Military Report on the Naga Hills*. Simla, Govt. Press, 19p. (*2nd Edition*) published in 1913 from Simla with 39p.)

1326. ———, 1914 : *History of Upper Assam, Upper Burmah and North-Eastern Frontier*. London, Macmillan & Co., 272p.

1327. ———, 1929 : *History of the Assam Rifles*, London, Macmillan (*Reprinted* in 1981 by Spectrum Publications, Gauhati), 301p. (*Reprinted* also by Tribal Research Institute, Aizawl through Firma K.L.M., Pvt. Ltd., Calcutta in 1977)

1328. Sharma, Abhimanyu, 1955 : Notes on Kachin Kinship and Linguistic Categories. *The Anthropologist*, 2(2) : 55-62

1329. Sharma, B.D. 1985 : Eco Development in Bastar and North Eastern Hill Areas. *South Asian Anthropologist* (Ranchi), 6(1), March : 49-61.

1330. ———, 1989 : Shifting Cultivators and their Development. (*In*) *North East Hill University Journal of Social Sciences and Humanities*, April-June.

1331. Sharma, H. 1974 : *District Statistical Hand Book*. Imphal, Manipur South District.

1332. Sharma, Ranbir 1975 : The Politics of Statehood : A Search of Identity. *Political Science Review*, July-Sept. and Oct.-Dec., 1975.

1333. Sharma, Tarun Ch. 1986 : Recent Advances in Prehistory and Archaeology of North East India. *Jour. of the Assam Research Society*, XXVIII (1984-'85) : 1-28.

1334. Shastri, Dharma Dev, 1960 : Assam ke Mizo Jile men (*in Hindi*). *Vanyajati*, 8(2), April 81-4 and 106-09 of vol. 8(3), July, 1960.

1335. Shaw, William 1929 : *Notes on the Thadou Kukis*. (*Edited* with Introductory Notes, Appendices, Illustrations and Index by J.H. Hutton). Calcutta, Asiatic Society of Bengal on Behalf of the Govt. of Assam, 175p. (7 plates, tables, map etc.) [*Reprinted* in 1980 by TRI, Aizawl].

1336. Shaw, W. 1928 : Notes on the Thadou Kukis. *Proc. Roy. As. Soc. Beng.*, (*N.S.*), Vol. 24, Appendix-H : 159-62.

1337. Shillong Times 1984 : North Eastern Affairs : Chakmas Get Hell in Mizoram Border. *The Shillong Times*, July 14 : 2.

1338. ———, 1986 : Editorial : Mizo Talks in Final Round. *The Shillong Times*, March 15 : 2(1-2).

1339. ———, 1986 : Editorial : Stagrant Mizo Talks. *Shillong Times*, May 24 : 2(1-2).

1340. ———, 1987 : Election Bell Rings in Mizoram. *Shillong Times*, January 17 : 1(1-2).

1341. ———, 1987 : Editorial : The Chakma Problem. *Shillong Times*, January 17 : 2(1-2).

1342. ———, 1988 : Uncertainty Looms Large Over Mizoram, *Shillong Times*, Sept. 2 : 1(2-3).

1343. ———, 1989 : North East is not a Haven for Drugs Peddlers. *Shillong Times*, March 18 : 5(1-4), 6(4).

1344. ———, 1989 : Lalthanhawla Refutes Poll Rigging Allegation. *Shillong Times*, April 15 : 2(5-6), 3(4).

1345. ———, 1989 : Editorial : Jhuming Reconsidered. *Shillong Times*, June 2 : 2(1-2).

1346. ———, 1989 : Mizo Mountaineers Felicitated. *Shillong Times*, June 15 : 4(2).

1347. ———, 1989 : NH 44 to be Converted into 4 Way Lane. *Shillong Times*, July 14 : 1(1).

1348. ———, 1989 : Editorial : Hmars' Move for Autonomy. *Shillong Times*, Aug. 10 : 2(1-2).

1349. ———, 1989 : Editorial : MNF to Join NF. *Shillong Times*, Aug. 22 : 2(1-2).

1350. ———, 1989 : Pawi District Council CEM Voted out of Power. Shillong Times, Aug. 22 : 3(3).

1351. ———, 1988 : Editorial : Mizoram Ministerial Crisis. *Shillong Times*, Sept. 2 : 2(1-2).

1352. ———, 1989 : TNCF Advocates United Struggle. *Shillong Times*, Sept. 22 : 3(5-6). [*Zoro*].

1353. ———, 1989 : Journalists' Conference Ends : Concern over Proposed Mizoram Press Bill. *Shillong Times*, Sept. 25 : 1(2-4).

1354. ———, 1989 : To The Editor : Arunachal's Harassment of Chakmas by an Affected Chakma. *Shillong Times*, Sept. 26 : 2(5-6).

1355. ———, 1989 : Insurgents Active in Narcotics Trade in Burma Border. *Shillong Times*, Oct. 4 : 3(2-3).

1356. ———, 1989 : NE States Need Special Economic Norms. *Shillong Times*, Oct. 5 : 3(4).

1357. ———, 1989 : Invitation Football : Aizawl Lifts Trophy. *Shillong Times*, Oct. 12 : 4(4).

1358. ———, 1989 : Chakma Students' Union. *Shillong*

Times, Oct. 16 : 2(1). [Meghalaya : *Chakma*].

1359. ———. 1989 : Editorial : Failure of an Experiment. *Shillong Times*, Oct. 17 : 2(1-2).

1360. ———, 1989 : Jampui Mizos Plan their Own self Government. *Shillong Times*, Dec. 29 : 3(1-2) [Tripura : *Mizo*].

1361. ———, 1990 : I' Card for all Border States. *Shillong Times*, Feb. 6 : 1(4).

1362. ———, 1990 : NE Cultural Meet at Aizawl. *Shillong Times*, Feb. 8 : 3(1-2).

1363. ———, 1990 : Centre Defends Appointment of Mizoram Governor. *Shillong Times*. Feb. 13 : 1(1).

1364. ———, 1990 : Editorial : New Governors *Shillong* Feb. 13: 2(1-2).

1365. ———, 1990 : Capt. Sangma's Appeal to Hmars for Abjuring Violence. *Shillong Times*, Feb. 16 : 3 (1-2) [Meghalaya : *Hmars*].

1366. ———, 1990 : Jampui Mizos up in Arms. *Shillong Times* April 25 : 3 (1-3) [Tripura : *Mizo*].

1367. ———, 1990 : Editorial : The Hmar Case. *Shillong Times*, May 1 : 2 (1-2).

1368. ———, 1990 : Editorial : Forest Cover on Decline. *Shillong Times*, June 16 : 2 (1-2).

1369. ———, 1990 : NE States to Formulate Joint Tourism Development Plan. *Shillong Times*, June 26 : 3 (1-2).

1370. ——, 1990 : NE States Demand Inner Lines Permit Withdrawal. *Shillong Times* July 4 : 1 (3-4).

1371. ——, 1990 : Mizo Pastor Holds Prestigious NCCI post. *Shillong Times*. July 6 : 3(6).

1372. ——, 1990 : Laldenga Dies in London. *Shillong Times*, July 8 : 1 (2-3), 4(5).

1373. ——, 1990 : Rajiv characterises Laldenga as True Patriot. *Shillong Times*, July 9 : 1 (2-3).

1374. ——, 1990 : New MNF Chief. *Shillong Times*, July 10 : 1(3).

1375. ——, 1990 : State Funeral for Laldenga on July 12. *Shillong Times*, July 10 : 1(4).

1376. ——, 1990 : Editorial Laldenga. Shillong *Times* July 10 : 4(1-2).

1377. ——, 1990 : Fernandes to Attend Funeral of Laldenga. *Shillong Times*, July 11 : 1 (1).

1378. ——, 1990 : President, PM Pay Pomage to Laldenga. *Shillong Times*, July 12 : 1 (4).

1379. ——, 1990 : Editorial : Lawlessness in Border Areas. *Shillong Times*, July 12 : 2 (1-2).

1380. ——, 1990 : JD Leader Urges Dispersal of Cha kma Refugees. *Shillong Times*, July 12 : 3 (1-2).

1381. ——, 1990 : Laldenga Laid to Rest. *Shillong Times*, July 14 : 1(2), 4 (6).

1382. ———, 1990 : Editorial : End of a Romantic Career. *Shillong Times*, July 18 : 2 (1-2).

1383. ———, 1990 : Rokamlova Elected Speaker of Mizoram Assembly, *Shillong Times*, July 18 : 3(2).

1384. Shrikant, L.M., 1961 : Tribal Welfare Under Panchayati Raj. *Vanyajati*, IX (4), Oct. : 136-44.

1385. Shukla, B.P., 1980 : *What Ails India's North East?* New Delhi, Suruchi Sahitya,

1386. Shukla, S.P. and A.K. Agarwal, 1983 : The Magnitude of the Problem of Agricultural Labour in the N.E. Region. *Jour. NEICSSR*, 7 (1), April : 34-8.

1387. Shwe Mang Ling, 1960 : Haka Hram Thawkehnak. *Hill Chin Students' Union's Annual Magazine* (Rangoon), Haka Section : 21-4.

1388. Siama, V.L. (*Ed.*), 1975 : *Mizo History*. Aizawl, Lalrinliana and Sons. 65p.

1389. Singh, Ajay, 1986 : Laldenga story. *Hindustan Times* August 31.

1390. Singh, B.P., 1987 : *The Problems of Change : A Study of North East India*. Delhi, Oxford University Press.

1391. Singh, G.P., 1990 : *The Kiratas in Ancient India*. Delhi, Gian Publishing House.

1392. Singh. Jhaljit, 1962 : *History of Wampur*. Imphal, O.K.Store, (1965). 67p.

1393. Singh, Jogendra P., : Levels of Human Resources in

1980 North East India. *Jour. NEICSSR*, IV (II), Oct. : 1-6.

1394. Singh, Kunj Bihari, 1964 : Traces of Pre-Hinduism in the Meitei Society. *Folklore*, 5 (6), June : 201-06.

1395. Singh, K.M., 1990 : *History of Christian Missions in Manipnr and Other Neighbouring States*. New Delhi, Mittal Publications.

1396. Singh, K. Suresh, 1972 : General Background and Situation in North East India, (*In*) *Tribal Situation in India : Proceedings of a Seminar*, (*Ed.*) by K.Suresh Singh. Simla, Indian Institute of Advanced Stud : 534-40.

1397. ———, 1972 : Integration and Understanding in the North East, (*In*) *Tribal Situation in India : Proceedings of a Seminar*, (*Ed.*) by K. Suresh Singh. Simla, Indian Institute of Advanceed Studys : 616-24.

1398. Singh, K.S. (*Ed.*), 1982 : The Post Script, (*In*) *Tribal Movements in India, vol. I.* New Delhi, Manohar Publications, 361p.

1399. ———, 1989 : Research Note : Ethnicity and Polity Formation in Tribal India. *Human Science*, 38 (1), March : 77-82.

1400. ———, (*Ed.*), 1990 : Computer Diskette on All the Communities in India with Four Volumes on *Specific Communities and a Bio-antpropological Survey* (2nd Oct. 1990). Delhi, Anth.

Surv. of India, (*People of India*, National Project).

1401. Singh, Prakash, 1972 : *India, the Land and People : Nagaland.* New Delhi, National Book Trust (India) : 125, 132, 162. (*Kuki*).

1402. Singh, P.P., 1975 : Aizawl Outrage : Letters to the Editor. *North Eastern Affairs*, 3(4), Jan.-March : 5.

1403. Singh, Ram Gopal, 1985 : *The Kukis of Tripura : A Socio-Economic Survey.* Agartala. Directorate of Research, 58p.

1404. Singh, R.K. Ranjit, 1982 : Problems of Ethnic Identity Among the Tribes of Manipur During the Post-Independence Period, (*In*) *India's North East : A Multi-faceted View*, (*Ed.*) by Pankaj Thakur. Tinsukia, Prakash Publishing House : 197-208.

1405. ———, 1990 : Emergent Ethnic Processes in Manipur : A Reappraisal, (*In*) *Nationality, Ethnicity and Cultural Identity in North East India*, (*Ed.*) by B. Pakem. New Delhi, Omsons Publications : 233-251.

1406. Singh Suryavanshi, Bhagwan, 1959 : Romances in the Tribals. Indian Folklore, 2(III), July-Sept. : 223-25.

1407. Singh, S.J. 1933 : Habitations of the Maitais. *Man in India*, 13 : 165-88.

1408. Sinha, A.P. 1972 : Politics and Economic Development in the Hill Districts of Assam, (*In*) *Tribal Situation in*

India : Proceedings of a Seminar, (*Ed.*) by K. Suresh Singh, Simla, Indian Institute of Advanced Study : 336-51.

1409. Sinha, Kamaleshwar, 1970 : *Meghalaya*. Delhi. Publication Division : 92-103, 168-69.

1410. Sinha, M, 1990. : Fishing in the Fallow N-E. *Amrita Bazar Patrika*, July 31 : 7(3-6).

1411. Sinha, Surajit, 1970 : Study of Tribal Solidarity Movements : General Proposition, (*In*) *Research Programme on Cultural Anthropology & Allied Disciplines*. Calcutta, Anthropological Survey of India.

1412. ———, 1972 : Tribal Solidarity Movement in India : A Review, (*In*) *Tribal Situation in India*, (*Ed.*) by K. Suresh Singh. Simla, Indian Institute of Advanced Study.

1413. Soil Conservation 1973 : *Scheme for Permanent Settlement of Jhumia Cultivators Through Development of Plantation Crops by Fifth Year Plan, 1974-'75 to 1978-'79*. Gauhati, Soil Conservation Deptt., Assam [September].

1414. Som, Tapan Kumar, 1989 : Book Review : Homeless Since Partition, '*The Chakmas : Life and Struggle*' by S.P. Talukdar, Gian Publishing House, 29/6, Shakti Nagar, Delhi-110007, Rs. 150/-. *Amrita Bazar Patrika* (*Sunday Magazine*) : 2 (5-7).

1415. Songate, Hranglien, 1956 : *Hmar Chanchin.* Imphal, Mao Press.

1416. ———, 1977 : *Hmar Chanchin* (Hmar History). Churachandpur, Manipur (*Reprinted*).

1417. Soppitt, C.A., 1884 : *A Short Account of the Kuki and Lushai Tribes on the N.E. Frontier.* Shillong, Govt. Press.

1418. ———, 1885 : *A Short Account of the Kachcha (Empeo) Tribe, in the North Cachar Hills, with an Outline Grammar, Vocabulary and Illustrative Sentences.* Shillong, Assam Secretariat Press.

1419. ———, 1887 : *A Short Account of the Lushai Kuki Tribe of the North East Frontier (Cachar, Sylhet, Naga Hills etc. and the North Cachar Hills), with an Outline Grammar of the Rangkhol Lushai Language and a Comparison of Lushai with other Dialects.* Shillong, Assam Secretariat Press, 88p. (*Reprinted*) in 1978 by Firma K. L. M. Pvt. Ltd., Calcutta on behalf of Tribal Research Institute, (Aizawl).

1420. Spearman, H.R., 1880 : *The British Burma Gazetteer, vol. 1.* Rangoon, Govt. Press.

1421. Special Report, 1978 : Special Report, Insurgency : Trouble in the Hills. *India Today* June 16-30.

1422. Spiro, M.E., 1967 : Burmese Supernaturalism. *N.J.* : 247-80.

1423. Spolia, Kamla, 1984 : Women of Mizoram. *MNM*, 1, August : 56-9.

1424. Srivastava, A.K., 1987 : Incidence of Left-handedness Among Mizo Children : Examining Ecology and Urbanisation Effects. *Personality Study and Group Behaviour*, 5 : 33-44.

1425. Srivastava, Ashok Kumar, 1989 : A Study on Field Dependence : Independence Among Mizo Children. *P S : Psychological Studies* (Calicut, Kerala), 34 (1), March : 55-8.

1426. Srivastava, A.K. and C. Lalbiaknungi, 1988 : Culture and hand preference : A Study of Mizos. *Jour. of Cross Cultural Psychology*.

1427. Srivastava, S.C., 1987 : *Demographic Profile of North East India*. New Delhi, Mittal Publications.

1428. State Bank of India, 1972 : *Lead Bank Scheme : Survey Report on Mizoram*. Shillong, State Bank of India, (May).

1429. Statesman, 1952 : Mizoram. *The Statesman*, Nov. 10 (*Editorial Page*).

1430. ———, 1966 : Lushai Hills. *The Statesman*, March 4.

1431. ———, 1966 : Mizo Hills District. *The Statesman*, March 6.

1432. ———, 1966 : What happened in the Mizo Hills. *The Statesman*, April 18.

1433. ———, 1983 : Chakma Influx a Political Issue in in Mizoram. *The Statesman*, July 1.

1434. ———, 1985 : Mizoram to Restrict Area Under Jhum Cultivation. *The Statesman* Feb. 23 : 4.

1435. ———, 1988 : Mizoram : Era of Peace and Progress, (1st Anniversary of its Statehood). *The Statesman*, Feb. 20 : 7 (1-8).

1436. ———, 1988 : MNF to Join National Front. *The Statesman*, Aug. 15 : 9 (2-4).

1437. ———, 1989 : Mizoram's Problem Economy. *The Statesman*, April 4 : 7 (2).

1438. ———, 1989 : Nagaland and Mizoram Against General Act. *The Statesman*, April 4 : 9 (6-7).

1439. ———, 1989 : Hmar Youths Clash with Mizo Police. *The Statesman*, May 30 : 4 (3-4).

1440. ———, 1989 : Mizoram Group to Intensify Campaign. *The Statesman*, June 13 : 4 (1) (Hmar).

1441. ———, 1988 : Laldenga Says He is Still in Control. *The Statesman*, August 31 : 1 (2-3).

1442. ———, 1989 : Centre Urged to Take up Chakma Issue with Dhaka. *The Statesman*, July 10 : 9 (3-5).

1443. ———, 1989 : Worst Landslides in Mizoram in 60 years. *The Statesman*, August 3 : 1 (7-8).

1444. ———, 1989 : Chakma Repatriation Uncertain. *The Statesman*, August 7 : 9 (2-4).

1445. ———, 1989 : Mizoram Trying to Grab Cachar

Areas. *The Statesman*, August 10 : 4 (2-4).

1446. ———, 1989 : Laldenga's Legend Beginning to Fade. *The Statesman*, Sept. 18 : 9 (5-7).

1447. ———, 1989 : Laldenga Calls on V.P. *The Statesman*, Dec. 10 : 7 (4-6).

1448. ———, 1990 : The Iron Horse Travels to the North East. *The Statesman*, January 15 : 11 (2-4). [Railway, Mizoram].

1449. ———, 1990 : Burmese Troops Seize Karen Rebels' Base. *The Statesman, Sunday Miscelany*, Feb. 4 : 5 (2-5).

1450. ———, 1990 : Mtzo Party. *The Statesman*, Feb. 10 : 9 (1).

1451. ———, 1990 : 'Burma Road' Turned into Heroin Route. *The Statesman*, April 2 : 5 (1-2).

1452. ———, 1990 : Mizo Youths Threaten Militant Agitation. *The Statesman*, April 3 : 7 (7-8).

1453. ———, 1990 : Mizoram Speaker to Contest Poll. *The Statesman*, June 26 : 4 (1).

1454. ———, 1990 : Obituary : Laldenga. *The Statesman*, July 8 : 9 (5).

1455. ———, 1990 : System Forced Laldenga to Choose Violence : Fernandes. *The Statesman*, July 14 : 14 (3-5).

1456. Statistical & Economic Deptt., 1979 : *Statistical Hand Book of Mizoram*, Aizawl, Statistical and Economic Deptt.

1457. ———, 1985 : *Chhimtuipui District At a Glance, 1985*. Saiha, Dist. Statistical Office.

1458. ———, 1985 : *Statistical Hand Book of Mizoram, 1985*. Aizawl, Statistical and Ecomics Deptt.

1459. Sten, H.W., 1973 : Why Some Nagas and Mizos Become Rebels. *Himalaya News Round Up* (New Delhi), 2 (3) March : 6-7.

1460. Stern, T., 1955 : A Provisional Sketch of Sizang (Siyin) Chin. *Eugene. Ore. State Museum of Anthropology*, University of Oregon, 56p.

1461. ———, 1957 : Resin Glazed Pottery in the Chin Hills. *American Anthropologist*, 59 (4) : 511-14.

1462. Stevens, E., 1836 : A Description of Assam : Extent and Boundaries of its Three Principal Divisions, with notes of the States and Tribes Bordering of the North and South. *Chinese Repository*, 5 : 49-55, 97-104.

1463. Stevenson, H.N.C., 1943 : *The Economics of the Central Chin Tribes*. Bombay, Times of India Press for Govt. of Burma (*in Exile*). [*Reprinted* in 1987 by TRI, Aizawl).

1464. ———, 1944 : *The Hill Peoples of Burma, Pamphlet No. 6*). London, Longmans Green & Co.

1465. Stewart, R., 1855 : Notes on Northern Cachar. *J.A.S.B.*, XXIV (7) : 617-49, 656-75, 685-91.

1552. Vanlalauvi, 1988 : *The Traditional Mizo Society*. (*Unpublished*) M. Phil Dissertation, History Deptt. NEHU, Shillon under Dr. M.S. Sangma

1553. Vanlawma, R. (*Ed.*), 1965 : *Ka Ram leh kei* Aizawl, Zalen Printing House, 79p (*2nd Edition* Pub. in 1972 with 196p.) [*in Mizo*].

1554. ———, (*Ed.*), 1972 : *My Country and I.* Aizawl, Zalen Printing House (*in Mizo*).

1555. ——— (*Ed.*), 1985 : Who and What are the Mizos ? *Mizoram News Magazine.* Issue No. 23.

5556. Vanthanga and Zemana, 1978 : From the Underground : Mizo National Army Version (Announced to the Mizo National Army personnel). (*In*) *The Mizo Dilemma* by Amit Kumar Nag. Silchar, Tribal Mirror Publications (1984): 57-72.

1557. Vara, V. Hmar, 1967 : *Hmar Hla Hlui Bu* (Collection of Traditional Songs of *Hmar*). Churachandpur, Manipur.

1558. Verma, B.,1988 : *Insurgency and Counter Insurgency.* New Delhi, Uppal Publishing House.

1559. Vickers, A., 1927 : Among the Kukis. *Blackwood's Magazine.*

1560. Vidya, Binode *and* Padma Nath, ? : *A Critical Study of Gait's History of Assam.* Sylhet.

1561. Vidyarthi, L.P., 1975 : The Future of Traditional "Primitive" Societies : A Case Study of

1476. Swami, K.S.K., 1965 : Tea : An International Beverage. *Mirror* (Bomboy), IV (12), October.

1477. Sword, V.H., 1935 : *Baptists in Assam : A Century of Missionary Service, 1836-1936.* Chicago.

1478. Syam Choudhuri, N.K., 1967 : Anthropology and the Tribes of Assam. (*In*) *A Commn Perspective for North East India,* (*Eds.*) by Rathin Mitra and B. Das Gupta. Calcutta, Pannalal Das Gupta : 58-63.

1479. Syam Choudhuri, N.K. and S.K. Biswas, 1963 : A Trait of Making Earthen Wares in the Mizo District and its Cultural Evaluation in Assam. *Bulletin : Anthropological Survey of India,* XII (1-2), January-June : 57-64.

1480. Syam Choudhury, N.K., 1968 : Tribal Solidarity Movement in Assam : An Appraisal of the Movement, (*In*) *Seminar on Research Programmes in Cultural Anthropology and Related Disci. pline,* (*Ed.*) by S.C. Sinha. Calcutta, Anthroplogical Survey of India.

T

1481. Talukdar, S.P. 1974 : The Place of Chakmas in Mizo Society. *North Eastern Affairs,* 3 (2-3). July-Dec. 27-8 and 34.

1482. Telford, J.H, 1937 : Animism in Kengtung State. *Jour. Burma Research Society* (Rangoon), XXVII, pt. 2, August : 135.

1483. Tewari, C.P. 1978 : Need for a New Model of Development for Hill Areas. *Himalaya Man & Nature,* 1(11), April : 25-7.

1484. Thakkar, A.V. 1941 : Census of Assam Tribals. *Man in India* XXI (4), Oct.-Dec. : 243-47.

1485. Thakur, Pankaj (Ed) 1982 : *India's North East.* Tinsukia Prakash Publishing House, Assam.

1486. Thangkhangin, S. Ngaihte, 1979 : *History of the Zomi of Mizoram and the Surrounding Areas : Aspects of Pre-Colonial Society.* (*Unpublished*) M. Phil Dissertation of Jawaharlal Nehru University, New Delhi.

1487. ———, 1980 : Comments, (*In*) *Discovery of Zoland* by T. Gougin. Churachandpur, Published by the Author (T. Cougin), Churachandpur, Zomi Press.

1488. ———, ? : *Colonial System of Indirect Rule : A Case Study of British Administration in Chin Lushai Country.* (*Unpublished*) Ph. D. Thesis, Jawaharlal Nehru University, New Delhi.

1489. Thangkhangin, S. 1980 : Why Should We be Called Zomi ? *Zomi Today*, Churachandpnr (Manipur).

1490. ———, 1986 : Why Should We be Called Zoumi, (*In*) *In search of Identity*, (*Eds.*) by H. Kamkhenthang et al. Imphal Kuki Chin Baptist Union 52-66.

1491. Toanglura, A., (Ed) 1983 : *Zoram Politic Lumlet Dan.* (*In Mizo*). Aizawl, Thakthing Bazar Press.

1492. Tiankham, T.C. 1948 : *English Paite Manipuri Word Book.* Imphal, Pub. by the Author.

1493. Thanga, L.B., 1971 : An Episode from the History of the Mizos. *Pines* (Shillong), 1 (1), March : 33-9.

1494. Thanga Lal, Biak 1977 : The Mizos. *The North Eastern Spectrum*, II(I), July : 29-37.

1495. Thanga, L.B. 1978 : *The Mizos : A Study in Racial Per*

1583. Wolfenden, Stuart N., 1929 : *Outlines of Tibeto Burman Linguistic Morphology with Special Reference to the Prefixes, Inffixes and Suffixes of Glassical Tibetan and the Languages of the Kachin, Bodo, Naga, Kuki-Chin and Burma Groups*, London, Royal Asiatic Society, 216p. (*Royal Asiatic Society*, Prize Publication Fund, vol. 12).

1584. Wood, R., 1953 : The Hill Tribes of Assam. *Jour. of the Royal Asiatic Society of Bombay*, 28 : 187-214.

1585. Woodthorpe, R.G., 1873 : *The Lushai Expedition, 1871-1872.* London, Hurst and Blackett, 338p. (*Reprinted* by Spectrum Publications, Gauhati in 1980 and also, Firma K.L.M. Pvt. Ltd, Calcutta in 1978 on behalf of Tribal Research Institute, Aizawl.). 338p.

1586. ———, 1873 : *Report to Capt. Badgley, Officiating Deputy Superintendent i/c Survey with the Lushai Expedition : Extracts from Notes to Accompany Capt. Badgley's Report. General Report on the Operations of the Survey of India, 1871-72, Appendix-A.* London, Hurst & Blackett.

1587. ———, 1890 : The Lushai Country. *Jour. of United Services Inst.*, (Ind.). No. 79.

People. The *North Eastern Sepectrum*, 1 (1), July : 31-4.

1505. Thaosen, J.K., 1985 : Introduction. (*In*) *Kuki Life and Lore* by Tarun Goswami. Haflong, North Cachar Hills District Council : i-iii.

1506. Thatsavunga, A.H., 1979 : *Thu leh Hla*. Aizawl, Mizo Academy of Letters.

1507. Thawma, Sr. Capt. 1984 : *Mizoram Salvation Army Chauchin*. Aizawl, Pub. by the Author. (*in Mizo*) [*Mimeographed*] about History of Salvation Army in Mizoram.

1508. Thiangzau Zakaia Pawi, 1975 : *Zoram Kohhran Tual to Chanchin*. Aizawl.

1509. ———, ? : *Mizo Israel*.

1510. ———, ? : *Zoram Maicham*.

1511. ———, ? : *Zathungvunga Pawi*,

1512. ———, ? : *Isua Krista Kohhran*.

1513. Thiek, Sumhlihrwng, 1982 : Practice of Head Hunting Among the Hmar Tribe. *Proceedings of North East India History Association*, (Imphal) : 73-6.

1514. Thomas, M.M. and R.W. Taylor. (*Eds*), 1965 : *Tribal Awakening : A Group Study*. Bangalore.

1415. Thompson, W.H., 1923 : Chakma. (*In*) *Census of India 1921, vol. V, Bengal, pt.-I : Report*. Calcutta, Govt. Printing Press, 362p.

1516. Thongehinthang, ? : *Zokhang Simna.*

1517. Thought, 1967 : Mizo People. *Thought* (Delhi) Oct. 14.

1518. Thuama, 1971 : Nau Awih Hla (A Lullaby of the Mizos). *Pines* (Shillong), 1 (1), March : 91.

1519. Tiankham, T.C., 1980 : Foreward. (*In*) *Discovery of Zo-land by* T.Gougin. Churachandpur, Published by the Author, Printed at Zomi Press : iv.

1520. Tickell, S.R., 1853 : Notes on the Heuma or Shendoos, a Tribe Inhabiting the Hills North of Arakan. *Jour. Asiatic Society of Bengal*, XXI.

1521. T'ien Juk'ang, 1986 : *Religious Cults of the Pai-i Along the Burma Yunnan Border.* Ithaca (N.Y.), Cornell.

1522. Times of India, 1970 : Mizos. *The Times of India* (New Delhi), June 13.

1523. ———, 1972 : Mizo Rebel. *The Times of India*, January 3.

1524. ———, 1986 : Agreement Uncertain on Mizo Issue. *The Times of India*, March 12 : 1 (5).

1525. ———, 1986 : Status of Mizoram, The Main Issue. *The Times of India*, March 15 : 3 (4-5).

1526. ———, 1986 : Laldenga to Meet P.M. *The Times of India*, March 16 : 1 (3-5).

1527. ———, 1986 : Chittagong Hill Tribals Urge End to Colonisation. *The Times of India*, May 11 : 5 (1-2).

1528. Tiwari, S.P. and D.K. Chauhan, 1989 : Vanishing Floral Wealth and Necessity of a Green Museum in North East India. *Jour. of Indian Museums* (New Delhi), XLV : 32-40

1529. Tlangchhuaka, 1972 : *MNF Pawl Thil tumte Hrilhfiahna.* Aizawl, MNF Hqrs. (*in Mizo*).

1530. ———, 1973 : *Mizoram Politic Chanchin* (Booklet). Aizawl, Mizo National Front, 19p. [29th Sept. 1973].

1531. ———, (*Ed.*), 1974 : *Mizoram politics.*

1532. Toky, O.P. and P.S. Ramakrishnan. 1981 : Gropping and Yields in Agricultural System of the North Eastern Hill Region of India. (*In*) *Agro Eco Systems.* Amsterdam, Elsevier Scientific Publishing Company.

1533. Touche, Tom D. La. 1891 : Note on the Geology of the Lushai Hills. *Records of the Geological Survey of India*, XXIV, pt. 2.

1534. Touthang, L., n.p. : *Kuki-Chin : Search for an Identity.* Ph. D. Thesis (*in Progress*), History Deptt., NEHU, Shillong Under Dr. M.S. Sangma.

1535. Trant, T.A., 1827 : *Two Years in Ava.* London, John Murray.

1536. Tribal Research Institute, 1980 : *Collections on Some Interesting Correspondences on Mizoram. 1890-1896.* Calcutta, Firma K. L. M. Pvt. Ltd. Published on Behalf of Tribal Research Institute, Aizawl. (*Reprinted*).

1537. ———, 1978 : *Lushais and Manipoorees.* Aizawl, Tribal Research Institute (Mizoram) [*Reprinted*].

1538. ———, 1978 : *The Lushai 1878-1889. op. cit.* (*Reprinted*).

1539. ———, ? : *The Chief and his Administration. op. cit.* (*Mimeo.*)

1540. ———, ? : *Zawlbuk as a Social Institution in the Earlier Mizo Society. op. cit.* (*Mimeo.*)

1541. ———, ? : *Status of Women in the Earlier Mizo Society. op. cit.* (*Mimeo.*)

1542. Trong, Cam *and* U'ng, Hu'u, 1976 : Essay on the Evolution of the Thai Political System. *Ethnos,* 41 (I-IV) : 21-2.

1543. Turner, W., 1899 : Contributions to the Craniometry of the People of the Empire of India-I : The Hill Tribes of the North East Frontier and the People of Burma with Three Plates. *Trans. Roy. Soc.*, (*Edinb.*), 39. pt. III 703-47.

U

1544. University of Delhi, 1971 : *Sociology of North Eastern Hill Areas, (Proceedings of the 3rd Summer School, Kohima, 1973*]. [Centre of Advanced Study in Sociology), Delhi, University of Sociology, 41p.

1545. Upadhyay, Baldev, : Assam ke Adivasi (*In Hindi*). *Ajkal*, June : 37.

1546. Upadhyay, K.K., 1986 : *Development Problems and Prospects of Mizoram*. New Delhi, Inter India Publications, 64p.

V

1547. Vaasanthi, 1989 : *When Bamboo Blossoms*. (*Translated* from the Tamil Original by Gomathi Narayanan), Guwahati, Span Publications, 66p.

1548. Vaghaiwalla, R.B., 1952 : *Census of India 1951, Assam, District Census Hand Book, Lushai Hills*, Shillong, Assam Govt. Press, 76p.

1549. Vaiphei, S. Prim *et al* (*Eds*.) 1986 : *In Search of Identity*, Imphal, Kuki Chin Baptist Union, 66p.

1550. Vanchhunga, 1955 : *Lusei leh a Vela Haam Dangte Chanchin*. Aijawl, Pub. by the Author, Zoram Printing Press. *in Mizo*) : 92-93, 94, 95, 100.

1551. Vanlalauva, C., 1982 : *Religious Beliefs and Customs Among the Mizos Before the Advent of Christianity*. (*Unpublished*) Ph.D.Thesis, Gauhati University.

1552. Vanlalauvi, 1988 : *The Traditional Mizo Society*. (*Unpublished*) M. Phil Dissertation, History Deptt. NEHU, Shillon under Dr. M.S. Sangma

1553. Vanlawma, R. (*Ed.*), 1965 : *Ka Ram leh kei* Aizawl, Zalen Printing House, 79p (*2nd Edition* Pub. in 1972 with 196p.) [*in Mizo*].

1554. ———, (*Ed.*), 1972 : *My Country and I.* Aizawl, Zalen Printing House (*in Mizo*).

1555. ——— (*Ed.*), 1985 : Who and What are the Mizos? *Mizoram News Magazine.* Issue No. 23.

5556. Vanthanga and Zemana, 1978 : From the Underground: Mizo National Army Version (Announced to the Mizo National Army personnel). (*In*) *The Mizo Dilemma* by Amit Kumar Nag. Silchar, Tribal Mirror Publications (1984): 57-72.

1557. Vara, V. Hmar, 1967 : *Hmar Hla Hlui Bu* (Collection of Traditional Songs of *Hmar*). Churachandpur, Manipur.

1558. Verma, B.,1988 : *Insurgency and Counter Insurgency.* New Delhi, Uppal Publishing House.

1559. Vickers, A., 1927 : Among the Kukis. *Blackwood's Magazine.*

1560. Vidya, Binode *and* Padma Nath, ? : *A Critical Study of Gait's History of Assam.* Sylhet.

1561. Vidyarthi, L.P., 1975 : The Future of Traditional "Primitive" Societies : A Case Study of an Indian Shifting Cultivation Society. *Eastern Anth.*, 28(3), Oct.-Dec. : 313-26.

1562. Village Councils Act, 1953 : *Lushai Hills Act. No. V* (The Lushai Hills District [Village Councils'] Act., 1953).

1563. Viswam, S., 1986 : Mizoram : A Stormy Ear Ends. *Indian and Foreign Review*, July 15 : 8-11.

1564. Viswanath (*Ed.*), 1967 : Demand of Separate Regional Council by Chakmas of Mizo Hills. *Caravan* (New Delhi), June, no ii, 61p.

1565. Vivek Publishing, 1978 : *Hill Tracts Between Assam and Burma*. Delhi, Vivek Publishing Co., 342p (*Reprinted*).).

1566. Vumkhohau, 1963 : *Profile of a Burma Frontier Man.* Bundung (Indonesia) : 135, 214, 297, 301.

1567. Vummang *and* Jam, Khogin, 1957 : *The Jou Custom Book.* Nengjakham, 14p.

1568. Vumson, 1984 : *Zo History*. Aizawl.

W

1569. Wade, J.P., 1805 : *A Geographical Sketch of Assam.* London.

1570. ———, 1927 : *An Account of Assam.* (*Ed.*) by Benudhar Sharma. Sibsagar (Assam).

1571. Waddell, L.A., 1901 : *The Tribes of the Brahmaputra Valley. J.A.S.B.*, LXIX, pw. III (1900). [*Reprinted* in 1975 by Sanskaran Publications, Delhi, 127p.].

1572. Wadia, F.K., 1980 : Control of Shifting Cultivation in the North Eastern Region. (*In*) *Tribal Economy of the North Eastern Region*, (*Ed.*) by T. Mathew. Gauhati, Spectrum Publications : 62-79.

1573. Walker, E.O., 1894 : The Chin-Lushai Country. *Gentleman's Mag.*, 276 : 227-42.

1574. Walker, G.D., *et. al.* 1935 : Notes on Some Assam Hill Tribes. (*In*) *Census of India, vol. I, India, pt. III-B, Ethnographic Notes, (Ed.)* by J. H. Hutton. Simla, Govt. of India Press : 126-46.

1575. Walli, R.L., 1975 : The Process of Power Distribution and Resources Distribution. *The Thinker : Jour. of Thinkers Forum* (Kohima).

1576. ———, ? : Relationship Between the Process of Power Distribution and Resources Distribution. *The Thinkers Jour. of Thinkers Forum.*

1577. Ward, S.R., 1884 : *A Glimpse of Assam.* Shillong, Pub. by the Author.

1578. Watt, D.G., 1887 : The Aboriginal Tribes of Manipur. *J.R.A.I.* XVI : 349-50.

1579. Way, G.A., 1885 : *Supplementary Report on the North East Frontier of India, Notes on the Lushai Tribes.* Simla, Govt. Printing Press.

1580. Webb, C.M., 1912 : The Kuki Chin Group. (*In*) *Census of India, 1911, vol. IX Burma, Pt. I : Report.* Rangoon, Govt. Press: 266-67.

1581. Welsh Foreign Mission, 1899 : *Statistics of Aizawl District.* Shillong, Welsh Foreign Mission.

1582. Wilcox, R., 1855 : *Memoir of a Survey of Assam and the Neighbouring Countries Executed in 1825-28 (Selections From the Records of the Bengal Govt.),* Calcutta, vol. 23 : 19-.38.

1583. Wolfenden, Stuart N., 1929 : *Outlines of Tibeto Burman Linguistic Morphology with Special Reference to the Prefixes, Inffixes and Suffixes of Glassical Tibetan and the Languages of the Kachin, Bodo, Naga, Kuki-Chin and Burma Groups*, London, Royal Asiatic Society, 216p. (*Royal Asiatic Society*, Prize Publication Fund, vol. 12).

1584. Wood, R., 1953 : The Hill Tribes of Assam. *Jour. of the Royal Asiatic Society of Bombay*, 28 : 187-214.

1585. Woodthorpe, R.G., 1873 : *The Lushai Expedition, 1871-1872.* London, Hurst and Blackett, 338p. (*Reprinted* by Spectrum Publications, Gauhati in 1980 and also, Firma K.L.M. Pvt. Ltd, Calcutta in 1978 on behalf of Tribal Research Institute, Aizawl.). 338p.

1586. ———, 1873 : *Report to Capt. Badgley, Officiating Deputy Superintendent i/c Survey with the Lushai Expedition : Extracts from Notes to Accompany Capt. Badgley's Report. General Report on the Operations of the Survey of India, 1871-72, Appendix-A.* London, Hurst & Blackett.

1587. ———, 1890 : The Lushai Country. *Jour. of United Services Inst.*, (Ind.). No. 79.

Y

1588. Y.M.A. 1978 : *Dan Bu (Constitution o, Y.M.A.)*, Aizawl, Central Y.M.A. Headquarters.

1589. ———, 1979 : *General Secretaty's Report,' 1978-79. op. cit.*

1590. ———, 1980 : *Chanchin Bu*. Feb.-June, 1980. *op. cit.*

1591. ———, 1978 : *Chanchin Bu*. Nov., 1978. Aizawl, Pub. by Central Y.M.A. Headquarters.

Z

1592. Zadeng, K., 1971 : Customs and Cultural Life of the Mizo. *Pines*, 1(1), March : 17-21.

1593. Zairema, Rev. n.p. : *The Mizo Problems*. Aizawl. (*Unpublished*).

1594. ———, 1945 : *The Religion of the Lushais*. Chandernagore, Serampore College (*Unpublished*).

1595. ———, 1978 : *God's Miracle in Mizoram* (*A Glimpse of Christian Work Among Head Hunters*). Aizawl, Synod Press and Book Room, 23p.

1596. Zaithanga, Rev. 1981 : *From Head Hunting to Soul Hunting*. Aizawl. Pub. by the Author.

1597. Zatluanga, 1966 : *Mizo Chanchin*. Aizawl, Khuma Printing Press. 20p. (*in Mizo*).

1598. Zawla, K. 1964 : *Mizo Pipute leh an Thlahte Chan-*

chin. Aijal, Modern Printing Press : 119-20, 229-37.

1599. ———, ? : *Ancient History and Culture of the Mizo People.*

1600. Zomuana, K. 1989 : *Baptist Missionary Society in Mizoram, 1903-1968.* (*Unpublished*) M. Phil Dissertation Submitted, History Deptt., NEHU under Dr. M.S. Sangma.

1601. Zonunmawia 1988 : *The Formation of District Council in Mizo Hills.* (*Unpublished*) Dissertation for M. Phil., History Deptt., NEHU under Dr. J.B. Bhattachar jee.

1602. Zoramthanga, 1980 : *Zoram zalenna Lungphun.* Aizawl, MNF Hqrs. (*in Mizo*).

1603. ———, ? : Srihatter Itibritta, vol. II, chapter-II, : 209-211.

Addenda

1604. Acharya, S.K., 1984 : Ethnic Process in Central Hill States of North Eastern India : An Overview. Proceedings of a Seminar on *Question of Nationality and Cultural Identity in the Context of North East India,* held on December, Organised by NEICSSR, Shillong, (*Mimo*).

1605. Agarwal, A.K., (Ed.) 1987 : *Economic Problems and Planning in North East India.* New Delhi, Sterling Publishing.

1606. ———, 1988 : Shifting Cultivation in Mizoram. Proceedings of *Review and Reappraisal Seminar on Ṣhifting cultivation in North East India* Organised by NEICSSR, Shillong during 13-14 May, (*Mizo.*)

1607. Agarwal, A.K., *and* R.N. Prasad, 1990 : *Political and Economic Development in Mizoram,* Delhi, Mittal Publications (*in Press*).

1608. Agarwala, Prahlad, 1986 : Letters : Mizoram Accord. *Amrita Bazar Patrika*, July 10 : 6(3-4).

1609. Aggarwal, S.P., 1976 : *Enquiry Report of the Enquiry Commission on the Pawa District Council Affairs.* Aizawl, Mizoram Local Administration.

1610. Amrita Bazar, Patrika, 1986 : Mizoram Accord by June Likely : Laldenga. *Am. Baz. Pat.* Feb. 26 : 7(2-3).

1611. ———, 1986 : Mizo Talks Resume. *Am. Baz. Pat.* May 20 : 1(7-8).

1612. ———, 1986 : Future of Mizo Peace Talks Hazy. *Am. Baz. Pat.*, May 23 : 1(2-5)

1613. ———, 1986 : Laldenga Blames CM for Mizoram Tangle. *Am. Baz. Pat.*, June 1 : 7(4-5),

1614. ———, 1986 : Editorial : Talks Again on Mizoram. *Am. Baz. Pat.*, June 5 : 5(1-2).

1615. ———, 1986 : Laldenga Signs Accord with Delhi. *Am. Baz. Pat.*, July 1 : (5-6).

1616. ———, 1986 : Mizoram Opposition in a Quandary. *Am. Baz. Pat.*, July 6 : 6(4-8).

1617. ———, 1986 : Mizo Accord may put TNV off Gear. *Am. Baz. Pat.*, July 7 : 7(1-5)

1618. ———, 1986 : Ershad may Seal off MNF Foxholes. *Am. Baz. Pat.* July 15 : 1(4) & 12(3).

1619. ———, 1986 : Stern Steps if Mizo Rebels don't

Give in : Rajiv. *Am. Baz. Pat.*, July 10 : 1(1-3), 12(5-6).

1620. ———, 1986 : 600 to Lay Down Arms : MNF Amends Party Constitution. *Am. Baz. Pat.*, July 12 : 1(4-5).

1621. ———, 1986 : TUJS Objects to Laldenga's Remark. *Am. Baz. Pat.*, July 12 : 7(6-7).

1622. ———, 1986 : Greater Mizoram : PM Rejects Laldenga's Demand. *Am. Baz. Pat.*, July 13 : 1(7-8) & 7(3).

1623. ———, 1986 : Editorial : Accord and Discord. *Am. Baz. Pat.*, July 15 : 6(1-2).

1624. ———, 1986 : Mizo Accord Opens a New Chapter : Azad. *Am. Baz. Pal.*, July 22 : 12(1-3).

1625. ———, 1986 : The 'General' is Back Home with his Boys. *Am. Baz. Pat.*, July 25 : 7(1).

1626. ———, 1986 : Greater Mizoram. *Am. Baz. Pat.*, July 25 : 7(1).

1627. ———, 1986 : Laldenga May Take Oath in August. *Am. Baz. Pat.*, July 28 : 1(1).

1628. ———, 1986 : Church Played Crucial Role in Mizoram Accord. *Am. Baz. Pat.*, July 29 : 7(2-4).

1629. ———, 1986 : Hero's Welcome. *Am. Baz. Pat.*, Aug. 3 : 7(1).

1630. ———, 1986 : MNF Meet on Monday : Laldenga Still Drams about Greater Mizo-

1770. Assom Tribune, 1987 : Chakmas in Mizoram Feeling Unsafe. *A.T.*, Feb. 13 : 4 (1-2).

1771. ——, 1987 ; Mizoram Needs a Strong Govt. : PM. *A.T.*, Feb. 14 : 1 (7-8).

1772. ——, 1987 : Issues Before Mizoram Electorate. *A.T.*, Feb. 15 : 7 (3-6).

1773. ——, 1987 : Economic Measures for Mizoram. *A.T.*, Feb. 15 : 1 (7-8).

1774. ——, 1987 : Mizoram Goes to Polls Today. *A.T.*, Feb. 16 : 1 (3-6).

1775. ——, 1987 : 70 P.C, Cast Votes in Mizoram. *A.T.*, Feb. 17 : 1 (1-3).

1776. ——, 1987 : MNF Forging Ahead of Congress (I) : Twin Victories for Laldenga. *A.T.*, Feb. 18 : 1 (1-3).

1777. ——, 1987 : Saikia Appointed Governor of Mizoram. *A.T.*, Feb 18 : 1 (1).

1778. ——, 1987 : MNF Captures Absolute Majority in Mizoram. *A.T.*, Feb. 19 : 1 (2-5) 8 (5).

1779. ——, 1987 : Editorial : Laldenga Ministry. *A.T.*, March 7 : 4 (1-2).

1780. ——, 1987 : Jhum Cultivation in Mizoram may be Closed Down. *A.T.*, March 10 : 6 (3-5).

1781. ——, 1987 : Goitre : Mizoram Tops the List. *A.T.*, April 14 : 6 (4).

1782. ——, 1987 : Constraints in Harnessing Natural Wealth in N-E. *A.T.*, April 14 : 4 (1-2).

1642. ———, 1986 : Editorial : Extraordinary Experiment. *Am. Baz. Pat.*, Aug. 26 : 6(1-2).

1643. ———, 1986 : Laldenga Clarifies Greater Mizoram Stand. *Am. Baz. Pat.*, Sept. 1 : 1(4-5).

1644. ———, 1986 : Mizoram Accord Unique in Insurgency World. *Am. Baz. Pat.*, Sept. 9 : 7 (2-4).

1645. ———, 1986 : Mizoram Water Flow. *Am. Baz. Pat.*, Sept. 20 : 7(5).

1646. ———, 1986 : Rajiv's Steps Generate New Spirit in N-E Region. *Am. Baz. Pat.*, Dec. 27 : 7(2-4).

1647. ———, 1987 : Mizoram Assembly Poll on February 16. *Am. Baz. Pat.*, January 18 : 4(7-8).

1648. ———, 1987 : Mizoram polls : A Test of Laldenga, MNF. *Am. Baz. Pat.*, Feb. 15 : 5(5-6).

1649. ———, 1987 : Congress Can Make a Stronger Mizoram. *Am. Baz. Pat.*, Feb. 15 : 1(2-4) & *12*(4-5).

1650. ———, 1987 : Relief at Laldenga's Win. *Am. Baz. Pat.*, Feb. 25 ; 6(3-6).

1651. ———=' 1987 : Mizoram Voters Have Shown Sound Judgment. *Am. Baz. Pat.*, March 3 : 3(1-2).

1652. ———, 1987 : Editorial : Bloodshed in Mizoram. *Am. Baz. Pat.*, March 5 : 6(1-2).

1653. ———, 1987 : Move to Close Down Jhums. *Am. Baz. Pat.*, March 9 : 3(1-2).

1796. Assam Tribune, 1988 : Drug Addiction Increasing in Mizoram. *A.T.*, Feb. 5 : 8 (6-7).

1797. ——, 1988 : Mizoram, Arunachal to Celebrate Anniversary of Statehood. *A.T.*, Feb. 19 : 7 (4-6).

1798. ——, 1988 : Laldenga Criticises Centre. *A.T.*, Feb. 22 : 1 (5-7).

1799. ——, 1988 : Mizoram Festival [*Chamcharkut.*] *A.T.*, Feb. 27 : 1 (8).

1800. ——, 1988 : Rs. 332-27. Cr Deficit Budget for Mizoram. *A.T.*, March 5 : 1 (1-2).

1801. ——, 1988 : Schemes for Small-Scale Industries in Mizoram. *A.T.*, March 14 : 3 (2-3).

1802. ——, 1988 : Court of Inquiry into Aizawl firing. *A.T.*, April 4 ; 1 (6-8) 8 (7).

1803. ——, 1988 : Zomi Reunification Body Formed. *A.T.*, May 29 ; 5 (1-2).

1804. ——, 1988 : Mizoram Govt's Concern Over Drug Adicts. *A.T.*, June 14 : 7(3-6).

1805. ——, 1988 : ZRV involment Drive Launched. *A.T.*, June 15 : 7 (1-2) Zomi Reunification Voluntеer.

1806. ——, 1988 : Assam-Mizoram Ground Demarcation by December. *A.T.*, June 19 : 6 (6).

1807. ——, 1988 : 144 Cr. P.C. in Mizoram Issued for Two Years. *A.T.*, Junc 26 : 3(4).

1808. ——, 1988 : Goodbye to 'Jhum' Cultivation. *A.T.*, July 13 : 7 (4-5).

1666. ———, 1988 : Hardcore Drugs Reach N-E Areas Through Burma. *Am. Baz. Pat.*, March 30 : 7(1-4).

1667. ———, 1988 : Editorial : Tragedy at Aizawl, *Am. Baz. Pat.*, April 2 : 8(1-2).

1668. ———, 1988 : Burma May Ban Free Movement of Mizo People. *Am. Baz. Pat*, April 2 : 8(6-8).

1669. ———, 1988 : Editorial : Right Step in Mizoram. *Am. Baz. Pat.*, Sept. 8 : 6(1-2).

1670. ———, 1988 : Burmese Students Crossing Over to Mizoram. *Am. Baz. Pat.*, Nov. 3 : 12(5-6).

1671. ———, 1988 : Laldenga to Consult Basu on Legality of Centre's step. *Am. Baz. Pat.*, Nov. 7 : 7(5-6).

1672. ———, 1988 : Laldenga's Dictatorial. *Am. Baz. Pat.*, Nov. 24 : 7(1-3).

1673. ———, 1988 : Editorial : Relations with Burma. *Am. Baz. Pat.*, Dec. 8 : 6(1-2).

1674. ———, 1988 : Aizawl Water Supply Scheme. *Am. Baz. Pat.*, Dec. 28 : 7(2).

1675. ———, 1988 : Rajiv's Policy on Trial in Nagaland, Mizoram. *Am. Baz. Pat.*, Dec. 28 : 12(1-3).

1676. ———, 1989 : Rajiv Criticises Former Mizoram Government. *Am. Baz. Pat.*, January 6 : 12(1).

1677. ———, 1989 : Editorial : Distrust in Mizoram. *Am. Baz. Pat.*, January 10 : 6(1-2).

1678. ———, 1989 : PM Rejects Demand for Greater Wizoram. *Am. Baz. Pat.*, January 19 : 1(2-3).

1679. ———, 1989 : Minority Communities Represented in Lalthanwala Ministry. *Am. Baz. Pat.*, Feb. 6 : 7(5-6).

1680. ———, 1989 : Saikia rigged Mizoram Elections : Laldenga. *Am. Baz. Pat.*, Feb. 25 : 7 (5-6).

1681. ———, 1990 : N-E States Plan to Boost Tourism. *Am. Baz. Pat.*, June 26 : 6(2-4).

1682. ———, 1990 : Chakma DPs Creating Law and Order Problem. *Am. Baz. Pat.*, July 2 : 5(1).

1683. ———, 1990 : Karen Insurgency in Burma : Amar Jit, *Am. Baz. Pat.*, July 3 : 6(7-8).

1684. ———, 1990 : Editorial : Of Two Rebels. *Am. Baz. Pat.*, July 11 : 6(1-2).

1685. ———, 1990 : Laldenga to be Buried Near War Memorial. *Am. Baz. Pat.*, July 14 : 5(1-3) & 5(1-3).

1686. ———, 1990 : Mizoram CM Wants Special Attention from Planners. *Am. Baz. Pat.*, Aug. 5 : 5(4-6).

1687. ———, 1990 : Rly Board's Decision Disheartens North Eastern States. *Am. Baz. Pat.*, Sept. 24 : 5(1-3).

1688. ———, 1990 : Non-Mizo Traders in Trouble. *Am. Baz. Pat.*, Oct. 22 : 9 (6-8).

1689. Aristide, Marre, : *The Hill Tracts of Arakan, Par*

1883 : *Aristide Marre*. Louvain, Extrait du Musion.

1690. Assam Secretariat, 1889 : *The Lushais, 1873 to 1889*. Shillong, Assam Secretariat Press, 59p.

1691. Assam Tribune, 1947 : Lushai Hills. *Assam Tribune*, Oct. 5.

1692. ———, 1977 : On 4 March 1977, About 118 Mizo Detenus Were Reported to be in Jail. *Assam Tribune*, March 5.

1693. ———, 1981 : Central Team's Suggestions to Control Rat Menace in Mizoram. *A.T.*, April 7.

1694. ———, 1981 : Eleven Crores Project for Railway line in Mizoram. *A.T.*, Dec. 5.

1695. ———, 1986 : MNF Refuses to Include TNV in Peace Talk. *A.T.*, Jan. 16 : 1 (2-5).

1696. ———, 1986 : Final Settlement of Mizo Problems Urged. *A.T.*, Feb. 15 : 3 (6)

1697. ———, 1986 : Mizos Want Permanent Peace : Antony. *A.T.*, Feb. 15 : 7 (4).

1698. ———, 1986 : Mizo Accord Likely by June. *A.T.*, Feb. 26 : 1 (2-4).

1699. ———, 1986 : Mizoram CM Delaying Signing of Accord : Loldenga. *A.T.*, May 31 : 1 (5-6).

1700. ———, 1986 : Influx of Chakmas in Mizoram. *A.T.*, May 31 : 4 (6).

1701. ———, 1986 : Top Cong-I Leaders Join Mizo Talks. *A.T.*, June 4 : 1 (5-7).

1702. Assam Tribune, 1986 : Editorial : Mizoram Puzzle. *A.T.*, June 11 : 4 (1-2).

1703. ———, 1986 : Mizo Settlement Soon : Laldenga Likely to Head in Interim Govt. *A.T.*, June 18 : 1 (1-3).

1704. ———, 1986 : Mizo Accord Awaiting Cabinet Panel approval. *A.T.*, June 23 : 1 (1-2).

1705 ——— 1986 : Mizoram to be Conferred Statehood soon A. T, , July 4: 1[1-3]

1706. ———, 1986 : Mizoram Peace Accord Constitutional; *A.T.*, July 5 : 4 (1-2).

1707. ———, 1986 : Laldenga Confident Full Laying Down of Arms. *A.T.*, July 6 : 1 (1-3) 6 (6).

1708. ———, 1986 : Mizoram Accord Ends Decades of Insurgency. *A.T*, July 10 : 1 (3).

1709. ———, 1986 : Laldenga for Greater Mizoram. *A.T.*, July 10 : 4 (7-8).

1710. ———, 1986 : Every Aspect of Mizo Accord to be Implemented ; PM. *A.T.*, July 11 : 1 (2-3).

1711. ———, 1986 : In Mizoram : District Councils will Continue : PM. *A.T.*, July12 : 1 (1-3).

1712. ———, 1986 : CM, Opposition. *A.T.*, July 12 : 1 (3),

1713. ———, 1986 : MNF Constitution Amended. *AT.*, July 12 : 1 (1(2).

1714. ———, 1986 : Chakma District should give PC. *A.T.*, July 12 : 1 (6).

1715. ———, 1986 : PM Rules out Demand for Greater Mizoram. *A.T.*, July 13 : 1 (1-3).

1716. Assam Tribune, 1986 TUJS Against Demand for Greater Mizoramr *A.T.*, July 13 : 4 (1-2).

1717. ———, 1986 : Opposition Doubts Over Success of Mizo Accord. *A.T.*, July 22: 1 (2-3) 6 (5).

1718. ———, 1986 : Six Central Ministers at Aizawl. *A.T.*, July 27 : 1 (7-8).

1719. ———, 1986 : Centre to Implement Accords. *A.T.*, July 30 : 1 (5).

1720. ———, 1986 : No Special Status to Mizoram : Buta Singh. *A.T.*, July 30 : 1 (6-7).

1721. ———, 1986 : Editorial : Hope in Mizoram. *A.T.*, July 31 : 4 (1-2).

1722. ———, 1926 ; All MNF Men Have Come Overground : Laldenga. *A.T.*, Aug. 1 : 1 (2-3) 8 (7).

1723. ———, 1986 ; Laldenga's Appeal to Mizo People. *A.T.*, Aug. 1 : 3 (3).

1724. ———, 1986 : Rs. Four Crores Likely for Mizo Village Scheme. *A.T*, Aug. 1: 3 (3).

1725. ———, 1986 : No Problem in Accord. Implementation. *A.T.*, Aug. 2: 1 (7-8) 6 (6).

1726. ———, 1986 : Laldenga Visits Peace Camp. *A.T.*, Avg. 2 : 3 (5).

1727. , ———1986 : Hero's Welcome to MNF Retur— nees. *A.T.*, Aug. 3 : 1 (2-4).

1728. ———, 1986 : Lok Sabha Passes Mizoram Statehood Bill. *A.T.*, Aug. 6 : 1 1-3).

1729. Assam Tribune, 1986 : Mizoram Statehood Bill Passed. *A.T.*, Aug. 8 : 1 (1-3).

1730. ———, 1986 : MNF Returnees not Happy at Arrangement. *A.T.*, Aug. 8 : 1 (1) 6 (3).

1731. ———, 1986 : Laldenga Heads New MNF Office Bearers. *A.T.*, Aug. 9 : 8 (6).

1732. ———, 1986 : MNF Extends Support to Coalition partner. *A.T.*, Aug. 9 : 1 (6-7) 12 (5).

1733. ———, 1986 : Central Assistance for Development of Mizoram. *A.T.*, Aug. 11 : 6 (3).

1734. ———, 1986 : Greater Mizoram not Absolutely, Impossible : Lalthanwala. *A.T.* Aug. 15 : 1 (1-2).

1735. ———, 1986 : Laldenga to Form Govt. Today. *A.T.*, Aug. 21 : 1 (2-4).

1736. ———, 1986 : Nine-Member Mizoram Ministry Sworn in *A.T.*, Aug. 22 : 1.

1737. ———, 1986 : Editorial : Change in Mizoram. *A.T.*, Aug. 22 : 4 (1-2).

1738. ———, 1986 : Profile of Laldenga. *A.T.*, Aug. 23 : 4 (7-8).

1739. ———, 1986 : Laldenga Seeks People's Co-operation *A.T.*, Aug. 23 : 1 (4-6) 8 (6).

1740. ———, 1986 : Laldenga Could Have Signed Accord in 1986, *A.T.*, Aug. 25 : 1 (2-5).

1741. ———, 1986 : Mizo Coalition Govt. Seeks P.M's Help. *A.T.*, Aug. 29 : 1 (5-7).

1742. Assam Tribune, 1986 : Laldenga's Plea to Journalists. *A.T.*, Sept. 1 : 3 (3).

1743. ——, 1986 : Trust to Help Rural Poor in Mizoram. *A.T.*, Sept. 2 : 5 (3).

1744. ——, 1986 : Release of Detained MNF Men Under Consideration. *A.T.*, Sept. 4 : 4 (7-8).

1745. ——, 1986 : Mizoram Assembly Welcomes Accord. *A.T.*, Sept. 5 : 8 (4).

1746. ——, 1986 : All MNF Prisoners Cases to be Considered. *A.T.*, Sept. 5 : 5 (4-5).

1747. ——, 1986. : More Autonomy to Mizoram District Council *A.T.*, Sept. 6 : (1).

1748. ——, 1986 : United Parliamentary Party in Mizoram. *A.T.*, Sept. 6 : 6 (1).

1749. ——, 1986 : Mizoram Preparing New Farming Scheme. *A.T.*, Sept. 15 : 1 (3-4).

1750. ——, 1986 : Mizoram Preparing New Farming Scheme. *A.T.*, Sept. 15 : 1 (3-4).

1751. ——, 1986 : Laldenga Meets Central Leaders. *A.T.*, Sept. 11: 4 (7-8).

1752. ——, 1986 : Mizoram Assembly Poll May be Held on Feb. 15. *A.T.*, Oct. 6 : 7 (1).

1753. ——, 1986 : Acts on Mizo Situation Either Repealed or Not Extended. *A.T.*, Oct. 18 : 1 (2) 6 (4).

1754. ——, 1986 : Laldenga's Appeal to People. *A.T.*, Nov. 11 7 (6-8).

1755. ——, 1986 : NSCN Condemns Mizo Accord.

A.T., Nov. 12 : 6 (3-4).

1756. Assam Tribune, 1986 : Tripura's Mizos Want Regional Council *A.T.*, Dec. 9 : 1 (5-7).

1757. ——, 1986 : Editorial : Mizoram Scene. *A.T.*, Dec. 10 : 4 (1-2).

1758. ——, 1986 : MNF Resents Centre's Decision *A.T.*, Dec. 19 : 1 (3-5).

1759. ——, 1987 : Mizoram Assembly Poll on Feb. 16. *A.T.*, January 13 : 1 (6-7).

1760. ——, 1987 : Mizoram Govt. Doctors' Indefinite Strike. *A.T.*, Jan. 23 : 1 (1).

1761. ——, 1987 : MNF Seeks "Tiger" Symbol for Poll. *A.T.*, Jan. 25 : 7 (4).

1762. ——, 1987 : GSI's Scientific Expedition. *A.T.*, Jan. 26 : 6 (1).

1763. ——, 1987 : Mizoram Poll to be Peaceful : Saikia, *A.T.*, Jan. 31 : 1 (5-6).

1764. ——, 1987 : PM to Campaign in Mizoram from Feb. 12. *A.T.*, Feb. 6 : 9 (58).

1765. ——, 1987 : Poll Compaign in Mizoram. *A,T.*, Feb. 6 : 5 (2-4).

1766. ——, 1987 : Editorial : Mizoram Poll. *A.T.*, Feb. 8 : 4 (1-2).

1767. ——, 1987 : Triangular fight Likely in Mizoram. *U.T.*, Feb. 11 : 4 (7-8).

1768. ——, 1987 : State Day on Feb. 20. *A.T.*, Feb. 13 : 1 (5) 6 (5).

1769. —— . 87 : High Stakes in Mizoram Elections. *A.T.*, Feb. 13 : 1 (3-5).

1770. Assom Tribune, 1987 : Chakmas in Mizoram Feeling Unsafe. *A.T.*, Feb. 13 : 4 (1-2).

1771. ——, 1987 ; Mizoram Needs a Strong Govt. : PM. *A.T.*, Feb. 14 : 1 (7-8).

1772. ——, 1987 : Issues Before Mizoram Electorate. *A.T.*, Feb. 15 : 7 (3-6).

1773. ——, 1987 : Economic Measures for Mizoram. *A.T.*, Feb. 15 : 1 (7-8).

1774. ——, 1987 : Mizoram Goes to Polls Today. *A.T.*, Feb. 16 : 1 (3-6).

1775. ——, 1987 : 70 P.C, Cast Votes in Mizoram. *A.T.*, Feb. 17 : 1 (1-3).

1776. ——, 1987 : MNF Forging Ahead of Congress (I) : Twin Victories for Laldenga. *A.T.*, Feb. 18 : 1 (1-3).

1777. ——, 1987 : Saikia Appointed Governor of Mizoram. *A.T.*, Feb. 18 : 1 (1).

1778. ——, 1987 : MNF Captures Absolute Majority in Mizoram. *A.T.*, Feb. 19 : 1 (2-5) 8 (5).

1779. ——, 1987 : Editorial : Laldenga Ministry. *A.T.*, March 7 : 4 (1-2).

1780. ——, 1987 : Jhum Cultivation in Mizoram may be Closed Down. *A.T.*, March 10 : 6 (3-5).

1781. ——, 1987 : Goitre : Mizoram Tops the List. *A.T.*, April 14 : 6 (4).

1782. ——, 1987 : Constraints in Harnessing Natural Wealth in N-E. *A.T.*,, April 14 : 4 (1-2).

1783. Assom Tribune, 1987 : Cardamom Nursery in Mizoram. *A.T.*, April 17 : 5 (3-4).

1784. ——, 1987 : Editorial : Fear in the Hills. *A.T.*, April 18 : 4 (1-2).

1785. ——, 1987 : Rampant Corruption : A Major Problem in Mizoram. *A.T.*, May 7 : 4 (7-8).

1786. ——, 1987 : Anti-Drunken Squad to be Set Up *A.T.*, June 6 : 5 (6).

1787. ——, 1987 : Laldenga Never Wanted Greater Mizoram. *A.T.*, June 17 : 1 (7-8).

1788. ——, 8987 : Editorial : Enough is Enough. *A.T.*, June 18 ; 4 (1-2).

1789. ——, 1987 : Editorial : Rebels in North East. *A T.*, Aug. 21 : 4 (1-2).

1790. ——, 1987 : Central Team in Mizoram to Study Allegation. *A.T.*, Sept. 12 : 6 (3-4).

1791. ——, 1987 : Editorial : Inner Line Regulations. *A.T.*, Sept. 21 : 4 (1-2).

1792 ——, 1987 : Ordinance to Safeguard Tribal People. *A.T.*, Sept. 25 6 (5-6)

1793. ——, 1988 : Laldenga to Attend Non-Cong (I CMs Conference. *A.T.*, January 9 : 6 (5).

1794. ——, 1988 : Chittagong Insurgency Gaining Momentum. *A.T.*, January 11 : 1 (1-4).

1795. ——, 1988 : Jhum uCltivators to be Settled Permanently *A.T.*, January 19 : 3 (4-5).

1796. Assam Tribune, 1988 : Drug Addiction Increasing in Mizoram. *A.T.*, Feb. 5 : 8 (6-7).

1797. ——, 1988 : Mizoram, Arunachal to Celebrate Anniversary of Statehood. *A.T.*, Feb. 19 : 7 (4-6).

1798. ——, 1988 : Laldenga Criticises Centre. *A.T.*, Feb. 22 : 1 (5-7).

1799. ——, 1988 : Mizoram Festival [*Chamcharkut.*] *A.T.*, Feb. 27 : 1 (8).

1800. ——, 1988 : Rs. 332-27. Cr Deficit Budget for Mizoram. *A.T.*, March 5 : 1 (1-2).

1801. ——, 1988 : Schemes for Small-Scale Industries in Mizoram. *A.T.*, March 14 : 3 (2-3).

1802. ——, 1988 : Court of Inquiry into Aizawl firing. *A.T.*, April 4 ; 1 (6-8) 8 (7).

1803. ——, 1988 : Zomi Reunification Body Formed. *A.T.*, May 29 : 5 (1-2).

1804. ——, 1988 : Mizoram Govt's Concern Over Drug Adicts. *A.T.*, June 14 : 7(3-6).

1805. ——, 1988 : ZRV involment Drive Launched. *A.T.*, June 15 : 7 (1-2) Zomi Reunification Volunteer.

1806. ——, 1988 : Assam-Mizoram Ground Demarcation by December. *A.T.*, June 19 : 6 (6).

1807. ——, 1988 : 144 Cr. P.C. in Mizoram Issued for Two Years. *A.T.*, Junc 26 : 3(4).

1808. ——, 1988 : Goodbye to 'Jhum' Cultivation. *A.T.*, July 13 : 7 (4-5).

(*or*) Zomi nam pi. *Sionsinpawl*, vol. 12 : 15·7 (in Paite).

1933. Choudhury, Neerja, 1979 : MNF Blamed for Violence in Mizoram. *Himmat*, 17 : 7.

1934. ———, 1979 : Mizo Problem Cannot be Solved Militarily. *Himmat*, Nov. 16 : 8-9.

1935. ———, 1980 : Mizoram : Search for Peace with Honour. *Himmat*, May 16 : 8-9.

1936. Choudhury, : MNF Volte face on Prohibition. *Shillong T*, July 29 : 1 (2-3).

1937. ———, 1988 : Pressure for Autonomy of Jampui Hills. *Shillong T.*, Nov. 24 : w (3-5).

1938. ———, 1988 : Burmese Mizos Support Unification of Mizoram, *Shillong T.*, Dec. 7 : 3 (1).

1939. Cock, C., 1968 : Mizo and Naga Problems. *Eves Weekly*, May-June : 13-9.

1940. Commerce, 1976 : Mizoram : New Political Era. *Commerce*, Aug. 14 : 3-4.

1941. Dahrawka, P.S., : *Mizo Thanthu*. Aijal, Salem Book Stall.

1942. Das, Arunava, 1988 : Social life. *Am. Baz. Pat., Sunday* Magazine, Dec. 18 : 8 (1-8).

1942. ———, 1988 : Highland Charm. *Am. Baz. Pat., Sunday* Maga. Dec. 18 : 17 (1-8).

1945. ———, 1988 : Mizoram Today : Focus. *Am. Baz. Pat.. (Sunday*Magazine), Dec. 18 : 15 7 18-19 (1-8).

1945. Das, A.K., M.K. Chaudhuri *and* Bose, S., 1982 : Anthropology of Development : Socio-Economic Condition of the Scheduled Tribes and Scheduled

Laldenga. *A.T.*, January 18 : 7 (2·5).

1822. Assam Tribune, 1989 : Man Eats Dog , What's New ? *A.T.*, January 22 : 4 (3-6). Phillippines, S. Korea, Hong Kong, Indonesia, Thailand, Singapore, Malaysia.

1823. ———, 1989 : Mizoram Denies Charges of Rigging Assembly Polls. *A.T.*, March 5 : 3 (4-5).

1824. ———, 1990 : Mizoram Govt. Ready for Talks With HPC. *A.T.*, June 28 : 5 (4).

1825. ———, 1990 : Permanent H.C. Bench in Mizoram Opened. *A.T.*, July 6 : 1 (4·5).

1826. ———, 1990 : Laldenga : A Leader of Insurgency. *A.T.*, July 8 : 6 (6-7).

1827. ———, 1990 : Laldenga Dead. *A.T.*, July 8 : 1(5-6) 6(4).

1828. ———, 1990 : Demand for Full-fledged H.C. in Mizoram. *A.T.*, July 9 : 3(1-2).

1829. ———, 1990 : State Funeral to Laldenga on July 12. *A.T.*, July 10 : 1(8).

1830. ———, 1990 : Laldenga's Body Received at Aizawl. *A.T.*, July 12 : 1(2).

1831. ———, 1990 : J.D. Activities Unauthorised : Fernandes. *A.T.*, July 17 : 6(6).

1832. ±———, 1990 ; Laldenga's Tomb desecrated. *A.T.*, July 27 : 3(4).

1833. ———, 1990 : Hmar 'Leaders' Talks with Mizo Govt. Today. *A.T.*, 7uly 31 : 1(7).

1834. Assam Tribune, 1990 : Autonomous Council for Hmar Tribes Soon. *A.T.*, Aug. 31 : 5(5-6).

1835. ———, 1990 : Reconstitution of Mizo Village Councils Justified. *A.T.*, Oct. 22 : 3(4).

1836. ———, 1990 : Assam's Help Sought on Non-Mizo Sponsor Impass. *A.T.*, Oct. 22 : 3(4-5).

1837. ———, 1990 : Kuki Chavang Kut Festival Celebrated. *A.T.*, Nov. 15 : 5(5-7).

1837a. Assam Tribune, 1990 : Heroin Seized. *Assam Tribune*, Dec. 20 : 3(3).

1837b. Assam Tribune, 1990 : Peace Again May Evade Mizoram. *Assam Tribune*, Dec. 21 : 5(4-6).

1838. Athparia, R.P. 1985 : Hmar : Tribal Identity. *Jour. of Social Research* (Shillong), 5 : 14-22.

1839. Athparia, R.P. *and* S. Sengupta, 1990 : The Hmars of Assam : A Preliminary Appraisal on Identity Orientation. (*In*) *Nationality, Ethnicity and Cultural Identity in North-East India*, (*Ed.*) by B. Pakem. New Delhi, Omsons Publications : 187-90.

1840. Bali, Suyakanta, 1987 : Kaye Larte Hai Purbachal Kee Sat Bahane (*in Hindi*). *Naba Bharat Times*, Nov. 7 : 4(3-6).

1841. Bandopadhyay, P.K. 1986 : Press in North Eastern Region : *A* Review, (*In*) *Social and Economic Development in North East India*, (*Ed.*) by Shashi Ahluwalia. Delhi, Gian Pubg. House : 103-10.

1842. ——, 1987 : Land Relations and Land Use Pattern : The Mizo Dimension (*In*) *Land Relations in North East India* (*Eds.*) by B.B. Dutta *and* M.N. Karna. New Delhi, Peoples Publishing House : 184-92.

1843. ——, 1987 : The Mizoram Accord and After. *Jour. NEICSSR*, 11(1), April : 14-22.

1844. ——, 1987 : The Mizoram Accord and After. *Jour. NEICSSR*, XI(1), April : 14-22.

1845. Banerjee, Dhaneswar, 1986 : Letters : Mizoram Accord. *Am. Baz. Pat.*, July 10 : 6(4).

1846. ——, 1986 : Letters : Mizo Accord. *Am. Baz. Pat.*, July 12 : 6(5).

1847. Banerjee, Nirmalya 1987 : No Tension in Mizo Poll Campaign *Statesman* (Calcutta), Feb. 13 : 9(4-7).

1848. ——, 1987 : Chance of Coalition in Mizoram. *States.*, Feb. 14 : 9(2-5).

1849. ——, 1987 : Lukewarm Reception to Rajiv in Mizoram. *States.*, Feb. 15 : 1(2-4).

1850. ——, 1987 : Mizoram Peaceful on Poll Eve. *States.*, Feb. 16 : 1(2-4).

1851. ——, 1987 : MNF Romps Home with Majority. *States.*, Feb. 19 : 1(2-4) 9(6-7).

1852. ——, 1987 : Mizoram to Have Cabinet of Four. *States.*, Feb. 20 : 1(6-8) 9(5).

1853. ——, 1987 : Mizoram and Arunachal Celebrate

Statehood. *States.*, Feb. 21 : 1(6-8) 9(2-3).

1854. Banerjee, Nirmalya 1987 : MNF secured 36.5 Per Cenvt of Votes. *States.*, Feb. 23 : 9(7-8).

1855. Banerjee, Saumitro, 1980 : In Mizoram the Tricolour was not flown on 15th August 1947. *Sunday*, Aug. 24 : 20-21.

1856. Bardoloi, B.N., 1988 : The Hmars and The Kukis, (*In*) *Assam, part II, TRI Popular Series* by B.N. Bardoloi *and* G.C. Sharma Thakur, Guwahati, Tribal Research Institute (Assam). 20-41. 44-54.

1857. Barkatakis' S., 1962 : *The Escapades of a Magistrate.* Calcutta, Orient Longmans.

1858. Barman, Bhaskar, 1972 : Mizoram : The Struggle Continues *Frontier*, April 15 : 5-6.

1859. B. M. 1977 : Mizo Grievances. *Link*, July 13 : 19

1860. Barua, P.C. (*Ed.*), 1990 : *Development Planning of North-East India (Agricultural, Economic, Environmental, financial. Industrial, Manpower and Rural).* Delhi, Mittal Publications.

1861. Barua, S.N., 1990 : *Tribes of Indo-Burma Border.* Delhi, Mittal Publications (*in Press.*)

1862. Basumatari, K.K. 1985 : To the Editor : Assam Mizoram Solutions : A Common Factor. *Shillong Times*, March 2 : 2(3-5).

1863. Bhagabati, Annada : Emergent Tribal Identity in North

C. 1982 East India, (*In*) *Tribal Development in India : Problem and Prospect* (*Ed.*) by Buddhadeb Chaudhuri. Delhi, Inter India Pubs : 213-32.

1864. Bhalla, H.R. 1986 : Letters to the Editor : MNF and Mizoram are not Synonymous. *Shillong* T., Aug., 15 : 2(3-5).

1865. Bhattacharjee, Ajit 1975 : Misconduct in Mizoram. *Indian Express*, April 7.

1866. ———, 1975 : Misconduct in Mizoram. *Ind. Exp.*, April 10 : 6(4).

1867. Bhattocharjee, Anil 1986 : Tribal Inliltration Continued. *Am. Baz. Pat.*, June 3 : 7(1-4).

1868. ———, 1986 : Sailo-Laldenga Clash in the Offing. *Times of India*, Oct. 10 : 5(1-4).

1869. ———, 1986 : Parties Preparing Poll Strategies : Mizoram. *Am. Baz. Pat.*, Oct. 15 : 7(1-5).

1870. ———, 1986 : Relaxed Atmosphere in Mizoram. *Times of India*, Oct 18 : 5(5-6).

1871. ———. 1987 : National Party Gains Popularity Over Regionalism in N-E India. *Am. Baz. Pat.*, Dec. 9 : 7(4-6).

1872. ———, 1989 : Laldenga Faces Tough Opposition in Mizoram Elections. *Am. Baz. Pat.*, January 16 : 7(1-3).

1873. ———, 1989 : Mizo Tribes in Tripura Demands Separate Council. *Am. Baz. Pat.*, Feb. 22 : 7(4-5).

1874. Bhattacharyya, Nitya, 1986 : Letters to the Editor : The Mizoram Accord. *A.T.*, Aug. 1 : 4(3-4).

1875. Bhattacharyya, S.K., 1985 : The Paite of Mizoram (*P.O.I. Seminar*, An. SJ., *Unpublished Report*).

1876. ———, 1986 : The Mara (Lakher) (*Unpublished Report*).

1877. ———, 1986 : The Pang (*Unpublished Report*).

1878. ———, 1986 : The Chakma of Mizoram (*Unpublished Report*).

1879. ———, 1986 : The Riang of Mizoram (*Unpublished Report*).

1880. ———, 1990 : Population Heterogeneity and Ethnic Identity in Mizoram, (*In*) *Nationality, Ethnicity and Cultural Identity in North East India*, (*Ed.*) by B. Pakem. New Delhi, Omsons Publications : 299-308,

1881. Bhattacharjee, Tanmay, 1988 : The Dimasa and the Hmar Political Movement. Proceedings of a Seminar on *Regional Political Parties in North East India* held during 9-10 Dec. 1988 by NEICSSR, Shillong (*Mimeo*).

1882. Bhuyan, S.K. 1951 : *Kachari Buranji*. Gauhati, Deptt. of Historical & Antiquarian Studies, 149p.

1883. Brown, R. 1870 : Selection from Records of the Government of India. *Foreign Department*, No. LXXVIII .

1884. Business Standard, 1980 : Mizo Middle. *Bus. S*, June 20 : 5(1).

1885. Candeth, K.P. 1978 : Insurgency in Mizoram. *Indian Express*, April 25 : 4 (7).

1886. Cantlie, Keith, 1949 Foreword. (*In*) *Lushai Chrysalis* by A.G. Mc Call. London, Luzac & Co.

1887. Carey, B.S. N. Tuck, 1976 : *Chin Hills, vol. I.* Aizawl, Tribal Research Institute.

1888. ———, 1976 : *Chin Hills, vol. II.* Aizawl, T.R.I.

1889. ———, 1895 : *The Chin Hills (A History of the People, Our Dealings with them, their Customs and Manners and a Gazetter of their Country).* [*Reprinted* in 1976 by T.R.I, Aizawl]

1890. Carvan, 1969 : Mizo Problem. *Carvan*, Jan. 1 : 54-5.

1891. ———, 1971 : Amnesty to the Mizos. *Carvan*, Oct. 1 : 67.

1892. Chakraborty, Anirban, 1989 : President's rule to Benefit Congress in Mizoram poll. *Am. Baz. Pat.*, Jan. 18 : 1 (2-3)

1893. ———, 1989 : MNF Supporters Raid Deb's Suite. *Am. Baz. Pat.*, Jan. 22 : 1 (2-3).

1894. ———, 1989 : Nine-men Coalition Ministry in Mizoram. *Am. Baz. Pat.*, Jan. 25 : 1 (2-4).

1895. Chakravorty, B.C., 1958 : *British Relations with the Hill Tribes of Assam* Calcutta, Firma KLM Pvt. Ltd.

1896. Chakrabarty, Saroj : 1984 *The Upheaval Years in North East India : A Documentary in*-depth *study of Assam* Halocausts Calcutta, S. Chakrabarty & R. Chakraborty : 1, 13, 86, 95, 99, 100, 101, 105, 118, 120, 141, 152, 166, 188, 205, 206.

1897. Chakrabarti, Satyabrata, 1988 : Development Projects in Mizoram. *Statesman*, Ma rch 8, 4(5).

1898. Chakraborty, Swadesh, 1988 : MNF Wants Immediate Elections. *Stateman*, Nov. 10 : 4 (4).

1899. Chaliha, Amttav, 1988 : Festivals and Dances of Mizoram. *A T.*, Feb. 5 : I (8).

1900. Chanda, Arup, 1988 : Cong-I Stakes Claim : Mizoram Rebels Face Dismissal. *Statesman*, Sept. 1 : (2-3).

1901. ———, 1988 : Saikia Asks Speaker to Prove Validity of Show Cause. *Statesman*, Sept. 2: 1 (6-7).

1902. ———, 1988 : Laldenga Trying to Contact V.P. and Rajiv. *Statesman*, Sept. 3 : 1(5).

1903. ———, 1988 : Laldenga Warns of Fresh Insurgency *Statesman*, Sept. 41 : 1 (5-6).

1904. ———, 1988 : Laldenga Blind to Writing on the Wall. *Statesman*, Sept. 13 : 16 (3-5)

1905. ———, 1988 ; Is Laldenga Still a Rebel *Statesman* Sept. 18 : 1 (2-4)

1906. ———, 1988 : The fleeing Burmese : Sanctuary in India. *Statesman (Saturday* Magazine), Dec. 10 : I(1-8) 4(-14).

1907. ———, 1988 : Laldenga Fears Rigging by Cong (I). *Statesman*, Dec. 29 : 1 (2-5).

1908. ———, 1988 : Laldenga Inviting Leaders of All Parties. *Statesman*, Dec. 30 : 9 (6-7).

1909. ———, 1989 : Burmese Refugees Will Try to Meet Rajiv Gandhi. *Statesman*, Jan. 4 : 9 (7-8).

1910. Chaliha Amttav, 1989 : Mizoram Poll Scene- I Congress(I) Communal Campaign. *Statesman*, Jan. 16 : (2-4).

1911. ———, 3989 : Mizoram Poll Scene-II : Clear Majority May Elude Parties. *Statesman*, Jan. 17 : 14 (1-4).

1912. ———, 1989 : Outright Victory for Cong-I, MNF Unlikely. *Stattesman*, Jan. 20 : 14 (3-4).

1913. ———, 1989 : Lalthanhawla Sworn in. *Statesman*, Jan. 25 : 1 (7-8) 9 (6).

1914. ———, 1989 : Congress (I) Became a Party for Christians' in Mizoram. *Statesman*, Jan. 30 : 9 (2-7).

1915. Chandola, Harish, 1980 : Towards settlement in Mizoram *Mainstream*, Aug. 9 : 5-6.

1916. Chandrakanta, 1971 : Mizo Hills : India's Eastern Frontier. *Mirror*, 10 (10), Aug. : 34-6.

1917. Chaphekar, S.G., 1967 : Another Nagaland in Making. *Triveni*, January : 13-6.

1918. Chatterjee, Suhas, 1988 : Banaithangi : Romantic Mizo Princess of Cachar Frontier. *A.T.*, Feb. 22 : 8 (5-8) 9 (4-5).

1919. Chatterji, Suniti, Kumar, 1951 : *Kirata-Jana-Kriti*. Calcutta, *Jour. Royal Asiatic Society of Bengal, Letter*, XVI (2). 1950 : 1-94.

1920. Chaube, Shibanikinkar, 1973 : *Hill Politics in North East India*. Bombay, Orient Longman :35, 75 119, 160, 161.

1921. ———, 1980 : Peace in North East. *Statesman*, June 6.

1922. Chaube Shibani-kinkar, 1982 : Ethnicity and Political Development in North East India, (*In*) *Tribal Development in India : Problem and Prospect*, (*Ed.*) by Buddhadeb Chaudhuri Delhi, Inter India Pullratins : 127-47.

1923. ——, 1985 : *Electoral Politics in North East India*. Bombay, Orient Longman.

1924. Chaudhuri, Buddhadeb (*Ed.*), 1982 *Tribal Development in India : Problem and Prospect*. Delhi, Inter-India Pullratins : 55, 217, 224, 289, 313, 330, 354, 355.

1925. Chaudhuri, K.C., 1988 : Letters to the Editor : What Gaidiliu Really Wants. *Statesman* may 25 : 8 (4).

1926. ——, 1988 : Uniting the Mizos : Fear of Cross-Border Agitation. *Statesman*. July 26:6 (4-6) [Zou, Zomi, Lushais].

1927. Choudhury, Rabijit, 1987 : Greater Mizoram Demand and Danger ahead. *Shillong T.*, April 25 : 2(3-6).

1928. ——, 1989 : Cong (I) Goes Christian in Mizoram. *Shillong T.* Jan. 20 : 1 (5-6) 4 (2-3).

1929. Chaudhuri, S.B., : Then and Now *Shillong, T.*, May 2 : 2 (3-6).

1930. Chetiya, Anima, 1990 : Laldenga : A Chapter of Mizo Politics. *A.T.*, Oct. 7 : 4 (3-6) 6 (1-2).

1931. Chhwana, S., 1984 : Education in Mizoram. *Jour. of North Eastern Council* (Shillong), 6 (3), May-June : 34-7.

1932. Chinenthang, : Ei Zomite in ih Ngei na Leh ih zolai baug cih leng Khang to ding (*or*) Zomi nam pi. *Siomsinpawl*, vol. 12 : 15.7 (in Paite).

1933. Choudhury, Neerja, 1979 : MNF Blamed for Violence in Mizoram. *Himmat*, 17 : 7.

1934. ———, 1979 : Mizo Problem Cannot be Solved Militarily. *Himmat*, Nov. 16 : 8-9.

1935. ———, 1980 : Mizoram : Search for Peace with Honour. *Himmat*, May 16 : 8-9.

1936. Choudhury, : MNF Volte face on Prohibition. *Shillong T*, July 29 : 1 (2-3).

1937. ———, 1988 : Pressure for Autonomy of Jampui Hills. *Shillong T.*, Nov. 24 : w (3-5).

1938. ———, 1988 : Burmese Mizos Support Unification of Mizoram, *Shillong T.*, Dec. 7 : 3 (1).

1939. Cock, C., 1968 : Mizo and Naga Problems. *Eves Weekly*, May-June : 18-9.

1940. Commerce, 1976 : Mizoram : New Political Era. *Commerce*, Aug. 14 : 93-4.

1941. Dahrawka, P.S., : *Mizo Thanthu*. Aijal, Salem Book Stall.

1942. Das, Arunava, 1988 : Social life. *Am. Baz. Pat.*, *Sunday* Magazine, Dec. 18 : 18 (1-8).

1942. ———, 1988 : Highland Charm. *Am. Baz. Pat.*, *Sunday* Maga. Dec. 18 : 17 (1-8).

1945. ———, 1988 : Mizoram Today : Focus. *Am. Baz. Pat.*. (*Sunday*Magazine), Dec. 18 : 15 7 18-19 (1-8).

1945. Das, A.K., M.K. Chaudhuri *and* Bose, S., 1982 : Anthropology of Development : Socio-Economic Condition of the Scheduled Tribes and Scheduled

Castes of Eastern India, (*In*) *Tribal Development in India : Problem and Prospect.* (*Ed.*) by Buddhadeb Chaudhuri. Delhi, Inter India Pubs. : 353-70.

1946. Das, J.N., 1980 : *Mizos* Proceedings of a Seminar on *Development Strategies* etc (Advent of the British in North East India, Notes on the N-E History, Shillong.

1947. ———, 1990 : *A Study of Administration of Justice Among the Tribes and Races of North-Eastern Region (Excluding Nagaland and Meghalaya).* Gauhati, Law Research Institute, Gauhati High Court (Sponsored by North Eastern Council, Shillong) [1987].

1948. ———, 1990 : *A Study of the Land System of Mizoram*, Gauhati, Law Research Inst., Gau. High Court (Sponsored by N.E.C., Shillong) [1986].

1949. Das, N.K., 1989 : *Ethnic Identity, Ethnicity and Social Stratification in North East India.* Delhi, Inter India Publications.

1950. Das, Rajat Kanti, 1982 : Changiung Patterns in Tribal Life in Manipur.(*In*) *Tribal Development in India : Problem and Prospect,* (*Ed.*) by Buddhadeb Chaudhuri. Delhi, Inter India Pubs. : 409-18.

1951. Das, R.K., 1990 : Tribal Identity in Manipur, (*In*) *Nationality, East India,* (*Ed.*) by B. Pakem. New Delhi, Omsons Publications : 257-63.

1952. Das Gupta, Malabika, 1990 : Nationalities, Ethnicities, and Cultural Identity . A Case Study of the Mizos of Tripura, (*In*) *Nationality, Ethnicity and Cultural Identity in North-East India*, (*Ed.*) by B. Pakem. New Delhi, Omsons Publications : 365-76.

1953. Data India, 1981 : Mizoram : Laldenga Submits Five Point Plan to Prime Minister. *Data India*, March 16 : 144.

1954. Datta, P.S., 1982 : A Note on the Pattern of Land Ownership in Mizoram. *North Eas Quarterly*, 1 (1), Aug. . 78-84.

1955. Datt, Parthasarathi, 1987 : Future of the East : A Few Words in Anticipation on Land Ownership Pattern in Mizoram, (*In*) *Land Relations in North East India*, (*Ed.*) by B.B.Dutta *and* M.N. Karna. New Delhi, Peoples Publishing House . 176-83.

1956. David Kyles, 1944 : *Lorrain of the Lushais Romans and Realism in the North East Frontier of India*, London. The Carey Press.

1957. Democratic World 1975 : Editorial : Feeding on Fear. *Democratic World*, Feb. 2 : 1-2.

1958. Dev, S.G., 1984 : Change in Mizoram. *Statesman*, June 1.

1959. Dewan, Vijay Kumar, 1976 : *North East Region : Local Acts of Assam, Nagaland, Meghalaya, Manipur, Tripura, Mizoram and Arunachal Pradesh, voi. I* Allahabad, Orient Law House, 785 p.

2085. Jafa, Jyoti, 1978 : Towards Peace With Understanding. *Statesman*, June 8 : 6(4).

2086. Jones, P.H. n.d. : *The Lushai Hills*. Londonm Baptist Missionary Society.

2087. J.T. 1986 : Laldenga May Still Surprise. *Times of India, Sunday Review* : V(1-5).

2088. Kahin, George Mc Turnan (*Ed.*) 1956 : *Government and Politics of South East Asia*. New York. Cornell University Press.

2089. Kailiana, B.S. 1980 : Economy of Mizoram : Agriculture, (*In*) *Tribal Economy of the North Eastern Region*, (*Ed.*) by T. Mathew. Gauhati, Spectrum Publications : 174-77.

2020. Kakati, Satiss Ch. 1986 : The Mizoram Accord : Hopes and Fears. *A.T.*, July 5 : 4(3-6) 7(3-5).

2091. 1987 : Mizoram Poll : Issues at Stake. *A.T.*, Feb. 16 : 4(3-8) 7(4 5).

2092. Kalbag, Chaitanya 1980 : Mizoram: Is Laldenga Fooling Mrs. Gandhi ? *New Delhi Fortnightly* Oct. 27 : 18-23.

2093. Kamkhenthang, H. 1969 : Concept of Time and Space in Paite Chrysalis. *Siamsinpawl*, vol. 7 : 7-11.

2094. Kamkhenthang, Hauzel 1974 : Some Aspects of Paite Customs and Traditions. *Siamsinpawl Annual Magazine of Siamsinpawlpi*, vol. 12 : 33-4.

2095. Khanna, K.C. 1968 : Long Haul in Mizo Hills : Anatomy of Revolt, *Times of India*, March 15 : 6(3).

2096. , 1968 : Long Haul in Mizo Hills : Re-

1971. Economic and Political Weeky, 1978 : Editorial : Mizoram, the Relevance of Laldenga. *Eco. & Pol. Weekly* Oct. 21 : 1750.

1972. —— 1979 : Mizoram : Back to Square One. *Eco. & Pol. Weekly* May 5 : 790.

1973. —— 1979 : Mizoram : Political Failure. *Eco. & Pol. Weekly*, June 30 : 1066-67.

1974. —— 1979 : Mizoram : Bad Morality, Bad Politics. *Eco & Pol. Weekly*, July 14 : 1139-40.

1975. —— 1980 : Mizoram : A Gesture but What Next? *Eco. & Pol Weekly*, Feb. 23 : 410-11.

1976. —— 1980 : Mizoram : Another Arrangement *Eco. & Pol Weekly*, July 12 : 1158.

1977. Economic Times, 1974 : Editorial Trouble in Mizoram. *Eco. Times*, Nov, 5 : 5 (1).

1978. —— 1975 : Editorial Tragedy in Mizoram. *Eco. Times*, January 17 : 5 (1).

1979. Elly, E.B. 1978 : *Military Report on the Chin Lushai Country*, Aizawl, Tribal Research Institute.

1980. Enlite, 1967 : More Violence on Border. *Enlite* April 8 : 6(6).

1981. ——, 1967 : Feeling of Fringe People. *Enlite*, April 8 : 4(5)

1982. ——, 1967 : Settling Uprooted Mizos. *Enlite* June 24 : 6.

1983. Evidence ? : Report of Baordoloi Sub-Committee. *Evidence*, Part I.

1984. Financial Express 1976 : Editiorial : Tasks Ahead. *Financial Express*, July 6 : 4(1-2).

1985. Financial Express, 1980 : Laldenga's Ways of seeking Political Settlement. *Financial Express*, 11(8), Aug. : 24.

1986. Fischer, E.C. 1978 : *The Flora of the Lushai Hills.* Aizawl, Tribal Research Institute.

1987. Folklore, 1990 : Mizo Life and Culture : Their Folk Superstitions, Beliefs & Proverbial Sayings. *Folklore*, vol. 31.

1988. Frontier 1975 : Editorial : Rebels Strike in Aizawl. *Frontier*, January 25 : 1-2

1989. Gage, A.T. 1978 : *A Botanical Tour in South Lushai Hills.* Aizawl, Tribal Research Institute.

1990. Gaitondes, M.G. 1982 : Tribal Economy, (*In*) *Economics of the Tribes and Their Transformation*, (*Ed.*) by K.S. Dingh. Delhi, Concept Pub. Com. ; 28-39

1991. Ghosh, Sailendra Kumar, 1951 : *Clouds over Assam.* Calcutta, One India Society, 75p.

1992. Hosh, Santanu, 1979 : Mizo Insurgency : Is there any End of Tunnel? *Hindustan Standard*, Aug. 31.

1993. ———, 1980 : Symphony of Violence. *Sunday*, May, 11 : 36.

1994. ———, 1986 : No Estimate of MNF Arm. *The Telegraph* (Calcutta), July 18 : 5(3-5).

1995. Ghosh, S.P. 1984 : *Horticulture in North Eastern India.* New Delhi, Associate Pubg. Com., 230p.

1996. Glower, Dorothy : *Set on a Hill : The Record of fifty*

F. 1944 *Years in the Lushai Country.* Bristol.

1997. Godden, G.M., 1897 ; Nagas and Frontier Tribes of North East India. *Jour of Anthropological Institute*, vol. xxvi (2) : 161-201 and vol. xxvii.

1998. Gokhale, Nitin 1987 : Low-key Electioneering in Mizoram Urban Areas. *The Sentinal* (Guwahati), Feb. 10 : 1(4-5).

1999. Gole, H.W.G. 1965 : Ethnographic Notes, (*In*) *Census of India 1961, vol. III, Assam. pt. V-A, Scheduled Tribes and Scheduled Castes (Reprints from Old Census Reports and Special Tables* by E.H. Pakyntain. Delhi, Controller of Pub. : 123.

2000. Goswami, B.B. : Kinship System of the Lushai. Proceedings of *All India Sociological Conference*, Delhi, held on 9th November, 1969.

2001. ———, 1978 : Hill Tribes Plainsmen Relations in an Area of North East India. *Samatat* (Calcutta).

2002. ———, 1980 : Hill Tribesman of North East, (*In*) *The Impact of Christianity in the Tribal World and its Transformation*, (*Ed.*) by Bhupinder Singh *and* J.S. Bhandari. Delhi,

2003. ———, 1983 : Correspondence : Script and Language. *Man in India*, 63, 313-17.

2004. ———, 1987 : The Mizo in the Context of State Formation, (*In*) *Tribal Politics and*

State Systems in Pre-Colonial Eastern and North Eastern India, (*Ed*). by Surajit Sinha. Calcutta, Centre for Studies in Social Sciences (Calcutta, K.P. Bagchi & Company) : 307-28.

2005. Goswami, 1987 : Survival and Revival of Ethnic Identities of Chakmas and Mizos of Mizoram, (*In*) *Anthropology Development and Nation Building*, (*Eds*.) by A.K. Kalla *and* K.S. Singh. New Delhi, Concept Pubg. Com. : 71-86.

2006. Goswami, M.C. *and* Kamkhenthang, H. 1967 : Ritual Experts S(iampi) Among the Paite. *Bull. of the Deptt. of Anthropology, Gauhati University*, vol. V.

2007. Goswami, P.C. (Ed.) 1969 : *Rural Life in Assam Hills : Village Survey Reports on Kanther Terang, Mawtnum, Huumpui and Benshdue*. Jorhat, Agro Economic Research Centre.

2008. Goswami, Tarun 1986 : *Kuki Life And Lore*. Halflong (Assam), North Cachar Hills District Council, 648p.

2009. Gougin, T. 1980 : *Discovery of Zoland*. Churachandpur, Zomi Press.

2010. Govt. of Assam 1959 : *Report of the Committee Appointed to examine the Measures Required to be Undertaken for Rehabilitation of the Economy of the People living in the Borders of Mizo District and Adjoining East Pakistan*. Shillong, Govt of Assam.

2011. Govt. of Mizoram 1959 : *Yearwise Basic Data Information for Ten Years (1967-'77) of Mizoram.* Aizawl. Planning and Development Department.

2012. ———, 1980 : *Draft Sixth Five Years Plan, 1980-'85.* Aizawl, Planning & Development Deptt.

2013. Grierson, George A. (Ed.), 1903 : *Linguistic Survey of India, vol. III Tribe to Burman Family, pt. 2, specimens of the Bodo, Naga and Kachin Groups.* Calcutta, Office of the Sudt. of Govt. Printing.

2014. Guha, Amalendu 1985 : Foreword (*In*) *Mizoram Under the British Rule* by Subas Chatterjee. Delhi, Mittal Publications.

2015. Guha, Seema 1987 : Mizoram Poll Crucial for Cong. *Times of India*, Feb. 11 : 5(1-3).

2016. ———, 1987 : Mizoram Cong. Banking on Rajiv. *Times of India*, Feb. 15 : 1(2-5) 7(1-3).

2017. ——, 1987 : Heavy Polling in Mizoram. *Times of India*, Feb. 17 : 1(5-7).

2018. ——, 1987 : MNF gets Absolute Majority. *Times of India*, Feb. 19 : 1(1-3).

2019. ——, 1987 : MNF Aim Transformation of Mizos. *Times of India*, March 20 : 14(1-4).

2020. Guide (Dutta, Gita and, Mrinal Dutt, 1982 : *Vraman Sangi (in Bengali).* Calcutta, Asia Publishing Company : 444-48.

2021. Gupta, M.G. 1980 : Mizo Problem. *Mainstream*, Feb. 10 : 21-3.

2022. Gurudev, S. 1975 : Stalemate in Mizoram. *Stateman*, Jan. 12 : 6(4).

2023. ——, 1988 : Laldenga's Revivalist Slogans disturbing. *Statesman*, May 8.

2024. ——, 1988 : Laldenga's Revivalist Slogans disturbing. *Statesman*, May 10 : 14(3-6).

2025. Hariharan, A. 1974 : A Trouble in the Mountain. *Far Eastern Economic Review* (Hongkong), Aug. 9 : 21-2.

2026. Haugo, S.T. 1971-'72 : Some Random Thought About our People, our Language, our Culture. *Chin Literature and Culture Sub-Committee Magazine* (Rangoon).

2027. Hawla, V. 1969 : *Zoram Hmar Chan Zosapte Chanchin* (History of the Missionaries in North Lushai Hills). Aizawl.

2028. Henderson, E.A. 1965 : *Tiddim Chin*. London, Oxford University Press.

2029. Himalaya 1976 : Mizo Peace Accord. *Himalaya*, 5(6), June : 7.

1978 Work for Peace in Mizoram. *Himalaya*, 3(3), Aug. : 1.

2030. Himmat, 1979 : Mizoram : Balanced Atop a Volcano. *Himmat*, Aug. 31 : 14-5.

2031. ——, 1980 : Editorial : Peace in Mizoram. *Himmat*, Aug. 8 : 5.

2032. ——, 1980 : Mizoram : The Search for Peace with Honour. *Himmat* (*Supplement*) : 28-32.

2033. Hindu, 1967 : Editorial : Mizo Hostiles. *Hindu*, Aug. 2 : 6(1-2).

2034. ——, 1968 : Chaliha and the Mizos. *Hindu*, Jan. 5 : 6(3),

2035. ——, 1975 : Editorial : Dealing With Rebels. *Hindu*, June 7 : 6(2)

2036. ——, 1969 : Editorial : Mizo Rebels. *Hindu*. Dec. 23 : 6(2-3).

2037. ——, 1970 : Editorial : Mizo Terrorism. *Hindu*, March 12 : 8(2).

2038. ——, 1971 : Editorial : Setback in Mizo Hills (Re-grouping of Mizo Villages). *Hindus*, Feb. 7 : 8(1-2).

2039. ——, 1971 : Mizo Demand for a Full Statehood *Hindu*, July 22 : 8(4).

2040. ——, 1975 : Mizoram Dilemma. *Hindu*, Feb 10 : 6(4).

2041. ——, 1975 : Spurt in Mizo Rebel Activity. *Hindu*, June 3 : 6(4).

2042. ——, 1975 : Editorial : Mizo Rebels. *Hindu*, July 2 : 6-(2).

2043. ——, 1975 : Editorial : Dwindling Rebels. *Hindu*, Sept 12 : 6(1).

2044. ——, 1977 : Are Mizos Bargaining For More ? *Hindu*, July 19 : 8(4).

2045. ——, 1978 : Editorial : What Next in Mizoram? *Hindu*, March 23 : 8(2).

2046. ——, 1980 : Editorial : Mizoram Question *Marks Hindu*, Aug. 1 : 2.

2047. Hindu Weekly, Review, 1967 : Constructive fight With the Mizo Rebels. *Hindu Weekly Review*, Web. 27 : 7.

2048. Hindustan Times, 1967 : Editorial : Trouble in the Hills. *Hin. Times*, June 10 : 7(1-2).

2049. ———, 1969 : Editorial : Next Step in Mizo Hills. *Hin. Times*, January 11 : 7(1-2).

2050. ———, 1969 : Editorial : Next Move in Mizo Hills. *Hin. Times*, Dec. 26 : 9(1-2).

2051. ———, 1971 : Editorial : New Deal for Mizos. *Hin. Times*, July 17 : 7(1-2).

2052. ———, 1974 : Editorial : Restive Mizos. *Hin. Times*, April 12 : 5(1-2).

2053. ———, 1974 : Editorial : More Than Insurgency. *Hin. Times*, Dec. 17 : 5(1-2).

2054. ———, 1975 : Editorial : Long View Mizoram. *Hin. Times*, June 5 : 1(1-2).

2055. ———, 1977 Editiorial : Honouring an Accord. *Hin. Times*, July 30 : 7(1-2).

2056. ———, 1978 : At Game's End. *Hin. Times*, March 22 : 9(6).

2057. ———, 1978 : Editorial : Justified Action. *Hin. Times*, Nov. 14 : 7(1-2).

2058. ———, 1990 : Mizo Govt. Accused of Corruption. *Hin. Times*, Oct. 23 11(1-2).

2059. ———, 1990 : Editorial : Mizoram Bandh. *Hin. Times*, Oct. 23 : 11(1-2).

2060. Hluna, John Vanlal 1986 : *Education in Mizoram : 1804-1947 (A Historical Study with Special References to the Role of Christian Missions)*. *Unpublished* Ph. D.

Thesis, Gauhati University. History Deptt.

2061. Hungyo, P., 1987 : Land Tenure System in the Hills of Manipur : A Comparative Study of the Tangkhul Naga and the Thadou Kuki, (*In*) *Land Relations in North East India*, (*Ed.*) by B.B. Dutta *and* M.N. Karna. New Delhi, Peoples Pubg. House : 65-70.

2062. Hunter, W.W. 1976 : *A Statistical Account of Bengal, vol. VI : Chittagong Hill Tracts, Chittagong, Noakhali, Tipperah, Hill Tipperah.* Delhi, D.K. Publishing House.

2063. Hunthapa, C. 1974 : Mizoram : MNF Holds to Political Stability. *Economic and Political Weekly*, Dec. 14 : 2053-54.

2064. Inderjit, 1980 : Laldenga and The New Game. *A.T.*, Sept. 1 : 3(4).

2065. ———, 1980 : Laldenga and The New Game. *Economic Times*, Aug. 26 : 5(7).

2066. ———, 1986 : Mizoram, Peace and Laldenga. *A.T.*, Feb. 6 : 4(3-6).

2067. ———, 1986 : Mizoram Accord : Facts and Fiction. *A.T.*, July 10 : 4(3-6) 5(3-4).

2068. ———, 1987 : Mizoram Poll, A Lesson For All. *A.T.*, Feb. 25 : 4(3-6) 5(3-6).

2069. Indian Express, 1967 : Editorial : Mizo Problem (Kidnapping of Officials). *Ind. Express*, Jan. 24 : 6(1).

2070. Indian Express, 1967 : Editorial : Resettling the Mizos. *Ind. Express*, Feb. 16 : 6(1-2).

2071. ——, 1967 : Editorial : Danger in the East. *Ind. Express*, Nov. 20 : 6(1-2).

2072. ——, 1969 : Editorial : Pointless Proposal. *Ind. Express*, March 3 : 6(1-2).

2073. ——, 1972 : Editorial : End of a Rebellion. *Ind. Express*, January 5 : 5(1-2).

2074. ——, 1975 : Editorial : Aijal. *Ind, Express*, January 15 : 4(1-2).

2075. ——, 1975 : Editorial : In Perspective. *Ind. Express*, June 5 : 4(1-2).

2076. ——, 1976 : Editorial : Peace in Mizoram. *Ind. Express*, July 3 : 4(1-2).

2077. ——, 1977 : Editorial : Laldenga's Volte Face. *Ind. Express*, July 9 : 4(1-2).

2078. ——, 1978 : Editorial : Dealing with the Mizos. *Ind. Express*, March 23 : 6(1-2).

2079. ——, 1978 : Editorial, MNF Without Laldenga. *Ind. Exptess*, July 12 : 6(1-2).

2080. ——, 1978 : Editorial : Dissident to the Fore. *Ind Express*, Nov 14 : 6(1-2).

2081. ——, 1980 : Editorial : Unhelpful *Ind. Express*, Aug. 20 : 6(1-2).

2082. ——, 1980 : Editorial : Laldenga's Antics. *Ind. Express*, Oct. 10 : 6(1-2).

2083. India Today, 1976 : Mizos : Return of the Hostile Prodigals. *India Today*, July 15 : 14-5.

2084. , 1980 : Mizoram : Killings With a Message. *India Today*, July 16 : 16-7.

2085. Jafa, Jyoti, 1978 : Towards Peace With Understanding. *Statesman*, June 8 : 6(4).

2086. Jones, P.H. n.d. : *The Lushai Hills*. Londonm Baptist Missionary Society.

2087. J.T. 1986 : Laldenga May Still Surprise. *Times of India, Sunday Review* : V(1-5).

2088. Kahin, George Mc Turnan (*Ed.*) 1956 : *Government and Politics of South East Asia*. New York. Cornell University Press.

2089. Kailiana, B.S. 1980 : Economy of Mizoram : Agriculture, (*In*) *Tribal Economy of the North Eastern Region*, (*Ed.*) by T. Mathew. Gauhati, Spectrum Publications : 174-77.

2020. Kakati, Satiss Ch. 1986 : The Mizoram Accord : Hopes and Fears. *A.T.*, July 5 : 4(3-6) 7(3-5).

2091. 1987 : Mizoram Poll : Issues at Stake. *A.T.*, Feb. 16 : 4(3-8) 7(4-5).

2092. Kalbag, Chaitanya 1980 : Mizoram: Is Laldenga Fooling Mrs. Gandhi ? *New Delhi Fortnightly* Oct. 27 : 18-23.

2093. Kamkhenthang, H. 1969 : Concept of Time and Space in Paite Chrysalis. *Siamsinpawl*, vol. 7 : 7-11.

2094. Kamkhenthang, Hauzel 1974 : Some Aspects of Paite Customs and Traditions. *Siamsinpawl Annual Magazine of Siamsinpawlpi*, vol. 12 : 33-4.

2095. Khanna, K.C. 1968 : Long Haul in Mizo Hills : Anatomy of Revolt, *Times of India*, March 15 : 6(3).

2096. 1968 : Long Haul in Mizo Hills : Regrouping for Peace. *Times of India*, March 16 : 6(3).

2097. Khanna, S.N. 1978 : Peace Returning to Mizoram. Overseas. *Hindustan Times*, May : 25 : 10.

2098. Khatkhojam, H. 1979 : Paite and Other Languages. *Siamsinpawl Annual Magazine* (Churachandpur, Imphal), vol. 17 : 10-5.

2099. Khotahng, T. Jam *and* Kamkhenthang, H. 1978 : A Brief Introduction to the Language and Culture of the Paites [Tedim Chin]. (*In*) *An Introduction to Tribal Language and Culture of Manipur* (7 *Tribes*). (*Ed.*) by K.B. Singh. Imphal, Manipur Kala Accademi.

2100. Krishna, K.S., 1963 : *Report of the Development in the Mizo District of Assam*. New Delhi, Planning Commission.

2101. Kundu, Dilip, 1988 : Ethnic Politics in North East India : A Study of MNF. Proceedings of Seminar on *Regional Political Parties in North East India*, Held During 9-10 Dec., 1988 by NEICSSR, Shillong (Mimeo)

2102. Laldenga, R ; D. Pradhan *and* Lahkalma, 1986 : Cengre-MNF Agreement. *Shillong* 7., July 12 : 2 (3-5) 3 (.),

2103. Lalhmachhuana, 1980 : Economy of Mizoram : Prospects for Development (*In*) *Tribal Economy of the North Eastern Region*, (*Ed.*) by T. Mathew. Gauhati, Spectrum Publications : 185-90.

2104. Lalhmuaka, 1981, : *Zoram Zirna lam Chhinehhiahna.* Aizawl. Tribal Research Institute.

2105. Lalkhama, 1971 : *Report on Development of Industries in Mizo Hills.* New Delhi, Small Scale Industries Development Organization, Ministry of International Development and International Trade.

2106. ———, 1976 : Key Note Address to the Seminar on *Strategy for Planned Economic Development of Mizoram,* Held During 29-31 July 1976, in Aizawl.

2107. ———, 1984 : Nula-Rim : Mizo Customary Practice of Courting Girls. *Mizoram News Magazine,* Aug. : 18-21.

2108. Lalnithanga, P., 1983 : *Census of India 1981, Series 31, Mizoram, Pt. II-B, Primary Census Abstract.* Delhi, Controller of Pubs., 61p.

2109. ———, 1984 : *Census of India 1981, Series 31, Mizoram, Pts. XIII A and B, Village and Town Directory, Village and Townwise Primary Census Abstract : Aizawl District.* Delhi, Controller of Pubs., 187p.

2110. ———, 1984 : *Census of India 1981, Series 31, Mizoram, Pts. XIII-A and B, Village and Town Directory, Village and Townwise Primary Census Abstract : Lunglei District.* Delhi, Controller of Pubs., 86p.

2111. ———, 1984 : *Census of India 1981, Series 31, Mizoram, Parts XIII-A and B, Village and Town Directory,*

Village and Townwise Primary Census Abstract : Chimtuipui District. Delhi, Controller of Pubs., 95p.

2112. Lalnithanga, P. 1986 : *Census of India 1981, Sereis 31, Mizoram, Paper I of 1985 : Household Population by Religion of Head of Household (Upto C.D. Block and Town Level).* Delhi, Controller of Pubs., 17p.

2113. Lalramchuani Sena, 1974 : *The Mizo Independence Movement. Unpublisned* M.A. Dissertation Submitted to the California State University.

2114. Lalringkeema, 1984 : To the Editor : Mizoram Statehood Not Played Up At All and Why Not. *Shillon T.*, May 5 : 2 (3).

2115. Lalthangliana, B., Mizo., 1977 : *Mizoram Today*, II (1-2).

2116. Law Research Institute, 1982 : *Report of Mizo Customary Laws and Practices.* Gauhati, Law Research Institute, Gauhati High Court. (*Mimeo.*)

2117. Lehman, F.K., 1980 : *Structure of Chin Saciety.* Aizawl, Tribal Research Institute.

2118. Lewin, Thomas H., 1869 : *Progressive Collonial Exercised in the Lushai Dialect of Dozo or Kuki Language, With Vocabularies and Popular* Tales. Calcutta.

2119. ———, 1978 : *Wild Race of S.E. India.* Aizawl, Tribal Research Institute.

2120. ———, 1984 : *Progressive Colloquial Exercise.* Aizawl, Tribal Resear Inst.

2121. Lewin, Thomas, H., 1977 : *A Fly on the Wheel.* Aizawl, Tribal Research Inst.

2122. Liankhohau, T., 1990 : *Social, Cultural, Economic and Religious Life of a Transformed Community : A Study of the Paite tribe.* Delhi, Mittal Publications (*in Press*).

2123. Link, 1966 : Mizoram State. *Link* (New Delhi), March 13.

2124. ———, 1975 : Conspiracy in Mizoram. *Link*, Feb. 9 : 15.

2125. Lorrain, J.H. *and* Savidge, 1976 : *A Grammer and Dictionary of the Lushai Language.* Aizawl, Tribal Research Inst.

2126. ———, 1983 : *Pu Buauga Dictionary.* Aizawl, Research Inst.

2127. Luaia, Rev. H.S., 1945 : *Mizoram Baptist Kohhran Chanchin.* Lunglei (*Ed.*) by Rev. H,W. Carter. (*In Mizo*). Aijad, Published in 1981 in Revised and Enlarged Edition.

2128. Lyngdoh, U.C., 1986 : To the Editor : Centre-MNF Agreement on Border trade. *Shillong T.*, July 26 : 2 (3-5).

2129. Mahajan, V.S., (*Ed.*), 1987 : *Emerging Pattern of North Eastern Economy.* New Delhi, Deep and Deep Pubs.

2130. Mainstream, 1980 : Pre-requisites for Normalcy. *Mainstream*, Aug. 9 : 6-7.

2131. Majumdar, A., 1985 : To the Editor : Alternative Rail Link-up to Cachar-Tripura. Mizoram. *Shillong T.*, July 27 : 2 (3-5).

2132. Malik, Amita, 1971 : Encounter with Mizos. *Illustrated Weekly*. Oct. 10 : 5-12.

2133. Malik, Harjit, 1972 : New Bearings in Mizoram. *Indian Express*, April 21 : 6 (3).

2134. ———, 1972 : New Bearings in Mizoram. *Indian Express*, April 23 : 6 (3).

2135. ———, 1980 : Endless Violence in Mizoram *Times of India*, May 16 : 5 (6).

2136. ———, 1980 : Endless Violence in Mizoram-II. *Times of India*, May 17 : 6 (6).

2137. Marshall, H., 1945 : *The Karens of Burma*. Calcutta, Longmans Green.

2138. Mc Call, A.G., 1977 : *Lushai Chrysalis*. Aizawl. Tribal Research Inst. (*Reprinted*)

2139. ———, 1980 : *Lushai Hills District Cover*. Aizawl, Tribal Research Inst. (*Reprinted*).

2140. ———,1980 : *Collection of Some Interesting Correspondance*. Aizawl, Tribal Research Inst. (*Reprinted*)

2141. Medhi, Birinchi Kumar, 1980 : *Akhan Desh, Alekh Manuh*. (*in Assamese*). Mangaldai, J.N. Chakrabarti, Chakrabarti Brothers : 63-6.

2142. Miglani, Sanjeev. 1988 : The Battle Continues in the North East. *Statesman* (*Saturday Magazine*), Feb. 6 : I (1-8) II (4-8).

2143. Misra, Bani Prasanna, 1982 : Kirata Karyokinesis : An Introduction to the Political Economy of Tribal Societies in North East India, (*In*) *Economies of the Tribes and their Transformation*, (*Ed.*) by K.S. Singh Delhi, Concept Publishing Comp. : 43-62

2144. Mizoram News Magazine, 1984 : Mizo Festival and Dance. *Mizoram News Magazine*, Aug. : 56-9.

2145. Mukherjee, Chinmoy, 1988 : Letters to the Editor : Crisis in Mizoram. *Am. Baz. Pat.*, Sept. 26 : 6 (4-5).

2146. Mukherjee, Deba Prasad, 1982 : Some Biological Dimensions of Tribal Economy in India, *(In) Economies of the Tribes and their Transformation*,(*Ed.*) by K.S.Sing. Delhi, Concept Pubg. Comp. : 21-7.

2147. Mukherjee, Dilip, 1976 : Peace Returns to Mizoram : End of a Prolonged Insurgency. *Times of India*, July 3 : 6 (3).

2148. Naba Bharat Times, 1986 : Laldenga Ne Sahajog Manga (*in Hindi*). *Naba Bharat Times*, July 15 . 1 (7-8).

2149. ———, 1986 : Mizo Samjhote Par Bipakhya Ko Shankayen : Sarkar Par Samarpan Ka Arop (*in Hinai*)-*Naba Bharat Times*, July 22 : 1 (7-8).

2150. ———, 1986 : Mizoram : Chah Mahine Kathin (*in Hindi*), *Naba Bhart Times*, Aug. 18 : 1 (4).

2151. ———, 1986 : Laldenga 21 August Ko Satta Sambhalenge. (*in Hindi*). *Naba Bharat Times*, Aug. 19 : 1 (6-8).

2152. ———, 1986 : Mizoram ke bare men chetabanee (*in Hindi*). *Naba. Bharat Times*, Aug. 20 : 7 (1).

2153. ———, 1987 : Editorial : Mizoram Chunav (*in Hindi*). *N.B.T.*, January 15 : 5 (1-2).

2154. Naba Bharat Times, 1987 : Laldenga Kee Pratigya (*in Hindi*). *N.B.T.*, Feb. 13 : 4 (1-2).

2155. ———, 1987 : Mizoram Kee Adhikatam Madad Denge : Rajiv (*in Hindi*). *N.B.T*,. Feb. 14 : (7-8).

2156. ———. 1987 : Congress Va Mizo Front Men China Jhapttee, (*in Hindi*). *N.B.T.*, Feb. 14 : 1 (5-7).

2157. ———, 1987 : Rajiv Kee Sabha Me La denga vi. *N.B.T.*, Feb. 15 ::1 (8).

2158. ———, 1987 : Rajiv Kee Khyati Se Laldenga Khema Chintit. *N.B.T.*, Feb. 15 : 1 (7-8).

2159. ———, 1987 : Editorial : Mizoram Men Nayeee Shuruat. *N.B.T.*, Feb. 20 : 4 (1-2).

2160. ———, 1987 : Mizoram, Arunachal Ko Purna Rajya Ka Darja. *N.B.T.*, Feb. 21 : 1 (5-8).

2161. ———, 1988 : Laldenga Ko Sathiyon Ke Punarbhas Kee Chinta. *N.B.T.*, March 8 : 3 (1-2).

2162. ———, 1988 : Editorial : Mizoram Men Nashabandi. *N.B.T.*, 4 (1-7).

2163. ———, 1988 : Editorial : Mizoram Men Rashtrapati Shasan. *N.B.T.*, Sept. 8 : 6 (1-2).

2164. ———, 1988 : Mizoram Men Nashabandi Ke Douran Sharab Niryat ? *N.B.T.*, Dec. 20 3 (1-2).

2165. ———, 1989 : Mizoram Chunav Men Sirf Teen Mahila Pratyashi. *N.B.T.*, January 18 : 5 (1-2).

2166. Naba Bharat Times, 1989 : Mizo Front Men Foot Ka Lav Congress Ko Mila : Samachar Bhisleshan. *N.B.T.*, January 28. 8 (7-8).

2167. ———, 1989 : Editorial : Laldenga Ki Rajniti. *N.B.T.*, Feb. 27 : 4 (1-2).

2168. ———, 1989 : Laldenga Phir Se Bagee Nahi Banenge. *N.B.T.*, Feb. 24 3 (1-2).

2169. Nag, Amit Kumar, 1986 : Mizo Accord May Run into Rough Weather. *Am. Baz. Pat.*, July 15 : 7 (7-8).

2170. ———, 1987 : Laldenga Shows Signs of firmness. *Am. Baz. Pat.*, March 20 : 5 (1-4).

2171. ———, 1988 : Delay in Assistance Can Cause Serious Trouble : Laldenga. *Am. Baz. Pat.*, March 3 : 7 (1-4).

2172. Narayan, H., 1983 : Mizoram With Little Banking Facilities. *Indian Express*, Nov. 23.

2173. Nath, Alokananda, 1987 : Women in Folklore of North-East India : Some Focus on the Position and Status. *Folklore*, 28 (6), June : 120-26.

2174. N.A.G., 1988 : Proceedings of a Seminar on *Environmental Management in Hill and Tribal Areas*, Organised by the National Association of Geographer (India), Geographical Society of N.E.H. Region and the Deptt. of Geography, NEHS during Oct. 14 to Oct. 16 in NEHU, Shillong.

2175. NCAER, 1962 : *Techno-Economic Survey of Assam.* New Delhi, National Council of Applied Economic Research.

2176. Nath, S.C. *and* Bordoloi, D.N., 1988 : North East India : An Ethno-Botanical Survey. *Himalaya : Man and Nature*, XI (8-9), Jan.-Feb. : 2-6.

2177. Nayar, Kuldip, 1986 : Mizoram Has Gone One Better Than Jammu and Kashmir. *The Telegraph*, July 18 : 3-(6).

2178. Nehru, B.K., 1978 : Foreword, (*In*) *The Mizos* by L.B.Thanga. Gauhati United Publishers : viii.

2179. News, 1987 : Expedition to the Blue Mountain : Mizoram. News (Shillong), *Geological Survey of India*, VI, Oct. : 1-2.

2180. Ngaihte, S.T., 1979 : *Mistory of the Zomi of Mizoram and the Surrounding Areas : Aspects of Pre-Calonial Society. Unpublished* M.Phil Dissertation Submitted to Jawaharlal Nehru University, Delhi.

2181. Ngin Suanh, S., 1968-'69 : Brie History of Laipian Pauchinhau and His Religion. Rangoon, Rangoon University, *Chin Literature and Cultural Sub-Committee Annual Magazine*.

2182. Ngul Kho Pau, H., 1970 : *Hatzaw Beh Laibu* (i.e. A History of Hatzaw clan). Tedim, Pub. by author.

2183. Nibedon, Niramal, 1980 : Uncertainity Grips : Mizoram. *Democratic World*, July 13 : 5-6.

2184. ———, 1980 : Text of the February 1976 Agreement, (*In*) *Mizoram : The Dagger Brigade* by Niramal Nibedon.

New Delhi, Lancers Publishers : 263-64 (Appendix-I).

2185. NEICSSR, 1990 : Proceedings of a Seminar on *Continuity and Change in the Hills of North-East India with a Special Reference to Garo Hills as a tribute to Dr. D.N. Majumdar*, Held During 14-15 Dec. 1990, in Shillong by NEICSSR.

2186. Now, 1967 : Editorial : Smoke Over Hills. *Now*, Jan. 13 : 3 (4-5).

2187. ———, 1987 : Mizos. *Now*, Sept. 1 : 8.

2188. Nunthara, C., 1981 : Grouping of Villages in Mizoram : Its Social and Economic Impact. *Eco. and Pol. Weekly*, July 23.

2189. Pakem, B., 1986 : Political Development and Change in North East India, (*In*) *Changing North East India*, (*Ed.*) by A.P. Sinha. Ludhiana, Gagan Publishers : 29-64.

2190. Pakhuongte, R., 1978 : *The Development of the Evangelical Free Church of India Among the Hmar tribes and Suggestions for Future Directions. Unpublished* M.A. Th. Dissertation Submitted to the Northern Baptist Theological Seminary, Illinois.

2191. Pal, S., 1968 : Precarious Security in Mizo Hills. *Hindustan Times*, May 21 : 16 (1).

2192. Pal, Samir, 1968 : Mizo Rivalries Be Devil Development. *Hind T.*, May 22 : 16 (1)

2193. ———, 1947 : Is it MNF Rule in Mizoram? *Overseas Hindustan Times*, Oct. 17 : 11.

2194. Palit, D.K., 1978 : Counter Insurgency At its Best. *Hind. T.*, June 27 : 7 (3).

2195 Pande, S.K., 1985 : To the Editor : Mizo Settlement, Plea for a Quick Deal Right Now. *Shillong T.*, Oct. 5 : 2 (3-5).

2196. Pardesi, Ghanshyam, 1987 : Sailo for Integration of Mizo Inhabited Areas. *Statesman*, January 20 : 9 (7-8).

2197. Parry, N.E., 1976 : *A Monograph on Lushai Customs and Ceremonies.* Aizawl, Tribal Research Institute (*Reprint*).

2198. Pathak, Ram Deo, 1981 : Conceptual Analyses of Lushai Language in the Context of Hindi Teaching in Hindi Language, (*In*) *Janajati Bhasaen aur Hindi Sikshan.* Agra, Kendriya Hindi Sansthan : 173-81.

2199. Pathak, Ram Deo *and* D.K. Mishra, 1981 : Hindi Aur Lushai Bhasaon Ka Tulanatmak Adhyayan in Hindi Language, (*In*) *Janajati Bhasaen aur Hindi Sikshan.* Agra, Kendriya Hindi Sansthan.

2200. Patranabis, Tushar Ranjan, 1975 : Roots of Rebellion in Mizoram, *Organiser*, Feb. 15, 6 (11).

2201. Phookan, Surenram, 1988 : One year of Mizoram's Statehood. *A.T.*, Feb. 20 : 4 (3-4).

2202. Phukan Barua, Indira, 1988 : Mizo National Front. Proceedings of a Seminar on *Regional Political Parties in North East India*, Held During 9-10 Dec., 1988 by NEICSSR, Shilloug : 16 (*Mimeo.*)

2203. Pillai, M.P. Narayana, 1967 : Bamboo Tensions. *Far Eastern Economic Review* (Hongkong), Aug. 3 : 233-34.

2204. Platform, 1980 : Editorial : Restoration of Peace in Mizoram. *platform*, Aug. 7 : 2 (1).

2205. Poonte, B., 1965 : *Zoram Thliranga.* Aijal. Deputy Commissioner, Mizo District.

2206. Prasad, N.N., 1988 : Mizo National Front Party and its Activities : A Study. Proceeding of a Seminar of *Regional, Political Parties in North East India,* Held During 9-10 December, 1988 by NEICSSR, Shillong : 1-5 (*Mimeo.*)

2207. Prasad, R.N., 1986 : Soil Fertility Under Shifting, Terrace and Permanent Valley Cultivation. *(In) Land use pattern in North East India (Ed.)* by B.B. Dutta. Ludhiana, Gagan Publishers : 85-92

2208. Purbanchal Prahari, 1990 : Mizoram Men Ugrabhadi Gati Bidhiyon Nehi : Bedi. *Purabanchal Prahari,* Sept. 4 : 1 (5-8) [*In Hindi*].

2209. Rajan, K.R. Sundar, 1986 : Loose ends in Mizo Pact : A print of View. *Am. Baz. Pat.*, July 16 : 6 (3-6).

2210. Ramala, L.S. *and* Kankachary, M., 1990 : *Tribal Linguistics in India : International Resources*, Delhi.

2211. Ramunny, Murket 1978 : Similar Problems, Different politics. *Hindu*, May 16 : 8 (4).

2212. Rangasami, Amritha, 1978 : Mizoram : Tragedy of Our Own Making. *Econom'c and Political Weekly*, April 15 : 653-62.

2213. Rao, V. Venkata, 1980 : Slavery in North Eeast India. *The Thinkers.* 8 (1-2).

2314. Ray, A, 1972 : *Mizoram*. Calcutta, Pearl Publications.

2215. Raza, Moonis *and* Aijayuddin A., 1990 : *An Atlas of Tribal India with Computed Tables of District Level Data and its Geographical Interpretation*. Delhi.

2216. Reid, Robert. 1978 : *The Lushai Hills*. Aizawl, Tribal Research Institute.

2217. Rengsi, Vanlalruata, 1988 : Traditional Craft and Technology of the Mizos. Proceedings of a National Seminar on *Archoeology of North East India* (October 26-28, 1988), *Papers and Abstracts* (*Ed.*) by Jai prakash Singh. Deptt. of History, NEHU. Shillon (*Mimeo.*)

2218. ———, 1990 : Techniques of Food Production in Precolonial Mizo Society. Proceedings of *XIth Session of North East India History Association* (*Imphal*) held during October 25-27, 1990 in Manipur Univesity History Deptt.

2219 Resistance, 1980 : Case-fire Agreement in Mizoram. *Resistance*, Aug. 5 : 1(3).

2220. Roy, Asok Kumar, 1988 : *The Problem of Legitimacy in the Thadou Kuki Tribal Society in Manipur*. (*Unpublished* Ph D. Thesis, Burdwan University West Bengal).

2221. Roy, Khiren, 1986 : Mizoram Scene-II : Accord and Other Extremists. *A.T.*, July 19 : 4(3-6).

2222. Roy, Rati Ranjan 1988 : Laldenga's Dictatorial. *Am. Baz. Pat.*, Nov. 24 ; 7(1-3).

2223. Roy, Rati Ranjan 1989 : North East in the grip of Heroin fever. *Am. Baz. Pat.*, January 4 : 7(1-2).

2224. Roy Burman, B.K. 1984 : Crisis of Identity Among Mizos. *Mainstream*, 22(46), July 14 : 26-32.

2225. ———, 1987 : Foreword. (*In*) *Demographic Profile of North East India* by S.C. Srivastava. Delhi, Mittal Publications.

2226. ———, 1988 : Foreword, (*In*) *The Paite : A Transborder Tribe of India and Burma* by H. Kamkhenthang. Delhi, Mittal Pubs. : vii-xix.

2227. ———, 1989 : Introduction, (*In*) *North East Frontier of India* by Alexander Mackenzine. Delhi, Mittal Publications (*Reprinted* 2nd time).

2228. Roy Burman, J.J. 1988 : Impact of Grouping of Villages on the Jhum Culture of Mizoram. Proceedings of *Review and re-appraisal Seminat on Shifting Cultivation in North East India* organlsed by NEICSSR, Shillong during 13-14 May 1988 (*Mimeo*).

2229. Sagheer, Beddar 1975 : Murders in Mizoram. *Radiance*, June 26 : 9.

2230. Saha, Akshaya Kumar, 1986 : How accord May Help Mizos. *Am. Baz. Pat.*, Aug. 5 : 6(3-6).

2231. ———, 1990 : Destination North East. *Am. Baz. Pat.*, (*Sunday Magazine*), Nov. 4 I I(1-8).

2232. Sahlins, H.D., 1968 : *Tribesman*. London, Prentice-Hall International ; 6.

2233. Saiaithanga 1974 : *Mizo Kohram Chanchin : History of Mizo. Unpublished* M.A. Dissertation Submitted to the California State University.

2234. Sailo, Zoparmawii 1987 : Letters to the Editor : Leh to Lungleh. *Stateman*, April 25 : 2(5-6).

2235. Samanta, R,K. *and* Adhikary M.M. 1988 : Marriage Systems Among Tribals of North East India : An Overview. *Man in India*, 68(4), Dec. : 401-12.

2236. Sangkima, 1990 : A Mizo Uprising : A Significant Event in the History of Chieftainship in Mizoram. Proceedings of *XIth Session of North East India History Association (Imphal)*, Held During Oct. 25-27, 1993 in Manipur University by History Deptt.

2237. Sangma, Milton S. 1987 : *History of American Baptist Mission of North East India (vol. I)*. Delhi, Mittal Pubs.

2238. Sareen, H.K. 1980 : *Insurgency in North East India : A Study of the Sino-American Role.* New Delhi, Sterling Publishers.

2239. Sarin, VIK 1967 : Focus on Mizo Hills. *Indian Express*, May 28 : 1(2).

2240. ———, 1967 : Focus on Mizo Hills. *Indian Express*, May 28 : 1(2).

2241. ———, 1970 : Mizo Problem Still Unsolved. *Indian Express*, Dec. 29 : 8(5).

2242. ———, 1977 : Mizo Rebels flouting Peace Accord. *Indian Express*, March 17 : 5(6).

2243. Sarkar, Jayanta 1975 : Subcontintent : To New Delhi, A Manifesto of Murder. *Far Eastern Economic Review* (Hongkong), Feb. 7 : 36.

2244. ———, 1988 : Marriage System in North East India, (*In*) *Marriage in India : Tribes, Muslims and Anglo Indians*, (*Eds.*) by B.B. Goswami, J. Sarkar and D. Danda. Calcutta, Anthropological Survey of India : 47-55.

2245. Sawa Pau. G,H.T. 1973-,75 : Research on Some Aspects of Tiddim Chin Culture. *Chin Magazine* (Rangoon).

2246. Saw Shwe Boh, 1972 : Khawnusam, the Mistry Mountain *Forward* (Rangoon), Dec. 15.

2247. Secular Democracy, 1976 : Editorial : Mizos Join the Mainstream. *Secular Democracy*, July 1 : 14.

2248. ———, 1978 : Mizoram, New Outlook on Ending Insurgency. *Secular Democracy*, April 1 : 29-30.

2249. Sen, D. 1984 : Early History of Lushais With a Speeial Reference to Lushai Chiefs. *Social Research*, 4(3-4), July-Dec. : 13-7.

2250. Sen, Kranti, 1967 : Need for a New Approach. *Mainstream*, Sept. 30 : 13-6.

2251. Sen, Sipra, 1937 : *Bibliography of Mizoram.* (Bibliography Submitted to Anthrepological Survey of India, Shillong for Publication in *People of. India* Book of Anth. Surv. of India).

2252. Sen, Sumit, 1987 : MNF Move to Weed Out Corruption, *Statesman*, May 6 : 1(2-5) 9(4-5),

2253. Sen Sumit, 1990 : The Drug Tail. *Statesman, Sunday Miscellany*. Oct. 28 : 1(1-5), 2(1-5), 3(1-4) and 4(1-5).

2254. ———, 1990 : Khun Sa, Druglord of Shah State. *Statesman, Sunday Miscellany*, Oct. 28 : 3(1-4).

2255. Sen Gupta, N N. 1990 : *Finger Dermatoglyphics of Three Communities of the Mizos. Unpublished* mss., Anthropological Survey of India, Shillong.

2256. Sentinal 1984 : Youth Welfare Schemes in Mizoram. *Sentinal* (Guwahati, Aug. 25

2257. Serajuddin, A.M. 1984 : The Chakma Tribe of the Chittagong Hill Tracts in the 18th Century. *Jour of the Royol Asiatic Society.*

2258. Seth, R.N. 1967 : Village Grouping in Mizo Hills : Off to a Good Start. *Yojana*, March 12 : 15-8.

2259. Shakespear, J. 1990 : Folktales of the Lushais and Their Neighbours. *Folk Lore*, 2 C4 : 338-420. (Illustrated with Notes by T.C. Hodson).

2260. Shambuk 1975 : Torture in the North East. *Eves Weckly*, May 18 : 9.

2261. Sharma, Vijay Prakash, 1988 : Buonzawl : A Vanishing Institution of Hmar : Some Points About Youth Dormitories. *Folklore*, 29 (10), Oct. : 230-33.

2262. Shaw, W. 1980 : *Notes on the Thadou Kukis.* Calcutta, Firma KLM Pvt. Ltd.

(*Reprinted* on Behalf of Tribal Research Institute Aizawl).

2263. Shillong Times 1981 : Sailo's Plea for Greater Mizoram. *Shillong T.*, Dec. 19 : 1(4-5).

22 4. ———, 1982 : Editorial : MNF Banned at Last. *Shillong T*, January 30 : 2(1-2).

2265. ———, 1982 : Mizoram Scene : Laldenga's Limited Options. *Shillong T.*, March 6 : 1(1-4).

2266. ———, 1982 : Mizoram on Threshold of Agricultural Break-through. *Shillong T.*, May 1 : 1(1-3).

2267. ———, 1982 : MNF Circular for Bank raid. *Shillong T.*, June 5 : (1-2).

2268. ———. 1982 : Laldenga's Brother Arrested : Chaos in Mizoram Again. *Shillong T.*, June 19 : 1(3-5) 8(5) .

2269. ———, 1982 : Editorial : Rumblings in Mizoram. *Shillong T.*, June 26 : 2(1-2).

2270. ———, 1982 : Sailo explains MNF Antics. *Shillong T.*, Aug. 21 : 8(3-4).

2271. ———, 1982 : Mizo Student Leader Held in Shillong. *Shillong T.*, Sept. 11 : 1(4-5).

2272. ———, 1912 : Pilot Project for Control of Jhum. *Shillong T.*, Oct. 20 : 3(1-2).

2273. ———, 1982 : Editorial : One Ambush and Many Versions. *Shillong T.*, Nov. 6 : 2(1-2).

2274. ———, 1983 : Orders to Expel Aliens in Mizoram. *Shillong T.*, May 21 : 1(1-3).

2275. Shillong Times, 1983 : Editorial : Aizawl on Air map. *Shillong T.*, June 11 : 2(1-2).

2276. ———, 1983 : Editorial : Border Vigil. *Shillong T.*, Aug. 20 : 2(1-2).

2277. ———, 1983 : The Relevence of District Council-II. *Shillong T.*, Sept. 24 : 2(3-5).

2278. ———, 1984 : Editorial : The Mizoram Poll. *Shillong T.*, April 14 : 2(1-2).

2279. ———, 1984 : Mizoram Elections : Congress (I) Going the Whole Hog. *Shillong T.*, April 14 : 1(1-2).

2280. ———, 1984 : Tourism Newsletter. *Shillong T.*, April 21 : 5(1-5) 6(5).

2281. ———, 1984 : North Eastern Affairs : Mizoram Grabs Assam Territory. *Shillong T.* May 5 : 4(4-5), 6(4-5).

2282. ———, 1984 : North Eastern Affairs : The Triple entente. *Shillong T.*, May 5 : 4(1-4).

2283. ———, 1984 : Mizo Election And After : Brigadier Sailo in a New Role. *Shillong* T., May 12 : 2(3-5).

2284. ———, 1984 : Editorial : Change-over in Mizoram. *Shillong T.*, May 12 : 2(1-2).

2285 ———, 1984 : Editorial : Mizo Reconciliation. *Shillong T.*, June 23 : 2(1-2).

2286. ———, 1984 : Initiation for Peace Talks in Mizoram. *Shillong T.*, July 7 4(4-5) 6(3).

2287, ———. 1984 : Entrepreneurship Development in Mizoram. *Shillong* T., Aug. 25 : 3(1-2).

2288. Shillong Times, 1984 : Editorial : MNF's Wider Dimension. *Shillong T.*, Aug. 25 : 2(1-2).

2289. ———, 1984 : Editorial : Killing the Patient, *Shillong T.*, Sept. 8 : 2(1-2)

2290 ———, 1984 : Editorial : The Mizo Dialogue. *Shillong T.*, Oct. 20 : 2(1-2).

2291. ———, 1984 : Editorial : Laldenga in New Delhi. *Shillong T.*, Nov, 17 : 2 1-2l

2292. ——— 1984 : Editorial : Election Scene : North East. *Shillong T*,, Dec. 8 : 2(1-2).

2293. ———, 1985 : Editorial : 'Donations' for Insurgency. *Shillong T.*, April 6 : 2(1-2)

2294. ———. 1985 : Editorial : Strike the Iron Now. *Shillong* T., April 27 : 2(1-2)

2295. ———, 1985 : Fake Currencies Were Printed in Burma. *Shillong T.*, May 18 : 1 (3-5).

2296. ———, 1985 : Mizoram Accord Round the Corner. *Shillong T.*, Aug. 24 : 1 (4-5).

2297. ———, 1985 : Spectacular Youth Festival in Aizawl : A Correspondent. *Shillong T.*, Nov. 16 . 6 (2). 8 (2).

2298. ———, 1986 : Editorial : Elusive Mizo Accord. *Shillong T.*, Feb. 8 : 2 (1-2).

2299. ———, 1986 : Editorial : Commendable Gestures. *Shillong T.*, March 1 : 2 (1-2).

2300. ———, 1986 : Editorial : Mizo Talks in Final Round. *Shillong T.*, March 15 : 2 (1-2).

2301. Shillong Times, 1986 : Editorial: New Tangle in Mizoram *Shillong T.*, April 19: 2 (1-2).

2302. ———, 1986 : Editorial: New Tangle in Mizoram *Shillong T.*, April 19 : 2 (1-2).

2303. ———, 1986 : Editorial : Stagnant Mizo Talks. *Shillong T.*, May 24 : 2 (1-2).

2304. ———, 1986 : Editorial : A New Dawn in Mizoram. *Shillon T.*, July 5 : 2 (1-2).

2305. ———, 1986 : Mizoram's Hour of Reckoning. *Shillong T.*, July 10 : 1 (1-4).

2306. ———, 1986 : Mizoram's Hour of Reckoning. *Shillong T.*, July 12 : 1 (1-4).

2307. ———, 1986 : Editorial: The Accord and its Fall out. *Shillong T.*, July 12 : 2 (1-2).

2308. ———, 1986 : Centre-MNF Agreement. *Shillong T.*, July 12 : 2 (3-5), 3(1).

2309. ———, 1986 : Editorial: PM's Focus on Mizoram *Shillong T.*, July 19 : 2 (1-2).

2310. ———, 1986 : Efforts to Develop Air Transport : Tourism in Mizoram. *Shillong T.*, Aug. 15 : 1 (4-5) 8 (5).

2311. ———, 1986 : Laldenga Pledges Clean Govt. *Shillong T.*, Aug. 23 : 1 (1 2).

2312. ———, 1986 : Editorial : In True Spirit of Accord *Shillong T.*, Aug. 30 : 1 (1-3) 8 (1).

2313. ———, 1986 : Laldenga Defends Accords. *Shillong T.*, Aug. 30 : 1 (1-3) 8 (1).

2314. Shillong Times, 1986 : Editorial : On Way to Statehood. *Shillong T.*, Sept. 6 : 2 (1-2).

2315. ———. 1986 : Call for Strengthening Church : Govt. Ties in Mizoram. *Shillong T.* Oct. 4 : 1 (1-2).

2316. ———, 1986 : Mizo Contingent for National Festival. *Shillong T.*, Oct. 4 : 4 4 (1-3).

2317. ———, 1986 : Editorial : Two Welcome Gestures. *Shillong T.*, Oct. 4 : 2 (1-2).

2318. ———, 1986 : Editorial : Saikia's Rehabilitation. *Shillong T.*, Dec. 13 : 2 (1-2).

2319. ———, 1987 : Election Bell rings in Mizoram. *Shillong T.*, January 17 : 1 (1-2).

2320. ———, 1987 : PM : More Powers for District Councils. *Shillong T.*, Feb. 14 : 1 (4-5).

2321. ———, 1987 : Mizoram Poll Scenario : Centre Keen on Seeing Laldenga in Power *Shillon T.*, Feb. 14 : 3 (1-4[.

2322. ———, 1987 : Laldenga Assumes Office Today. *Shillong T.*, Feb. 19 : 1 (1-2).

2323, ———, 1987 : No Merger With Cong-I. *Shillong T.*, Feb. 19 : 1 (3-5).

2324. ———, 1987 : 500 Jhumias to Benefit From Cardamon Planting in Mizoram. *Shillong T.*, March 12 : 3 (1-2).

2325. ———, 1987 : Mizo Youths Tilt Scales for Laldenga. *Shillong T.*, March 12 : 3 (1-3).

2326. ———, 1987 : Editorial : Burmā Rice for Mizoram. *Shillong T.*, June 15 : 2 (1-2).

2327. Shillong Times, 1987 : Editorial: Mystery That is 'Seawind *Shillong T.*, June 25 : 2 (1-2).

2328. ———, 1987 : Centre Clears Mizoram Hycel Project. *Shillong T.*, July 1 : 3 (3).

2329. ———, 1987 : First Anniversary of Mizo Accord. *Shillong T.*, July 3 : 5 (1-4).

2330. ———, 1987 : Focus on Mizoram : How Laldenga Deals with Hostile Bureaucracy. *Shillong T.*, July 7 :3 (3-5-.

2331. ———, 1987 : Editorial : Laldenga in New light. *Shillong T.*, July 31 : 2 (1-2).

2332. ———, 1987 : Editorial : Corruption at Top. *Shillong T.*, Aug. 10 : 2 (1-2).

2333. ———, 1987 : Tribal Insurgents Form New Organisation. *Shillong T.*, Sept 28 : 1 (2-5).

2334. ———, 1988 : Laldenga Attributes Congress (I): Victory to Dissension Among People. *Shillong T.*, Nov. 3 : 3 (1-3).

2335. ———, 1987 : Editorial : Solution of the Chakma Problems. *Shillong T.*, Dec. 4 : 2 (1-2).

2336. ———, 1988 : Mizo Students Threaten NEHU V.C. *Shillong* T., January 29 : 3 (4).

2337. ———, 1988 : Mizo PCC (I) Plea for Effective Enforcement of Inner Line system. *Shillong* T,, Feb, 15 : 3 (1),

2338, ———, 1988 : Railway Expansion Projects in North East. *Shillong* T., Feb. 23 :3 (1).

2339. Shillong Times, 1988 : Editorial : Mizoram's Deficit Budget. *Shillong* T., March 11 : 2 (1-2)

2340. ———, 1988 : Mizoram Changes Capital Site. *Shillong T*., March 30 : 3 (2),

2341, ———, 1988 : No Renewal of Liquor Licences in Mizoram, *Shillong T*,. April 5 : 3 (1).

2342, ———, 1988 : Editorial : Laldenga in Calcutta. *Shillong T*,, 2 (1-2) About Greater Mizoram,

2343. ———, 1988 : Editorial : Mahanta's Barak Visit. *Shillong T*., June 6 : 2(1-2) lHailakandi (Assam) for Mizoram[.

2344. ———, 1988 : Cenre for Autonomy of Jampui Hills. *Shillong T*., June 7 : 3(1-2) [Tripura].

2345. ———, 1988 : Editorial : Aizawl flare-up. *Shillong T*., June 9 : 2(1-2).

2346. ———, 1988 : Editorial : Church in New Role *Shillong T*., July 4 : 2(1-2).

2347. ———, 1988 : Editorial : A Choked Highway, *Shillong T*., July 26 : 2(1-2).

2348. ———, 1988 : Centre Irked by Interference With District Councils in Mizoram. *Shillong T*., Aug. 22 : 1(2-4) 4(2).

2349. ———, 1988 : Editorial : Wanted a Positive Initiative. *Shillong T*., Aug. 27 : 2(1-2) [MNF].

2350. ———, 1988 : Laldenga Reduced to Minority, PR in the Offing ? Political Crisis in Mizoram. *Shillong T*., Aug. 30 : 1(2-4).

2351. Shillong Times, 1988 : Uncertainty Looms Large Over Mizoram. *Shillong T.*, Sept. 2 : 1(2-.).

2352. ———, 1988 : Editorial : Mizoram Ministerial Crisis. *Shillong T.*, Sept. 2 : 2(1-2).

2353. ———, 1988 : PR Likely in Mizoram. *Shillong T.*, Sept. 4 : 1(2-3).

2354. ———, 1988 : 6th Schedule Amendment Bill Only for Mizoram, Tripura. *Shillang T.*, Sept. 5 : 1(4-6).

2355. ———, 1988 : President's Rule in Mizoram. *Shillong T.*, Sept. 8 : 1(2-4).

2356. ———, 1988 : Editorial : Defection Law Side-linked. *Shillong T.*, Sept. 17 : 2(1-2).

2357. ———, 1988 : North East Ideal for Spices Cultivation. *Shillong T.*, Oct. 3 : 1(2-4).

2358. ———, 1988 : Editorial : Nagaland and Mizoram Polls. *Shillong T.*, Oct 8 : 2(1-2).

2359. ———, 1988 : Parliament Approves President's Rule in Mizoram. *Shillong T.*, Nov. 3 : 4(3-4).

2360. ———, 1988 : Editorial : Lalduhoma's Distinction *Shillong T.*, Dec. 6 : 2(1-2).

2361. ———, 1988 : Cong (I)-TUJS Differs on Mizo Council Demand. *Shillong T.*, Dec. 12 : 1(2-3) [in Tripura].

2362. ———, 1988 : Editorial : VI Schedule Amendment. *Shillong T.*, Dec. 12 : 2(1-2).

2363. ———, 1988 : Christmas festivity saps election

tempo in Mizoram. *Shillong T.*, Dec. 21 : 3(3-4).

2364. Shillong Times, 1988 : Editorial : Naga and Mizo polls. *Shillong T.*, Dec. 24 : 2(1-2).

2365 ———, 1989 : Laldenga's Charges Baseless : Saikia. *Shillong T.*, January 6 : 15(-6) 4(6).

2366. ———, 1989 : Greater Mizoram Move Unproductive. *Shillong T.*, Jonuary 6: 1(5-6) 4(6.)

.2367. ———, 1989 : Editorial : Naga, Mizo Polls. *Shillong T.*, January 16 : 2(1-2).

2368. ———, 1989 : Political Parties Say it With Bible. *Shillong T.*, January 16 : 1(2-3).

2369. ———, 1989 : Cong-I Wooes Church., *Shillong T.*, January 18 :3(2-3).

2370. ———, 1989 : Editorial : A Serious Lapse. *Shillong* T., Feb. 9 : 2(1-2).

2371. ———, 1989 : Laldenga Not to Take to Arms again. *Shillong T.*, Feb. 24 : 1(23.

2272. ———, 1989 : PM Sets Up Three-men Body on N.E. Tribal Institutions· *Shillong T.*. March 2 : 1(1) [Mizram Village Council Act].

2373. ———, 1989 : Editorial : Church Initiative in Mizoram. *Shillong T.*, March 4 : 2(1-2).

2374. ———, 1990 : Village Council Elections : MNF Gains at Cong(I)s Expense. *Shillong T.*, Nov. 6 : 32-3) Villages of Mizoram].

2375. Shillong Times, 1990 : Show Cause to Mizoram Law Secretary. *Shillong T.*, Dec. 1 : 3(1-2).

2376. ———, 1990 : Vignettes From Mizoram. *Shillong T.*, Dec. 4 : 3(1-4).

2377. Shukla 1974 : Mizo Problem : The Unknown Dimension. *Frontier*, Sept. 14 : 3(5).

2378. Shukla, S.P. *and* A.K. Aggarwal 1986 : *Agriculture in North Eastern Region*. New Delhi, National Pubg. House.

2379. Siang Lian, R. 1973 : Chin Choose to be Free. *Working People's Daily* (Rangoon), Feb. 24.

2380. Singh, Ajay 1978 : Mizoram : A Quest for Peace. *India Today*, May 16 : 2[illegible]-6.

2381. Singh Ajay *and* Mandira Purie 1978 : Laldenga : An Uneasy peace. *India Today*, Jan. 16 : 43.

2382. Singh, Bhawani 1984 : *Politics of Alienation in Assam*. Delhi, Ajanta Pubs. : 28-39.

2384. Singh, G.P. 1990 : *The Kiratas in Ancient India : Spotlight on North-east*. Delhi, Gian Publishing House 506p.

2384. Singh, J.D. 1978 : Insurgency in Mizoram *Times of India*, May 8 : 6(3).

2385. ———, 1982 : *Human Resources of North Eastern India*. New Delhi, Inter-India Pubs. : 160-69.

2386 Singh, K.M. 1990 : *History of Christian Missions in Manipur and Other neighbouring States*. Delhi, Mittal Publications (*in Press*).

2387. Singson' 1989 : *The Origin of the Thadou.* Imphal, (*Unpublished* mss).

2388. Sinha, A.P. (*Ed.*) 1986 : *Changing North-East India.* Ludhiana, Gagan Publications.

2389. ———, 1986 : Social Change in North East India, (*In*) *Changing North East India*, (*Ed.*) by A.P. Sinha. Ludhiana, Gagan Publications : 65-92.

2390. Spearman, H.R. 1987 : *Gazetteer of Burma, 2 vols.* Delhi, Gian Publishing House.

2591. Spolia, Kamla : Women of Mizoram. *Mizoram News Magazine*, August.

2392. Srinivas, M.N. 1984 and R. C. Sanwab, 1970 : Some Aspects of Political Devellopment in the North Eastern Hill Areas of India. *North Eastern Research Bulletin, Dibrugarh University*, I, Svmmer : 1-10

2393. Srivastava, S.C. 1987 : *Demographic Profile of North East India.* Delhi, Mittal Publicātions.

2394. Statesman 1973 : Editorial : Disturbed Area. *Statesman*, 6(2-3).

2395. ———, 1974 : Editorial : Price of Expediency. *Statesman*, March 15 : 4(2-3).

2396. ———, 1974 : Editorial : Ten ion in Mizoram. *Statesman*, April 20 : 6(2-3).

2397. ———, 1974 : Editorial : Stalemate in Mizora *Statesman*, Sept. 17 : 6(2-3).

2398. ———, 1974 : Editorial : Outsider in Mizoram. *Statesman*, Dec. 21 : 6(2-3).

2399. ———, 1974 : Editorial : Outrage in Aizawl. *Statesman*, January 16 : 4(2-3).

2400. ———, 1975 : Editorial : Task in Mizoram. *Statesman*, January 29 : 6(2-3).

2401. ———, 1977 : Editorial ; Stability in Mizoram. *Statesmān*, May 5 : 6(2-3).

2402. ———, 1978 : Editorial : Caution of Mizoram. *Statesman*, March 22 : 5(2-3).

1403. ———, 1978 : Editorial : Mischief in Mizoram. *Stateman*, April 21 : 6(2-3).

2404. ———, 1978 : Union Home Minister, Charan Singh's Statement in Parliament in March 1978. *Statesman*, March 21.

2405. ———, 1979 : Mizoram Causerie. *Statesman*, Nov. 24 : 5(1).

2406. ———, 1680 : Mizo Quest for Peace. *Statesman*, March 31 : 8(2).

2407. ———, 1983 : Chakma Influx : A Political Issue in Mizoram. *Statesman*, July 1.

2408. ———, 1985 : Mizoram to Restrict Area Under Jhum Cultivntion. *Statesman*, Feb. 23 : 4(3-4).

2409. ———, 1986 : Mizo Accord Approved. *Statesman*, Aug. 6 : 1(2).

2410. ———, 1987 : Laldeng's Legend Beginning to fade. *Statesman*, June 18 : 9(5-7).

2411. Statesman, 1987 : Insurgency Bid Foiled in Mizoram. *Statesman*, Aug. 14 : 12(6).

2412. ———, 1988 : Mizoram Era of Peace and Progress : 1st Anniversary of its Statehood. *Statesman*, Feb 20 : 7(1-8).

2413. ———, 1988 : Nine Killed in Aizawl firing, Night Curfew Clamped. *Statesman*, Aug. 31 : 1(2-4).

2414. ———, 1988 : Editorial : Coup in Aizawl ? *Statesman*, Sept. 1 : 6(2-3).

2415. ———, 1988 : ULP Threatens to Resign in Mizoram. *Stateman*, Sept. 5 : 1(6-7).

2516. ———, 1988 : Editorial : End of Mizo Accord ? *Statesman*, Sept. 8 : 8(2-3).

2417. ———, 1988 : Laldenga Keeps Options Open. *Statesman*, Sept. 22 : 9(6-8).

2418. ———, 1988 : More Powers for Tripura, Mizoram Councils. *Statesman*, Dec. 6 : 1(2-4).

2419. ———, 1989 : Laldenga Alleges Murder Conspiracy. *Statesman*, January 1 (Sunday).

2420. ———, 1989 : Editorial : Battle in Mizoram. *Statesman*, January 3 : 8(2-3)

2421. ———, 1989 : Fernandes Alleges Massive Rigging in Mizoram. *Statesman*, Feb. 9 : 9(6-7).

2422. Statesman, 1990 : Religious Revival in Mizoram *Statesman*, Dec. 24 : 9(6-7).

2422. State Soil Survey Organisation, 1984 : *Watershed Management Project : Darlawn Mamit.* Aizawl, State Soil Survey Organisation, Directorate of Agriculture.

2423. Stevenson, H.N.C. 1937 : Feasting and Meat Division Among the Zahau Chins of Burma. *Jour of Anthropological Institute*, LXVII.

2424. ———, 1987 : *The Economy of Central Chin Tribes.* Aizawl, Tribal Research Institute, (*Reprinted*).

2425. Sunday, 1980 : Mizoram the Chess Game for Peace. *Sunday*, Aug. [illegible]4 : 18-20.

2426. Talwar, Ashwani 1987 : Railways Branching out in N.E. States. *Times of India*, Feb. 20 : 18(1-6).

2427. Thanglhangin 1979 : Zomi Tenna Mun Masa. *Siamsinpawl Annual Magazine* (Churachandpur, Imphal), Vol. 17 : 1-7 (*in Paite, Tedim Chin*).

2428. Thangkhawkhai T. 1969 : The Chin-Paite Customary Law. *Siamsinpawl*, Vol. [illegible] : 16-20.

2429. Thangmawizuala, H. 1976 : Economy of Mizoram, (*In*) *Some Aspects of Economy of Hill Areas in North Eastern, Region*, (*Ed.*) by T. Mathew. Shillong, North Eastern Hill University : 355-56 (*Mimeo*).

2430. ———, 1980 : Economy of Mizoram : Industries, (*In*) *Tribal Economy of the North Eastern Region*, (*Ed.*) by T. Mathew. Guwahati, Spectrum Publications : 177-85.

2431. ———, 1981 : Land Reforms in Mizoram. (*In*) *Land Reforms in Eastern India*, (*Ed.*) by Manjula Bose. Calcutta, Jadavpur University : 28-32.

2432. Thought, 1967 : Assam : Amnesty That Failed : Mizo rebels. *Thought*, March 25 : 7-8.

2433. ———, 1967 : Background of Mizo Uprising. *Thought*, Oct. 7 : 7(8).

2434. ———, 1967 : Political Aspect of Mizo Uprising. *Thought*. Oct. 14 : 9-10.

2435. Times of India 1967 : Editorial : Security Belt (Mizo Hills). *T.O.I.* January 5 : 6(1-2).

2436. ———, 1967 : Editorial : Trap (Mizo Hills). *T.O.I.*, May 13 : 6(2-3).

2437. ———, 1967 : Editorial : Warning From Aijal. *T.O.I.*, June 20 : 6(1-2).

2438. ———, 1968 : Editorial : Arming the Mizos. *T.O.I.*, January 3 : 6(1-2).

2439. ———, 1968 : Editorial : Timely Offlcer. *S.O.I.*, Sept. 30 : 6(1-2).

2440. ———, 1968 : Editorial : In a Mess. *T.O.I.*, Nov. 14 : 8(1-2).

2441. ———, 1969 : Editorial : Feeler. T.*O.I.*, January 9 : 6(1-2).

2442. ———, 1969 : Editorial : Mizo Realities. *T.O.I.*, January 16 : 6(2-3).

2443. ———, 1970 : Editorial : Helpless Mizos. *T.O.I.*, June 17 : 6(2-3).

2444. ———, 1971 : Editorial : Unfortunate (Regrouping of Mizo villages). *T.O.I.*, Feb. 3 : 6(1-2).

2445. ———, 1971 : Editorial : Needless Fear. *T.O.I.*, Sept. 22 : 6(1-2).

2446. ———, 1973 : Editorial : Peace Move. *T.O.I.*, July 4 : 6(2-3).

2447. ———, 1975 : Editorial : Murders in Mizoram. *T.O.I.*, January 15 : 4(1-2).

2448. ———, 1976 : Editorial : Rebels on more. *T.O.I.* July 3 : 6(1-2).

2449. ———, 1977 : Editorial : End of Peace ? *T.O.I.*, July 14 : 6(2).

2450. ———, 1978 : Editorial : Mess in Mizoram. *T.O.I.*, Nov. 10 : 6(1-2).

2451. ———, 1978 : Editorial : No Other Way. *T.O.I.*, Nov. 14 : 6(1).

2452. ———, 1986 : No Compromise On Conditions in Mizo Accord : P.M *T.O.I.*, July 10 : 1(1-3).

2453. ———, 1986 : Editorial : Distracting Demand. *T.O.I.*, July 17 : 8(1-2),

2453. ———, 1986 : Laldenga Assails Oppcsitions Stand. *T.O.I.*, July 17 : 2(2-3).

2455. ———, 1986 : Laldenga Ministry to be Sworn in Today. *T.O.I.*, Aug. 21 : 1(7).

2456. ———, 1986 : Mizo Accord a 'Sell Out' *T.O.I.*, July 22 : 1(5-7).

2457. ———, 1986 : Parliament Ractifies Mizoram Accord. *T.O.I.*, Auh 8 : 7 (1-2).

2458. ———, 1986 : MNF-Cong Govt. Sworn in *T.O.I.* Aug. 22 : 1 (1).

2459. ———, 1986 : Laldenga Sticks to Stand on "*Greater Mizoram*". *T.O.I.*, Aug. 23 : 1 (4).

2460. ———, 1986 : Lalthanhawla Wants to Qu t. *T.O. I.*, Dec. 21 : 7 (1-3).

2461. ———, 1987 : Cong., MNU Promise "*Greater Mizoram*" ? *T.O.I.*, Feb. 4 3 (2-3).

2462. ———, 1987 : P M Promises Massive Aid to Mizoram. *T.O.I.*, Feb. 14 : 1 (6-8).

2463. ———, 1987 : "*Greater Mizoram*" Revived, *T.O.I.*, Feb. 15 : 1 (3-5).

2464. ———, 1987 : Saikia Governor of Mizoram. *T.O.I.*, Feb. 18 : 1 (3).

2465. ———, 1987 : Mr. Laldenag's Victory. *T.O.I.*, Feb 19 : 6 (1-2).

2466. ———, 1987 : Arunachal, Mizoram Gain Statehood. T.*O.I.*, Feb. 21 : 1 (5-7) 7 (5).

2467. ———, 1987 : Laldenga Sworn in C M. *T.O.I.* Feb. 21 : 1 (7).

2468. Toky, O.P , P.S. Ramakrishnan, B.K. Mishra *and* Saxena, K.G., 1981 : Slash and Burn Agriculture in North Eastern India, (*In*) *Fire Regimes and Ecosystem Properties*, (*Eds.*) by H.A.Mooney, T.M. Bonnicksen, N.L. Christensen, J.B. Loten *and* W.A. Reiners. Honolutu, Hawaii: Forest Service, General Technical Report No. 26 : 470-87.

2469. Tombing, Vung : A Treatise on the Tribal Families

Douthong, 1969 in the Indo-Burma border. *Siamsinpawl*, vol. 7 : 3-7.

2470. Tribal Research Institute, ? : *Sing Chiang*, Aizawl T.R.I. (*in Mizo*).

2471. ———, 1978 : *Puan the pride of Mizoram*. Aizaw T.R.I.

2472. ———, 1979 : *Monoliths and Landmarks of Mizoram*. Aizawl, T.R.I.

2473. ———, 1980 : *Foreign and Political Deptt, Repor 1874*. Aizawl, T.R.I. (*Reprinted*)

2474. ———, 1980 : *Foreign Dept., Report 1892* Aizawl, T.R.I. (*Reprinted*).

2475. ———, 1982 : *Know Your Own Land Series, vol. III*. Aizawl, T.R.I.

2476. ———, 1982 : *Know Your Own Land Series, vol IV*. Aizawl, T.R.I.

2477. ———, 1983 : *Mizo Sakhua*, Aizawl, T.R.I.

2478. ———, 1983 : *'Zu' in Mizo Society*. Aizawl T.R.I.

2479. ———, 1984 : *Mizo Irfiamvca*. Aizawl, T.R.I.

2480. ———, 1985 : *Mizo Lam Thenkhat e*. (*in Mizo*) Aizawl, T.R.I.

2481. ———, 1987 : *A Brief Account of Riangs in Mizoram*, Aizawl, T.R.I.

2482. ———, 1987 : *Paite in Mizoram*. Aizawl, T.R.I

2483. Upadhyaya, K.K., 1984 : *Pre-Capitalist Agricultural Formations in North East India : Mizoram*. Proceedings of a Semina Held in March, 1984 (*Mimeo*.)

2484. ———, 1984 : Options in Development Strateg for Mizoram in 1980s. Proceeding of a Seminar on *Strategy of Development of North East India* Sponsored by Planning Commission and Indian Economic Association, Shillong, NEHU, 9-12 April, 1984 (*Mimeo.*)

2485. ———, 1989 : *Semi Primitive Economy of an Indian Village : A Study of Lungdai in North East India*. Delhi, Mittal Publications.

2486. Van Gwladys, 1947 : *The Lushai Medical Mission.* Report of F.M. (WCMFMS).

2487. Varma, Ramkishore, 1986 : Mizoram ke Prakritiksanskritik bhu drishyon ka Bhougolik Bishleshan (*in Hindi*). *Himalaya : Man and Nature*, X (5), Oet. : 29-30, 35.

2488. Verghese, C.G., 1976 : The Mizoram I dream of. Proceedings of a Seminar on *Strategy for Planned Economic Development of Mizoram*. Aizawl, July 29-31 (*Mimeo.*)

2489. Vidyarthi, L.P., 1987 : *Art and Culture of North East India.* New Delhi, Business Manager, Publication Division.

2490. Warjri, Kynsai Maxmillian, 1987 : *A Study on the Parent-Child Relationship in the Khasi (Matrilineal) and Mizo (Patrilineal) Societies with Special References to its Relevant on the Adjustment Education of Children.* (*Unpublished*) Ph. D. Thesis, Education Deptt. NEHU, Shillong under Dr. P.P. Goku lanathan.

2491. Weisman, Steven R., 1988 : People : The Jews of Mizoram. *Am. Baz. Pat. Sunday Magazine*, Oct. 16 : 3 (1-3).

2492. Welsh Mission, 1946 : *Mizo Thawnthu*. Aijal, The Welsh Mission Bookroom.

2493. Winzler, Robert L., 1976 : Ecology, Culture, Social Organisation and State Formation in Southeast Asia. *Current Anthropology*, 17 (4).

2494. Working Peoples Daily, 1968 : Operation Chin Hills. *Working Peoples Daily* (Rangoon), Dec. 30.

2495. Zatu, R., 1973-'74 : Facts about the Chin State. *Chin Magazine* (Rangoon).

2496. Zirliana, D.R., (*Ed.*), 1968 : *Mizo Aw*. Aizawl, Pub. by the Author.

PART III

APPENDIX--A

Glossary of Words and Short Notes

Abanasong :- The price to be paid when a man marries his deceased brother's wife.

Adeuna :- An additional due payable when a woman marries into a strange village.

Amakia :- A marriage procession.

Angtong :-House posts.

Aparupa :-Theft.

Aphei :-Adultery.

Arakhei :-Elopement

Asu :-House post supporting the ridge pole.

Athiki :-Dead men's village.

Awithangpa Zai :-Composition of poetry by the Mizo poet Mr. Hmarawna.

Bai :-The basket used for measuring paddy.

Batla :- Beam of loom.

Beu :- A mole on the face.

Baitai :- A promise.

Bongchhi :-The sacred tree.

Bouinu :- It is a name of *Kolodyne* river in Lusha language.

Bongchhi :- The sacred ficus (external soul of the village).

Buhchhun :- Paddy contribution from each house-hold of a village to Mizo *Chief.*

Basan :-Nobleman of a raid or head of a raid.

Bawi :- An individual dependent upon a Mizo *Chief* or a sort of retainer.

Chhinlung :- Covering rock of a hole in the earth (in Mizo mythology).

Chibai :- Greetings.

Chemsenboi :- A slave for life in the house of a Lushai *Chief.*

Chhara :- Kachari synonym for small stream.

Chin :- A tribe of Chin Hills of Burma. It is derived from the Burmese word' *Khyn*' which is pronounced as '*Chin*'. *Sokte, Kanhow, Shindu* etc. are the important clans of the *Chin* tribe.

Chin levy :- Special Police system established in Chin Hills after the Chin Lushai expedition of 1889-'90.

Chick :- Curtain made of straws.

Chhuar :- A shelf which is near to the bed.

Chawng :- Feast.

Chheih Lam :- The Mizo dance.

Chawng Chen Zai :- Lament of a person who is holding a feast.

Chhura :- A funnry man of the Mizo legendry.

Chapchar kut :- Agricultural festival performed in the month of March to get blessings of *Pathian* for future cultivation. The *jhums* are ready by then for burning.

Chai dance :- It is a dance by boys and girls by holding hands and moving in circles.

Doong :- Watershed.

Darbar :- An assembly of a *Chief.*

Dao :- Sharp and heavy curved hand-made iron weapon.

Dulian :- A dialect of the Lushai people. It is also called *Dulhian.*

Gam :- An elected village-headman of the *Old Kukis.*

Howlong :- A clan of the Lushai tribe inhabited in the South Lushai Hills.

Hranghul :- A clan of *Old Kuki* tribe. This is also called *Rangkhol.*

Hang :- Lushai synonym for the word "black".

Huais :- Evil spirit or a demon.

Hringlang Tlang :- A hill from which a dead man could get a good view of the land of the living creature.

Hawilo :- A flower which helps a dead man not to turn back.

Hlamguihs :- A powerful spirit for dead infants.

In Lam Thangchhuah :- A high status of a person of Mizo village.

Indu-h Zan :- The first night of a bride who went to her husband from her father's house is called *Indu-h zan* or *Lawi zan* ceremony.

Jhum cultivation :- This *Jhum* or *Jhoom* is a kind of natural cultivation practised by the hill tribes in the hilly areas. The jungle in a hill is cleared by the people and burnt. The burnt ashes serve as the only manure. The seeds are sown there by the people. In this field they are culti vate for a year or two or so and thereafter they leave that field for a considerable period to gather fertility in that soil by natural way after a new growth of jungle on them. This is also known as "shifting cultivation".

Khazangpa :- The creator of this world.

Khawhring :- A spirit which is living in certain women.

Kolowme :- Thanks.

Khuangchawl :- A ceremony for newly constructed houses. In this ceremony they get windows in their house.

Khawpui :- Principal and biggest village where the *Chief* is residing.

Khawper :- Small sub-villages where the *Chief* is not residing.

Kapu :- Sir.

Khawhringneis :- Beautiful women of a Mizo village who possesses evil eyes to do harm to people.

Kapi :- Madam.

Karbari :- A legal representative of a *Chief.*

Khumi :- A tribe for *Arakan* frontier.

Khumpui :- Big sized family bed of the Mizos.

Khuang Chawl :- *Machang* or platform making ceremony in the Mizo house to drive out evil spirit.

Khawhar Zai :- Lament of grief sentiments.

Khual Lam :- Mizo dance.

Kawrchei :- Multi coloured full sleeved Mizo blouse which is put during ceremonial occasions.

Khuang Chawi :- To perform a big expensive 7 days feasts by a villager to obtained his high status among the people of the whole village.

Keimi :- Tiger like person.

Kelmei :- A tuft of a tail of a sacrificed goat. It is an important symbol of the Mizo who follows the old indigenous religion.

Khuarang :- A Lushai god with less power than *Pathian.*

Lunglo :- A river. The Mizos belief that it is heartless, feelingless, having clear transparent water.

Laisizawls :- People who are the expert on supernatural powers. They are big hunters and can command the wild animals.

Lawichal :- A portion of bride-price. It is given to some person who acts as a master of marriage-ceremony and escorts the bride to her husband's home.

Lal :- Lushai *Chief.*

Lushai .- It is a generic term to denote the Mizos. In Lushai language *Lu* means head and *shei* means cut ; thus Lushai means head cutter. Another philological meaning of the term is long hair. During 1840 to 1890 they were the ruler group among the Mizos when their land was annexed by the British in the latter part of the nineteenth century. *Dulian* is their language.

Lungdawh :- An erected ceremonial platform of stone to sit on it and hold a feast.

Lungphun :- A ceremony of feasts during the construction of a memorial in honour of a dead person.

Lenkhawm Zai :- Religious hymn.

Lawi Zan :- The first night of the bride who went to her husband from her father's house and performed a ceremony which is called *Lawi Zan* ceremony.

Lawi That Zan :- The second night of a bride who went to her husband's house from her father's house.

Luh Khung :- A type of marriage in which there is no formal ceremony or negotiation about bride price.

Lam Pui Sial :- A religious ceremony performed by the village priest to invoke the blessings of *Pathian* for a huntin party.

Mim Kut :- This is a yearly '*shradh*' (funeral) ceremony. It is celebrated in the month of July. In this ceremony the Mizos offers their cooked food and *zu* to the departed souls. In old days they had kept bones of dead person in their house within a basket and displayed those during *Mim Kut* ceremony to pay their homage to those bones.

Mak Pa Chung Khung :- A type of marriage. In this, bride's father can admit a son-in-law to his house without getting the marriage price.

Machan :- *Machang* or platform.

Mizoram :- Mizo land.

Mizo :- It is a generic term to denote all the clans, sub-clans, tribes of the *Lushai* people. They are inhabited in Mizoram, Cachar district of Assam, Tripura, Chittagong Hill Tracts of Bangladesh and Chin Hills of Burma. The name *Mizo* is derived from the Lushai word *Mi*=people, *zo*=hill.

Mithun :- A bison.

Mullian Pui :- An analogous tribe.

Machas :- The selected elders of a village.

Mipatawng :- A common language of the Mizos. It is a *lingua franca* of Mizoram.

Mithikhua :- Dead men's world ; inferior world of the evil spirit ; hell.

Mithun : A bisam.

Mautam :- Famine (*Mau*=Bamboo, *tam*=to die).

Ngote Kherh :- A garment. It is decorated with black and white stripes and put by women like a *sarong*.

Nula Rim :- Boys come to their lover's house to sit round the hearth and chat with the girl.

Ni Ar :- After *Pusum's* (i.e. bride price to maternal uncle of a bride) share, next share of the bride-price which is given to sister of the bride's father is called *Ni Ar*.

Nwengals :- A clan of the *Chin* tribe.

Ni Len Zai :- Lament of love and passion.

Naupuak Pūan :- A portion of the bride price which is given to the cousin-sister of the bride's mother.

Pathian :- Lord Supreme being God the creator of this world.

Pawla :- An immortal being.

Punachei :- Mizo women's garment which is to cover the lower part of their body from waist to heel. It is a decorated cloth which seems to be an Assamese *mekhala*.

Puithiam :- Village priest.

Piangthar :- New born Christian.

Puan :- Ladies multi coloured hand woven Mizo long sized skirt which reaches below the knee. It is to put along with a big sized blouse which seems to be a shirt of upper garment.

Pusum :- A share of a bride price. It is to given to a maternal uncle of the bride.

Palal :- A portion of a bride price, This is to given to a member of the groom's locality who belongs to the same clan of the bride with an expectation that this clan-person may look after the welfare of the bride in future.

Pu :- Mister.

Posa :- Blackmail.

Punjee :- A village.

Patta :- Land deed.

Pytoo :- It is the *Paite* tribe.

Pathlawi :- Young married man.

Puanchei :- A costly blouse of the Mizo ladies. It has some design like *Kawrchei.* Its put like a *sarong* to match their blouse.

Puan Dum :- A cloth, with black and red stripes for men. They put it during ceremonial occasions which is wrapped around their shoulder. Both ends of this cloth is embroidered.

Puan Ngo :- It is an indigo coloured cloth with white stripes. They use it during ceremonial time.

Puan Fui : Mizo rug.

Pial Ral :- Dead men's world Paradise the abode of the bliss.

Pu Paw la :- *Zam.* A deathless male summoner of death to a live-person of the earth to die.

Pawl Kut : Thanks giving agricultural festival performed in the month of December January.

Rapaw :- A due which is payed to a *Chief* for cultivation of land.

Ram Lam Thangchhuah :- A brave huuter of a Mizo village who has high status among the people of his village.

Ram Huai :- Spirit of the forest.

Rains :- Female *Chiefs*.

Rawchhem :- To play a bag-pipe.

Ral :- A dead man's sitting position with fully stretched legs and kept against a wall. It is called *ral.* People visit to pay their homage by giving money and gifts to the family of the dead person. Visitors are entertained with tea, snacks etc. as a token of honour of the dead person.

Ral ram :- Enemy country.

Rak Zu :- Stronger drinks.

Ropuiliani of Maullungthu :- Female *Chief* who became the head of her village after the death of her father.

Ramhual :-The best agriculturist of a village who is entitled to choose a *jhum* land for *jhum* cultivation for a year or so.

Siahriapang :- A blanket of very coarse cotton which is used by the *Lakhers*.

Sachhiah : A contribution of a right fore-leg of an animal, killed by the villagers to give to their village *Chief*.

Sirthe Tlang :- *Dhaleswari* river in Lushai language. This is known as *Katakhal* in Cachar district of Assam.

Syloo :- It is also called as *Sailo*. It is a ruling clan of the Lushai tribe.

Se Chhun :-Window opening ceremony in Mizo new house to drive out evil spirits.

Sum Hmun :- The whole area of Mizo cottage.

Sailo Zai :- Lament of the Sailo *Chief*.

Salu lam zai :- Lament of hunting.

Selu Phan :- A symbol fixed outside on the door of a Mizo house which is to make at the window opening ceremony.

Sechhum :- To perform a ceremony by *Thangchhuah*. In this he is to sacrifice one *mithun*.

Sakei Lu Lam :- A ceremonial dance performing to kill a spirit of a tiger.

Tong :- Small river.

Thing Thiang : A sign of a house to warn the stranger about not to enter the house who do not belong to the clan member of that house.

Tungyas : Periodic cultivation like the *Chin* people.

Tin Zu : Stronger drink.

Thlim : A male culprit.

Thangchhuah : High status.

Tawlhloh Puan : An indigo coloured cloth with red and white stripes. It was put in earlier days by the Mizo warriors.

Tlang Lam : Mizo dance.

Thian Man : A portion of bride price which is given to the friends of the bride.

Thanglowa : The Lushai clan. They are also known as *Rutton Poeas*.

Tlangs : Rivers. It is a synonym.

Tehsil : Revenue office.

Thirdeng :- Village blacksmith.

Tlang Au :- Village announcer. He announces the order of the *Chief* in a loud voice.

Thangchhuah :- A powerful spirit of a dead honourable person.

Thitin rite :- Farewell to the spirit of a deceased.

Tunusa :- Seniority in age.

Upas :- A council of village elders.

Upa Min :- Prime Minister.

Ugo :- White colour. It is a synonym.

Vai hlo :- Mizo tobacco which is locally grown.

Vai Pawis :- Foreign Pawis. This is usually callcd to a *Sikh* man with long hair tied as bun above the forehead.

Vais :- This indicates non tribal plain people.

Zadeng :- An extinct *Lushai* clan.

Zalen :- A superior person who is a near relative of a *Chief*. He has a right to choose first, a *jhum* land even before *Ramhuals*. He gets some privileges.

Zawlbuk :- Bachelor's dormitory.

Zakhapa :- The *Pawi Chief*.

Zufang :- A mild type of *Zu*.

Zu :- Wine brewed from rice.

Zen :- Guilty person about sex.

Zu Pui :- Stronger drink.

Zawlneis :- Women who are skilled on witchcraft. They can tell about the forthcoming events.

Zingvawan :- A spiritual village.

Vai Upa :- An administrator of *Zawlbuk*. He is responsible for good conduct of all the young boys of his *Zawlbuk* as they are under him.

APPENDIX-B

The following are the Scheduled Tribes of Mizoram according to *Census of India, 1981*:-

Lushai,
Lakher (Mara),
Pawi (Poi),
Vaiphei,
Ralte,
Hmar,
Paite,
Gangte,
Thado,
Simte,
Zou,
Kuki,
Mag,
Riang,
Chakma.

There are, however, some more tribes and sub-tribes inhabited in Mizoram which were not listed in the Census of India, 1981. They are :-

Awzia, Baite or Beite, Chongther, Chawngthu, Changsen, Chhakchhuak, Darlong, Fanai, Hrashel, Halam, Hualngo, Jansen, Kelma, Khiangte, Khawlring, Nagente, Pam, Pangs, Pachuau, Pautu, Pante, Lolong, Rangkhol, Roite, Reuthlei, Sailo, Tlaw, Vanchhia, Tochhawng, Zawngle, Zahaus.

The following are the immigrant caste people of Mizoram. Their total population is 06.453 per cent (*1981 Census*) :-

Nepali,
Assamese,
Bengali,
Behari,
Punjabi,
South Indians.

Most of these afore said caste people are government job holders, businessmen, contractor, *Assam Rifles*' personnel and *Central Reserved Police Force (CRPF)*.

The following tribes and sub-tribes are inhabited in Mizoram. They are also resided in the State of Manipur along with the other tribes and sub-tribes of that State. It is observed in the modified *Order No. SRO 2477 A*, dated *New Delhi, the 29th October, 1956* of the *Ministry of Home Affairs, Government of India* that there are the following 37 numbers of *Kuki* group of tribes. These had been listed in the *Constitution of India* and was amended in 1976 under the head *Any Kuki* tribes. Practically it is very much difficult to give a single character of the tribes and sub-tribes under *Any Kuki* tribe. All these tribes and sub-tribes under *Any Kuki* tribe have their own ethnic identity and culture. The names under *Any Kuki* tribes are as follows :-

Baite or Beite,
Changsen,
Chongloi,
Doungel,
Gamalhou,
Gangto,

Guite,
Hanneng,
Haokip or Haupit,
Haolai,
Hengna,
Hongsungh,
Hraugkawal or Rongkhol,
Jongbe,
Khawehung,
Khawathlang or Khothalong,
Khelma,
Kholhau,
Kipgen,
Kuki,
Lengthang,
Lhangun,
Lhoujen,
Lhouvun,
Lupheng,
Mangjol,
Misao,
Riang,
Sairhen,
Semnam,
Singson,
Sitlhou,
Sukte,
Thado,
Thangou,
Uibuh and
Vaiphei.

APPENDIX--C

General information for tourists and those who are new-one to Mizoram :-

1. Entry Formalities :-

Without *Inner Line Permit* no outsiders of Mizoram could enter inside the State. Indians may get their *Inner Line Permit* for a limited period from any *Mizoram House* which are situated at *Silchar, Guwahati, Shillong, Calcutta, Delhi* etc. There is a prescribed application form which is to be filled up. Two passport size photographs are necessary to get the same. Re. 1 (Rupee One) is the Permit Fee per head. Signature is to be put by the Indian passengers in their Register which is maintaining for their records about permit matter. Foreign tourists may get their *Special Permission* from Central Government's Home Ministry (New Delhi), for a limited period to visit Mizoram.

Recently, Government of India is trying to improve their travel and civil aviation departments. The State Government have a proposal to withdraw this *Inner Line Permit* system. Thus, there is much possibillity to nullify this *Inner Line Permit* system by the Government soon for the Indians and to be very much liberalised for the foreign tourists.

2. Travel Agents :

(a) *Khuma Air Travels*, Upper Khatla, Aizawl, Phone : 2297/448.

(b) *Tourism Department*, Mizoram Government, Aizawl, Phone : 3161, 3162, 3163.

3. Communications :

(a) Daily *Vayudoot* Air Services from *Calcutta Aizawl-Silchar Aizawl Calcutta* is there. Helicopter Services are also available from *Silchar Aizawl Lunglei Zemabawk Champhai Aizawl Imphal Guwahati Shillong*. Mizoram's Helipad is situated at *Tuirial*. Nearest Airport is *Silchar* (Assam).

(b) Daily Bus Service between *Shillong* and *Aizawl via Silchar* is there. State Transport Buses are playing in between *Aizawl* and *Silchar* and advance tickets are available at *Aizawl*. There are other bus services on different routes within the State Mizoram.

The distance of *Silchar* to *Aizawl* is 180 km., *Aizawl* to *Lunglei* 235 km, and *Lunglei* to *Saiha* 140 km. Buses generally take 8 hours and light vehicles 6 hours from *Silchar* to *Aizawl*. Private Taxis and Buses are plying in the town of Mizoram. *Silchar* to *Bhangabazar* (Assam) is 43 km. The hilly area of the State Mizoram is started soon after crossing this *Bhangabazar*. A Checkpost is there at *Vairengte* (Mizoram) after 3 km. for *Bhangabazar* (Assam) to see the *Inner Line Permits* of the travellers. After running 95 km. from *Silchar* (Assam) a journey break *cum* Lunch-break is given by all the vehicles at *Kolasib* (Mizoram). *Nepali, Gorkha, Mizo* Hotels are there. Rest House is also available here at *Kolasib*.

(c) Nearest Railhead is *Silchar* (Assam). A railway Out Agency is there at *Aizawl*. A rail line would be there within the year 1990 of 18 km. long metre-gauge *N.F. Railway* line in between *Lalabazar* (Assam) to *Bairabi* (border site of Mizoram and Assam) *via Katlicherra* and *Jamira* (both are in Assam).

(d) S T D Telephone facility is there at *Aizawl*.

(e) T V Transmission Centre and Radio Station are there at Aizawl.

4. **Accommodations** :-

MLA Hostel, Aizawl.
Hotel RRAJJ [T V Set attached]. Treasury Square, **Aizawl.**
Hotel Embassy, Chanmari, Aizawl.
Hotel Moonlight, Chaltlang.
Tourist Lodge, Aizawl.
Aizawl Lodge, Aizawl.
Hotel Hill View, Aizawl.
Air Lines Hostel, Aizawl.
Aizawl Club Rest House, Aizawl.
Dak Banglows ; *Circuit Houses* etc. are also available in all districts of Mizoram.

5. **Climate** :

Mizoram is under the influence of the South West Monsoon from *Bay of Bengal*. Summer temperature is 19°C to 29°C and Winter is 11°C to 21°C. Rain starts here during the month of May to September and average rainfall is 250 cm. Favourable time for touring is during October to May.

6. **Distance from the Capital town Aizawl** :

Champhai to *Aizawl* 204 km.,
Thenzawl (*Vantawng fall*) to *Aizawl* 135 km.,
Lunglei to *Aizawl* 235 km.,
Tlabung via Lunglei to *Aizawl* 320 km.,
Lawngtlai via Lunglei to *Aizawl* 305 km.,
Saiha via Lunglei to *Aizawl* 375 km .

7. **Post and Telegraph** :

G.P.O. (General Post Office), Treasury Square, *Aizawl*,

There are several Sub Post Office.
C.D.T.O. (Central Division Telegraph Office), **Chandmary,** *Aizawl*,

8. Hospital :

Civil Hospital, Upper Bazar, *Aizawl.*
Synod Hospital, *Durtlang.*

9. Languages Which are Commonly Spoken :

Generally they speak *Mipatang, Dulian, Mizo* languages. Educated youths talk *English* language among other educated tribal and non tribal people. Rarely they speak *Hindi* inside their State *Mizoram.*

10. Comparison of Price-Index till March, 1985 (Base year 1960=100) :

Mizoram=661 ; All India=540 ; Guwahati=515 ; Shillong=577.

11. Banks :

State Bank of India, *Aizawl.*

State Bank of India, *Champhai* and also at *Kolasib.*

United Commercial Bank, *Aizawl.*

Vijaya Bank, *Aizawl,* Phone : 2542.

Co-operative Apex Bank, *Aizawl:*

12. Shopping Areas :

Bara Bazar and New Market of *Aizawl* area.

13. Animal Husbandry and Veterinary Department till 1984-85 :

(i) Animal Husbandry Complex, Selesih *Aizawl.*

(ii) Poultry Demonstration Farm, *Champhai.*

(iii) District Poultry Farm, *Lunglei.*

(iv) Poultry Demonstration Farm, *Kolasib.*

(v) Duck Multiplication Farm, *Thenzawl* and several other farms are there in Mizoram.

14. Name of the Newspapers of Mizoram :

(a) Mizo Aw, Romei Highlander. Remna Eng, Jupiter, Zo Awi, Chhim Eng, Kan Ram etc. are daily newspapers ;

(b) Deiva, Tawih, Zo En etc. are bi-weekly ;

(c) Khawpui Aw, Lenkawl Lai Ram etc. are tri-weekly ;

(d) Aizawl, Youth Herald, Mizoram Weekly, Sports Weekly, Zo Eng, Vox, Sourhern Express etc. are weekly

15. Places of worship :

Each locality has its own Church for Christians.
Temple for Hindus is situated in Zodin Square, *Aizawl.*
Mosque for the Muslims is situated in Bara Bazar, *Aizawl.*

16. Voluntary Organisations till 1984-1985 :

MHIP, YMA, Central YMA, YMCA, ZUP, ZCYCA, AJAS, MWO, DYO etc.

17. Common Fruits and Crops of Mizoram :

Citrus fruits, Bananna, Pineapple etc.

Maize, Sugercane, Ginger, Oilseeds, Chillies, Pulses, Potato etc.

18. Cinema and Amusements :

J.L.Cinema, Upper Khatla Road, *Aizawl.*

Zodin, Zodin Square, *Aizawl.*

Zoram Theatre, A. R. Ground, *Aizawl.*

Pushpak Hall, Zemabawk, *Aizawl.*

Sulu Theatre, Bawngkawm.

At *Aizawl* there is a Mini Zoo

State Museum is also there at *Aizawl.*

19. Some Political Regional Parties of Mizoram

Mizo Union (MU),

Mizo Common Peoples' Union (Mizo Commoners' Union) (MCU),

United Mizo Freedom Organisation (UMFO),

Eastern India Tribal Union (EITU),

Pawi-Lakher Tribal Union (PLTU),

Mara Freedom Party (MFP).

Chin National Front (CNF).

Kalai National Council (KNC),

Mizo Democratic Party (MDP),

Mizo Integration Council (MIC).

Mizo National Front (MNF),

Mizo National Front (D) (MNF-D),

Mizo National Union (MNU),

Mizo Labour Party (MLP),

Mizo Integration Party (MIP) etc.

20. A Brief Note About MNF Leader Late Laldenga :

David Laldenga was born on 11th June, 1926 at *Pu Ui* near *Lunglei* in *South Lushai Hills*. He was popularly known as Laldenga. He was a member of the *Pawi* tribe (*Fanai*). He studied upto class VIII in a Missionary School at *Jowai* in *Meghalaya*. During 2nd world war, he joined in British Indian Army and was promoted to the rank of havildar in 1944. He was a witness, in that capacity, in the Burmese action. After Independence, he was appointed as a Havilder-Clark in the Indian Army. After sometimes, he became an Accountant-cum Cashier in the *Lushai* District Council. In 1958, he resigned from the Council and formed the Mizo Cultural Society. He became the first Secretary of this Society.

During the famine of 1959-'60 in Mizoram, he formed *Mizo National Famine Front* (*MNFF*). Later on this Front was named as . *Mizo National Front* (*MNF*) on 12th October, 1962. He was the first President of this Front till his death. He was exiled from India twice, to *Dhaka* (East Pakistan, now Bangladesh) and *Karachi* (West Pakistan, now Pakistan). He returned to India on 24th January, 1976 and initiated peace talks with the Central Government, he signed an *Accord* with the Central Government on 30th June, 1986. He was an ex-Editor of *ThuLeh Hia* (Aizawl) newspaper,

He beeame the Chief Minister in 1986 in the Mizoram interim Government. He was elected from both *Aizawl North-II* and *Sateek* Constituencies in Assembly election in 1987. On 20th February, 1987, Mizoram became a "State" from the status of Union Territory and Laldenga was the first Chief Minister of Mizoram State. He died on 7th July, 1990, due to the disease, cancer, while he was in London on his way back to his home at *Aizawl* (Mizoram) from New York (U.S.A.) and was buried near *War Memorial* of Aizawl on 11th July, 1990.

APPENDIX-D

First Time in Lushai Hills (Mizoram) :-

1. Savidge and I first arrived in the Lushai Hills (*Sairang*) :- 11th January, 1894.
2. Opened first School (with two pupils) :- 1st April, 1894.
3. Commenced translating Scriptures (*St.Luke's* Gospel) :- 21st August, 1895.
4. I preached my first sermon in Lushai :- 16th September, 1895.
5. Began regular Lushai services :- 2nd October, 1895.
6. The first Lushai convent (Mentioned in letter dated 30.3.1896) :- 30th March, 1896.
7. Built first Lushai Church (Took nearly 2 days to build and cost £1-10-0 on spot where memorial now stands) :- 6th October, 1896.
8. Our Lushai written vocabulary reach approximately 5000 words :- 10th April, 1897.
9. Rev. D.E. Jones arrived in Aijal (to be started in the language by us and to take over our work) :- 10th September, 1897.

10. Savidge and I handed over our work to Rev. Jones of the *Welsh Mission* and left the Lushai Hills (*Sarang*) for Furlough in England, followed by pioneering work for the *Abor* and *Miri* Tribes around Sadiya, Upper Assam. :- 31st December, 1897.

11. Savidge and I arrived in *Lungleh* for work in the South Lushai Hills under the *B.M.S.* (*Baptist Missionary Society*). : 13th March 1903.

Sd/-J.H.Lorrain
8.5.34

Source : P.K. Bandyopadhyay (1985 : 260-61) & *Thu Leh Hla* (Aizawl), July, 1983

APPENDIX-E

"Somc Important Questions and their Answers"

by

J.H.Lorrain

How long after your arrival in Lushai Hills did you have a regular School running ?

In those early pioneering days, when we were still learning the language ourselves, and were reducing it to a system of writing which could be used by the people, our efforts at teaching them how to read and write their mother tongue could hardly be termed running a regular School. And yet, it was the remote source from which all the subsequent education in the Lushai Hills sprang. Savidge and I opened this first 'School' on or about 1st April 1894—2½ months after our first arrival in Aijal—with two pupils. Their names were Suaka and Thangphunga and they were the young men from whom we were learning the Lushai language. I have it on record that the 'School' was held from 9 till 11 each morning, and that before these two made the attempt to learn to read and write, all those whom we had tried to persuade to do so had excused themselves by saying that the Lushais were "like monkeys'' and could not possibly master such a difficult art. Suaka and Thangphunga quickly disproved that statement, for in one week they had learned the alphabet and could manage words of one Syllable, and before a month was over could read with understanding almost anything we wrote and were beginning themselves to write fairly. Two other pupils in those early days were the Sailo Chiefs Khamiliana and Khama. Their desire to learn, to read and write which first evinced itself amongst the young men (not amongst the boys) quickly spread, and although only a few could come to our School those who did so taught their friends at home, and, we were soon at our wits end to know how to supply them all with reading matter : for there was nothing yet printed in their language and we had to write or type everything ourselves.

From the day our 'School' started, I think I am right in saying that it went on without any big brake——though the pupils were often but few in numbers and it was impossible to keep any pupils very long. By the time we handed over our work to Rev. D.E.Jones of the Welsh Mission and left Aijal in December 1897, the Government had taken up the idea of Lushai Education and had got up a Bengali School master to learn the language and open a Government Sehool at Aijal. I do not know how long that continued, but 5½ years later, when we returned to the Lushai Hills (in March 1903) and settled at Serkawa, the Welsh Mission had a good boys' School running at Aijal, and in South Lushai the Government had one in Lungleh and another at Khawngbawk village—both run by Bengali School master teaching in Lushai. These were handed over to Savidge very soon after we arrived, and one of the Bengali masters (Nabin Chandra Barua) was with us for several years and did not leave even when we had a sufficiency of trained Lushai masters. Later, he became master of a School for Bengadi and Gorkha boys in the Lunglei station. It is interesting to note that a large proportion of the voluntary boy pupils——especially at Aijal—were members of the 'Bel nawt' fraternity——boys who were employed by the 'Sepoys' to scour their pots and pans. It was difficult to get ordinary village boys to come in either as day boys or boarders, and for some years the Government helped, first by ordering Chiefs to send in one or two from each village, the later by offering permanent freedom from enforced Kuli labour to every boy who should pass the Upper Primary Examination. When the Chiefs had orders to send boys to the Central School they found such difficulty in getting even one or two that they were in the habit of bribing parents to let their boys attend the Serkawn School by getting the whole village to supply such parents with rice. That was in the days when neither parents nor children saw any use in education, and the young men who were keen were content when they know how to read and write.

2. How far could Lushais count before the Schools came into being ? Did large numbers like 'Maktaduai' mean anything to them ?

I do not remember noticing that the Lushais were limited in any way in their power of counting. Their system is so simple that there was nothing to prevent a naturally intelligent man from going on from tens, to hundreds, and thousands and tens of thousands. I never tested anyone, but my impression is as stated above. I knew before I left Aijal that they had terms for all the above——i.e. sawm. za, sang, and nuai. It was left to the Welsh Missionaries to discover the terms maktaduai (1,000,000). Vaibel chhis (10,000,000) and Vaibel chhetak (100,000,000) and they were already printed in their School primer (Zirtir Bu) when we settled at Serkawn.

It is difficult to say what these vast numbers meant to the average Lushai—probably nothing more nor less that the same immence figures would mean to an ordinary uneducated Englishman. I don't think, however, that there is any doubt about them being genuine old fashioned Lushai words with the meanings as stated.

3. Who invented the present names of the days of the week ? Did the old Lushais have no names ?

There were no names whatever for the days of the week when we first went up ; but with the advent of the Sahibs, and Indian Sepoys and shopkeepers, the need for such names was being felt and a few were already beginning to call Sunday 'Rawsawt lak ai' (The day for drawing rations). It was, however during our absence from ths Lushai Hills, when we were working for the Abors, that names were given to all the days of the week—partly by the Welsh Missionaries and partly by the Lushais themselves. By the time we settled at Serkawa some of the days had more than one name. It was 20 months or so later, (at Xmas 1904), when Savidge and I and our wives went to Aija to confer with the Welsh Missionaries and Government officials, that the names were fixed more or less as they are today. They are really a selection made from the various names which had come into being during our Abor pioneering period away from the Lushai Hills.

4. The Assam Census report gives only 56,700 people speaking Lushai. The remainder are given as ;-

Hmar language	—	—	—	16,000.
Zahau	—	—	—	3,900.
Paite	—	—	—	6,600.
Ralte	—	—	—	16,000.
Unspecified Chin	—	—	—	14,000.

Are all these more or less dialects of Lushai ? Speakers of 'Hmar' are said to have increased rapidly since 1921 ?

I am surprised to hear that the Assam Census report gives only 56,700 people speaking Lushai. Probably that is the number of people to whom the Lushai or Dulian Tawng (which we work in) is their mother tongue But I cannot help thinking that the number of Lushai-speaking people far exceeds that figure. The other languages which you mention Hmar, Zahau, Paite and Ralte——I regard as more or less dialects of Lushai and it is my impression that these clans now-a-days are rapidly adopting the Lushai language in which the Scriptures are printed. They mostly live in the North and we see very little of them in the South. If you were to write to Rev. D.E.Jones, the Welsh Missionary who took over the work from Savidge and myself in December 1897, and who after many years of service in Aijal, is now living in retirement, he could give you more reliable information about them than I can and he might be able to suggest a reason why 'Hmar' speakers have increased so rapidly since 1921.I know that the British and Foreign Bible Society has been approached about a 'Hmar' version of the New Testament Scriptures, so I presume that there are some who do not feel quite at home with the 'Lushai' version as we have it. Jones, however, knows much more about all these clans than I do.

As for the item 'Unspecified Chin' almost the entire male Chin (or Pawi) population of South Lushai speaks Lushai as well as Chin, but many of the women folk still cling to their mother tongue. It is possible that the Lakhers—who do not speak Lushai to any extent—are included under this head.

Sd/- J.H. Lorrain
7th May, 1934.

Source : P.K. Bandyopadhyay (1985 : 262-266) and *Thu Leh Hla* (Aizawl), June. 1983,

Farewell Notes of Mr, J.H. Lorrain in the *Visitor's Book* at *Tlabung* Inspection Bungalow :-

SWEET MEMORIES

Mr. & Mrs. J.H.Lorrain Arrival

16-2-32

Going home to England perhaps never to return to these beautiful hills where so many happy years of our lives have been spent. When first arrived in Aijal in 1894 as one of the Pioneer Missionaries to the Lushai tribe there was not a single Christian anywhere. The Gospel message, however as fitted the needs of the people that today there are in the northern hills 43,972 Christians, here in the southern 12,125—a total of over 56,000 or above one half of the entire population. These figures exclude the Lakher Christians in Shenkor Circle who do not speak the Lushai language.

Date of Departure J.H.L.

17-2-32

Source : P.K.Bandyopadhyay (1985 267) and *Thu Leh Hla* (Aizawl), July, 1983.

APPENDIX-F

List of Periodicals and Newspapers (Used as Source Material)

1. Aizawl Times (Aizawl)
2. Ajkal (Calcutta)
3. American Anthropologist (Washington
4. Amrita Bazar Patrika (Calcutta) [Am. Baz. Pat.]
5. Anthropos (West Germany)
6. (The) Anthropologist (Delhi
7. Artha Vigyana (Poona)
8. Arunachal News (Shillong and Naharlagun)
9. Asian Survey (Washington, U.S.A.)
10. Asiatic Researches (Calcutta)
11. Asiatic Review (London)
12. Assam Academy Review (Gauhati)
14. Assam Anthropological Association (Gauhati)
14. Assam Review (Silchar)
15. Assam Quarterly (Gauhati)
16. Assam Tribune (Guwahati) [A.T.]
17. Baptist Missionary Review (Calcutta)
18. Bibliotheca Indica (Calcutta)

19. Black Wood's Magazine
20. Bulletin de la Societie des Missions Etrangeres de Paris (Hong Kong)
21. Bulletin : Anthropological Survey of India (Calcutta)
22. Bulletin of the Cultural Research Institute (Calcutta)
23. Bulletin of the Department of Anthropology, Dibrugarh University (Dibrugarh)
24. Bulletin of the Departnsevt. of Anthropology, Gauhati University, (Guwahati)
25. Bulletin of the Division of History (Imphal)
26. Bulletin of the Department of Tribal Cultural and Folklore Research (Guwahati)
27. Bulletin: Sch. Or. and Afr. Studies.
28. Bulletin: Tribal Research Institute (Guwahati)
29. Business Standard
30. Calcutta Review (Calcutta)
31. Carvan (New Delhi)
32. Chanchin Bu (Aizawl)
33. Chin Magazine (Rangoon)
34. Chinese Repository
35. China Quarterly
36. Citizen Voice (Kohima)
37. Col.
38. Comparative Studies in Society and History (The Hague
39. Current Biography
40. Current (Bombay)
41 Cultural Forum
42. Dan Bu (Aizawl)
43. Data India (Delhi)
44. Deccan Geography

45. Discovery
46. Eastern Anthropologist (Lucknow)
47. Eastern World (London)
48. Ecologist (Wadebridge, England)
49. Economic and Political Weekly (Bombay)
50. Economic Times
51. Ethnos (Stockholw)
52. Fugene : Oregcn State Museum of Anthropology (Oregon)
53. Folklore (Calcutta)
54. Folk lore (London)
55. Foreign Proceedings
56. Frontier
57. Frontline (Madras)
58. Geographical Journal (London)
59. Geographical Magazine (London)
60. Geographical Review of India (Calcutta)
61. Gentleman's Marg
62. Globus
63. Hiu Chin Student's Union's Annual Magazine (Rangoon)
64. Hiu Geographec (NEHU, Shillong)
65. Highlarder : The Bulletin of the Cultural Research and State Museum (Kohima)
66. Himalaya : Man and Nature (Delhi)
67 Himalaya News Round Up (New Delhi)
68. Hindi Vishwa Bharati
69. Hindu (Madars)
70. Hindustan Standard (Calcutta)
71. Hindustan Times (Delhi)

72. Human Science : Anthropological Survey of India (Calcutta)
73. India Abroad (New York)
74. Indian Antiquary (Bombay)
75. Indian Express (Delhi)
76. Indian Folklore (Calcutta)
77. Indian and Foreign Review
78. Indian Forester (DehraDun)
79. Indian Journal of the Medical Research (New Delhi)
80. Indian Journal of Political Science
81. Indian Journal of Social Work (Bombay)
82. Indian Linguistics (Poona)
83. Indian Studies : Past and Present (Calcutta)
84. Indo-Asia (Stutgurt)
85. Illustrated Weekly (Bombay)
86. India Today (Faridabad)
87. International Committee on Urgent Anthropological and Ethnological Research Bulletin (Vienna)
88. Janata (Bombay)
89. Journal of the Anthropological Society of Bombay (Bombay)
90. Journal of the Asiatic Society of Bengal (Calcutta)
91. Journal of Asiatic Society of Gereat Britain and Ireland (London)
92. Journal of Assam Political Science Association (Guwahati)
93. Journal of Assam Research Society (Guwahati)
94. Journal of Bombay National History Society (Bombay)
95. Journal of Burma Research Society (Rangoon)
96. Journal of Cross Cultural Psychology

97. Journal of Gauhati University (Guwahati)

98. Journal of the Royal Anthropological Institute of Great Britain and Ireland (London)

99. Journal of Indian Anthroplogical Society (Calcutta)

100. Journal of the Indian Archipelago and Eastern Asia

101. Journal of Indian History (Trivandrum)

102. Journal of North Eastern Council (Shillong)

103. Journal of North Eastern Council for Social Science Research (Shillong)

109. Journal of Political Studies (Jullandhar)

110. Journal of Royal Asiatic Society of Bengal (Calcutta)

111. Journal of Royal Asiatic Society of Bombay (Bombay)

112. Journal of Royal Central Asiatic Society (Calcutta)

113. Journal of Royal Society of Arts

114. Journal of Social Research (Ranchi)

115. Journal of United Services Institute (Indonesia)

116. Jugantar (Calcutta)

117. Khadigramodyog (Bombay)

118. Language

119. Leekha

120. Light of Life

121. Link (New Delhi)

122. Mainstream (Delhi)

123. Man (London)

124. Man and Life (Calcutta)

125. Man in India (Ranchi)

126. Manipur State Kala Akademi Quarterly Journal (Imphai

127. March of India (Delhi)

128. Memoirs of the Asiatic Society of Bengal (Calcutta)

129. Memoirs of the Geographical Survey of India (Calcutta)

130. Military Proceedings
131. Military Report
132. Mirror (Bombay)
133. Mitteilungen der Anthropologischen Gesellschaft (Wien)
134. Mitt. Geog. Ges. Jena
135. Mizo leh vai chanchin lehkhabu (Aizawl)
136. Mizo National Magazine (Aizawl)
137. Mizo News Magazine (Aizawl)
138. M·N.M. (Aizawl)
139. Mizoram Today (Aizawl)
140. Modern Review (Calcutta)
141. Naba Bharat Times (Delhi) [N.B.T.]
142. Naga News (Kohima)
144. Naga National (Dimapur)
144. News : Geological Survey of India (Shillong)
145. New Horizon (Aizawl)
146. North East Hill University Journal of Social Science and Humanities (Shillong)
147. North Eastern Affairs (Shillong)
148. North Eastern Economic Review (Gauhat)
149. North Eastern Research Bulletin (Dibrugarh)
150. North Eastern Review
151. North Eastern Spectrum (Gauhati)
152. North East Quarterly (Gauhati)
153. Organiser (Delhi)
154. Oriental Watchman and Herald of Health (Poona)
155. Paite Paunak (Imphal)
156. Patriot
157. Personality Study and Group Behaviour
158. Pine (Shillong)

159. Political Science Review (Jaipur, Rajasthan)

160. Proceedings of Royal Asiatic Society of Bengal [New Series] (Calcutta)

161. Proceedings of Royal Geographical Society (London)

162. Productivity News

163. P.S. : Psychological Studies (Culicut, Kerala)

164. Purbanchal Prahari (Guwahati)

165. Quast (Bombay)

166. Querterly Journal of the Mythic Society (Bangalore)

167. Rajasthan Patrika

168. Records of the Geological Survey of India (Calcutta)

169. R.E. : Review of Ethnology (Wien, Vienna)

170. Ropeca (Shillong)

171. Royal Asiatic Society (Calcutt a

172. Royal Central Asian Journal

173. Sainik Samachar

174. Science and Culture (Calcutta)

175. Seminar (New Delhi)

176. Shillong Times (Shillong)[Shillong T.]

177. Social Mirror

178. Sociologous (Berlin)

179. Social Research : Journal of tha Institute of Social Research (Shillong)

180. Social Scientist

181. Social Mirror

182. Social Welfare

183. South Asian Anthropologist (Ranchi)

184. South West Journal of Anthropology

185. (The) Statesman (Calcutta)

186. Sunday (Calcutta)

187. Surma Valley Magazine (Silchar)

188. (The) Telegraph (Calcutta)

189. (The) Times of India (Delhi, Bombay) [T.O.I.]

190. (The) Thinkers : Journal of Thinkers Forum (Kohima)

191. Thought (Delhi)

192. Thu Leh Hla (Aizawl)

193. Trans. N.Y. Acad. Sc. (New York)

194. Trans. Roy. Soc. (Edinburg)

195. Tribe (Udaipur, Rajasthan)

196. Tribal Mirror (Karimganj and Silchar)

197. Vanyajati (Delhi)

198. Weed Research

199. Week End Review (New Delhi, Bombay)

000. Word

201. Yojana (Delhi)

202. Zeitchrift der Duetschen Morgenlandischen Gosellshaft Wies baden

203. Zeitschrift fur Ethnologie

204. Z. Morph. Anthrop.

205. Z. Ethn.

206. Zoramthupuan (Aizawl)

207. Zomi Todoy (Churachandpur, Manipur)

Authorindex

(References to the serial number of entries in tke Bibliography)

Addenda